Handbook of Clinical Intervention in Child Sexual Abuse

This drawing is by a sixteen-year-old sexually active rape victim who had a spontaneous abortion and later became pregnant again. The picture was executed during a depressed period between pregnancies. The anatomically accurate penile form, its emphasis in central placement on the page and heavy shading, rising as it does from the bottom of the paper gives a quality of intrusion to the depiction. The even more strongly emphasized ovid form with its dark nucleus descending from the upper regions of the page more closely resembles ovulation than a human eye.

Handbook of Clinical Intervention in Child Sexual Abuse

Suzanne M. Sgroi, M.D.

LexingtonBooks
D.C. Heath and Company
Lexington, Massachusetts
Toronto

Library of Congress Cataloging in Publication Data
Main entry under title:

Handbook of clinical intervention in child sexual abuse.

    1. Child abuse—Services—United States.
I. Sgroi, Suzanne M.
HV715.H29   362.7'1   81–47707
ISBN 0–669–04720–1 Casebound   AACR2
ISBN 0–669–05213–2 Paperbound

Twelfth printing, September 1985

Published simultaneously in Canada

Printed in the United States of America on acid-free paper

Casebound International Standard Book Number: 0–669–04720–1

Paperbound International Standard Book Number: 0–669–05213–2

Library of Congress Catalog Card Number: 81–47707

Contents

During the last year that she spent on this earth, Clara Jo Stember dedicated every particle of her being to learning how the arts therapies could best be used to help sexually abused children. As a master of arts in psychology and as a registered arts therapist, she relentlessly pursued the goal of demonstrating that the arts therapies are essential diagnostic and treatment tools for children who have been neglected or abused. In her home territory of Suffolk County, New York, she had developed an Artmobile for a program called Extended Family Support Systems for Families under Stress; after filling a van with various arts materials, she drove it around the county for two years, bringing the arts therapies to maltreated children in their homes and schools. She began sharing her findings in articles and presentations. While engaged in the last stages of writing her doctoral thesis on the role of the arts therapies in treating child abuse in 1977, we invited her to serve as a consultant to Connecticut's Sexual Trauma Treatment Program; she accepted with alacrity. "Why not?" was her response, after telling us that she had identified a number of previously unsuspected cases of sexual abuse from the artwork of troubled children: "I want to learn more about it."

Why not, indeed? Why not commute more than 200 miles one way to spend two days each week (sometimes consecutive, sometimes separated, and often several days or the whole week) in a strange city where you know no one but your new colleagues, for a pittance in compensation that barely covers your travel and lodging expenses and arts materials, to work side by side with people who are largely ignorant of your specialty, unwilling to share turf, and with whom you must fight to prove your worth and gain access to the children you so desperately wish to serve and study? Why not fight Connecticut's worst winter of the 1970s and share the pains and frustrations of wallowing through the stifling bureaucratic strictures imposed by federal and state government on a pilot project to try to help sexually abused children and their families? Why not? Clara Jo Stember did all these things—with gusto, with excitement, with fury, with tenacity, with love—from November 1977 to the night in July 1978 she died in her sleep in a motel in West Hartford. We knew something serious had happened to her when she failed to show up at the office on the next morning to meet a therapist who planned to accompany her on a home visit to a sexually abused child. In eight months she had never missed an appointment.

Did she shorten her life by this activity? Probably yes. Could anyone have persuaded her to stop or to slow down, once launched into the project? I sincerely doubt it. Shortly before she died, she had decided to participate for a second year, despite a previously firm assertion to the contrary. "You need me and I need you," she said. "Besides, it's all beginning to come together now, and I need a little more time."

She did not have the time after all, as we were to discover. How did she accomplish as much as she did in the time allotted to her? She was a small woman with a youthful figure and softly waving white hair. She wore muted colors, mostly pastels. Although she moved with vigor, she looked frail. No one would ever have guessed from her appearance that she served as a Women's Air Service Pilot during World War II, piloting large bombers from the United States to England so that they would be immediately available from the factory to Allied Forces in Europe. Her delicate appearance belied her strengths.

When talking to an individual, Clara Jo Stember's eyes were alive and intense, reflecting every nuance of emotional expression. She used her voice as an instrument with great effectiveness, raising and lowering the pitch as she talked. In contrast, she was impatient with meetings and rarely contributed to group discussion of a case or problem. One-on-one interaction was her forte although she could, and did, present to a group with great effectiveness when asked to do so. She was consumed with interest about her subject and would talk about it hour after hour if allowed. She demonstrated, she described, she questioned, she teased, she pleaded, she cajoled, she sucked you in, she wore you down. Highly task oriented, she allocated time with great precision for clients and professional commitments. But during interaction with a colleague with no time constraints beyond mundane considerations of eating and sleeping and leisure, you finally had to call a halt and after you walked away or hung up the telephone, you knew that she would continue to pursue the topic mentally. She appeared never to stop searching and reflecting during the time that she was with us.

After fighting for the right to work directly with clients, Clara Jo Stember worked primarily out of her car while she was in Connecticut. She loaded it with arts materials and drove to the homes of clients in the thirty-three towns served by the program. Many of the children she worked with lived in the ghetto, but she went to them anyway, searching for poorly marked buildings and apartments. She would use her arts materials as a personal I.D. and as a means of entry. Sometimes she waited outside buildings or in hallways for an hour or more until people arrived or decided to let her in. As suspicious adults opened the door a crack (with chain lock still attached), "All they see of me is my hand, waving a pot of paint," she would joke. Usually, however, they finally let her in.

It took very little time for her to establish a relationship with children or adults in their families. Again, she used her arts media as entry tools. She would spread newspapers that she had brought if they were working with paints or clay. "I wouldn't dare make a mess," she said ironically, since many of the homes were dirty and disordered. Using great subtlety as she engaged a child with her media, she could create a small island of serenity occupied by the two of them in the midst of a chaotic or hostile home situation. She watched the youngster intently as he or she worked with crayons or paints or clay or used styrofoam or other materials to built or sculpt. Always an unobtrusive yet reassuring presence, she inspired confidence, anticipated but never directed the child's needs, responded to his or her comments or questions, supplied verbal or nonverbal support, and enabled the youngster to master each creative task and advance toward the next. The sessions usually lasted about one hour, sometimes more, often less. She was acutely aware of every nuance during those periods—the child, the family, the setting—nothing escaped her. Sometimes she needed another person with her to run interference with other family members so that she could focus on the child. "They see my white hair and expect me to do the grandmother bit with the baby," she would say, mimicking cradling and rocking motions with her arms.

After a session was over, she returned to her car and furiously dictated all of her impressions so that nothing would be forgotten. She left behind many hours of tapes, a boon to those who would understand her work. The tapes were lengthy and difficult to transcribe because she hastily poured out a stream of consciousness series of thoughts. Most of the transcriptions were done at her own expense because the project lacked secretarial time for them.

Although she also did many arts therapy sessions in an office setting, Clara Jo Stember believed that there was great value in working with the child in his or her own home. "Home is where it all happens," she would say. She saw the child's home as an arena where he or she must perform every day. She believed passionately that to enable a youngster to achieve even a tiny success in mastering a creative task with arts media in the home would assist that child in the battle to achieve mastery of self and environment. She practiced what she preached and extended herself ceaselessly to work with every child that she could. If she ever refused or turned aside a case referral, I am unaware of it. She made herself available to clients and staff at any time of the day or evening when access or opportunity arose.

Clara Jo Stember could be cryptic despite her great desire to share and communicate. Her mind worked so fast and she was so enthusiastic that oftentimes the words spilled out in a sort of verbal shorthand that was difficult to follow. She used technical phrases or terms that had meaning for her and perhaps to other arts therapists but meant little to the rest of us. "I know you probably just said something very profound, but I didn't understand it," I would tease her. More seriously, I said to her several times, "You are going to have to use language that the rest of us can understand because other clinicians will never bother to learn terminology used in your specialty." She listened to this criticism without apparent resentment and struggled to find the right words to convey her insights and observations.

After fighting for time to present her work at a panel sponsored by the project in May 1978, she listened quietly to several hours of presentation by others. When her turn came, it was almost lunchtime and everyone was feeling stale and tired. In a voice modulated so that all would strain their attention to hear her opening remarks, she said to the group: "Will you come with me now to a cave? Here a newly erect Homo sapiens is using the earth and his animals' blood to mark the place of his passing, what he did there, and something of his life and feelings. Feelings? Yes. The quality of line expresses his wonder at the grace and beauty of the other life that shares his space." There followed a lucid and concise presentation on applying arts therapies to a mesmerized audience. She was still engaged in that struggle to communicate on a level we could understand when she died.

During the last few months of her life, Clara Jo Stember was in a creative ferment. She confided in some of us that she felt as if she was on the verge of a significant breakthrough. She wrote three articles, she was in telephone contact with colleagues all over the country, and she produced a flood of notes and memos and messages. For nearly a year afterward, those of us who worked with her were still coming across notes she had scribbled to us during that time, which were interspersed with papers and products from meetings and cases. Perhaps she knew, somehow, that she would not be permitted enough time to finish her work. But she left behind a legacy of information and communiques for the rest of us in addition to her completed articles.

Once or twice in a professional lifetime, you are privileged to work with someone who stimulates you to do more or to go further than perhaps you otherwise would have done. Clara Jo Stember has had that effect on me and, I think, on at least a score of other colleagues. Her unfinished work stands as a challenge and an obligation to us all. As this personal memoir implies, I do not have the knowledge to assess her contribution in a scholarly fashion. I am indebted to Connie E. Naitove for preparing a sensitive professional interpretation of Clara Jo Stember's work in chapter 10 of this book. Hopefully, a more comprehensive assessment and presentation will follow. Another dimension of obligation will persist, nonetheless. I do not expect ever to forget or to discharge fully my personal and professional debt to this brave and talented and deeply caring lady. She lingers in the back of my mind and never fails to emerge to challenge me with fondness or irritation when I fall short (as often happens) of doing all that I could do with a task or a case or a commitment. I expect that she will support and prod me all my days.

Thank you, Clara Jo!

Acknowledgments

This book and the clinical work and community programming that led to it could not have been accomplished without the constant encouragement and unfailing support of my friend and colleague, Jeanette Dille, M.S.W.

I am grateful to Jerome Stember, who has generously permitted the use of notes, writings, slides, and photographs belonging to his wife, the late Clara Jo Stember.

Finally, I owe a debt of gratitude to my assistant, Alma Fitzsimmons, R.N., and secretary, Sharon Cousineau—their patience and devotion enabled me to keep writing in the midst of a busy office practice.

Introduction: The State of the Art in Child-Sexual-Abuse Intervention

Suzanne M. Sgroi

Ten years ago, it would have been possible to describe "the state of the art" in child-sexual-abuse intervention in a few paragraphs or less. Public and professional acknowledgment that significant numbers of children are sexually abused by their relatives and caretakers did not really begin to emerge until the mid-1970s. Only a handful of established child-sexual-abuse intervention programs exist in 1981; only one, the Child Sexual Abuse Treatment Program of Santa Clara County, California, has been offering offender and family treatment mandated by the criminal-justice system for more than five years.

When the Children's Division of the American Humane Association, under the leadership of its Director, Vincent DeFrancis, published a landmark study, "Protecting the Child Victim of Sex Crimes Committed by Adults," in 1968, few agencies or individual clinicians saw the need or felt a responsibility to develop skills and strategies to cope with the problem. More than a decade later, this attitude is slowly changing. Clinicians and investigators are learning that child sexual abuse exists within their communities and have become all too painfully aware that, in most instances, they and the community law enforcement and helping services systems are woefully unprepared to cope with the cases that come to the surface.

Why is this so? Why are we so poorly prepared to cope with child sexual abuse in the 1980s? A variety of factors are responsible.

Sex versus Power

There is much confusion among professionals and lay people alike regarding the nature of the problem. Child sexual abuse tends to be classified as a *sexual problem*. Textbooks on human sexuality often describe pedophilia as a sexual *variation*. Treatment of child sexual abuse therefore is traditionally oriented toward treatment of a sexual aberration.

However, individuals who are sexual offenders against children do not seem to be motivated primarily by sexual desires; instead, as well-documented by Drs. Ann Burgess and A. Nicholas Groth, they tend to engage in sexual behavior with children in the service of nonsexual needs, especially the need to feel

powerful and in control. Thus the dynamics of child sexual abuse involve a
sexual expression or acting out of nonsexual issues. Inevitably, the offender's
power position in relation to the child victim and the child's perception of his
or her subordinate role are the principal determinants of what occurs between
them, how it occurs, where, when, and why it occurs, whether or not the
activity is kept secret, when and under what circumstances (if ever) the secret
is disclosed and, finally, what occurs after the disclosure. Within this context,
it is far more appropriate to regard child sexual abuse as a *power problem* and
to plan and design intervention strategy accordingly.

All elements of society have been slow to deal realistically with issues
relating to human sexuality. The misperception of child sexual abuse as a sexual
problem has undoubtedly contributed to the reluctance of professionals to develop intervention skills. However, we are also notoriously ill-equipped to deal
with clients whose behavior is characterized by aberrations or disorders of
power. Such persons tend to be hostile and attempt to ward off interference by
exhibiting aggressive or threatening behavior. Most perpetrators of child sexual
abuse are successful in scaring off clinicians who, in turn, never feel pressed
or motivated to develop skills to treat disorders of power.

It is safe, then, to predict that as long as we persist in treating child sexual
abuse primarily as a *sexual problem* (which it is not), we will continue to
intervene inappropriately in cases which come to our attention. Further, we can
predict that the more functional perception of child sexual abuse as a *power
problem* represents only the necessary first step to more effective intervention.
The capacity to assess sexually abusive behavior toward children within the
context of misuse and aberration of power must be coupled with the willingness
and skills required to deal with this particular power disorder.

Involuntary Clients

Current philosophies of the helping professions deliberately exclude the *involuntary client*. Those who provide help for deeply troubled people usually eschew
outreach. Instead we require that an individual must first recognize that he has
a problem, then decide that he wants help for a problem, next, identify an
appropriate help source, and finally present himself at the appropriate place at
the appropriate time to receive the help. Needless to say, most participants in
child sexual abuse do not fit this description, are unlikely to seek help at all,
and are predictably likely to be unmotivated if intervention and help are forced
upon them.

Few professionals today have developed skills to deal with *involuntary
clients*. Such individuals are difficult to treat and are inclined to deny their need
for treatment. In other words, they tend to be *resistant* as well as *unmotivated*.
Behind a façade of belligerence and disinterest, they are frightened, lonely, and

desperately needy people who are as eager for someone to demonstrate a caring and knowledgeable approach to them as they are distrustful and evasive in response. Although modern social services began with an outreach approach to the involuntary client, it has been both unfashionable and "low status" to work with such people in recent years. Consequently, we are the inheritors of a fifty-to-sixty-year time lag in the development and refinement of skills for working with involuntary clients. Little attention has been paid to these skills since the 1920s. In addition to the power-sex misperception and the unwillingness and inability to deal with power disorders, another major gap in child-sexual-abuse intervention is lack of preparedness to cope both conceptually and practically with involuntary clients.

Authoritative Intervention

The key to working effectively with involuntary clients who exhibit disorders of power is *authoritative intervention*. Instead of sitting back and waiting for participants in child sexual abuse to come to us, we must be prepared to go to them. We can forget about looking for motivated clients to be recipients of our child-sexual-abuse intervention and therapy. A mandate for intervention and a willingness to work with immature, hostile, and dependent clients must be substituted for "client motivation" in these cases. No matter how attractive, competent, and optimistic we appear, these clients will turn to us only as an alternative to some pressure or sanction.

Authority tends to be a dirty word in the lexicon of most helping services professionals. Most of us prefer a professional self-image involving gentle and judicious application of finely honed skills made credible and palatable to the client by our obvious wisdom and pleasing personalities. The notion that we might actually be required to impose ourselves upon people who not only did not seek us out but also are unwilling to be treated is damaging to that self-image, to say the least. Most of us are uncomfortable with authority at best; we do not enjoy being subject to authority exercised by others, and when we exercise authority ourselves, we prefer that others gracefully accept our authoritative position without question and certainly without resistance. Somehow, to be allied with a person or an agency with statutory authority can feel uncomfortable indeed to the helping professional—it tends to undermine all of the gratuitous aspects of that cherished self-image.

Nevertheless, a combined authoritative and supportive approach to clients involved in child sexual abuse seems to be most effective. Although great initial resistance may be shown, most clients respond well (sometimes with relief) to "being told what to do," especially when the approach is firm, consistent, nonpunitive and generally upbeat, with emphasis on the positive aspects of the situation. Until helping professionals are willing to join forces with professionals with statutory authority, little effective treatment for child sexual abuse is likely to occur. It is manifestly unrealistic to suppose that individuals who depend upon abuse of power first to engage children in sexual activity and then to conceal the sexual abuse from others are likely to respond to nonauthoritative intervention.

This foregoing description of the state of the art in child-sexual-abuse intervention is admittedly gloomy. Since, in large measure, we have chosen to be incompetent, the gaps in professional skills are both shameful and unjustifiable. Still, a gradual acceptance of the responsibility to develop case management skills is now emerging. There are several reasons for this change. First, more cases of child sexual abuse are being recognized and reported each year, sometimes at a level that is impossible to ignore. Second, in response to congressional directives, the federal government is now funding a limited number of projects nationwide that are designed to improve services and to train professionals in essential treatment skills as well as to stimulate research on a few aspects of the problem. Lastly, consumer pressure to acknowledge and treat the trauma resulting from childhood sexual exploitation is slowly being felt by clinicians and agency administrators.

A Personal Perspective

Where are we going? How will child-sexual-abuse intervention proceed in the 1980s? It seems strange to be speculating about the future of a field that has been in existence for such a short time that it has virtually no past. One thing is certain, however. The field will undergo a rapid expansion in the next decade. In 1978 it was possible to gather most of the notable professionals involved in child-sexual-abuse intervention in the United States together in one room and have fewer than thirty persons present. This will not be the case in 1988; and it is unlikely ever to occur again.

It is difficult to describe how it felt to be a member of a small group of professionals who were contributing to a limited but rapidly developing human services field. In less than five years, child sexual abuse moved from the status of an obscure issue to a prominent one. So little had been written about clinical intervention that it was possible to secure national attention by the publication of a single paper or article. In such a milieu, it was also possible to be acquainted personally with most if not all of the people who were writing and speaking about the problem. Although universal agreement was unlikely, we could respect our colleagues and often share their perspectives. Usually we learned from each other and eagerly sought each other's opinions and experience.

How did it feel? It was often a lonely business, especially when you had to reach to another state, perhaps thousands of miles away, for the opportunity to obtain advice and support or to share experiences with someone else who "talked the language" and understood the issues. It could be frustrating and discouraging to experience the multiple setbacks encountered by all who attempt to establish child-sexual-abuse programs. It could be stimulating and exciting as well, especially when an approach you had struggled long to develop suddenly began to be effective or when identifiable progress at last was made.

For those who work with child sexual abuse on a daily basis, it is theoretically possible to become blasé about the subject. Practically speaking, the likelihood is small. The immediacy of the human suffering involved is hard to ignore. For example, if you lecture frequently on incest, it is not unusual to have a member of the audience appear at a break in the proceedings and identify himself or herself as a former victim. The impact of such disclosures is undeniable, especially when the person shares that this is the first time he or she has told the secret to anyone. It is sometimes possible to identify these people before they speak, simply by the unguarded and often relieved expressions on their faces. What they say on these occasions becomes so familiar: "You could have been talking about me. This happened to me when I was a child. It has affected me all of my life. I've never gotten over it. I've never told anyone before." It is as if hearing someone else describe the dynamics and mechanics of child abuse out loud "in front of God and everybody" both validates the sexually abusive experience and at the same time releases the victim from the burden of keeping the guilty secret forever.

Complacency is always dispelled as you become personally involved with new cases. Person-to-person contact with the individuals involved never fails to impress me because of the basic similarity of their histories and the common patterns of sexually abusive behavior. The same stories are heard again and again. The first, the tenth, the one-hundredth case—virtually all fit within an overall context of recurring dynamics and mechanics of child sexual abuse. Sometimes you cannot restrain your amazement that the patterns are so repetitive. Colleagues who are newly involved in investigation and validation sometimes express surprise when they observe the behaviors first-hand and find that they *do* fit within a conceptual framework. Shaking their heads, they marvel: "It's just like you predicted!" or "This is a textbook case!" Yet, regardless of familiarity, the enormity of the suffering implicit in these recurrent patterns is a palpable reality.

Intervention in the 1980s

Child sexual abuse is so perplexing, so disturbing, and so difficult to resolve that it is tempting for investigators and clinicians to seek assistance and direction from "experts." They would be well advised, however, to beware of "experts bearing expertise." The field is too new and the body of accumulated knowledge and skills is too small and inadequately tested for anyone to claim that he or she has *the* answers. We are many years away from evolving an intervention meth-odology that has stood the test to time. To say authoritatively that an approach "works" requires evaluation of the "results" of applying that methodology in a consistent fashion—preferably in the form of prospective longitudinal data collected on many hundreds or even thousands of cases over a minimum of ten years. No child-sexual-abuse expert can boast such expertise in 1981—none of us have been working in the field long enough, nor do we possess data collected from enough cases over time, to prove that the methodology we have evolved is more-or-less effective than the approach advocated by someone else.

Yet the individuals who must deal with the cases are clamoring for expert advice. In the absence of authoritative information backed by adequate data, how should professionals assess the appropriateness of guidelines and strategies for child-sexual-abuse intervention that are put forward? We are, after all, talking about a new field that is currently in a state of rapid evolution. Will today's tentative theories become widely accepted tomorrow or will they be discarded? Who can tell?

The sobering response to these questions is that there are no definitive answers. Every clinician and investigator who deals with cases of child sexual abuse today is, in a sense, a pioneer exploring largely uncharted territory. Any prudent explorer will obtain the best charts available and perhaps even employ guides before undertaking an expedition into a new land. Likewise, responsible professionals who must deal with child-sexual-abuse cases will seek the best advice available as they develop their own approach to the problems at hand.

It is always wise to identify the experience base of the expert in assessing the depth and quality of his or her expertise. How many cases of child sexual abuse has the expert seen? In what capacity has he or she worked with offenders, victims and/or their families? For how long? Was the expert working with cases alone or cooperatively with others? Were the cases reviewed regularly? Were approaches and methodologies tested before being used with more than a few cases? Once adopted, was the methodology consistently applied?

Although there are no uniform criteria, it is important to know what the expert has used to measure his or her own case experience. How were the cases investigated and by whom? Did the expert and his or her colleagues participate in case investigation? What criteria did they use to validate child-sexual-abuse cases? Was a child-protection assessment consistently made? How did they determine the impact of the sexually abusive behavior upon the child? What criteria were used to determine the extent of trauma to the victim, the degree of pathology of the offender, and the level of family functioning? Were the treatment approaches voluntary or authoritative? Was the treatment limited to a single therapeutic approach or was it multidimensional? What criteria were used to determine the outcomes of intervention? Was ongoing monitoring a part of the treatment plan? How long were cases followed?

The posture of any expert vis-à-vis child protection and the criminal-justice system is also important. Does he or she believe in working cooperatively with the police? With child-protective services? What is the expert's position on authoritative intervention in child-sexual-abuse cases? Does he or she believe it is helpful or harmful for clients to be involved in treatment mandated by an authoritative system such as child-protective services or the criminal court? If the expert advocates authoritative intervention, how does he or she recommend that other professionals engage clients in voluntary treatment?

At the present time, clinicians and investigators must be willing to assess critically the experience base of any so-called expert on child sexual abuse. Only then can the expertise of that person be used to advantage by the professionals who are responsible for case management in their own communities. At best, the expert can convey his or her current perspective on the state of the art in child-sexual-abuse intervention. It is then up to the listener to decide if the information and advice are credible and to what extent they can be applied.

This book attempts to convey a coherent and cohesive perspective on the state of the art in child-sexual-abuse intervention in 1981. It is not and never can be the final word on investigation, validation, case management and treatment of child sexual abuse. The observations, opinions, and recommendations expressed are based on my own clinical experience and the considerable experience of my colleagues, the contributing authors. Most of the chapters examine the various aspects of intervention and present information in a "here-is-how-we-do-it" format. This is not because any of us have deluded ourselves into believing that the approaches, guidelines, strategies, and methodologies that we describe are the only way to manage child-sexual-abuse cases, nor yet the best way. However, there does seem to be justification for offering a clinical handbook now since few such books or articles are available for professionals to consult.

The aim in all of the chapters is to emphasize the practical rather than the theoretical aspects of intervention. Whenever possible, case examples are used to illustrate the points made and the approach recommended. Chapter 1 was written because it seemed necessary and appropriate to present a conceptual framework to serve as a context for the clinical material presented in the other chapters. Chapters 2 and 3 cover validation of cases and case management. These topics are the sine qua non for child-protective-services workers—the key group in the field. They and they alone, of all clinical professionals engaged in child-sexual-abuse intervention, have an unassailable right to be involved in cases because of their mandated responsibility for child protection. Linda Canfield Blick and Frances Sarnacki Porter, both former child-protective-services workers, made valuable contributions to chapters 1 and 2. As co-authors of chapters 4 and 5, these social workers offer cogent guidelines for treatment of sexually abused children and adolescents, again based on their own case experience.

Dr. Carlos M. Loredo, a clinical psychologist, brings extensive case experience to chapter 6, which deals with sibling incest. Few clinicians can match the expertise of Dr. A. Nicholas Groth, who is well known for his work with sexual offenders and has made another valuable contribution in chapter 8, which deals with the incest offender. Natalie T. Dana, also a former child-protective-services worker, has contributed her treatment experience with mothers of sexually abused children to chapter 7. An overview of family treatment is presented in chapter 9. Connie E. Naitove, a leading proponent of the arts therapies, has made a very special contribution in chapter 10, which describes the work of Clara Jo Stember, a pioneer in using art therapy to help sexually abused children.

In chapter 11, Lieutenant Patricia A. Graves has contributed the law enforcement perspective on child sexual abuse—another essential element in intervention. Chapter 12 presents my own perspective on multidisciplinary team review based on five years of child-protection team experience. In chapter 13, Dr. Karen W. Bander, Edith Fein, and Gerrie Bishop discuss program evaluation and present data collected from the child-sexual-abuse intervention program in which most of us participated. The "how to" of starting a community child-sexual-abuse program and recommendations for staffing are covered in chapter 14.

To reiterate, professional readers of this book must judge for themselves the credibility of the expertise contained herein. No one is likely to read a clinical handbook on child sexual abuse unless he or she is genuinely concerned about the problem and wishes to expand his or her knowledge base in the interest of helping clients. Undoubtedly, the state of the art will change and readers must recognize this fact. In any event, it is the responsibility of all professionals to make a critical assessment of proffered information and advice and adapt what is learned to their own case experience. I salute you for your interest, concern, and critical appraisal. Keep them active as knowledge and skills advance in the years to come!

1

A Conceptual Framework for Child Sexual Abuse

*Suzanne M. Sgroi,
Linda Canfield Blick,
and Frances Sarnacki Porter*

Clinical intervention in child sexual abuse requires a basic understanding of the phenomenon—what it is, how it happens, when it is likely to occur and why, what circumstances determine disclosure of the activity, how participants may be expected to react, and so forth.

Effective investigation, validation, child-protection assessment, crisis intervention, planned intervention, and treatment all depend on a working knowledge of the mechanics and dynamics. This chapter will present a basic conceptual framework for child sexual abuse.

Definitions

What Is Child Sexual Abuse?

Child sexual abuse is a sexual act imposed on a child who lacks emotional, maturational, and cognitive development. The ability to lure a child into a sexual relationship is based upon the all-powerful and dominant position of the adult or older adolescent perpetrator, which is in sharp contrast to the child's age, dependency, and subordinate position. Authority and power enable the perpetrator, implicitly or directly, to coerce the child into sexual compliance.

Linda Canfield Blick, M.S.W., is the director of the Family Assessment and Treatment Program—Child Sexual Abuse in Montgomery County, Maryland. From 1977–1979 Mrs. Blick was a staff member of the Sexual Trauma Treatment Program of the Connecticut Department of Children and Youth Services where she specialized in working with child victims and was the implementer and coleader of a treatment group for adolescent incest victims. Mrs. Blick received the M.S.W. from the University of Connecticut School of Social Work and the bachelor's degree from Saint Joseph College, West Hartford, Connecticut.

Frances Sarnacki Porter, A.C.S.W., presently does program planning and policy development for the Connecticut Department of Children and Youth Services and from 1977–1979 was a staff member in its Sexual Trauma Treatment Program, working predominantly with sexually victimized children and adolescents, and serving as coleader of an adolescent-therapy group. Mrs. Porter provides training and consultation for child-sexual-abuse workers and treats adult and child victims in a private clinical practice.

What Is Incest?

Defined from a psychosocial perspective, incestuous child sexual abuse encompasses any form of sexual activity between a child and a parent or stepparent or extended family member (for example, grandparent, aunt, or uncle) or surrogate parent figure (for example, common-law spouse or foster parent). Incest is variously defined by statute as specific sexual acts (usually involving some type of intercourse) performed between persons who are prohibited to marry. In general, persons are not permitted to marry their parents, grandparents, aunts, uncles, siblings, or steprelatives. The crucial psychosocial dynamic is the *familial* relationship between the incest participants. This is especially important when the incestuous sexual relationship involves a child. The presence or absence of a blood relationship between incest participants is of far less significance than the kinship roles they occupy.

Mechanics

A Spectrum of Sexually Abusive Behaviors

Sexual activity between an adult and a child may range from exhibitionism to intercourse, often progressing through the following spectrum of behavior:

1. *Nudity:* The adult parades nude around the house in front of all or some of the family members.

    Stepfather paraded around the house nude in front of his 16-year-old stepdaughter despite protests from her mother that his behavior was provocative and seductive. He claimed that the mother had a "dirty mind," but later on the child revealed the secret of a 3-year sexual relationship with the stepfather.

2. *Disrobing:* The adult disrobes in front of the child. This generally occurs when the child and the adult are alone.

    Twice a week, while viewing television, father allowed his bathrobe to slip open, which exposed his naked body to his preadolescent daughter while her mother was attending a regularly scheduled meeting out of the home.

3. *Genital Exposure:* The adult exposes his or her genitals to the child. Here the perpetrator directs the child's attention to the genitals.

    Father came into his 11-year-old daughter's bedroom where he opened the front of his pants. He exposed his penis to her and requested that she "rub it."

4. *Observation of the Child:* The adult surreptitiously or overtly watches the child undress, bathe, excrete, urinate.

    Several times a week over a period of 8 to 10 years, the parents of an adolescent son and daughter gave their children enemas and then watched them excrete.

5. *Kissing:* The adult kisses the child in a lingering and intimate way. This type of kissing should be reserved for adults. Even very young children sense the inappropriateness of this behavior and may experience discomfort about it.

    During the interview, the adolescent reported to the clinician, "my father tried to French kiss me."

6. *Fondling:* The adult fondles the child's breasts, abdomen, genital area, inner thighs, or buttocks. The child may similarly fondle the adult at his or her request.

    "When I was eight years old, I was sleeping in my bedroom and woke up because my father was rubbing me all over."

7. *Masturbation:* The adult masturbates while the child observes; the adult observes the child masturbating; the adult and child observe each other while masturbating themselves; or the adult and child masturbate each other (mutual masturbation).

    A 16-year-old adolescent discussed her 9-year history of sexual abuse. Several times a week she masturbated her stepfather to ejaculation. Although he attempted mutual masturbation, she refused.

8. *Fellatio:* The adult has the child fellate him or the adult will fellate the child. This type of oral-genital contact requires the child to take a male perpetrator's penis into his or her mouth or the adult to take the male child's penis into his or her mouth.

    Nine-year old Jimmy told his mother, "Uncle Mark made me suck on his thing" [penis] and then he ". . . suck on mine."

9. *Cunnilingus:* This type of oral-genital contact requires the child to place mouth and tongue on the vulva or in the vaginal area of an adult female or the adult will place his or her mouth on the vulva or in the vaginal area of the female child.

    The police officer asked 6-year old Tommy to draw a picture of his mother and place X's where she made him kiss her. The child marked X's on the stomach, chest, and "pussy" (child's own word), making the largest X in the genital area.

10. *Digital (finger) Penetration of the Anus or Rectal Opening:* This involves penetration of the anus or rectal opening by a finger. Perpetrators may thrust inanimate objects such as crayons or pencils inside as well. Preadolescent children often report a fear about "things being inside them" and

"broken."

Christopher, a small child, revealed to his therapist that his mother had put her fingers into his rectum. He drew a picture describing this.

11. *Penile Penetration of the Anus or Rectal Opening:* This involves penetration of the anus or rectal opening by a male perpetrator's penis. A child can often be rectally penetrated without injury due to the flexibility of child's rectal opening.

Fourteen-year old Steve was sexually abused by his father on numerous occasions. This included the father penetrating Steve's rectum with his penis.

12. *Digital (finger) Penetration of the Vagina:* This involves penetration of the vagina by a finger. Inanimate objects may also be inserted.

When questioned by the clinician, four-year-old Barbara said that mother's boyfriend put ". . . a pen in my pookie." (vagina)

13. *Penile Penetration of the Vagina:* This involves penetration of the vagina by a male perpetrator's penis.

Thirteen-year-old Jennifer was taken to a doctor by her mother for an examination due to several missed menstrual cycles. Upon examination it was discovered that Jennifer was five months pregnant. She then disclosed that father had "been having sex with me."

14. *"Dry Intercourse":* This is a slang term describing an interaction in which the adult rubs his penis against the child's genital-rectal area or inner thighs or buttocks.

Sally's mother told the clinician that her husband was "dry screwing" her daughter. He rubbed his penis against her buttocks but did not penetrate.

The typical scenario is a progression from less intimate types of sexual activity (such as exposure and self-masturbation) to actual body contact (such as fondling), and then to some form of penetration. Oral penetration may be expected to occur early in this progression, which is often followed by digital penetration of the anus or vagina. Ejaculation by a male perpetrator, sometimes against the child's body can occur at any time in this progression.

Dynamics

The dynamics of sexual encounters between adults and children usually fall within a predictable pattern. This is particularly true of those cases of intrafamily child sexual abuse that come to light and are reported. The activity usually occurs in five separate phases: the engagement phase; the sexual interaction phase; the secrecy phase; the disclosure phase; and often a suppression phase following disclosure.

Engagement Phase

Access and Opportunity. Child sexual abuse is not a capricious, unplanned, unpredictable phenomenon. For the most part, the perpetrator is someone who is known to the child and who has ready access to the child. Opportunity to engage in sexual activity is essential and can usually be equated with privacy. The perpetrator and the child need to be alone with each other—in a room, in a house, or in some secluded place out of doors. Although these circumstances of access and opportunity may be accidental on their first encounter, the perpetrator can be expected to watch for, or to create, opportunities for private interaction with the child thereafter.

Relationship of Participants. Who is the perpetrator likely to be? Almost always it is someone in the child's own family who has access and opportunity by residing in the home or family circle. If not a relative, the perpetrator may be someone given access to the child by the parents or guardian—again someone within the child's daily sphere of activities. Where do we allow little children to be? And with whom? We let them be at home or in the homes of relatives, friends, and neighbors. We also let them go to school and permit them to engage in age-appropriate group activity—boy scouts, girl scouts, clubs, church-related activity, and so forth. Children outside their own homes are usually under the authority of adults who temporarily occupy caretaking or guardianship roles. Thus the dynamics of child sexual abuse most often involve a known adult who is in a legitimate power position over a child and who exploits accepted societal patterns of dominance and authority to engage the child in sexual activity. It is impossible to overemphasize the significance of the exploitation and misuse of accepted power relationships when assessing the impact of sexual abuse on the child.

Inducements. How does the perpetrator engage the child? How does he or she get the child to participate in some type of sexual behavior? Usually in a low-key nonforcible fashion, possibly by presenting the activity as a game or something that is "special" and fun. This always entails misrepresentation of moral standards, either verbally or implicitly (Burgess and Holmstrom, 1975). The power and authority of adulthood conveys to the child that the proposed behavior is acceptable and sanctioned. The perpetrator usually knows something about what children like and how to get children to fall in with some activity. Perhaps rewards or bribes will be offered. More often than not, the opportunity to engage in activity with a known and favored adult is sufficient incentive for the child to participate.

The successful perpetrator will manage to be coercive in a subtle fashion. The more adept the perpetrator, the less likelihood that threats will be used to induce compliance. Although physical force is rarely used to engage a child in the intrafamily situation, it is important, nevertheless, to assess the context of the overall family dynamics in which the sexual abuse occurs. In many of these families, force or threat of use of force are the most common mode of interaction between family members. When sexual abuse of a child occurs within the context of the violent family, implied force or threat of use of force if the child fails to comply may be an important aspect of the engagement process.

Sexual Interaction Phase

A list of sexually abusive behaviors has already been presented. The perpetrator exposed himself or herself, wholly or in part. The perpetrator then persuades the child to undress partially or completely and to expose his or her genitals. Then they look at each other. What comes next? On the first encounter, perhaps nothing. They may look at each other and stop there.

After exposure, what comes next? The activity may progress to autostimulation or masturbation. The perpetrator masturbates himself or herself and encourages the child to imitate the behavior. They may masturbate themselves at the same time or at different times in each other's presence. They may still never touch each other.

The activity may, however, progress to fondling. The perpetrator may fondle the child, touching him or her in a gentle stroking fashion. The fondling initially may involve the entire body but eventually focuses on body parts with erotic significance—breasts, buttocks, genitals, lower abdomen, inner thighs. The perpetrator may persuade the child to mimic this activity and fondle him or her.

Fondling is often accompanied by kissing. This can be generalized or limited to kissing on the mouth. The perpetrator may introduce the child to so-called French kissing, exploration of the other person's open mouth with the tongue.

The activity may also progress to penetration of the child's body in a variety of ways. Oral penetration occurs frequently since a child's mouth is the opening most amenable to penetration. A male perpetrator will persuade the child to take the perpetrator's penis into the child's mouth. Often the child will be invited to lick or suck the penis. This activity is termed fellatio. Alternately, a male or female perpetrator may fellate a male child, taking the child's penis into the perpetrator's mouth.

If another area of the child's body is to be penetrated, the next most likely opening is the anal or rectal opening. Penetration of the anal or rectal opening usually begins with finger penetration. It may progress to penile penetration if the perpetrator is a male. Or there may be penetration of the anal or rectal opening by an object. The essential elements are the size of the child, his or her previous sexual experience, and the degree of force used. If the child is carefully prepared and not hurt, an extensive level of anal or rectal penetration can occur without residual signs of trauma or abnormal dilation.

Vaginal penetration is, of course, limited to female children. All of the previous sexual behaviors could occur equally as readily with male or female victims. The perpetrator usually penetrates the vulvo-vaginal opening with a finger tip. A thin membrane of tissue, the hymen, extends over the vaginal opening. This usually is a ring of tissue with a central opening. Over time, the opening in the hymenal ring will enlarge until an adult's finger can be inserted entirely. Progressive dilatation will permit penile penetration by the male perpetrator. Penetration of the vulvo-vaginal region by the perpetrator's lips and tongue is called cunnilingus. Again, the extent of penetration will depend on the degree of dilatation. If the dilatation is gentle and occurs over time, it is unlikely to be painful or result in trauma. The only physical evidence that is likely to result is absence of the hymenal ring and a degree of vaginal dilation that is inappropriate for the age of the child.

Sometimes the male perpetrator will not attempt vulvo-vaginal penetration but instead will rub his penis against the genito-rectal region of the female child. This behavior is sometimes called "dry intercourse." Girls who are sexually inexperienced are likely to confuse dry intercourse with penile penetration of the vagina. These girls will sometimes tell investigators that vaginal penetration has occurred when, in fact, it did not. The child's mistake may later undermine her credibility if a physical examination fails to elicit signs of vaginal penetration.

Any of these sexual behaviors may be accompanied by ejaculation, sometimes into a body opening.

Although no one should expect a slavish adherence to this list of sexual behaviors in the exact order described, the engagement phase does encompass a progression of sexual activity. The progression of exposure to fondling to some form of penetration is very predictable. The interviewer can expect to elicit a similar progression of sexual activity in most intrafamily cases.

Secrecy Phase

After engaging the child in some form of sexual behavior, the activity then enters a secrecy phase (Burgess and Holmstrom, 1975). The primary task for the perpetrator after the sexual behavior has taken place is to impose secrecy. Why? Secrecy eliminates accountability—the perpetrator is unlikly to wish to be caught and held responsible for the sexual abuse. Secrecy also enables repetition of the behavior. The perpetrator, in all likelihood, is sexually abusing the child in order to meet nonsexual needs (Groth and Burgess, 1977). Desiring to feel important, powerful, dominant, knowledgeable, admired, wanted—all of these needs are likely to be recurrent. If the perpetrator can satisfy these needs easily with a readily accessible child who is unlikely to be very demanding and without the necessity of addressing the mutuality required by an adult relationship, he or she may be powerfully motivated to continue the behavior. Thus secrecy is essential. The perpetrator must persuade or pressure the child to keep their activity a secret over time.

The child usually *does* keep the secret. Some children never tell anyone. Others keep the secret throughout their childhood and only disclose the sexual behavior many years later. Why? Rewards have probably been offered and given. More important, the child may keep the secret because he or she enjoyed the activity and wants the behavior to continue. This premature introduction to sexuality by a known and valued perpetrator, a person who is a "significant other" for the child, may feel good on several levels—pleasurable sexual stimulation, enhancement of self-esteem, feeling important to another person in a special grown-up fashion, and so forth. Although not especially pleasing to contemplate, to deny that the pleasurable aspects of the sexual behavior may be self-reinforcing for the child, is to ignore the obvious and to nelect to consider one of the most important dynamics.

Threats may have been used to reinforce secrecy—in general, the less adept the perpetrator, the more likely he or she is to threaten the child. If threats were used, they should be carefully assessed for the degree of physical violence proposed, if any. Of course, many compelling threats made to a child do not include physical violence. For example, the threat of anger by a third party ("If you tell mommy, she'll be awfully mad!"). Separation is a potent threat, especially for a young child. A perpetrator might say to the child, "If you tell anyone, mommy may divorce me or I may be sent to jail." A threat of personal separation for the child may be particularly anxiety-provoking: for example, "If you tell anyone, they'll send *you* away." Or the threat may involve self-harm by the perpetrator ("If you tell anybody, I'll kill myself."). A variation might involve threat of harm to someone else ("If you tell anybody, I'll hurt your sister."). Finally the threat may entail violence against the child, ("If you tell anybody, I'll hurt you or kill you."). In assessing these threats, two elements deserve particular attention: the degree of physical violence involved and the extent to which any part of the threat was carried out.

The issue of implied threat by virtue of the overall context of family dynamics again deserves mention. Is this a family whose members routinely interact by use of physical force or threat of use of force against each other? If so, threat of forcible reprisal if the child fails to comply with the request (or order) for secrecy may well be implied without ever being verbalized. For some children, the sexual activity may be virtually the only interaction they ever have with an adult family member in the absence of overt physical force or threat of use of force. This sexual attention is frequently the only form of affectionate physical intimacy experienced by the child in the home. Although the mother may provide the child with discipline and physical necessities, there is often an absence of affection and emotional bonding between them. This void may be partially filled by the perpetrator by kissing, fondling, and other sexual activity.

For some combination of the foregoing reasons, the secrecy phase often lasts for months and years, especially in intrafamily child sexual abuse. The sexual behavior progresses over time, usually in the direction of greater intimacy. As the child grows older there may be a parallel increase in the frequency of incestuous sexual activity. It is helpful to think of child sexual abuse on a continuum over time. The chances are very great that the incident of sexual behavior that occurred at the time a case came to attention is unlikely to be the first incident of sexual activity for that child. Many situations of child sexual abuse remain secret forever. By definition, for the case to be reported, someone or something must interrupt the secrecy phase.

Disclosure Phase

There are two types of disclosure of child sexual abuse: accidental and purposeful. Each type of disclosure will be described.

Accidental Disclosure. In this type of disclosure, the secret was revealed accidentally, because of external circumstances. The key factor here is that none of the participants decided to tell the secret. Instead the secret was revealed in one of the following ways.

1. Observation by a third party. Someone else observes the participants and tells someone else.

Betty walked into her parents' bedroom looking for her sister. As she entered, Betty saw her father fondling her sister's buttocks. Betty quickly reported this to her mother.

2. Physical injury to the child. When this occurs it is usually not intentional. However, the signs of the injury then draw outside atention to the sexual behavior.

Five-year-old Carmen was taken to the hospital emergency room because her mother noticed vaginal bleeding. The examination revealed vaginal tearing due to trauma. When questioned, Carmen said, "My daddy did it."

3. Sexually transmitted disease in the pediatric age group. Sometimes sexual abuse is discovered because the child acquired a symptomatic infection.

Four-year-old Joey developed a pus-like discharge from his penis. Cultures revealed a gonorrhea infection of the urethra and throat. During a play interview, Joey said, "Sammy played with my pee-pee and I played with his and I sucked him." Sammy, Joey's 14-year-old cousin, had been babysitting for the younger boy after school.

4. Pregnancy. Sometimes the child becomes impregnated accidentally because the perpetrator did not take appropriate precautions or thought the girl

was too young to be impregnated. Occasionally, a perpetrator may withhold contraceptives to "punish" the child.

Marilyn, age 12 years, was brought to a clinic for recurrent stomach ache. On examination, she was found to be eight weeks pregnant. Although she did not understand the connection between vaginal intercourse and pregnancy, Marilyn named her stepfather when she was asked with whom she had vaginal intercourse.

5. Precocious sexual activity initiated by the child. This most often is seen when young children display precocious knowledge of sexual behavior with peers and/or adults.

Three-year old Tommy's mother became alarmed when her son began to fondle her breasts and try to suckle her, although he had never been breast fed. He also crawled on top of her while she was lying on the couch and began posturing and mimicking mounting behavior. Investigation revealed that Tommy's babysitter, an emotionally disturbed adolescent girl, had introduced him to this behavior.

Crisis Intervention. Accidental disclosure of child sexual abuse also means that none of the participants are prepared for the secret to be revealed. Since most professional people are equally unprepared to cope with sexual abuse on an emergency basis, the accidental disclosure most often precipitates a crisis. The first task of the clinician will frequently be crisis intervention. He or she can be most helpful by immediately going to the scene as soon as the referral is received.

In this situation, the clinician will have little prior information about the sexual abuse or the family. Depending upon the skills and attitudes of the individuals involved, a state of chaos, high anxiety, feelings of professional inadequacy, hostility, and even fear may predominate. The immediate tasks of the clinician skilled in child-sexual-abuse intervention are to diffuse the anxiety, reinforce the reality that sexual abuse *does* exist, participate in fact-finding, direct the validation process, and assist in initial intervention planning. The following case example demonstrates how a clinician responded during the crisis stage of an accidental disclosure of child sexual abuse.

Eleven-year-old Tricia was in the emergency room of a community hospital for evaluation of abdominal pain when the case was reported. Upon arrival at the hospital, the clinician was greeted by the medical staff and a police officer. They explained that the child's mother had just been sedated for a hysterical reaction upon learning that Tricia's discomfort was due to suspected pregnancy by her stepfather.

It was necessary for the clinician to offer some guidance, as no one knew how to handle the child's information. To minimize repetition of the story, a nurse, police officer, and the clinician were all present while Tricia explained the details of her sexual relationship with her stepfather. The police officer, although very supportive, kept using terms that Tricia did not understand (for example, intercourse). The clinician's sensitivity to this situation enabled her to clarify the meaning of several words for Tricia and to explain the child's level of understanding to the police officer.

This team approach under the clinician's direction during the crisis resulted in the immediate arrest of the stepfather, emergency-shelter placement of mother and all her children and much support for the family members. An initially chaotic situation, with proper direction, resulted in coordination of all the essential services: medical, law enforcement, child protective, and therapeutic.

In spite of the confusion and anxiety, several advantages may be derived from the crisis situation. First, it may enable the clinician quickly to establish a relationship with the child by presenting the concrete services of a skilled supportive advocate. Second, the clinician's entry at this stage reduces the number of times that the child must recite the story of sexual abuse. Finally, the clinician's skills may serve as role-modeling tools and teaching aids for the other professionals involved.

Purposeful Disclosure. In this type of disclosure, a participant consciously decides to tell an outsider about sexual abuse. In the cases that come to the attention of helping professionals, it is most often the child who decides to reveal the secret. Why might a child decide to disclose the secret? A young child may tell the secret to share it. The activity was so exciting or so stimulating that it simply must be shared with someone. An older child usually tells the secret for very different reasons. Often he or she is trying to escape or modify some family pressure situation. For example, in father-daughter incest, the sexual behavior usually begins early and extends into adolescence. The youngster who used to regard father as a warm, loving, and giving person may view him very differently when she reaches adolescence; now she sees him as a narcissistic, controlling individual. In earlier years she could be totally preoccupied by his attentions. Now she is more interested in peer and group relationships outside the family circle. She wants to have friends, to participate in social activities, to date, to stay out late. Her father, however, limits her peer and social activities and pressures her to continue to stay within the family circle and meet *his* needs. Now she feels imprisoned by, and angry at, her father for these restrictions; she senses that his restrictions are aimed at keeping her for himself.

As her frustration mounts, she may finally reveal the secret of their incestuous relationship. The aim of the disclosure may not be primarily toward stopping the incest, but rather toward attaining more freedom. This adolescent may be willing to continue the incestuous relationship with her father as a trade-off for being permitted to form peer relationships, to date, to socialize outside the family circle, and so forth. After the disclosure, the child may initially experience a sense of relief in discharging the burden of a long-kept secret. However, she may also experience guilt for having enjoyed the sexual relationship and perhaps feelings of disloyalty for betraying her father.

Darlene's story emphasizes these dynamics as she reveals the progressive nature of her relationship with her father and her final ambivalent feelings toward him:

> At age 14, Darlene described herself as being close to her father for as long as she could remember. She never felt she could turn to her mother who had not hugged or kissed her since before she was age 5. Father was always physically affectionate with her. She had especially enjoyed their tickling and wrestling matches which started at age 8 and occurrred until she was age 11. Even though mother disapproved of her frequent sitting in father's lap, he felt it was appropriate and accused mother of having a "dirty mind." Shortly after her 11th birthday, father would go into the bathroom whenever Darlene was bathing. By the time she was age 12, he would go into her bedroom late at night to fondle her breasts and genitals. Although she initially enjoyed the attention, by the time she was 13 and started to menstruate, she began to worry that father would press her further. Indeed he did and when she resisted he would physically abuse her into compliance. A year later, after an intense argument with father, she disclosed the incestuous secret. During a session with her clinician two weeks later, an emotionally distraught and very tearful Darlene said, "I feel like I lost my best friend. I miss him. . . . What am I going to do?"

Children sometimes decide to reveal the sexual abuse for other reasons. One girl finally told a school counselor about her incestuous relationship with her father because, at age 14 years, she was fearful of becoming pregnant. Although she had shared these fears with her father, he minimized the risk and refused to use any protection, saying "Don't worry honey, I'll take care of you if you do." Another girl revealed the secret to protect her younger sister.

> Lucy and Ann, sisters, were involved in a sexual relationship with their stepfather for approximately six years. Lucy age 17 years, learned her retarded sister Ann, age 15 years, was pregnant. Both girls had known about the other's sexual relationship with their stepfather, but had been afraid to seek help or even to discuss it with each other. When Lucy learned of her sister's pregnancy, she immediately reported the sexual abuse to the police. The pregnancy helped Lucy decide to risk the consequences of disclosure to protect Ann.

The clinician must determine the reason underlying a child's purposeful disclosure of sexual abuse. Failure to do so can be disastrous. The child who discloses sexual abuse may have completely unrealistic expectations of the person who received the information. He or she is frequently looking for a magical solution to the problem at home. The child usually wants the situation to change without confrontation, without outside interference, frequently without separation. Unless the clinician takes the time to find out why the child told and attempt to modify the youngster's expectations if they are indeed unrealistic, in all likelihood, the child will recant the story as soon as the threat of outside interference is indentified. Whenever possible, it helps enormously if even a small request can be granted for the child.

Planned Intervention. Purposeful disclosure of sexual abuse by a child, fortunately, often permits the case to be handled by planned intervention. When the child decides to share the secret with a professional person or supportive adult, a report should then be transmitted to the statutory child protection agency. If that agency utilizes clinicians who are knowledgeable about child sexual abuse, an opportunity exists to capitalize on the child's conscious decision to seek help from a trusted person. Instead of precipitating an immediate crisis, the clinician can meet with the child and the reporter in a calm, relaxed atmosphere and proceed with fact-finding and validation. This gives the child an opportunity to express his or her concerns, and together they may explore alternatives which are of the least detriment to the entire family system.

Planned intervention as a result of purposeful disclosure may occur in the following manner:

Jodi, a bright girl who had done well academically, was age 15 years when she was referred to the school guidance counselor because her grades were declining. Her parents were divorced three years earlier, and for the last year she had been living with her father and three brothers. After a while, Jodi formed a trusting relationship with the guidance counselor who filled the void left by her absent mother. Several months went by before Jodi told her guidance counselor about her father's sexual molestation of her and her desire to have him stop.

The guidance counselor contacted Child Protective Services immediately. The assigned social worker, who was skilled in child-sexual-abuse intervention, had a joint meeting with Jodi and the guidance counselor at Jodi's request. Because of this interview and a second one which transpired several days later, the social worker was able to validate that sexual abuse had occurrred. During this process, the social worker encouraged Jodi to express her fears and concerns about the situation. A plan was then made with Jodi regarding how and when the incestuous relationship would be revealed to the family.

In this case, the purposeful disclosure to her guidance counselor provided the victim with an opportunity to express her anxieties, as well as to prepare her emotionally for the anticipated familial disruption. It also allowed her to discuss with the social worker the circumstances by which her family would be told about the sexual abuse. And finally, this process enabled her to determine with whom she could live if she needed protection from her father and her mother was not available as an ally. Planned intervention rather than crisis intervention was thus possible in this case.

Family Reactions to Disclosure. Clinicians should anticipate a wide range of family reactions when sexual abuse of a child residing within the family circle is disclosed. What is happening? What are the reactions to disclosure? What are some of the motivations for the behavior that follows?

Perpetrators are likely to react to disclosure with alarm. Child sexual abuse is a crime and criminal penalties could ensue if the case finds its way into the legal justice system. Societal attitudes make exposure and publicity very threatening as well. The perpetrator must also fear loss of social status in the community and possibly loss of job, especially if he or she works in a field involving some type of care or supervision of children. Accordingly, he or she can be expected to react defensively to disclosure with self-protection as the primary goal. At the same time, the perpetrator can be expected to react with hostility toward the child and anyone else inside or outside the family who is supporting the child and acting as a child advocate. After disclosure, the perpetrator can be expected to exploit his or her power position to the fullest to control the child and other family members while undermining the credibility of the allegation and or neutralize negative effects or consequences that may ensue. The intrafamily perpetrator will, of course, be able to control the child far more effectively because of the likelihood of ongoing access to the child.

Parents of a child who has been sexually abused by someone other than a parent are likely to react in a more protective fashion toward the victim. The degree of protectiveness toward the child will depend in part on the identity of the perpetrator. If he or she was a family member (grandparent, uncle, aunt, older sibling or cousin), there may be conflicting loyalties involved as well. This issue has been thoroughly addressed by Burgess and Holmstrom (1979). In extrafamily child sexual abuse, there may be no conflicting loyalties involved. Nevertheless, the parents may fear the possibly negative consequences of publicity and exposure. They may also feel guilty about their own failure to protect the child and wish to deny or cover up their own culpability. Parents may also be exceedingly reluctant to address the issues of the child's premature introduction to sexuality and the negative impact of the sexual abuse upon him or her. Many parents prefer to handle these problems with denial. For all of these reasons, parents may refuse to cooperate with child protective services or the police. Instead, they may assert that they need no assistance in protecting the child from future sexual abuse and in dealing with the consequences to the victim. Also, parents often refuse to assist the legal justice system to deal with perpetrators, both in intrafamily and extrafamily cases, for many of the same self-protective reasons.

Mothers of victims of intrafamily child sexual abuse may initially react to disclosure by expressing many concerns for the child. They may cooperate fully in processes aimed toward child protection and helping the victim to recover from the effects of the sexual abuse. Clinicians should not, however, expect that all mothers will react in this way, nor should they expect that mothers whose initial reaction is protective will be able to sustain a posture of protection and concern without much support and encouragement from others. Self-interest and self-protection are powerful human responses that must be acknowledged. Some mothers may already be aware of the sexual abuse and may even have encouraged the activity or participated in it. Other mothers may have been previously told about the sexual abuse but failed to believe the child or to move effectively to stop the activity. If they fit within either of these categories, mothers may also react to disclosure with guilt and a desire to protect themselves. Even if there was no direct culpability, mothers of victims of intrafamily child sexual abuse must face the consequences of siding with the child, sooner or later. Often they must choose between protecting the child or protecting the perpetrator. If the perpetrator provides the mother with economic support, social status or emotional support, this choice may be painful indeed. If the perpetrator has been violent or abusive toward the mother in the past, she must fear physical retribution as well as loss of all the previously mentioned supports. If the perpetrator reacts to disclosure by exerting pressure on the child's mother, her reaction will also be affected by the type of pressure exerted. It is not at all unusual for mothers to collapse under these combined pressures, abandon responsibility, avoid decision making and withdraw as much as possible from the activities following disclosure, thereby affording more opportunity for the perpetrator to exert control over the family's response.

Siblings of victims may react protectively and with concern but they may also react defensively. Children fear disruption of family life, even if that has been traumatic and problematic for them. For children, especially, fear of the unknown and fear of separation usually outweigh their negative responses to a known situation. In extrafamily child sexual abuse, siblings of the victim may be angry at the perpetrator but may also be resentful of the disruption of family life, exposure, and publicity resulting from disclosure. In intrafamily child sexual abuse, siblings may also be forced to choose between siding with the perpetrator or siding with the victim. In either situation, the sibling who reacts with concern for the victim and anger at the perpetrator may still feel stigmatized or with reduced self-esteem or social status because at least one family member has been victimized and perhaps another family member has been revealed to be an abuser. Clinicians should remember that in some cases siblings of the victims may have previously been victimized themselves or may even have participated in the abuse or "set up" the victim. The following case example illustrates this point:

> Shirley, age 15 years, was being examined for child sexual abuse. Her mother had reported her father to the police 48 hours earlier, for sexual abuse of a sister, Angela, age 13 years. Shirley was sullen and hostile when interviewed. She reluctantly admitted that she also had been fondled by her father and had vaginal intercourse with him beginning when she was 11 years old. When she was 13 years old, Shirley volunteered to trade bedrooms with Angela, thereby placing Angela in a bedroom by herself while Shirley assumed Angela's bed

in the same room with their younger sister. Shirley further admitted that she switched bedrooms with Angela after telling her mother about the father's sexual advances and receiving a hostile response from her mother. At the time of the examination, Shirley expressed only anger about the events following disclosure. She had been forced, along with her mother and sisters to move into an emergency shelter and was missing school and the junior prom because the father's arrest had been reported in the newspapers and she was ashamed to face her friends. Shirley said of her sister Angela, "Why did she have to go and say something? If she had kept her mouth shut a little longer, there was always Susie."

In this case, the eldest daughter had extricated herself from the incestuous sexual abuse by her father by "setting up" her sister in the bedroom by herself. She was angry at her mother for failing to respond to her appeal for help but for responding positively to her younger sister's appeal. She was also angered by the disruption to *her* life that ensued after disclosure. She had fully expected that her sister Angela would extricate herself from the sexual abuse by substituting their younger sister instead.

Other extended family members may be expected to have the same combination of reactions to disclosure with protection and concern for the child vying with self-protective and defensive reactions. In-laws, brothers, sisters, and grandparents may also place pressure on the target family to react with denial and fail to cooperate with child-protective services and law-enforcement authorities. Such reactions are seen in both intrafamily and extrafamily child sexual abuse cases.

In summary, all family members can be expected to react to disclosure of child sexual abuse within the framework of a response to the question, "How will this affect me?" Only those who have great ego strength and security can be expected to sustain a posture of protection and concern toward the victim. All others will require enormous support and some pressure to maintain a victim-oriented response. In some cases, family members will not be able to react with support or concern for the victim, regardless of the circumstances.

Suppression Phase

Following disclosure, either accidental or purposeful, the dynamics of most child-sexual-abuse cases tend to enter a suppression phase. Even when the perpetrator is outside the family circle, the child's immediate and extended family are likely to react by trying to suppress publicity, information, and intervention. Sometimes this suppression may extend to denial of the significance of disturbances suffered by the child victim as a result of the sexual abuse in order to discourage further intervention by outsiders. The following case example illustrates such suppression in a case of extrafamily sexual abuse.

Ronnie, a 6-year-old boy, was lured into a vacant building by two adolescent boys and forced into sexual activity. Ronnie was forced to fellate one of his abusers while the other boy performed forced rectal penetration upon him. After repeated slapping and many threats, the older boys let Ronnie go. The child's physical injuries quickly drew attention to the sexual abuse and both the abusers were arrested. Although initially grateful for assistance from child protective services in the first 48 hours, Ronnie's parents withdrew and became hostile after medical attention had been rendered and depositions to the police were finished. Ronnie had a severe reaction to the incident—he had nightmares every night, developed a school phobia, and refused to go outside the house unless accompanied by his mother. Nevertheless, his parents refused to permit access to the child for individual and art therapy. When his obviously negative reaction to the sexual abuse was pointed out, his parents replied, "It's nothing to worry about—he'll forget about it soon."

A clue to the motivation for Ronnie's parents to suppress the sexual abuse incident can be found in their expressed determination that the child will "forget" about the sexual abuse. One interpretation of their behavior is that it is the parents themselves who wish to forget about the incident—perhaps in part because they feel guilty for real or imagined culpability in the sexual abuse of their child by outsiders. Their denial of their son's obviously disturbed behavior is a manifestation of their desire to forget or suppress the incident. Another possible explanation is that these people were themselves under pressure from neighbors or perhaps from relatives of the adolescent perpetrators to withdraw the sexual assault charges.

When the sexual abuse has occurred within the family circle, suppression is likely to be intense. The perpetrator can be expected further to exploit his or her power position by pressuring the child and any other family members who appear to be cooperating with outside authority figures. Sometimes the suppression is limited to verbal pressure calculated to induce feelings of guilt in the child for his or her part in the disclosure. Other family members may join in this process and "gang up" on the child. Feeling isolated and perhaps even ostracized, the child may give in and withdraw the complaint or simply stop cooperating with those who are trying to assist him or her.

Grace, age 13 years, told her mother that her grandfather had masturbated and fondled her on numerous occasions when she had stayed with him on summer vacations. On their last encounter, he had attempted vaginal penetration but failed. The mother initially reacted with concern for her daughter and with anger toward her own father for his behavior. After the mother realized, however, that addressing the impact on Grace would inevitably lead to examination of her own role in "setting up" the sexual abuse, she quickly lost interest in therapy for her daughter. The girl missed several sessions because her mother failed to provide transportation at the last minute. After the child declined to read several letters sent by the grandfather which explained the allegation of sexual abuse by describing Grace as "insane," mother then permitted a telephone confrontation to take place between the girl and her grandfather. When Grace asked her mother if she still believed that the sexual abuse had occurred, the mother replied that she "refused to take sides." Finally Grace told her therapist that she "didn't need" any more therapy and declined to return.

In the foregoing example, the behavior of Grace's mother suggests that her own needs were not being met after the disclosure when intervenors focused concern on the child. She at first attempted to sabotage her daughter's treatment program by last-minute failures to give her a ride. When this failed, she joined forces with the grandfather in suppressing Grace's allegation by reinforcing his attacks on the girl and withdrawing her support.

Sometimes the suppression phase is characterized by verbal pressure that is abusive or threatening. Threats may be similar to those described in the secrecy phase, variously invoking anger from a third party, separation, physical harm to the perpetrator, to a third party, or to the child. Again, the aim of the verbal abuse or threats is to pressure the child to recant or to stop complying with the intervention process. In some cases, children and compliant family members may be subjected to physical abuse as part of the suppression phase.

Jolene, age 16 years, made a complaint to the police in which she stated that her father had fondled her breasts and genitals. At the hearing for probable cause, she refused to speak, remaining silent in response to all questions. Charges against her father were dropped. Jolene later revealed that her mother, brothers, and sister all told her that they would refuse to live in the same house with her if she persisted in her complaint.

Regardless of the type of pressure employed, the primary aim of the perpetrator during the suppression phase is to undermine the credibility of the child and the allegation of sexual abuse. One obvious result may be for the child to withdraw the complaint or falsely declare that the complaint was a lie.

Eleven-year-old Tricia told investigators that she had been impregnated by her stepfather. When the case came to trial, the girl perjured herself on the witness stand by telling the judge that she had lied and that she had really been impregnated by her 15-year-old stepbrother. Later she revealed to peers in a support group that she had perjured herself because of repeated physical assaults by her stepfather during the period of time prior to the trial.

Sometimes the child stubbornly withstands pressure to withdraw the complaint. The suppression phase may also be characterized by various attempts to undermine the child's credibility. The child may be described by other family members as a pathological liar or as mentally disturbed or "crazy." Previous school problems or difficulties in interpersonal relationships may be cited as evidence that the child is untrustworthy or disturbed. If an adolescent victim has ever run away from home, skipped school, stayed out too late, or engaged in peer sexual activity, these behaviors may be cited to support the family's contention that the child's allegation of sexual abuse is untrue.

A Profile of Participants

Perpetrators. Psychological motivations of perpetrators of child sexual abuse are discussed in detail in chapter 8, "The Incest Offender." In general, perpetrators are likely to be "me-first" individuals who satisfy many nonsexual needs when they engage a child in sexual behavior. For a variety of reasons, the sexual relationship with a child feels safer, less threatening, less demanding, less problematic than a relationship with an adult. Gratification may be enhanced by the child's accessibility, naïveté, trust, affection, and compliance. Although some perpetrators enjoy being in control to the extent of being gratified by overpowering a resistant victim, most are content to persuade or entice the child into sexual behavior with their own position of power and dominance remaining implicit rather than directly expressed. A few perpetrators enjoy the process of forcibly overpowering the victim, terrifying him or her, and inflicting pain. Fortunately, the last group are in the minority.

Incest perpetrators tend to perceive the outside world as hostile and convey this perception to the child as both a reason and an excuse for the incestuous sexual behavior. The child is encouraged to trust only family members; interpersonal relationships with outsiders are discouraged and often severely limited. Incestuous families, at the behest of the perpetrator, are frequently very isolated. Family members tend to have few friends and few peer activities. The perpetrator often sets the style of family interaction by encouraging or even requiring all family members to meet their social needs within the family circle. This may even extend to use of the telephone. In one incestuous family, the father refused to permit any family member to place or receive telephone calls while he was at home. When the telephone rang in his presence, he answered it. If the call was for some other family member he immediately hung up. Consequently most telephone calls were for him. The perpetrator often dominates all family decision making and is the sole authority on where the family lives, how much is spent for clothing, food and household needs, vacation planning, part-time jobs for family members, contributions to charity, participation of the children in school activities, and so forth. Although physical force is rarely used to engage the child in sexual activity, force or threat of use of force may be used to maintain the perpetrator's authority over everyone else.

Although rarely psychotic, perpetrators frequently exhibit personality disorders. Alcohol abuse is common although few are frank alcoholics. Perpetrators are likely to appear to outsiders as quiet, unassertive, emotionally colorless individuals. An underlying core of rigid and dysfunctional behavior patterns can usually be discerned. However, since perpetrators tend to be hostile, mistrustful, and suspicious of outside authority, there is little chance that any clinician will have taken a good look.

Mothers. The incest victim's mother is usually in a subordinate position to the perpetrator since incest perpetrators in known cases are most frequently male power figures (for example, father, stepfather, uncle, grandfather, mother's boyfriend) in the home. A rare incest case will involve a mother as the sole sexual abuser of her own children or perhaps as a coperpetrator of child sexual abuse (usually with a male coperpetrator). In the coperpetrator situation, the mother nonetheless is still usually cast in a subordinate role.

Mothers can perhaps be most generally described as failing to protect the child victim. Assessment of Connecticut's Sexual Trauma Treatment Program (see chapter 13, "Evaluation of Child Sexual Abuse Program") showed that the extrafamily cases almost always involved single-parent families headed by mothers who failed to protect by exercising poor supervision or directly or indirectly exposed the victim to sexual risk. Mothers of incest victims fail to protect on several levels. Sometimes the mother is physically absent on a regular and predictable basis, thereby affording the opportunity for incest to occur. The classic example of this situation involves a mother who works a night or evening shift. Sometimes mother is psychologically absent, often ignoring overt seductive behavior between the incest participants that she should be curbing and redirecting and setting limits on at a very early stage. Some mothers fail to protect in a very direct fashion by deliberately setting up situations in which the incest participants are encouraged to engage in sexual behavior.

> Nancy, a 35-year-old mother of four girls, regularly encouraged her husband to go to her daughters' bedrooms late at night and "cover them up." One night when Nancy knew Cindy, her 14-year old daughter was sleeping in the nude, she nevertheless sent her husband into Cindy's bedroom, "to be sure she doesn't get cold."

The above case example illustrates a mother's intentional maneuver to encourage sexual behavior between her husband and daughter.

Although it is tempting to think of all mothers of incest victims as women who deliberately encourage their spouses to turn to their children for sexual gratification, this pattern probably occurs less often than we believe. Most mothers of incest victims are married to men who have unrealistic expectations of them. The "dependent husband" wants his wife to prop him up on every level; the "dominant husband" wants his wife to be so dependent that his own needs for power and control are continuously satisfied (see chapter 8, "The Incest Offender"). Wives who stay with such husbands may accept either the dependent or dominant role that is assigned to them. The likelihood that these women will seek relief from duress or boredom or frustration and meet their own needs elsewhere (by becoming psychologically absent or physically absent or both) is very great. In both patterns of husband-wife interaction, the wife frequently eschews a true maternal role with her children. She may often view the children as competitors and rivals while simultaneously meeting some of her own social needs by interacting with the children on a peer level.

Often mother escapes responsibility by being ill or by complaining that she does not "feel good." Indeed she does not feel good and one can anticipate a high level of functional physical complaints, often with no organic basis, from these mothers. Depression, either overt or masked, is also very common. Many of these women have poorly developed social skills, few friends or outside interests and in general, little aptitude for developing and maintaining a relationship. More often than not, they lack everyday living skills as well and cannot drive, handle money, balance a checkbook, interact with the retail business world as consumers, and so forth.

Most mothers of incest victims are aware, consciously or unconsciously, that the incest exists. Many of the mothers have been told by the children that the incestuous sexual behavior is occurring. Some of the mothers respond to this revelation with immediate hostility and disbelief and warn the child never to mention the matter again. Some make no response and discourage the child from pursuing the issue by their silence. Some mothers respond by initially believing the child, promising to intervene and protect the youngster, and then neglect to do so. Still others sincerely try to prevent further sexual abuse by "running interference" and attempting never to permit an opportunity for the perpetrator to be alone with the child again. This method is rarely successful, especially if the perpetrator is a dominant figure in the home. A few mothers respond to the child's complaint by taking immediate action, notifying outside authorities, separating from the perpetrator if necessary and preventing further sexual exploitation of the child either by prolonged separation or by setting limits and forcing the perpetrator to adhere to them. Few mothers have the strength or resources to accomplish this by themselves. Many mothers fear change, shrink from separation, dread retribution by the perpetrator, and shirk or feel inadequate to perform the tasks and fulfill the responsibilities required to stop the incest.

Child Victim. To refer to the child who is the subject of sexual attentions by an adult or "bigger person" as a victim reflects our view that children are always victimized by sexual abuse, even when they are willing and enthusiastic participants in the sexual behavior. Children lack the emotional, maturational, and cognitive development to assimilate or withstand premature introduction to sexuality by an adult. Although frequently described by the perpetrators as seductive ("She kept trying to turn me on, your Honor; I just couldn't help myself"), children who become incest victims have usually displayed no more than the ususal degree of age appropriate exploratory or acting out behavior.

Infants explore their own bodies and quickly discover their genitals. Toddlers have usualy discovered self-stimulation and masturbate freely unless limited by their caretakers. By ages two-and-one-half to three years, children begin to appreciate differences between males and females and be curious about their sex and genitalia. Their ever-expanding perceptions about the world around them (mostly stimulated by observing their own home life and viewing the television set) include an increasing awareness of sexuality tied to male-female roles. Slightly older children may see and mimic behavior that has sexual overtones, especially posturing and touching, in a diconcertingly accurate fashion. Although these actions may be aimed toward attracting attention and favor, it is unlikely that the young child conceptualizes their sexual connotations. By the same token, the child is unlikely to appreciate any relationship between affectionate or affection-seeking behavior and sexuality.

Despite society's tendency to blame the victim, even when the victim is a young child, it is not appropriate to hold a child responsible for exploratory behavior that stimulates an adult. The appropriate adult response is to acknowledge stimulation, deal with his or her own reactions on a personal level, and respond to the child by setting limits on or redirecting the child's behavior. It is never appropriate for adults to respond by engaging the child in a sexual relationship, even when the child appears willing and eager for the behavior to progress. The grossly seductive child who overwhelms the helpless adult with a degree of sensuality that cannot be ignored or denied and thereby stimulates a compulsive response from the adult that inevitably ends in a sexual relationship is a myth existing only in the minds of perpetrators and some defense attorneys. In fact, most victims do not behave in a seductive fashion. The attraction for the perpetrator is much more likely to be some combination of qualities that can best be termed childlike: immaturity; inexperience; defencelessness; and affectionate, trusting, confiding, playful behavior.

If the sexual abuse does not frighten or injure the victim, he or she will probably willingly engage in a progression of sexual behavior, repeatedly over time. As the child grows older and more experienced, he or she may perceive that the sexual behavior meets the perpetrator's needs at some level. The child may come to occupy a favored position vis-à-vis the perpetrator. If not intimidated, he or she may even attempt to manipulate that position of favor and limited power to some degree by withholding or avoiding participation in the sexual behavior or threatening to disclose the secret to outsiders. If other family members are involved in the sexual activity, the child may variously be intimidated by them or angry at them or regard them as fellow conspirators or perhaps even be contemptuous of them. An older child will probably eventually see the perpetrator as a narcissistic individual who exploited him or her. If the older child victim is being limited in peer activities or forced to remain within the family circle rather than develop and enjoy outside relationships and activities, he or she may be very resentful and frustrated indeed. The child victim who disclosed the sexual abuse secret to someone in authority (for example, mother) and received an inappropriate response can be expected to feel betrayed by that person.

Adolescent girls who are incest victims are frequently described as "pseudomature." Physically they may be fully developed by age twelve or thirteen years. These girls often assume much responsibility for management of domestic tasks: preparing meals, caring for younger children, and so forth. They often have special responsibilities to their fathers which are acknowledged by everyone else: bringing in his beer while he watches television, straightening his tools, preparing dad's favorite dessert, and so forth. In many ways, these girls function in quasimaternal, quasispousal roles at home. Nevertheless the girls are expected to eschew independent and "grownup" activities at school and outside the home.

The adolescent male victim of incest is a shadowy figure who has rarely been described. We have seen adolescent males, who were themselves previous victims of sexual abuse by a male perpetrator, engaging their sisters and younger children, both male and female, in sexual behavior. Much of this sexual behavior appeared to be in the service of a need to control or dominate another person, rather than to satisfy a sexual need. Much of this type of sexual behavior was abusive in fact as well as in name; force or intimidation was used with agemates as well as with younger children and trauma to the victim would often result. (See chapter 6, "Sibling Incest"). On the other hand, little information exists about adolescent males, who are being or have been victimized by women, especially in the mother-son incest situation. How do they appear to the clinician? It has been suggested that the impact of mother-son incest is the most pathological of all types of incest. We can neither confirm nor challenge this impression.

Other Family Members. With the social decline of large extended families living under one roof, pertinent other family members are usually children other than the child victim of incest. Frequently they also are aware of the incestuous sexual behavior. Sometimes other children are or were themselves victims of sexual abuse. By definition, such multiple incest victims will be siblings or stepsiblings. When more than one child is a victim, any of several patterns may emerge. First, the victims may be unaware that the incestuous behavior has involved another child in the family. Or they may be aware of other victims but be unwilling or afraid to discuss the situation with them. Or multiple victims may discuss their situations with each other and give mutual support or assistance. Sometimes, one child victim will "set up" or deliberately arrange the sexual victimization of another child in the family, usually with the aim of extricating himself or herself from the incestuous sexual relationship.

Even when they are not aware of the incestuous sexual behavior, other children in the family may discern a special or favored position of the child victim. This special position or privileges may serve to attract resentment from siblings toward the victim. Much sibling rivalry may be present.

Family Interaction. The incestuous family very closely resembles the pathological family described by Beavers (1976). It is a closed and generally pathological system, constantly draining more and more energy from the individuals who comprise the family and offering little that is positive in return. At the same time the individual family member's dependence on this pathological system is enormous and the difficulty in extricating himself or herself and maintaining a healthy independent existence is equally great. These families and their members develop few skills for coping with the outside world that are effective or adequate to meet the complex demands of daily living. The outside world is perceived as hostile; individuals outside the family are "out to get you" and not to be trusted. Any attempt by outsiders to interact with family members is viewed as intrusion that is threatening to everyone at home. Such attempts are greeted with hostility, suspicion, and fear. Family members who overcome their own hesitation and anxiety and attempt to interact with outsiders are greeted with hostility, scorn, and reprisals from those within.

Although power is often exerted within incestuous families in a predictable fashion as described above, it is also exerted capriciously at times. Powerful individuals within incestuous families are variously so ambivalent about their feelings and so unlikely to be able to move effectively to satisfy a conflicted need that they may rigidly demand a certain type of behavior on one day only to abandon that expectation and substitute another (usually without prior notice) on the next. Power is generally exercised by physical force or by intimidation. Children learn that power is all-important in human relationships and that powerful people can make their own rules and change them without warning. Instead of observing the legitimate use of power in conjunction with responsibility and the benevolent exercise of power for the common good, children in incestuous families tend to see power exercised irresponsibly and solely to meet the needs of the person who is in power. They tend to role model this behavior, especially with each other and often with mother acting as a peer participant in family battle.

In incestuous families when a father figure is the perpetrator, he may stand aside and observe the other family members as they act out with each other and maneuver for power. Sometimes the father may even initiate or "set up" such a battle and then withdraw to the sidelines. Eventually, he will take command of the situation, by out-shouting or out-punching all the other participants or perhaps by engaging in behavior that startles the others into quiescence or submission (for example, brandishing or firing a gun, breaking a window or a piece of furniture, or the like). With a fraction of the unbearable tension released, the family may then settle temporarily into a deceptively tranquil routine. Sooner or later, however, the tension can be expected to erupt again.

Sometimes power is exercised by withdrawal. The powerful individual ignores or refuses to speak to one or all family members.

George, an incestuous father, punished his wife and attempted to prevent her from participating in therapy by giving her the "silent treatment." On the night she would return from her group therapy session, he would refuse to acknowledge her return in any way or even speak to her. He would, however, sit across from her in the living room and openly masturbate himself for hours. Although they slept in the same bed he would continue to ignore her. The "silent treatment" would continue for several days and then he would begin to speak to her again. By the end of the week, their interactions were "normal" but as soon as she went to the next therapy session, the silent treatment would resume.

Power may also be exercised by belittling others and their efforts, often by previously setting up a situation in which the person would be likely to fail.

Jack had incestuous relationships with his two older daughters, ages 16 and 14 years. Angry with his 16-year-old daughter, he sent her on an errand in the family car when he knew the gas tank was nearly empty and with little money. When he finally "rescued" her he criticized her for calling him for help, saying "If you are old enough to drive, you should be able to take care of yourself."

Another way in which the perpetrator may keep family members in line is to react unexpectedly, catching the other person off balance.

Patricia stayed married to a man who had sexually molested her daughter for many years. Before the disclosure of incest occurred, Patricia decided to surprise her husband with a fancy dinner on the occasion of their wedding anniversary. She made other arrangements to feed the children and was alone in the house when her husband came home, table elegantly set, candles lit, and a roast beef dinner (his favorite meal) ready to be served. Her husband responded by slamming his fist on the table and yelling, "How dare you behave like a whore with me?" He refused to eat any of the dinner and prepared himself a hot dog instead.

Any permutation of the exercise of power can be seen within the incestuous family. The overriding theme, however, for the person in power is to meet his or her own needs first and to maintain control within a closed family system.

Denial is overused as a defense mechanism in incestuous families and frequently is the only coping skill available to family members. An enormous degree of denial is required, for example, for mothers to overlook the incestuous sexual behavior and the "special" positions occupied by the participants in relation to each other. Denial may actually be an extension of the secrecy phase of sexual abuse and even an expression of the secrecy. In other words, the sexual abuse is so secret that the participants deny its existence even to themselves. Father may think of the activity as "sex education"; the victim may call it "helping dad." Family members routinely deny their real feelings, especially when feeling angry or hurt or disappointed or frustrated. Projection of these feelings on others is very common. They tend to be concrete in the extreme, especially on a verbal level. Much denial is also used to maintain the false image that the incestuous home is a blissful haven of security and freedom in comparison to the hostile outside world.

Incestuous families are sometimes described as having no role boundaries. Because family members behave in a manner that is not in keeping with their traditional roles of father, mother, and child, and because they may temporarily exchange roles, the boundaries separating them are said to be blurred. Actually, the blurring of boundaries and lack of limits is likely to pervade every aspect of family life. Individuals are not often permitted to set limits on other family members with respect to their bodies, belongings, or personal space. People wander into bedrooms or bathrooms, opening closed doors, and walking in on others while they bathe, go to the toilet, and undress. Bedrooms, beds, closets, drawers, and clothing tend to be used interchangeably by everyone. In particular, parents have little respect for the privacy of the children or siblings for each others' privacy. Powerful family members have, in effect, no limits on observing less powerful individuals, or on touching their bodies or their belongings. Children and less powerful individuals usually have the benefit only of those limits that they can enforce themselves.

Recent papers have described the incestuous family as the multiproblem family or character-disordered family. This description certainly fits for the majority of incestuous families that we have seen. Despite internal tensions and flawed familial interpersonal relationships, these individuals seem to exhibit an array of dysfunctional behavior and methods of coping with stress that causes them to be viewed as a unit or entity. The multiplicity of problems and acting out behavior makes it tempting for the clinician to view the incestuous behavior as ''only a symptom'' and as one of a variety of problems that compete for attention. In reality, the incestuous family is most often a ''nonfamily'' in the cultural sense: a group of individuals of varying ages and sexes live under one roof, have a biological relationship with each other, and may even call each other by familial role labels (mother, father, daughter, son, sister, brother). However the real ties between them at the time of disclosure are the sharing of interdependent dysfunctional behavior patterns rather than traditional or functional intrafamily relationships. The existence of the abusive incestuous behavior is a reflection of their nonfamily status and usually serves as the sole leverage point for bringing about changes in the direction of healthier and more effective coping patterns.

Impact on the Child

In discussing the impact of sexual abuse upon the target child, it is necessary to make the distinction between known cases and cases in which the secret was never disclosed. It is possible that there are children who are not adversely affected by sexual abuse. Indeed, the absence of adverse effects upon the child may be related to the frequency of disclosure: that is, perhaps situations involving little or no psychological or physical trauma to the child are less likely to be disclosed to anyone else. Although cases are now being disclosed or identified with greater frequency, we cannot know the outcome unless someone reveals the secret or discloses the sexual abuse accidentally.

Ultimately, people who make judgments about the impact of sexual abuse upon the child must do so based upon their own clinical experience with known cases. We believe sexual abuse is nearly always a profoundly disruptive, disorienting, and destructive experience for the child with a degree of stimulation that is far beyond his or her capacity to encompass and assimilate. Consequently, there is interference with the accomplishment of normal developmental tasks. The progression of mastery of one's self, environment, and relationship with others is significantly disrupted by the child's permanently altered awareness and new role vis-à-vis the perpetrator.

Child sexual abuse is disorienting because profound blurring of boundaries inevitably follows when someone in a power position exploits the child by making him or her a sexual partner. These children cannot avoid questioning limits set for them and for others. They must be confused about the appropriate uses of power and authority. Their very identities are at issue as they ask: "Who am I, that I am both a child and a sexual partner of someone who is supposed to be parenting or nurturing or protecting me?"

Destructive effects of sexual abuse are readily identifiable. Most of the children we encountered seemed to have a very poor self-image. Strikingly attractive youngsters would describe themselves as ugly and express great doubt that they could appear attractive or appealing to others. Although some of the children displayed much pseudomaturity, they frequently possessed very poor social skills. Seductiveness was often displayed inappropriately and as a substitute for other social skills that were lacking. Victims tended to be isolated socially with poor peer relationships as well as unsatisfying social relationships. Many were hostile or depressed, and some were even suicidal. They commonly expressed reluctance or inability to trust any other human being.

Data on long-term impact of child sexual abuse are sadly lacking. Some individuals disclose the secret years later after reaching adulthood. We have not encountered anyone who has reported that a sexual abuse experience in childhood had a positive or even neutral effect upon their lives. On the contrary, many such individuals describe serious difficulty in attaining a satisfactory level of emotional self-sufficiency or independence as adults. Nearly all attribute a poor self-image and lack of confidence to their childhood victimization. Some are plagued by multiple phobic or psychosomatic problems often resulting in serious dysfunction or disability. Few incest victims report satisfactory relationships with members of their family of origin. Most incest victims report serious difficulty in establishing satisfactory interpersonal relationships with others. Sexual dysfunction is also commonly reported.

Although the data are incomplete, a significant proportion of parents in the incestuous families studied in Connecticut's Sexual Trauma Treatment Program (see chapter 13) reported that they themselves had been sexually abused in childhood. This raises two areas of concern. First, childhood sexual victimization may increase the likelihood that an individual will become a perpetrator later on. Second, it is disturbing to note the apparent tendency of women who were sexually victimized in childhood to select mates who, in turn, were likely to abuse them and sexually exploit their children. Prospective longitudinal studies are needed to determine the long-term impact of child sexual abuse and to project how often and under what circumstances deleterious effects may be expected.

Conclusion

The clinician who begins to work with child-sexual-abuse cases needs a conceptual framework for understanding the often bewildering array of behavior that he or she should expect to encounter. It requires much effort to enrich and augment one's store of useful knowledge about this problem. A conceptual framework should not be static. Instead, concepts should be continuously tested and revised in the light of one's experience as new information and insights emerge. A basic knowledge of the mechanics and dynamics of child sexual abuse nonetheless remains the cornerstone for effective intervention.

References

Anderson, Lorna M., and Shafer, Gretchen. "The Character-Disordered Family: A Community Treatment Model for Family Sexual Abuse." *American Journal of Orthopsychiatry* 49 (3), July 1979: 436–45

Beavers, W. Robert. "A Theoretical Basis for Family Evaluation." In Lewis, J.M. et al., *No Single Thread: Psychological Health in Family Systems.* New York:Brunner-Mazel, 1976.

Burgess, Ann W., and Holmstrom, Lynda L. "Sexual Assault of Children and Adolescents: Pressure, Sex and Secrecy." *Nursing Clinics of North America* (September 1975): 551–63.

Burgess, Ann. W., Holmstrom, Lynda L., and McCauseland, Maureen P. "Child Sexual Assault by a Family Member." *Victomology: An International Journal* 2 (1977): 236–50.

Groth, A. Nicholas, and Burgess, Ann W. "Motivational Intent in the Sexual Assault of Children." *Criminal Justice and Behavior: An International Journal of Correctional Psychology* 4 (1977): 253–64.

2 Validation of Child Sexual Abuse

Suzanne M. Sgroi,
Frances Sarnacki Porter,
and *Linda Canfield Blick*

Validation

Every reported case of child sexual abuse must be investigated to determine if the complaint is valid: that is, did sexual abuse of the target child actually occur or not? The process by which this happens is termed *validation*. It should be conducted in an orderly fashion by knowledgeable individuals who are prepared to deal with the consequences of the process regardless of the outcome.

Who Is Responsible for Validating Cases?

In every jurisdiction, there is a statutory child-protective-services agency which has the authority and responsibility for receiving reports of all types of child maltreatment (including sexual abuse), investigating cases, and validating the complaint. Law-enforcement agencies also have statutory responsibility for validation, although the process involves investigating to determine if a crime, *sexual assault* of a child, has been committed. (See chapter 11, "Law Enforcement and Child Sexual Abuse.") It is not unusual for both the child-protective-services agency *and* the law-enforcement agency to investigate the same case, often simultaneously, sometimes jointly, sometimes in parallel fashion, and not infrequently at cross purposes.

Responsibility for validation of child sexual abuse extends beyond these statutory agencies, however. Every clinician or professional person who works with children should be aware of the essential elements of validating child sexual abuse. Investigators or individuals who perform validation of cases may be personnel of the statutory agencies or clinicians or both.

Why Emphasize Validation of Cases?

Child-protection agencies need to determine if sexual abuse has actually occurred in order to fulfill their statutory responsibility for child protection. Law-enforcement agencies need to determine if sexual assault has occurred in order to fulfill their statutory responsibility to enforce the law. This simplistic definition is offered to illustrate the underlying compatibility of the tasks with which each agency is charged. Both agencies have a like charge to distinguish between valid and in-valid complaints in order to be certain that the appropriate cases receive intervention aimed at child protection and law enforcement, respectively. Since both types of intervention are authoritative in nature, there is great concern about protecting the rights of innocent parties. On the other hand, great danger or harm could occur if intervention is withheld due to error. Statutory agency personnel are thus understandably anxious to avoid mistakes in validation.

Components of Validation

Validation hinges upon one's ability to interpret behavior, physical signs, and information elicited from investigative interviews within a conceptual framework for child sexual abuse (see chapter 1, "A Conceptual Framework for Child Sexual Abuse"). It requires a fundamental understanding of the dynamics and mechanics of child sexual abuse, good interviewing skills, and a capacity to assess credibility of the information elicited. The remainder of this chapter will describe each of the following components separately: (1) behavioral indicators of child sexual abuse; (2) investigative interviewing; (3) credibility assessment; (4) physical indicators of child sexual abuse; and (5) medical examination.
Each of the above components will be presented and explained in this chapter. It should be noted that the methodology presented represents an expansion of some issues discussed in chapter 3, "An Approach to Case Management." The validation process is, of course, an integral part of initial case management.

Behavioral Indicators of Child Sexual Abuse

A child's behavior may directly indicate or strongly suggest that he or she is a subject of sexual abuse. Recognizing behavioral indicators is an important part of the validation process and should begin in the initial interview. Although the presence of some of these indicators may be helpful, they are not conclusive. Nevertheless, any professional person who works with children and observes these behavioral indicators has an obligation to ask if sexual abuse is occurring. The following behavioral indicators will be described:

1. Overly compliant behavior.
2. Acting-out, aggressive behavior.
3. Pseudomature behavior.
4. Hints about sexual activity.

5. Persistent and inappropriate sexual play with peers or toys or with themselves, or sexually aggressive behavior with others.
6. Detailed and age-inappropriate understanding of sexual behavior (especially by young children).
7. Arriving early at school and leaving late with few, if any, absences.
8. Poor peer relationships or inability to make friends.
9. Lack of trust, particularly with significant others.
10. Nonparticipation in school and social activities.
11. Inability to concentrate in school.
12. Sudden drop in school performance.
13. Extraordinary fears of males (in cases of male perpetrator and female victim).
14. Seductive behavior with males (in cases of male perpetrator and female victim).
15. Running away from home.
16. Sleep disturbances.
17. Regressive behavior.
18. Withdrawal.
19. Clinical depression.
20. Suicidal feelings.

Some combination of these behaviors may be observed in children who are victims of sexual abuse. In general, the behaviors may be seen in children of all ages unless otherwise indicated.

Unlike most children, the incest victim may display *overly compliant behavior*. These children have suffered significantly. Every aspect of their lives has often been subjected to control. These children may have no control over what happens to their bodies and no choices in every day events such as choosing their friends. The result is lack of assertiveness and inability to take control of their lives in any way. For example, in the Connecticut Sexual Trauma Treatment Program,[a] many of the adolescent girls who participated in group therapy were overly compliant. The therapists would attempt to help them become more assertive and to make decisions for themselves. Months after the incestuous behavior had ended and after months of group treatment, the girls would still raise their hands and ask permission to talk (behavior not encouraged by the therapist).

Conversely, some victims can be described as "actor-outers." Children who display *acting-out behavior* seem to have greater emotional strength than those children who are compliant. The acting-out children have made efforts to get help and to stop the incestuous behavior. Usually they have gone to another adult such as the nonoffending parent or even the police, but have failed to gain

[a]Sponsored in part by National Center for Child Abuse and Neglect, DHEW, Grant No. 90-C-399.

help. As their frustration and anger mounts, they begin to displace their feelings on others. These children begin to get a reputation at school as fighters and name-callers which often leads to expulsion from school and added problems.

> At age 12, Connie was molested by her father. She tried to tell her mother who could not accept it. Connie told her therapist that her mother's disbelief angered her. She said: "Something happened, I changed, I felt angry with everyone." She had fights at school and with neighborhood children, and her fighting led to numerous expulsions from school. Eventually, having no place to release this anger, Connie stole a car, was arrested, and ended up in the juvenile court system.

Often, as in Connie's case, the anger and frustration leads to increasingly negative behavior. Some of this negative behavior is a result of pent-up emotions. However, the acting-out behavior may also represent a cry for help.

Whether these children are compliant or acting-out, both groups exhibit *pseudomature behavior*. Their outwardly mature appearance is truly a façade. Incest victims have often been forced to take on responsibilities well beyond their years. They may be called upon to perform the majority of household chores and to care for their siblings. They often behave as quasi parents as well as quasi spouses. This added responsibility and premature introduction to sexuality creates an outwardly sophisticated appearance. When the pseudomature exterior is penetrated, a frightened, guilt-ridden, lonely child is revealed. This phenomenon occurs in all age groups and in varying degrees.

Some children will drop *hints about sexual activity* without offering a direct explanation of what has happened. One girl, while watching a television show which portrayed an older man who was making advances to a young girl, remarked to her mother, "He's a dirty old man, just like grandpoppy."

Young children who have been sexually abused may reveal this through *persistent and inappropriate sexual play with others or with toys or with themselves*. These children may initiate sex play with their peers or even with older persons.

> A four-year-old boy who had been involved in fellatio with his father was discovered to be exposing his genitals to adolescent boys. Several of these boys were from an incestuous family themselves and viewed this child's exposure as a sexual invitation to them.

Another little boy was observed to be holding a doll's face pressed to his genitals. Some of these children have become so focused on sexual activity that they masturbate almost continuously, openly and in public as well as when they are alone. When adults set limits on masturbatory activity, these children sometimes place objects inside their clothing so that they can masturbate surreptitiously. Although not conclusive evidence of sexual abuse, inappropriate sex play or excessive masturbation should always be carefully assessed with possible victimization of the child in mind.

Some sexually victimized children may actually become sexually aggressive and victimize others who are younger and smaller than themselves. The child who is a sexual offender should always be regarded as a probable victim of sexual abuse. Identification with the aggressor and resolving conflict about one's own powerlessness by acting out against others are well-recognized responses to victimization.

Other young victims of sexual abuse may reveal themselves by displaying *detailed and age-inappropriate understanding of sexual behavior.* A child who can describe cunnilingus, fellatio, or rectal or vaginal intercourse could only have obtained this information through observation of others or through participation in these sexual activities. Sometimes their precocious knowledge will be revealed in their drawings.

> Billy, who had recently turned seven years old, was referred to a clinician knowledgeable in sexual abuse for assessment of his advanced knowledge of sexual behavior. At the initial meeting, Billy drew two people engaged in vaginal intercourse. When questioned about this, he said it was his mother and a man. However, several sessions later, Billy revealed that he was the person in the picture with his mother.

Another child, a seven-year-old girl, also revealed precocious knowledge of sexual behavior through her drawings.

> A teacher had referred Lisa after she had observed several drawings that made her suspicious that sexual abuse was occurring. Lisa drew a picture for the clinician of two people in bed with "dots" all over the bed. When questioned about her picture, Lisa revealed that her stepfather had been masturbating against her in bed and that the "dots" were really ejaculated semen.

Of course, clinicians must be prepared to learn and use the child's own terminology in assessing the child's level of understanding of sexual behavior, as the above case illustrates.

School behavior and performance, patterns of attendance, and interaction with peers are all important indicators to explore. Since the incestuous family limits the outside contacts that the children may have, school is often the only place a child can be seen or observed outside of the home. Accordingly, it is very important to obtain data from school personnel who have contact with the child.

In an effort to escape the home situation, incest victims will often *arrive early at school and leave late.* Usually, they have few if any absences. While home is not a safe place for these children, school may provide them relief from the abuse they are suffering at home. Another reason for this attendance pattern is accessibility to peer contact. The children are usually limited by parents from having friends outside of school; therefore, their only peer contact is often at school. However, even though the children attempt to make friends at school, they often fail.

Poor peer relationships or inability to make friends can also be indicators. The incest victim yearns to be like his or her peers and to become friendly with them. This is not an easy task. One difficulty arises because of their prescribed limits outside of school. Children usually carry school friendships into the community. They meet after school to play games or just to get together and talk. The incestuous family does not afford this opportunity to its children. Secondly, it is difficult for sexual abuse victims to relate to peers who are more naïve than themselves. One girl victim spoke of her friends talking excitedly about kissing a boy for the first time. She felt alienated from the conversation as she had been involved sexually with her father for years.

Sexually abused children often *lack the ability to trust* anyone. They have not been allowed privacy of body or personal space. The children often reveal that they have had no place where they felt safe. This prevailing lack of trust creates a barrier to the establishment of trust relationships.

Nonparticipation in school or social activities may also be indicators. These children are often "loners" in school.

> Fourteen-year old Marcia maintained contact with only two girls at school and had no close friends. Marcia would sneak into the library at lunchtime, sit at a desk furthest from any activity, hunch down into the chair, and eat alone. She was referred to a sensitive school guidance counselor who was able to learn that Marcia had been engaged in a sexually abusive relationship with her stepfather for two years.

In addition to isolation during the school day, incest victims do not usually participate in social activities after school or on weekends. They are generally not allowed to participate in any activity that takes them away from home. Parents in the incestuous family may interfere with social activities by assigning household chores and babysitting responsibilities which do not allow the children very much free time.

> A typical day in Sallie's life consisted of getting ready for school, making her bed, and then feeding and dressing her younger siblings. After school, Sallie reported home immediately to clean the house and await the arrival of her three younger sisters from school. Often she would make dinner. Mother was usually home, either drunk or absorbed in soap operas, refusing to take on her adult
> .   responsibility.

The child's academic performance may be another important indicator. Children who are having emotional difficulty in coping with the sexual abuse may demonstrate *inability to concentrate in school*. These children are always anticipating the next encounter or are trying to think of ways to escape or are simply emotionally overloaded. They may report that there is so much on their minds that they are unable to focus on their studies or pay attention in the classroom.

Sudden drop in school performance may also be an indicator. Some children seem to have better coping methods and perform well academically. However, their grades sometimes drop markedly. This performance change may be related to a change in the sexual relationship. For example, there may be a progression in the sexual behavior from fondling to attempted intercourse. The victim may be reaching adolescence and evidencing interest in peers of the opposite sex. He or she may no longer want to continue the sexual relationship. This usually angers or threatens the perpetrator, who may resort to force or bargaining to maintain the relationship as it was.

> Sixteen-year old Susan told her therapist about her relationship with her father. She said, "I never liked it but I just put up with it [the sexual abuse] until I became older and wanted to date. My father was jealous. He used to say, "If you let me suck on your breasts, I'll let you go out." Susan said she would just stay home.

Conflict or change in incestuous behavior again affects the victim's concentration in school and is often reflected by a drop in academic performance.

The way a female victim interacts with males should also be assessed. Two types of behavior may indicate sexual abuse: *extraordinary fear of males or seductive behavior toward males*. Some child victims find men frightening. There does not seem to be any way to measure this fear in terms of the extent of the sexual trauma. The fear is based on the child's *perception* of the abuse and may be correlated to threats of violence or actual violence. This type of victim has usually had no other positive contact with male figures to demonstrate appropriate behavior.

> Wanda, age 12, would come to the female therapist's office for therapy. As a sexually abused victim, she had suffered physical beatings and had become pregnant by her stepfather. Wanda spoke clearly of the absence of any positive aspect of this relationship. There were no other adult males in her life. For many weeks during her initial therapy sessions, she would be introduced to or come in contact with male therapists. Wanda would lower her head, barely acknowledging their presence and move closer to her female therapist for "protection."

The seductive child or adolescent may suffer other complications. The victim learns to be seductive from the perpetrator and this behavior causes two problems. One, a seductive victim (particularly an adolescent) reporting sexual abuse is usually not believed by authorities, or worse, is *blamed* for causing the sexual abuse. Secondly, children who have learned this type of behavior may carry it over into relationships with other people, making them prime candidates for further sexual assault.

Nicki, a seductive 13 year old, revealed to her therapist that she had been sexually abused three times since the age of 7. The first time she was sexually assaulted by an unknown assailant in a park. Her parents, unable to cope with this, began blaming her and then alienated her emotionally from the family. Her behavior changed. Nicki became aggressive and seductive in an attempt to gain some attention. Her father then molested her three years later, stating that "she knew about sex anyway." He was arrested for this and removed from the home. Nicki's seductive behavior extended itself to people she knew and strangers. Less than one year after the abuse by her father, another unknown assailant tried to rape her at knife-point.

Running away from home may be an indicator of sexual abuse. As incest victims grow older and become adolescents, they make greater efforts to escape the sexual abuse. The runaway has usually exhausted all known sources of help and believes the only remaining solution is to leave home.

Fifteen-year-old Sandra had been a victim of father/daughter incest (including sexual intercourse) for seven years. Sandra had approached her mother on several occasions for help and had been ignored. She sought out community professionals who also failed her. Eventually, she ran away to a large city and became a prostitute.

Children who run away will rarely disclose sexual abuse as a reason. By the time they run away from home, the children are desperate and distrustful of adults. At this point, it takes an extremely sensitive person to engage this child. Only then, when asked about the possibility of sexual abuse, is the child likely to disclose this traumatic secret. As a result, the problem of sexual abuse goes undetected and therefore untreated for many runaways.

Sleep disturbances are another strong indicator of child sexual abuse. These indicators can only be observed by family members and must be elicited from them or from the victim. Child-sexual-abuse victims of all ages suffer from nightmares. Surprisingly, the nightmares are usually about falling, kidnappings, or violence rather than re-enactments of the sexual abuse. The children wake up in the night, crying and frightened. In young children this type of behavior is frequently known as night terrors.

Twelve-year-old Tauanda spoke to her therapist about nightmares. She explained, with much distress, that they occurred nightly. In describing the nightmares, the child did not relate scenes from her one-and-one-half year sexually abusive relationship with her stepfather, but of strangers chasing her with the implied threat of physical harm.

Sleep disturbance often results from the pattern of sexual abuse. Some perpetrators abuse children in the child's own bed during the night. Because of this behavior, children become fearful of falling asleep in anticipation of the next attack. When these children finally do fall asleep from exhaustion, their sleep pattern is fretful. Consequently, they awake tired and find it difficult to cope with school or other activities of the day.

> During the initial investigation of 11 year old Lisa's complaint about sexual abuse, she told the therapist and police officer of her father's nightly fondling of her in her bedroom. She tearfully described the abuse she had suffered and her inability to sleep because of it. Lisa said, "Every night I would lie awake in my bed and wonder when he would come tonight."

Sleeping long hours may be another indicator of sexual abuse. Some children attempt to escape reality through sleep and may sleep ten or twelve hours or more.

> After Patsy's father was arrested for sexually abusing her, her mother reported to her therapist that Patsy was sleeping ten hours a day or more. Patsy had suffered physical abuse and extensive sexual abuse which had caused her to become pregnant. After exploring alternatives for the pregnancy, Patsy had decided on an abortion. With the father out of the home and her abortion completed, Patsy became severely depressed. Even during sessions with her therapist, Patsy said she was embarrassed about what had happened and that she didn't want to talk about it. She said the only good time she had was when she was sleeping.

Sleep disturbances are often a part of *clinical depression,* another behavioral indicator of sexual abuse.

Children who have suffered such a severe level of emotional trauma usually exhibit *regressive behavior* and escape into a fantasy world during their waking hours. Patsy did this also.

> Patsy slowly continued with each session to explain to her therapist that when she was not sleeping, she was talking to her "dog" and "other friends"—all stuffed animals. Patsy had created a world for herself with these friends where she could be safe and express any emotions she wanted to with them. In observing this behavior, it was clear to the therapist that at times Patsy could not distinguish which world was "real" and which world was "make-believe."

Clinically depressed child victims require close monitoring by a supportive adult. Sometimes medication may be prescribed to help the victim overcome the depression in addition to outpatient therapy. Severely depressed or suicidal victims will probably require hospitalization.

Most child sexual abuse victims have *suicidal feelings.* These feelings should be brought out through appropriate questioning by a trained therapist. Again, as with many of the behavioral indictors, the child probably will not volunteer these feelings. Most children will reveal that, "I thought about killing myself, but I guess I really didn't want to." However, the more traumatized the child, the greater the risk of actual suicidal attempts.

> Fifteen-year old Carol cut her wrists in school. As a consequence of this behavior, she was hospitalized, and it was learned that she had been sexually abused by her grandfather. She revealed to the hospital physician that this was not the first suicide attempt, but that no one had noticed the other attempts.

It is difficult to predict which children will make suicide attempts as a result of sexual abuse. The type and extent of the sexual abuse seem less important than the child's perception of the behavior and presence or lack of emotional strengths.

Investigative Interviewing

Without a doubt, investigative interviewing is the most important component of the validation process. It requires the greatest skills and affords the best opportunity to collect pertinent information. In the past, physical evidence and findings from physical examination of the victim have been accorded greater weight than skilled investigative interviewing. This emphasis has been misplaced. In most child-sexual-abuse cases, there will be little or no physical evidence and few, if any, physical findings to support the allegation. A methodology for investigative interviewing will now be presented.

Interviewing the Child Victim

The techniques employed for investigative interviewing should impact upon the child in the following ways:

1. They facilitate a quiet engagement of the child.
2. They provide the first therapeutic session for the child.
3. They help to validate or to negate the allegation of sexual abuse.
4. They enable the interviewer to assess the child's need for immediate protection.

Although the primary purpose of investigative interviewing is fact-finding, there will be a clinical effect upon the child as well. From a clinical standpoint, interviewing for facts can be potentially traumatic or therapeutic. Since no professional person wishes to inflict a traumatic process upon a child, it is well to structure the interview in such a way that the net effect will be therapeutic. It is not necessary that the interviewing be done by a clinician to achieve this effect, but it is ideally done by a person who has both investigative and clinical skills.

The interviewer should concentrate on certain key issues and processes in working with child victims.

1. Continuum of exposure. *The first report is almost never the first incident*. Experience has shown that, regardless of what the child initially reports, it is highly unusual for the perpetrator to jump into bed with a child and engage in sexual intercourse as their first encounter. This is especially true in intrafamily sexual abuse. In general, the sexual abuse occurs multiple times over a span of several months to many years. A child as young as six months of age may be sexually abused. The sexual behavior may continue for many years before the secret is revealed. Some children may never disclose the sexual relationship. When this happens, they carry the trauma into adulthood and may never receive any help.

2. Setting for the interview. *Interview the child alone in a neutral setting or with a supportive adult ally*. Upon receiving a sexual-abuse referral, the child should be interviewed alone in a neutral setting. By interviewing a child alone, there is an avoidance of any pressure or influence that may be placed upon the child. Privacy eliminates corrections, additions, or deletions to the story by observers, as well as the influence of their looks of horror, embarrassment, or disgust. The one-to-one interview provides the child with a sense of relief in disclosing the secret in detail. It also conveys to the child that he or she is important and believable enough to be interviewed without an adult to corroborate the story.

Access to the child victim for the interview is usually effected through the referring party. (See chapter 3, ''An Approach to Case Management.'') Occasionally, when the child is unwilling or extremely uncomfortable about being interviewed alone, the interviewer may permit the presence of an adult requested by the child. The interviewer should have this adult assume a silent, supportive position by sitting next to the child, out of the child's view, with the interviewer sitting opposite both of them. This positioning will eliminate the child's awareness of the other adult's reactions to his or her story.

Regardless of whether a child is interviewed alone or with a supportive adult ally, the setting chosen is important and should be selected to place the child at ease. A neutral setting, such as a school, is frequently used for this purpose. Other neutral areas may be the social service agency, a relative's or neighbor's home or even a park or playground. Avoidance of the child's home as an interview site is imperative. Investigative interviewing of children in their own homes may be influenced by pressure upon the child to cover up or even by the child's fear that the interview will be overheard or interrupted by a powerful family member.

3. Interviewer credibility. *Tell the child you have spoken with others in the same situation*. A simple statement, such as, ''Connie, I've spoken to other children who have had this kind of problem,'' helps to relax the child and enhances the interviewer's credibility. Frequently, this is the first time that the child becomes aware that he or she is not alone, and that other children have experienced the same problems. It also enables the interviewer to introduce

areas of investigation in a nonthreatening and nonpressured way: for example, "Some of the children I have talked to were afraid of somebody."

4. Child's terminology. *Use the child's terminology and clarify its meaning.* In interviewing the child, the interviewer needs to be aware of the victim's terminology and to be able to clarify its meaning in relation to the sexual activity. Interviewing young children is a challenging experience, as they lack the necessary vocabulary for identifying body parts and sexual activity. The creativity and imagination of the clinician are quite important in eliciting the sexual abuse details from a young child. For example,

1. Have the child draw a picture of how and where the sexual abuse happened.
2. Have the child point to areas of his or her body that were violated.
3. Make a game out of the session, with the interviewer pointing to his or her own body and having the child say "yes" when a pertinent area is pointed out.
4. Use anatomically correct dolls to facilitate role playing between the interviewer and the child and to help identify the details of the sexual abuse.

Regardless of which technique is employed, the interviewer must always be sensitive to the child's terminology and use the child's words when speaking. Sometimes this is a difficult task, as in the case of Sharon, age four.

> The clinician was experiencing a great deal of frustration in ascertaining the details of the sexual abuse of Sharon. At the second interview it became apparent that in this child's mind, the word "monkey" meant penis and the word "pookie" meant vagina. So her statement that mother's boyfriend tried to put ". . . his monkey in my pookie" really meant he tried to put his penis in her vagina.

Clarifying terminology with an older child or adolescent is just as important as with a younger child. With the prevalence of sex education in schools and the exploitation of sexuality by the mass media, there is an often incorrect tendency to assume that older children understand sexual terms.

> When 14-year-old Wendy was asked if her father masturbated in front of her, she replied, "No." When the clinician rephrased the question, and asked if her father's penis became larger after he rubbed himself and then white stuff came out of it, she replied, "Yes." Wendy had had two years of sex education in school and claimed to know "everything" about sex.

Children, particularly adolescents, are too embarrassed to admit their ignorance about sexual terms. To one child "we had sex" means kissing, to another it might mean fondling, and to another child, sexual intercourse. In spite of a child's age, his or her access to sex education, or apparent sophistication, sexual terminology and sexual behavior need to be discussed during the interview and understood.

> Fourteen-year-old Meredith related to her clinician that she had engaged in "sexual intercourse" with her father. This went on for two years, between the ages of 9 and 11. Although medical examinations for sexual abuse tend to be inconclusive, in this case the medical examination indicated no vaginal intercourse had occurred. Further discussions between the child and her clinician revealed that what Meredith thought was "sexual intercourse" was the painful act of submitting to her father rubbing his penis between her thighs and against her vulva. (This is known as dry intercourse.)

Without proper clarification by the clinician, a misunderstanding such as this could create confusion and cause disbelief in the child's story.

5. Child's sense of time. *Be aware of the child's sense of time; use special events to pinpoint incidents.* In eliciting details of the sexual abuse, the clinician needs to be aware of the child's sense of time. Young children do not have the same concept of time and do not experience the passage of time in the same manner as adults. They are unlikely to be able to pinpoint exact dates or to translate elapsed time since a given event has occurred into the appropriate number of weeks or months without assistance. To a child who is five or six or seven years old, any time period lasting more than a week is "a long time."

One valuable way of assisting the child's recall is to help by connecting special events, holidays, or memorable occasions with the sexually abusive experience.

> Ten-year-old Paula was having difficulty remembering when her father began to molest her. Paula's clinician asked her if she remembered her teacher's name or what grade she was attending in school. She recalled being in second grade with Mr. Thompson and yet the behavior happened earlier. With some further questioning, she remembered that her mom went into the hospital to have her younger brother. It was during this time that her father began to fondle her. The clinician was then able to determine that the sexual abuse began around mid-August when Paula was age 7 years and about to enter the second grade.

The key is to help the child correlate the incident to a signficant event or time in his or her world: birthdays, grades in school, the birth of a younger sibling, and so forth.

6. Multiple interviews. As the child discloses details concerning the sexual abuse, there may be discrepancies in the story. Usually this is due to the child's sense of time or perhaps to confusion about what incident the interviewer is asking about. It is necessary to be certain that the interviewer and the child are discussing the same incident at the same time. *Multiple interviews may be necessary* to straighten out the sequence of events and fill in gaps in the story. Also, the younger the child, the shorter the expected attention span, even for neutral material. The child may react to discussion of emotionally charged

material in an approach-avoidance fashion. Typically, the child will vacillate and switch the subject to extraneous matters (for example, his or her day at school) as stressful topics are introduced. The interviewer should allow a brief digression on an unrelated topic to lower the anxiety level but then gently return to the sexual abuse. The interviewer must be sensitive to cues that the youngster is unable (rather than unwilling) to address a topic further during that session. It is better to plan to see the child on another day. A statement to the child could be, "I would like to see you on Friday so we can talk about this again." To an older child who has provided very fragmented material, the interviewer may add, "I'm a little confused about all the things you've told me and I would like you to help me put everything together at another time."

7. Duration and type of sexual abuse. *How extensive was the sexual abuse?* As indicated earlier, experience demonstrates that the sexual abuse can extend over a period of time from a few weeks to as long as fifteen years. It generally begins with less intimate forms of sexual behavior and then progresses to some type of intercourse. It is unlikely that an incestuous perpetrator would have intercourse with his own child in a single incident. The interviewer should be aware of these dynamics as illustrated in the following case example:

> Seventeen-year-old Dawn reported that her father "raped" her on two occasions. She made a sworn complaint to the police and her father was arrested for sexual assault. The clinician had great difficulty in eliciting any details of the sexual abuse. Dawn denied emphatically that any earlier incidents had taken place and did not supply any history indicating a progression of sexual activity over time. She became furious and regarded the interview and the questions as an intrusion. Both Dawn and her father agreed to take a polygraph test. Her father's responses supported his denial of the sexual abuse and he was able to produce witnesses who could testify that he was with them at one of the times that his daughter said he was "raping" her. After one month had elapsed, Dawn acknowledged that she had lied and that no sexual abuse had occurred. There had been serious family problems, she had been very unhappy at home, and she told the clinician that she had lied about the sexual abuse in order to try to force her family to get help.

We have had few cases of false allegations of sexual abuse by children and adolescents. In the above case, there were several clues to suggest that the complaint was false. First, the absence of progression of sexual activity, from less intimate forms of sexual behavior to sexual penetration, is unusual. Second, the girl insisted that "rape" had occurred on two occasions only, thereby eliminating the more usual history of multiple encounters over time. Lastly, the girl adamantly refused to discuss any details of the sexual abuse. Although every sexual abuse case presents a unique investigative and clinical challenge, a sensitive and knowledgeable interviewer should be able gently to elicit details of the sexual activity from even the most withdrawn or hostile victims. Severe emotional trauma may, of course, inhibit the child from discussing the sexual abuse. It is also possible that a child may hold back information because he or she is under substantial pressure exerted by a powerful family member. If indicators of severe emotional trauma are lacking and there is little pressure on the child to withhold information, refusal to discuss details of the sexual abuse should alert the interviewer to the possibility that the child may be lying.

8. Diffusing anxiety. Interviewing for child sexual abuse can be a stressful process for both the interviewer and the child. It is essential that both be relaxed enough to be able to communicate with each other openly and easily. *Responsibility for establishing a relaxed atmosphere and diffusing anxiety clearly rests with the interviewer.* It is extremely important for the interviewer to feel comfortable about sexuality and discussing sexual abuse. Any negative or uncomfortable feelings experienced by the interviewer during meetings with the child are either observed or sensed by the child and in turn inhibit the child's telling of the story. It can also intensify the child's guilt and embarrassment, and perhaps lead him or her to recant the story and reject any help.

As indicated earlier, the interviewer's own body is a good visual tool for helping the child identify the location of the sexual abuse. This technique is especially helpful with a younger child who lacks the vocabulary to communicate what has happened. With an adolescent, use of the interviewer's body can help to decrease the amount of embarrassment already felt by the victim.

Preliminary Considerations

Let us assume that the referring information has been received, the scene has been set, introductions have been made, and the child and the interviewer are alone together. Ideally they are in a quiet neutral place with privacy and a comfortable low-pressure atmosphere. Some type of game or drawing materials or both are available for use with younger children. The interviewer has introduced himself or herself to the child or a third person (perhaps the complainant) has introduced them. Now that all this groundwork is done, what comes next?

Interviewing children about sexual abuse necessarily encompasses several different phases. One or more tasks must be accomplished in each phase. First, a relationship of trust and communication must be established. Next, there must be a fact-finding phase, during which the interviewer elicits as much information about the sexual abuse and the family constellation as possible. After this, the child's expectations and wishes must be explored. The interview should close with a planning phase, during which the interviewer and the child discuss what will happen next.

Many factors will determine if all the necessary tasks can be accomplished and all of the phases encompassed during a single interview. The age and maturity of the child, his or her emotional state, the child's attention span, the duration and extent of the sexually abusive activity, the presence or absence of a crisis situation touched off by the disclosure, practical issues of the length of time the interview site will be available, how soon is the child expected home, and so forth—all are related factors. Preplanning by the interviewer, especially in cases of purposeful disclosure, is very important because it can eliminate many problems.

The skillful and experienced interviewer will continually be sensitive to the child's response to him or her and the interview situation. It is important to sense when a change of topic, a change of pace, or a temporary break in the proceedings is necessary. If the child is allowed to become too tired, too anxious, too depressed, too fearful, or simply emotionally overwhelmed by all that is happening, the interview process will have been traumatic. Instead, interviewing for validation should, on balance, have a therapeutic rather than a traumatic effect.

Circumstances may make it impossible to accomplish all the necessary tasks in a single interview. Multiple interviews may be required, especially around the initial phase of establishing a relationship. Child protection is, of course, the primary issue in a validated case of sexual abuse. When purposeful disclosure of sexual abuse has taken place, there may be more flexibility regarding multiple interviews. The key issue then involves keeping the disclosure a secret among those who are working with the child until the planning phase is completed. In an incest case, it is essential to avoid a confrontation between powerful family members and the child who has disclosed sexual abuse until the case is validated and intervention planning is complete. Premature confrontation can endanger the child and interfere with the validation process. Experience with child sexual abuse quickly teaches that cases become "noncases" very quickly if the child must endure intense pressure by the perpetrator and other powerful family members in the absence of equally intense support and assistance.

The following description of interviewing for child sexual abuse is a distillation of our experience. Readers are also referred to Burgess and Holmstrom (1978) and Stevens and Berliner (1976) for guidance in formulating their own strategies and methodology. All of our strategies evolved from the conceptual framework for child sexual abuse described in chapter 1. The material that follows will focus on the two phases that comprise interviewing for validation: establishing a relationship and fact-finding. Although issues of child-protection assessment and intervention planning are usually addressed simultaneously with interviewing for validation, these last two phases will be discussed in chapter 3, "An Approach to Case Management."

Phase I: Establishing a Relationship

Methodology. Experienced professional persons are likely to agree that the degree of success one has in working with children is directly proportional to the extent that he or she enjoys the process. To put it in the vernacular, people who "like to work with kids" will probably be more successful in their work with children than people who "don't like to work with kids." Establishing a good relationship with a child depends on the adult's ability to convey interest, warmth, sincerity, and respect for the youngster. Some people seem to have a "knack" for this. They proceed intuitively without ever having been taught and without ever seeming to need to work at establishing a relationship with a child. Others can be taught how to do so, even if they do not initially have the required skills. A third group of individuals seem to have significant barriers to acquiring these skills; it seems like busywork to them or feels demeaning or like a waste of time. In the vernacular, these people "can't stand kids." They should not be working with children in the first place, and it is tragic (for the professional person *and* the child) if such individuals actually wind up interviewing children for sexual abuse.

People in the first group who have the "knack" or intuitive bent usually gravitate to activities that involve a great deal of direct interaction with children. These are the persons who look forward to encounters with children, who go out of their way to speak to youngsters and to try to engage them in conversation, and who derive real satisfaction and gratification from these contacts. The second group is comprised of people who are not "turned off" by encounters with children but who lack some of the skills required to establish a relationship. How do you know if you can be taught the skills required to work satisfactorily with children? Here is a simple check list of questions to ask yourself.

1. *General feelings.* How do I feel toward children in general? Do I like being with children? Do they make me nervous? Am I exhausted afterwards? Did the encounter feel like hard work? Did it feel like a challenge but still satisfying? Did it feel like fun?

2. *Communication.* Do I reach out to communicate with children? Do I spontaneously stop and talk with children when I meet them? Am I apt to fail to recognize a young child's presence unless or until it is brought to my attention by the child or someone else? Does a young child's conversation seem important to me? Do I take the time to stop and listen and find out what the child is trying to communicate? Is a child's description of a place or an event apt to strike me as amusing or interesting or as silly or irritating? Do I really ever care about what a child is *thinking?* Am I willing to take the trouble to find out?

3. *Use of media.* Can I do it? Do I like to play games with children? Does it feel like too much trouble to sit down on the floor with a young child or at a table with an older child and play a game? Does it seem like a waste of time to look at a child's drawing and figure out what the picture represents and to talk about it with him or her? Do I find such activities boring or threatening or perhaps even demeaning? Or do these activities seem purposeful and meaningful or perhaps even enjoyable to me?

4. *Praise versus criticism.* What is my reaction? Do I remember sponta-

neously to praise a child for good behavior or good performance? If not spontaneously, can I do it methodically? Do I instead have the tendency spontaneously to be critical and deprecrating of a child's behavior or performance? Do I have to stop myself from automatically being critical of him or her? Does the process of constantly praising and reinforcing good or even neutral behavior bore me?

5. *Interest level.* Am I interested in children? Do children strike me as being intrinsically interesting as human beings? Do I think of children as *children?* Am I more likely to think of children as shorter, less capable, less interesting, less useful, less reliable, and more troublesome than adults?

6. *Personal reaction.* How do children affect me? Do children have a tendency to make me angry? Do I feel resentful of extra effort they require of me? Does a child's dependency make me feel protective or annoyed or burdened? Does a child's behavior ever make me feel out of control of the situation or with myself?

Persons who are "good with kids" are likely to answer yes to questions on this checklist that describe interactions with children in a positive fashion. People who "can't stand kids" are likely to answer yes (if they are honest with themselves) to questions on the checklist that describe interactions with children in a negative fashion. Individuals who are not "turned off" by children but who lack some of the necessary skills to work effectively with youngsters will not answer yes to those quesitons that describe interactions with children as boring, threatening or demeaning. They are likely to be people who have never considered the skills required for successful interaction.

Acquiring Basic Skills. How does one acquire these skills? *Observing* and working alongside someone who is "good with kids" is a logical first step. The observer can decide what patterns of behavior he or she can try to imitate. Good opening phrases, ways of putting the child at ease and initiating activity, words of praise, strategies for redirecting inappropriate behavior—all can be learned by observation.

Asking questions of the person who is "good with kids" is also helpful. Ask why he or she decided to praise or redirect a certain type of behavior, why an active game was proposed at a given time instead of a more quiet activity, and so forth. In particular, try to find out what cues from the children he or she is picking up and responding to at intervals.

Practicing these skills is essential. No one acquires interpersonal skills solely by observation. Anyone who wishes to improve his or her interactions with children must do so via practical experience. People who are interested in doing this should try to practice initially in some sort of play or recreational setting or perhaps in a daycare center for experience with younger children. Working on a volunteer basis affords the luxury of trial and error experience without direct program responsibility.

Performance critique by a knowledgeable person is invaluable to the learning process. It is extremely helpful to have feedback from someone who is "good with kids" when one is trying to acquire the skills. The second person can be an observer or even a participant within the setting.

Role playing with another adult is less effective than direct practice with children for the purpose of acquiring basic skills. However, as one prepares to do investigative interviewing for sexual abuse, role playing with a knowledgeable adult can be extremely helpful—to gain confidence, to identify the interviewer's inhibitions or hangups and to practice saying the words required. It is astonishing how often professional persons find at the last minute that they have difficulty articulating terms that are part of their passive vocabulary! Children are apt to use slang or scatological terms to describe sexual behavior—sometimes matter-of-factly, sometimes with shame. The interviewer must be conversant with this terminology as well as with the appropriate anatomical terms. For the purpose of investigative interviewing, it is as important to be able to say fuck or cunt or asshole without flinching as it is to be able to say penis or vagina or ejaculate. Role playing is excellent preparation for this task.

Establishing a relationship with a child for the purpose of investigative interviewing for sexual abuse should be no different than the process required for any child of that age group, with one exception. The interviewer must be sensitive to all the underlying issues related to the sexual abuse. Unpalatable as it may seem, the interviewer's task is similar to that of the perpetrator of sexual abuse: he or she must engage the child's interest, confidence, and cooperation. How to begin?

1. *Introduce yourself.* Tell the child your name. If you are comfortable on a first-name basis with children, tell the child your first name. If you are not comfortable on a first-name basis with children, acknowledge this to yourself and proceed accordingly. Children are not generally accustomed to addressing adults by their first names. They are unlikely to perceive a self-introduction using "Miss" or "Mrs." or "Mr." or "Dr." as unfriendly. If your surname is difficult to pronounce, you may wish to tell the child, "You can call me Mr. K." or "I'm Mrs. T."

2. *Demonstrate interest in the child.* Most people (children included) are disarmed and flattered when someone appears genuinely to be interested in them. Ask the child his or her name and ask if there is a special name or nickname that he or she prefers. Indicate a willingness to make the child feel comfortable and, in a sense, entertained. A young child can usually be put at ease by playing a game or drawing a picture. The interviewer may say, "I knew you were coming today and I thought you might like to look at these with me (pictures) or play with these (toys or games) or draw with these (crayons, magic markers, paper). This activity serves as an ice breaker, gives both adult and child something to do with their hands, and provides diversion, if necessary, when a pause or "rest" is necessary.

Children like to be able to choose between activities if this is possible. The activity selected by the child is a good opening to learn something about the child's likes and dislikes. Simple initial information about the home and family can also be elicited at this time. For example, the interviewer may ask, "Do you like to draw pictures? Do you draw at home? By yourself or with your brothers and sisters? How many brothers and sisters do you have? Do you show the pictures to your mommy and daddy?" and so forth.

Questions should be asked casually and a "third-degree" atmosphere with questions fired rapidly, one following immediately after another, should be avoided. Listen attentively to the child's responses and let your facial expressions and body language reinforce *your* attentiveness and interest along with your comments. Be prepared to answer the child's questions as you proceed so that the interchange is truly a conversation instead of an interrogation.

As the interview proceeds, space and time your questions so that they are not obtrusive. Again, *respond genuinely* to the child. Children will quickly sense perfunctory responses or a pressured quality to the interchange. If this occurs, the child may in turn respond by withdrawing or by becoming absorbed in something else. Watch for cues that a lightening of the atmosphere or a change of pace is needed.

In addition to establishing a relationship, this strategy for engaging the child lays the groundwork for the fact-finding phase of the interview. The child must be persuaded later that the interviewer is eliciting information about sexual abuse because he or she really *cares* about what has happened and cares about the youngster. A genuine atmosphere of interest in the child and caring about the child must be established at the outset.

Older children should also be put at ease in the early stages of the interview. Games or media will probably not be required to engage most older children. Instead the interviewer might begin by asking, "Do you know why we are here today?" Most older children will respond directly to this question and the interviewer can then demonstrate interest and concern by asking, "How do you feel about discussing this with me?" It may be appropriate to comment that it is not unusual for people to feel uncomfortable or apprehensive in similar situations. If the older child indicates extreme discomfort or resentment at this point, these feelings must be dealt with directly. A process of bargaining may ensue. Some youngsters may not be willing to proceed beyond this point on a initial interview. The next steps should, however, be tried in any case.

3. *Establish credibility.* It is important for the child to know that you are an experienced and knowledgeable person. Tell the younger child, "I've talked to a great many boys and girls who have had things like this happen to them." An older child should hear a similar message, conveyed at an age-appropriate level. Identify yourself to the child as experienced in this fashion, even if you

are not. Saying that you have talked to children in similar situations establishes *your* credibility. It is appropriate to tell the child the name of the agency or institution that you represent but do not overwhelm the youngster with lengthy or confusing titles or explanations. It may help an older child to receive a brief explanation of your professional responsibilities pertaining to investigative interviewing.

4. *Clarify initial expectations.* The child's expectations of what will transpire during the interview should be clarified. For a very young child, this may boil down to the statement: "You're here to ask me some questions." However, the older child may need to know *why* the questions are being asked and for what purpose information is being elicited. Some children may have unrealistic or inaccurate expectations. The interviewer must be careful to avoid conveying a false impression to the child. For example, it is essential to explain at the outset that the information elicited from the child cannot be kept secret; it must be shared with appropriate authorities.

Try to find out what the child wants to have happen to him or her. If there has been a purposeful disclosure by the child, the primary task of the interviewer is to find out *why* the child decided to disclose the secret of sexual abuse. This question should be raised in the early stages of the interview and should be repeated later on after the details of the sexual abuse have been described and the interviewer and the child have learned more about each other.

It is very helpful to be able to grant some aspect of the child's request(s). The interviewer should search carefully for something he or she can do that the child wants to have accomplished. On the other hand, the interviewer must never promise to do anything that he or she is not certain can be done.

5. *Convey willingness to help.* The child needs to understand that you are interested in helping him or her. The fact-finding phase of the interview must be linked to something that feels like help to the child. It is usually easier and safer to offer help of the following types:

1. *Providing information.* There may be many issues about which the child lacks information or finds confusing. You can legitimately offer to supply information at a level that he or she can understand.
2. *"Feeling better."* Youngsters usually are uncomfortable or guilty about what has already happened. The interviewer can be supportive and reassuring and assist the child in dealing with discomfort and guilt.
3. *Dealing with fear.* Youngsters are often fearful that they have been damaged, that no one will ever like them again, that tremendous disruption will result from the disclosure. All of these fears are legitimate; the interviewer cannot promise magically to solve the problems they represent but he or she can promise to help the child deal with these fears.

4. *Belief in the child*. Most sexually abused children are convinced that no one will believe their stories. If the interviewer believes that the complaint is valid, believing the child and letting him or her know that you believe may be the single most therapeutic thing that can or will happen as a result of the disclosure.

Willingness to help is conveyed both directly and indirectly. For the younger child, willingness to help is often conveyed by the interviewer's attitude and demonstration of interest and caring. The older child may require direct negotiation between his or her expressed request(s) and the help that the interviewer is able to promise to give.

Phase II: Fact-Finding

Methodology. After establishing a relationship with the child, the interviewer can move into the fact-finding phase. Careful and complete recording of the facts elicited is essential. The interviewer should be prepared to take notes or perhaps to tape-record the interview. Most children readily accept the necessity of recording information and quickly adjust to the tape recorder or to the note-taking process.

The interviewer should ask the child to describe the sexually abusive behavior from the beginning. Encourage the child to use his or her own words. Be attentive and supportive. Try to avoid leading the child or introducing bias. Instead of asking direct questions about what happened, introduce generalizations about sexually abusive behavior and note the child's response. The following outline and questions may be helpful.

Nature and Extent of Sexual Abuse. 1. How did it begin? Ask the child to describe the initial encounter. Comment that sometimes adults talk to children about the sexually abusive activity and see if the child volunteers what was said. Ask about touching in the same general fashion. Distinguish between touching the child on top of his or her clothes or underneath them. Note whether the child volunteers information about masturbatory activity. Use drawings or point to your own body or anatomically correct dolls to determine exactly which areas of the child's body were involved.

2. What happened after that? Explore subsequent encounters. Ask if the activity stayed the same. If not, ask how it changed. Note if the child volunteers information to indicate that progression of sexual activity occurred. If not, describe fellatio in general terms ("Sometimes men ask children to lick them or to suck them"). Describe digital penetration in the same general fashion

("Sometimes people try to stick their fingers inside you"). Cunnilingus should also be explored for female victims ("Sometimes people put their mouths on a little girl's bottom"). Remember to determine what names the child uses for penis, vagina, anus, and so forth. Note if the child volunteers a description of ejaculation by a male perpetrator. If not, comment that "sometimes a man's penis will stand up and get big and white stuff comes out" and note the child's response.

3. Where did it happen? Ask the child where the activity occurred. If at home, determine where the activity took place (the child's bedroom and the bathroom are frequent sites). If out of the home, determine the location. Ask if there was any reason for the selection of the site(s). Note all volunteered information before asking more leading questions. If in the bedroom, did the sexual activity take place in bed? on the floor? If in the living room, did it happen on the couch or in a chair or on the floor? If in the bathroom, did either party sit down or lie down? If so, was it on the toilet seat, on the edge of the bathtub or on the floor?

4. Where was everyone else? If the sexual activity occurred at home, was anyone else in the house? Were there any witnesses? Were there any other participants? If at home, find out where all the other family members were at the time the sexual abuse occurred. If out of the home, find out if anyone else was present in the general location or was a witness or perhaps a participant.

5. When did it happen? Find out the general time of day or night or day of the week when the sexual abuse was likely to occur. Elicit as much information as possible about patterns of family activity or regularly occurring absences of family members (for example, mothers who regularly work the night shift). Look for times when the perpetrator was likely to have both access to the child and opportunity (privacy) for the sexual abuse to occur.

6. How long has this been going on? Again, when did the sexual activity begin? Remember a young child's sense of time. If necessary, try to correlate the occurrence of the sexual abuse with holidays or times that have special meaning for the child. Try to learn if the activity stopped for a period of time and then was resumed again. Grades in school may be useful blocks of time with which to correlate sexual activity. Try to determine the frequency of sexual abuse (every night, once or twice each month, and so forth).

7. Did anyone else know? Try to determine if the child told anyone else. If not, ask why not. This is a good way to assess the important element of secrecy. Does the child volunteer anything about secrecy? If not, again ask in a general way about secrecy ("Sometimes people try to get children not to tell about what has been happening.") and note the child's response. Try to find out if the child has told anyone else about the sexual activity. If so, how did that person respond to the disclosure? It is especially important to determine if other family members were aware of the sexual abuse. If so, they may corroborate the child's story. Since other family members may have reason to deny that

they knew about the sexual abuse, it is helpful to know as many details as possible about the disclosure.

8. Why did you go along with this? It is important to learn the child's reasons for participating in the sexual activity. This is a good way to elicit information about the types of pressure or coercion used to engage the child in sexual activity and to maintain secrecy. Information may be volunteered about rewards, bribes, special favors, or threats. If threats were made, they should be carefully assessed. Was threatened violence to the child or some other family member involved? If threats were made, was any aspect of the threat ever carried out? Ask the child about other family activities or interactions. Do other aspects of family life involve threats or violence?

9. How did it feel to have this special relationship? Try to determine how the child feels about the perpetrator, about family members, about himself or herself. Were any aspects of the sexual activity positive or negative? If so, which aspects? Is the child angry at anyone? If so, why? What aspects of the child's relationship with the perpetrator were positive or negative? The interviewer should avoid conveying a bias against the perpetrator or giving the child the impression that it is wrong to have enjoyed the sexual relationship or to feel positively toward the perpetrator.

10. Were there special physical aspects? The child should be asked if he or she was ever injured as a result of the sexual activity. Was there ever any bleeding or pain or interference with urination, defecation, or menstruation? If so, how was it handled or treated? Has the child ever had a sexually transmitted disease? If so, how was it dealt with? If the child is an adolescent female, was any method of birth control used? Has she ever been pregnant? If so, what happened? Has a child of either sex been sexually active with any other adults? with peers?

11. Why tell now? The timing of the present disclosure is an extremely important issue. The interviewer must determine if the disclosure was accidental or purposeful. If the disclosure was purposeful, the interviewer needs to find out what the child expects will occur or what the child wishes will occur as a result. As previously discussed, the child may have expectations that are totally unrealistic. Never assume that a child purposefully disclosed sexual abuse solely to stop the sexual abuse. Anticipate the underlying reason; the chances are very great that the child wants something else to happen.

Needless to say, many factors will determine if all these categories of information about sexual abuse can be covered in a single interview: age of the child, degree of trauma or inhibition, circumstances and setting of the interview, accidental versus purposeful disclosure situation, and so forth. Multiple interviews may be required to complete the fact-finding phase. The following case example required three interviews for fact-finding in the case of a 7-year-old girl. The first interview was conducted by a female child-protective-services worker.

Interviewer:	Hello. What's your name?
Mary:	Mary. What are we going to talk about?
Interviewer:	Whatever you'd like to talk about.
Mary:	Well, uh, what do you say?
Interviewer:	What grade are you in?
Mary:	First.
Interviewer:	Do you like school?
Mary:	Yeah.
Interviewer:	What do you like about school?
Mary:	Well, once we went to the zoo.
Interviewer:	Well, that's a nice thing.
Mary:	And what else. What do *you* like about school?
Interviewer:	Well, I don't go to school right now.
Mary:	Oh yes, you do too. You've got to go to school sometime.
Interviewer:	What do you do when you're not in school?
Mary:	Well. (She gets up and starts to leave the room).
Interviewer:	You've got to stay here, my dear. Can you stay over here? Otherwise we can't hear you. (She brings her back to the table and gives her crayons and drawing paper).
Mary:	I make things.
Interviewer:	Like—what do you mean?
Mary:	Well, like things like I'm making now.
Interviewer:	And what are you making now?
Mary:	A house.
Interviewer:	That's a very pretty house.
Mary:	In a picture.
Interviewer:	Whose house is this?
Mary:	Nobody's.
Interviewer:	Hmm.
Mary:	Just a picture.
Interviewer:	Mmm Hmmm. You like to draw pictures?
Mary:	Yeah. Enh, enh, Polly wants a cracker? (She laughs).
Interviewer:	Who's that?
Mary:	It's Polly.
Interviewer:	Polly, the parrot?
Mary:	Yeah.
Interviewer:	Mnn.
Mary:	Polly, be quiet.
Interviewer:	Do you think Polly will say anything else?
Mary:	Well, yeah. Polly wants a cracker. (She laughs again).
Interviewer:	Want to listen to this? (She offers her a toy with a recording inside).
Mary:	Yup.

Interviewer: O.K.

In this initial interview, the interviewer has the task of establishing a relationship with a seven-year-old girl. She begins by asking her name and a few questions about school. The child is restless and finds it hard to settle down. The interviewer gently draws Mary back to the table and offers drawing materials. This provides a diversion and lessens the tension. The interviewer then tries to engage Mary in conversation about what she is drawing. She avoids the opportunity to describe the house that she had drawn as her own house. Instead Mary firmly states that it is "just a picture." She then deftly changes the subject by speaking in the voice of Polly, the parrot. The interviewer attempts to direct the interchange once more by asking Mary if she thinks Polly will say anything else. A child sometimes finds it less threatening to speak in the person of someone else (for example, a puppet or a character in a story or drawing). When invited to project herself as Polly, Mary responds "Polly be quiet" and once again changes the subject. At this point, the interviewer correctly decides that Mary is not ready to talk to her and directs Mary to a toy and terminates the visit shortly thereafter.

If a younger child is unwilling to be engaged in a meaningful fashion on the first attempt at investigative interviewing, it is well to heed his or her cues. Children are usually quite adept at turning inquiries aside and are capable of being extremely evasive. Pressuring the child at that point can make it impossible to establish a relationship that will permit fact-finding later on. Instead, it is better to respect the child's wishes, avoid pressuring him or her and redirect the activity in a positive way so that the child is not made to feel pressured or guilty. Conveying anger, impatience, or frustration to the child under these circumstances is worse than nonproductive; it can be down right detrimental. It is far better to withdraw gracefully and try again.

In the case of Mary, the interviewer talked to her again several days later in a joint interview with a police officer. This time, Mary was able to discuss the sexual abuse by her uncle. The officer and child-protective-services worker used an anatomically correct drawing of a male figure to help Mary describe the sexual activity that took place. In a third interview in the following week, the same interviewer spoke to Mary again. Once again, she is drawing pictures as they talk.

Mary:	*Well, what are we going to talk about?*
Interviewer:	We want to talk about what we talked about last time when we got together with Officer Jones.
Mary:	Yes. Is that tape recording now? (She points to the tape recorder).
Interviewer:	It is. O.K. Now the last time we got together we talked about when you were over at Uncle . . .
Mary:	Tom's

Interviewer:	Tom's house.
Mary:	T-O-M, Tom.
Interviewer:	Right. O.K. You told us about two times when you were over there, now let's talk a little bit about the second time when you were there. And you were there and . . .
Mary:	Oh, that stuff happened.
Interviewer:	Right. And your Mom went to work and you spent the night with your Uncle Tom and his friend, Anne, and they were. . . . Can you tell me where they were and where you were?
Mary:	First of all, Tom took me into the bedroom. Right? And let me make me another one of them signs, so I won't have to talk.
Interviewer:	No. We need to talk. It's just you and me and the tape recorder here and that's all. And we're friends. Right? Hmm? You're my buddy?
Mary:	Yes, I guess. Finish this flower.
Interviewer:	O.K.
Mary:	Now, no nonsense—no nonny no. How am I doing?
Interviewer:	Very nice. So.
Mary:	So.
Interviewer:	You went in the bedroom with Uncle Tom.
Mary:	Yeah.
Interviewer:	And then what happened?
Mary:	He did some bad stuff to me. Bad, bad, bad, too bad stuff.
Interviewer:	O.K. What happened. What did Uncle Tom do?
Mary:	What did Uncle Tom do? He hurt me.
Interviewer:	And how did he hurt you?
Mary:	With his finger.
Interviewer:	And what did he do with his hands?
Mary:	Stuck it up in my pee-pee.
Interviewer:	And that hurt?
Mary:	Yeah.
Interviewer:	Mmm.
Mary:	Y-E-S. Yes!
Interviewer:	And what did you do when he did this?
Mary:	I pushed him away.
Interviewer:	And then what happened?
Mary:	He started to do it to me again. And I pushed him away again.
Interviewer:	And was anyone else there when this happened? This was when you and Tom were there alone. And where was your Mom? Where was Anne?
Mary:	At the store. First they went to wash clothes, then they went to the store. I wanted to go but Mom wouldn't let me. I didn't want it to happen any more.

Interviewer:	Had it happened before that?
Mary:	Yes.
Interviewer:	What had happened before that?
Mary:	He hurt me. The same way he did last time.
Interviewer:	Darling, come over here and sit by me. Here sit on my knee here. O.K. Can you tell me about the time when Anne was there, and she was in, uh. . . .
Mary:	Bedroom.
Interviewer:	What happened that time?
Mary:	Anne was in bed, she was drunk, Tom was too and he hurt me.
Interviewer:	And how did he hurt you?
Mary:	Same way he did last time.
Interviewer:	And that was how? What did he do?
Mary:	Hurt me with his finger. Pinky, pinky.
Interviewer:	What did he do with his finger.
Mary:	Stuck it up in my pee-pee.
Interviewer:	Did Uncle Tom do anything else or ask you to do anything else?
Mary:	Yes.
Interviewer:	What was that?
Mary:	He made me suck his thing.
Interviewer:	He made you suck his thing?
Mary:	UmHm.
Interviewer:	And what is his thing?
Mary:	Dick.
Interviewer:	His dick. He made you suck his dick? That's what he called it?
Mary:	UmHm.
Interviewer:	And did he ask you to do that?
Mary:	Yes, but I said no and he pushed my head on it.
Interviewer:	He asked you to do it and you said no?
Mary:	Yes, and he pushed my head on it.
Interviewer:	He pushed your head on his dick?
Mary:	UmHmm.
Interviewer:	And then what did you do?
Mary:	I took my mouth off it and he did it again and I ran.
Interviewer:	You took your mouth off of it and then he did it again? He pressed your head down on his uh, on his dick?
Mary:	UmHmm.
Interviewer:	Did any other part of your head touch his dick? Your face, your nose, your eyes, mouth?
Mary:	Nothing, but my mouth.
Interviewer:	He pressed your mouth down on it?
Mary:	UmHmm. Then he made me put my mouth on it and his thing in my mouth.

Interviewer:	His thing? You mean his dick?
Mary:	UmHmm.
Interviewer:	Was in your mouth?
Mary:	UnHuh.
Interviewer:	And how did it get in your mouth?
Mary:	He pushed my head down on it.
Interviewer:	He pushed your head down on it?
Mary:	Yes. Then I said no and then he stuck it in my mouth when it was open.
Interviewer:	Then he stuck it in again? For very long?
Mary:	For two minutes.
Interviewer:	Maybe two minutes?
Mary:	Or an hour.
Interviewer:	Maybe two minutes or an hour? Did anything come out of his dick?
Mary:	(No audible answer)
Interviewer:	And then what did you do? When he pushed it in your mouth again?
Mary:	Then I kicked him.
Interviewer:	Where did you kick him?
Mary:	On his legs.
Interviewer:	On his legs? And then what did he do?
Mary:	He chased me into the living room and then I ran out the door.
Interviewer:	He chased you into the living room and you ran out what door?
Mary:	The one that you go out of.
Interviewer:	That you go to where? Outside?
Mary:	Yeah.
Interviewer:	And then what happened?
Mary:	I ran and hid behind the car.
Interviewer:	And then what?
Mary:	I stayed there and then he went back inside. Then I came out and then Mom had come home and I didn't tell her. I just told her. And Don and Billy was outside playing too. They told me to stay outside. And then Mom came home and I told her that I was playing hide and seek.
Interviewer:	So you didn't tell your Mom what happened? You told her you were playing hide and seek?
Mary:	UmHmm.
Interviewer:	Did your Uncle Tom ever do anything like that again?
Mary:	Only twice.

By the time of their third encounter, the interviewer had established a good working relationship with Mary. She trusted her and was accustomed to the routine of drawing and talking with her and apparently enjoyed their interaction. The interviewer introduced the topic of sexual activity that Mary had described in the second interview. Her goal was to have Mary describe the behavior in her own words. Mary tried to avoid this by asking to use the diagram that the interviewer and the police officer had offered as an aid before. This time, however, the interviewer firmly encouraged her to verbalize the details of the sexual abuse instead of pointing to a picture to describe what had occurred. Her willingness to talk about the activity thereafter indicated how much trust had been developed.

As Mary began to describe the sexually abusive activity, she told the interviewer that it was "bad" and that it had hurt her. Mary became agitated as she described and, in a sense, relived the experience. At a crucial point, the interviewer gave Mary direct support by drawing the child to her and allowing her to sit on her lap. She skillfully continued to elicit information by supplying just enough connecting phrases to encourage her to relate the story.

At no time did the interviewer lead Mary as she described the sexual abuse by her uncle Tom. The child volunteered all the details herself about digital penetration of the vagina and fellatio. A progression of sexual activity was thus elicited. The interviewer facilitated the flow of information frequently by repeating the child's last phrase or sentence in the interrogative mode. She allowed her to use her own terminology (for example, pee-pee meant vaginal opening) and clarified when necessary (Mary used both "dick" and "thing" to describe the perpetrator's penis).

The interviewer was also able to determine who else was present during the sexual abuse and the whereabouts of other family members as well. In this case, there is the possibility of direct corroboration of Mary's story by her uncle's girlfriend and Mary's brothers can corroborate that she ran out of the house and hid behind the car. Mary's mother can corroborate that she came home and found her behind the car and that Mary told her at that time that she had been playing hide and seek.

A young child's sense of time is vividly illustrated in this case example. First Mary said that the fellatio lasted two minutes; then she said it lasted an hour. The interviewer repeated this but did not pursue the issue further. Instead she redirected the story by asking what happened after that.

This case illustrates how many details can be elicited from a seven-year-old victim by skillful investigative interviewing. The crucial elements include the skills of the interviewer, the use of media and games to relax the child and facilitate the interviewing process, the use of a diagram initially to pinpoint details of the sexual activity, the technique of doing multiple interviews and letting the cues from the child set the pace: that is, no fact-finding in the first interview, use of a diagram to describe sexual behavior in the second interview, verbalization of details of sexual abuse when the child was prepared to do so in the third interview. Multiple interviews are easier to arrange, of course, if there is a supportive parent who consents to the process and protects the child from being pressured not to reveal information about sexual abuse.

Phase III: Child-Protection Assessment

This phase of investigative interviewing examines those elements of the situation which determine if the child will be safe after the disclosure. Will the child be safe in his or her own home now that the secret of sexual abuse has been disclosed to outsiders? This question must be asked in both extrafamily and intrafamily cases, although the incest victim is likely to be at a greater risk.

Chapter 3 "An Approach to Case Management," describes the elements of a child-protection assessment in detail. The age and condition of the child, the duration and extent of the sexual abuse, a past history of use of force or violence, the potential for use of force or violence, the child's expectations of the response of other family members to the disclosure, the presence or absence of a functioning adult ally for the child at home—all are factors to be considered.

Phase IV: Intervention Planning

The first three phases of investigative interviewing set the stage for the last phase. Both timing and logic make it appropriate for some measure of intervention planning with the child to be addressed by the person who established a relationship, obtained the facts about sexual abuse, and made a child-protection assessment. All of these tasks were, after all, accomplished with the expressed goal of helping the child. Now the interviewer and others must plan what will happen next with the child. The victim's age, physical and emotional condition, and wishes must be considered in conjunction with the child-protection assessment and the legal responsibilities of the participants. Intervention planning will be discussed in detail in chapter 3.

Credibility Assessment

Credibility assessment follows the fact-finding phase of investigative interviewing. Validation of child sexual abuse depends almost entirely upon investigative interviewing of the child. Determining the validity of an allegation of child sexual abuse is first and foremost a matter of belief. You either believe the child's story or you do not. If you require that there be corroboration of the child's story by physical evidence, witnesses, or a confession by the perpetrator, you will turn many cases into "noncases." Corroborating physical evidence or witnesses are rare. Perpetrators hardly ever confess unless they are persuaded that others believe the child. When perpetrators and powerful family members perceive that investigators have not yet made up their minds about the validity of the allegation, they will almost invariably deny that sexual abuse has occurred and pressure the child to recant the allegation.

Great stress is thus placed on assessing the credibility of a child's story of sexual abuse when the facts have been obtained by a knowledgeable interviewer. The credibility of the facts elicited should be assessed within a conceptual framework of child sexual abuse (see chapter 1). The interviewer and others must ask themselves if the story fits within such a framework. Are the dynamics and mechanics described by the child believable in this context? Does the child's past and present behavior with respect to the sexual abuse follow the patterns noted in other cases? Does the behavior of the perpetrator and other family members follow familiar patterns? If discrepancies and changes in the child's story have been noted, do these correlate with pressure placed on the child by others or with the interviewer's failure to clarify terminology or sequence of events? Were the facts elicited by someone who knew how to interview children for sexual abuse? Did the circumstances of the interview(s) facilitate fact-finding or the reverse?

The experienced and knowledgeable interviewer assesses credibility within the context of his or her knowledge base and previous experience with child-sexual-abuse cases. The knowledgeable but inexperienced interviewer stands a fair chance of eliciting the facts of the case but will need the assistance and support of another professional person who is both knowledgeable and experienced for the credibility assessment. The interviewer who is neither knowledgeable or experienced is unlikely to be able to elicit facts about sexual abuse from children in a fashion that permits credibility assessment to take place. Lacking the knowledge and skills required, the last interviewer is instead much more likely to elicit information that is confusing and likely to discredit the child. The interviewer who lacks both experience and knowledge is also likely to place the child at greater risk than ever before as a result of the disclosure.

There should be multidisciplinary team review of cases in which validation is questionable. Chapter 3, ''An Approach to Case Management,'' and chapter 12, ''Multidisciplinary Team Review of Child Sexual Abuse Cases,'' both address this subject.

How to determine credibility of a child-sexual-abuse complaint? The presence of the following tend to enhance the credibility of a child's story.

Multiple Incidents over Time. Most sexual abuse involves multiple incidents occurring over time. Although the initial information may indicate that only one incident occurred, careful questioning of the child usually reveals that more than one sexually abusive incident took place over a period of weeks, months, or even years. Sometimes the child withholds information about previous incidents because of fear or embarrassment. Sometimes questions about previous incidents are not asked or the child does not perceive the sexually abusive nature of the activity (for example, as in incidents of exposure, fondling, or masturbation). In any event, the experienced and knowledgeable interviewer will anticipate that previous incidents probably *did* occur and frame questions accordingly.

Progression of Sexual Activity. In general, most cases of child sexual abuse involve a progression of sexual activity, from less intimate types of behavior to more intimate interaction. More often than not, the progression of sexual activity occurs over time rather than during a single encounter. For example, initial incidents may involve exposure or masturbation. The sexual activity in later incidents may begin in the same way but then progress to fondling or to some form of penetration of the child's body. Absence of a history of progression of sexual activity over time is apt to make the experienced and knowledgeable interviewer suspect that the allegation of sexual abuse may be false. This is especially true in intrafamily cases and in situations where no force or threat of use of force was involved. It is important to be certain that questions were asked in a manner to elicit progression ("How did it begin? Did anything change?") Although not impossible, it would be highly unusual for sexual abuse of a child to begin with full vaginal or rectal intercourse without some prior elements of exposure, fondling, or digital penetration.

Elements of Secrecy. It is unusual to encounter a case of child sexual abuse involving multiple incidents occurring over time that does not also have elements of secrecy. It greatly enhances the credibility of a child's story of sexual abuse if he or she volunteers that there was a direct or implied understanding between the participants that the activity should be kept secret. With careful questioning, a skilled interviewer can elicit elements of secrecy in most cases without leading the child directly or putting words in his or her mouth. Conversely, the absence of any secrecy aspect should raise questions about the credibility of a history of repeated sexual encounters with a child.

Elements of Pressure or Coercion. Few cases of child sexual abuse lack elements of pressure or coercion (Burgess and Holmstrom, 1975). The perpetrator misuses the power, dominance, and authority legitimately accorded to adults in our society in all phases of the activity (see chapter 1, "A Conceptual Framework for Child Sexual Abuse"). In the engagement phase, the perpetrator misrepresents moral standards and bribes or pressures or coerces the child into some type of sexual activity. Similar tactics are used during the secrecy phase to prevent the secret from begin disclosed. Once disclosure has taken place, pressure or coercion is used in the suppression phase which usually follows with the goal of undermining the child's credibility and forcing withdrawal of the complaint. Elements of pressure or coercion are present in most cases. Knowledgeable interviewers with adequate skills can elicit these elements and assess them on several levels: credibility, safety of the child, and so forth. Absence of any elements of pressure or coercion should raise significant doubt about the validity of the allegation.

Explicit Details of Sexual Behavior. When explicit details of sexual behavior are elicited from a young child, the credibility of the allegation of sexual abuse is definitely enhanced. The skill of the interviewer is particularly critical here. Persons who are responsible for validation of child sexual abuse should review the methodology used for investigative interviewing. Were the setting and circumstances of the interview conducive to obtaining this information? Were media or other aids employed (drawing, dolls, diagrams, puppets)? Was the investigation a "one-shot-deal" or were multiple interviews conducted if necessary?

Collateral interviews may be part of the validation process in come cases. Careful timing of these interviews is essential. It may be helpful to obtain information from siblings (especially if they are outside of the home) or other persons named by the child who may be able to corroborate some of the facts. Investigators who choose to defer making up their minds about the validity of a child's complaint of sexual abuse until after they have confronted the perpetrator or others who occupy power positions should understand exactly what this process entails. A person who occupies a power position over a child is being invited to respond to a damaging allegation by behaving in an innocent or outraged or righteously indignant fashion. This person will quickly pick up cues that the investigator has not yet made up his or her mind and is likely to respond accordingly by further exploitation of the power position. The technique of validation by confrontation should be avoided for two reasons. First, it places the child at great risk for retribution. Secondly, only an extremely naïve person would be likely to fail to exploit this opportunity to discredit a damaging allegation. Chapter 3, "An Approach to Case Management," describes an approach which avoids these problems.

In summary, most cases can be validated by investigative interviewing and by assessing the credibility of the history of sexual abuse elicited from the child. In our experience this can be done with children in the age range of five years and older. A skilled interviewer can sometimes elicit helpful information from an unusually articulate younger child (age range three to five years). However, a child who is that young frequently lacks the verbal and conceptual skills required for investigative interviewing to have validity.

We have encountered very few false allegations of sexual abuse made by child victims. In the small number of cases of false complaints by children that we have encountered, the facts elicited by investigative interviewing did not fit within a conceptual framework of child sexual abuse. The information elicited in these cases was so different from the usual pattern as to excite immediate skepticism and concern.

Physical Indicators of Child Sexual Abuse

A few sexually abused children come to attention because physical indicators are present. These may include the following symptoms or signs.

Trauma to the Genital or Rectal Area. Although infrequent, child sexual abuse may occasionally result in genital or rectal trauma. This may take the form of soft tissue injury or lacerations to the urethral (urinary) vaginal, or rectal openings. The child with urethral trauma may experience pain or discomfort on urination, unusual frequency of urination, or have blood appear in the urine or be unable to pass urine. If rectal trauma is present, the child may be constipated or have pain on defecation or have rectal bleeding. Trauma to the vagina may be associated with pain, bleeding, or difficulties with urination or defecation. The children may voice complaints of any of these conditions or they may remain silent. These youngsters may have blood stains on their underwear. Physical discomfort may alter their behavior (for example, a child with genital or rectal pain may limp or perform poorly in gym or drop out of strenuous play activities or perhaps even have difficulty in sitting still).

Foreign Bodies in the Genital, Rectal, or Urethral Openings. Sexual abuse sometimes involves the insertion of foreign bodies in the genital, rectal, or urethral openings. In addition to causing local irritation or trauma, foreign bodies can also obstruct the passageway in which they were inserted. Such foreign bodies are sometimes detected by accident in very young children. The presence of a foreign body in a child's urethra, vagina, or rectum should always alert the examiner to the possibility of sexual abuse.

Abnormal Dilatation of the Urethra, Vaginal, or Rectal Openings. Child sexual abuse may involve gradual dilatation of the urethra, vaginal, or rectal openings. If the openings are dilated gently, nonforcibly, and on multiple occasions over time, it is unlikely that pain or discomfort or trauma will result. Unusual dilatation of the vaginal opening may be noted accidentally. The hymenal ring, a thin membrane of tissue across the vaginal opening, may become dilated from digital pressure or penetration. Although not conclusive evidence, abnormal dilatation of these openings would suggest the possibility that sexual abuse may be occurring.

Sperm in the Vagina. If vaginal penetration, however slight, has occurred, there may be sperm in the vagina. This is of special concern if the sexual abuse occurred a very short time before disclosure was made. If the sexually abusive activity included ejaculation against the perineum, semen may enter the vaginal pool through the opening in the hymenal ring even if penetration of the vagina by a male perpetrator's penis has not occurred. Under these circumstances, examination of secretions in the vaginal pool may reveal sperm. If sperm are present in the vagina of a prepubertal child this is conclusive evidence that sexual assualt or statutory rape has occurred. Occasionally, sperm will be isolated from the urine of a female victim as well.

Trauma to Breasts, Buttocks, Lower Abdomen, or Thighs. If force or violence have been employed in the sexually abusive activity, there may be soft tissue injury to the breasts, buttocks, lower abdomen or thighs (in addition to the genital or rectal area). These victims may have bruises, scratches, or abrasions in the aforementioned areas of the body. Presence of such injury may corroborate the child's description of the activity. If the child was beaten or whipped with a belt or strap or electric cord, the soft tissue injury may be characterized by telltale marks on the skin left by the instrument used. If the child reports being physically restrained or tied up, there may be imprints left on the extremities as well.

Sexually Transmitted Diseases. A child who has been victimized by an infected person may contract a sexually transmitted disease. Direct physical contact with a person who has infectious syphilis will probably result in a syphilis infection. If a male perpetrator has a gonococcal infection of the urethra, the child may contract gonorrhea. If the activity involved fellatio, the child may acquire a gonococcal infection of the pharynx or throat. If the activity involved penile penetration of the rectal or vaginal openings, the child may acquire a gonococcal infection in either area. If the infected perpetrator masturbated himself or herself and then rubbed the child's genital or rectal area with hands that were covered with secretions or semen, a gonococcal or syphilis infection may be transmitted to the child in this way. Herpes virus infection of the genital or rectal area, characterized by painful blister-like lesions, is also sexually transmitted. Presence of herpes virus lesions in these areas is also an indication that sexual abuse has occurred. Some female children may also have yeast (Candida) or *Trichomonas* or mixed bacterial infections in the vulvo-vaginal area. Although the latter may occur as a result of sexual transmission, there are several other predisposing factors for these conditions (presence of a coexisting illness, overgrowth of yeast or *Trichomonas* organisms as a result of antibiotic treatment for some other medical problem, swimming in heavily chlorinated water, bathing in water mixed with bubble-bath preparations, and so forth). Accordingly, yeast or *Trichomonas* or mixed bacterial infections of the vagina in young children do not necessarily indicate that the child has been sexually abused.

Pregnancy. A female victim may become impregnated as a result of sexual abuse. This often occurs by accident, especially when the child is 10 or 11 or 12 years old and the perpetrator has not considered pregnancy a great risk. Some girls do not acquire obvious secondary sexual characteristics prior to beginning menstruation. Most perpetrators are not aware that some girls as young as nine years of age may become impregnated. Pregnancy itself is an indicator of sexual activity. It behooves all professional persons who work with children and adolescents to consider the possibility that pregnancy may be an indicator of sexual abuse. At the present time, it is the custom to assume that a girl became pregnant as a result of peer or consenting sexual intercourse. Instead, a professional person should be prepared to consider a variety of circumstances that may explain the pregnancy, including sexual abuse. The younger the pregnant girl, the more consideration should be given to the possibility that she was pressured or forced into sexual activity.

Medical Examination for Child Sexual Abuse

The dynamics and mechanics of child sexual abuse are such that most victims do not have physical changes as a result. Unless there has been some element of force employed, especially forcible penetration, or unless the child becomes impregnated or contracts a sexually transmitted disease as a result, the physical examination can be expected to identify few, if any, signs of sexual abuse.

For years, attorneys, judges, police officers, and child-protective-services workers have relied upon the presence or absence of physical signs to validate child sexual abuse. The emphasis upon physical examination is totally misplaced from the perspective of validation. Instead, the validation process should emphasize investigative interviewing.

Nevertheless, a physical examination should be performed for every child if sexual abuse is suspected. The purpose of the physical examination is threefold:

1. To identify physical trauma or conditions that will require medical attention (for example, pregnancy).
2. To collect corroborating evidence of sexual abuse if such signs exist.
3. To reassure the child and his or her parents that the youngster is all right— unharmed and undamaged (or if injuries or associated conditions are present that they have been identified and treated.)

The utilization of a comprehensive physical examination by a competent and compassionate examiner as a treatment tool is further described in chapter 4, "Treatment of the Sexually Abused Child."

It is not appropriate to rely upon findings of a physical examination to rule in or out a diagnosis of child sexual abuse. A physician or other medical professional who performs physical examinations can never invalidate a sexual abuse case by reporting that there are no findings to suggest that sexual abuse has occurred. In fact, physical findings will be present in very few cases. Use of the presence of physical findings as a standard of proof of child sexual abuse is totally inappropriate. Medical professionals should vigorously resist attempts by others to require adherence to such a standard of proof.

Numerous protocols for medical examination for child sexual abuse have been published (Burgess, Groth, Holmstrom, and Sgroi, 1978). Despite a mystique attached to medical examination, the process in fact should be simple and straight forward. The following elements should be included.

Consent of the Child. No one should attempt to examine an unwilling or resistant child. Force or restraint should never be used to compel the child's compliance. It is necessary for the examiner and others who are working with the child to establish enough of a relationship that the child consents and cooperates. In those rare cases when a child has been traumatized so severely that he or she cannot be persuaded to comply, the youngster should be admitted to the hospital and examined under anesthesia. We have never encountered such a case.

Context of the Examination. Always, a medical examination for sexual abuse should be performed within the context of a complete physical examination. This practice deemphasizes the genital and rectal examination and enables assessment of the youngster's overall condition.

Examination for Trauma and Foreign Bodies. The child's entire body should be inspected minutely for trauma. Any injuries or foreign bodies should be carefully documented and recorded and, of course, treated if necessary. Use of diagrams is helpful in documentation. Taking colored photographs may also be helpful. Abnormal dilatation of the urethral vaginal or rectal openings should be noted and recorded. In female children, the presence and condition of the hymenal ring, the diameter of the hymenal opening, and the diameter of the vaginal opening should be recorded.

Examination for Sperm and Pregnancy. Female children should have a swab or aspirate of vulvo-vaginal secretions examined for sperm. Girls aged ten years and up should be checked for pregnancy if the history or physical findings indicate that the child might be pregnant.

Testing for Sexually Transmitted Disease. Cultures for gonorrhea should be obtained from the throat, urethra, vagina (in prepubertal females), cervix (in postpubertal females), and rectal opening. A urine specimen consisting of the first few drops voided by the child may be cultured for gonorrhea if no urethral discharge is present. A moistened swab should be inserted 1 to 2 cm into the rectal opening and left there for 5 to 10 seconds to obtain material to culture for gonorrhea. These specimens should be plated immediately on appropriate media and incubated. A blood specimen should be obtained for serologic test for syphilis.

Baseline tests for gonorrhea and syphilis should be done in all cases, as outlined above. In some cases, follow-up examination should include repetition of these tests after a four-to-six-week interval. If a sexually transmitted disease is identified, it should of course, be treated. Physicians are encouraged to treat uncomplicated gonococcal infections in children with an oral dosage regimen of amoxicillin, 50 mg/kg and probenecid, 25 mg/kg given as a single dose (Gonorrhea Treatment Regimens, Center for Disease Control, 1979). The single dose regimen of oral medication has been shown to be effective and is preferable to treating the child with injections. A follow-up examination and cultures for test-of-cure should be scheduled one to two weeks after treatment.

History-Taking. It is difficult, although not impossible, to combine investigative interviewing and medical examination. Under ideal circumstances, investigative interviewing takes place prior to the medical examination. Physicians should avoid taking a history regarding sexual abuse in the presence of family members. Even in cases involving extrafamily perpetrators, the child may be reluctant to discuss details of the sexual abuse in front of a family member. In intrafamily cases, the presence of a parent or family member may create a level of pressure that makes it impossible to elicit accurate information from the child. Whenever possible, details of sexual abuse should be elicited from the child by himself or herself. It is well to avoid unnecessary repetition for the child; if an adequate history has already been taken by a reliable person, the physician may elect to defer questioning the child again. With careful planning and appropriate preparation for the child, it may also be possible for a physician to be present during the part of the investigative interviewing that focuses on the sexual abuse. Sometimes it may suffice for the physician to listen to a tape recording of the interview with the child.

A clear separation should be made between history-taking and the physical examination. It is preferable to allow the youngster to remain dressed while a history is taken. Later on, during the physical examination, it may be helpful to verify parts of the history as one is examining the child (for example, "Show me where he touched you." or "Did anything happen here?").

Reassurance. An integral part of any medical examination is to reassure the subject that he or she is all right or, if necessary, an abnormality is being treated. It is particularly important to reassure a child who is being examined for sexual abuse that he or she is all right—intact, undamaged, normal. If abnormalities are found, the message should be that, with treatment, "You will be all right." Youngsters need this reassurance and support desperately. A physician or person who performs medical examinations can be a most authoritative source of reassurance. These children and their families need to receive a message that emphatically states: "You're OK; you're not different; you're not bad; you're not dirty; you're not damaged for life." They will need to hear this multiple times from more than one professional person, but it helps immeasurably to receive this message from an examining physician in the early stages of intervention.

Summary

Validation of child sexual abuse depends upon recognizing behavioral indicators, the capacity to perform investigative interviewing, the ability to do credibility assessment, recognizing physical indicators, and the capacity to perform comprehensive medical examinations. Behavioral indicators of child sexual abuse may be helpful but are rarely conclusive. Investigative interviewing is the single most important component of validation. Credibility assessment is dependent on the investigator's previous experience with child sexual abuse and rests primarily with information elicited by investigative interviewing. Physical indicators of child sexual abuse are exceedingly helpful when present; their absence, however, does not necessarily invalidate the complaint. A comprehensive medical examination of the child is essential for all cases. Nevertheless, validation should proceed independent of the medical examination; medical findings, by themselves, will rarely validate the case.

References

Burgess, Ann W., and Holmstrom, Lynda L. "Sexual Assault of Children and Adolescents: "Pressure, Sex and Secrecy." *Nursing Clinics of North America* (September 1975):551–63.

Burgess, Ann W., and Holmstrom, Lynda L. "Interviewing Young Victims." In Burgess et al, *Sexual Assault of Children and Adolescents,* Massachusetts: Lexington Books, D.C. Heath and Company, 1978, 197–204.

Gonorrhea Treatment Regimens, Center for Disease Control, 1979.

Sgroi, Suzanne M., "Comprehensive Examination for Child Sexual Assault." In Burgess et. al., *Sexual Assault of Children and Adolescents,* Massachusetts: Lexington Books, D.C. Heath and Company, 1978, 143–57.

Stevens, Doris, and Berliner, Lucy. "Harborview Social Workers Advocate Special Techniques for Child Witness." *Response* 1, December 1976. (A publication of the Center for Women's Policy Studies, Washington, D.C.).

An Approach to Case Management

Suzanne M. Sgroi

Most cases of child sexual abuse are managed badly. Those who are responsible for case management tend to have limited knowledge of the problem and an inadequate understanding of the issues involved. They also tend to work for agencies that are reluctant to be responsible for child-sexual-abuse cases and are unwilling to make the commitment to train their staff properly and to develop appropriate community resources. The four essential components of a good case management of child sexual abuse are:

1. Willingness to accept responsibility for the cases.
2. Adequate knowledge of the dynamics and mechanics of the phenomenon and the statutes which govern it.
3. Input of well-trained professional staff with good investigative and clinical skills.
4. Coordinated use of authoritative and supportive services within the community.

Without these capabilities, it is not really possible to manage a case of child sexual abuse adequately. Instead, one can only react to the events following the disclosure in a knee-jerk fashion, often precipitating crises and failing to accomplish the goals of intervening in the first place: that is, adequate investigation and validation of cases, child protection, alleviation of sexual and emotional trauma, and prevention of further sexual abuse.

I firmly believe that the responsibility for case management of child sexual abuse resides within the statutory child-protection agency. In other words, the local agency which, by statute, is required to receive complaints of child abuse, investigate and validate the complaints, protect the child(ren) involved and take steps to remedy the situation, is the logical group to be responsible for case management of sexual abuse. Accordingly, this chapter on approach to case management is written for child-protection agencies and their staff. Although primarily addressed to the statutory child-protection agency, the issues raised should also be of interest to clinicians and to law enforcement and legal justice system personnel.

It is not at all surprising that professionals who encounter child-sexual-abuse cases are often unsure about how to proceed. The considerations are many and complex and two are particularly anxiety-provoking: those pertaining to human sexuality and those which relate to the safety of the child victim. Some of the tasks to be accomplished must be worked on simultaneously. Pursuing some tasks prematurely can lead to confusion or invalidate responses or findings related to other tasks. Small wonder that some professionals are paralyzed by the situation while others rush in precipitously. These cases tend to create so much anxiety and discomfort that those who must respond to them very naturally succumb to the human impulse to alleviate tension by moving at breakneck speed, hoping that by rushing toward closure, the problems will be resolved. Usually they are not and the erroneous notion that a speedy response is preferable to a well-planned methodical response is hard to disspell.

The first part of this chapter will be devoted to a discussion of my own philosophy of case management. The second part will present a step-by-step methodology for approaching cases. Essential tasks for successful case management will be presented in the last section. This chapter is meant to be read in conjunction with chapters 1 and 2. Case management issues are best considered within the context of a conceptual framework for child sexual abuse (see chapter 1) and with a clear understanding of all of the components of validation of cases (see chapter 2).

Philosophy

Fundamental Premises

Although every case of child sexual abuse deserves individual consideration, it is possible to identify some fundamental premises that are generally applicable. First, all sexual misuse or exploitation of children is abusive in nature. This is true even when elements of physical assault are absent and even when the sexual behavior is of the affectional type. Second, the consequences of childhood sexual victimization are both serious and long-lasting. Third, our current sexual assault and child-abuse reporting statutes reflect a societal conviction that child sexual abuse is harmful and that society has a right to intervene, when necessary, on behalf of child victims to remedy the stituation and to prevent further abuse as well as to curb and sometimes punish the offenders. Fourth, child sexual abuse is primarily a disorder of power rather than a sexual aberration; it represents a sexual expression of the gratification of nonsexual needs that is achieved by the offender's misrepresentation of moral standards and misuse of the power that society legitimately accords to adults over children. Fifth, effective intervention into a disordered power system can only be accomplished in an authoritative fashion and from a position of power; other intervention methodologies invite the offender to misuse power further to suppress the allegation, to undermine the child's credibility and to ward off outside interference.

Risk of Intervention

The classic admonition to medical practitioners, *primum non nocere* (first, do no harm), is particularly pertinent in child sexual abuse. Nevertheless, the argument that intervention is intrinsically harmful and that cases are better left undiscovered or ignored is a specious one. Unskilled, clumsy, poorly timed and ill-considered intervention *can* be harmful. However, this is no excuse to continue to ignore cases and to decline to develop competency in intervention. It takes time to develop the skills and resources required. Intervention programs do not spring up full-bloom overnight; they must be built and developed slowly over time. They begin when a few courageous individuals elect to make a start. The risk of intervention also involves the risk of personal commitment to an open-ended process. This is especially true when community resources have not been developed and the intervenor has few committed colleagues or supporters. Yet the professional who proceeds with honest commitment to identify the facts, validate the complaint, and to do his or her best to remedy the situation represents an essential first step in effective intervention within any community.

Methodical Approach to Assessment and Planning: Application of a Problem-Oriented Medical Model

It is easy to become so overwhelmed by the enormity of the allegation of child sexual abuse that the methodical approach to assessment and planning falls by the wayside. This is a mistake. Every case should be approached first with a step-by-step assessment followed by intervention planning, and lastly the implementation of a treatment plan which includes continuous monitoring. There are many similarities between case management in internal medicine (an intensive diagnostic and treatment process) and the management of a child-sexual-abuse case. An analysis of these similarities is now in order.

Medical illness and child sexual abuse are both situations involving multiple variables. A rapid yet comprehensive analysis of these variables must be made and their relative importance determined—whenever possible before new variables (in the form of remedies or other types of intervention) are introduced. However, both situations may involve danger to life and well being and sometimes require that emergency measures be instituted right away. The involved subjects may be acutely uncomfortable or even in pain, frightened, ambivalent, and often resistant or hostile; their cooperation must be enlisted or induced. The overall approach must be based upon an underlying methodology of practice, yet must be adaptable to the unique situation at hand. Internal medicine has developed such an approach aimed at analysis and problem solving for a wide range of disorders of human well being. This approach can encompass the immediate and specific ("I just got this terrible pain in my chest and now I can't breathe.") as well as the chronic and vague ("I haven't felt good for a long time.")

An internist evaluates a patient's medical status by first taking a detailed history about the chief complaint. He or she begins by asking the patient to articulate the problem "in your own words." Then the physician asks a series of questions designed to elicit the symptoms as specifically as possible. Exactly what are the symptoms? When did they appear? How often have they reoccurred? Under what circumstances? With what activities are the symptoms associated (eating, sleeping, various types of exercise, and so forth)? As the patient responds, the physician categorizes the symptoms and identifies the body systems that they reflect. He or she then asks questions that relate to common disorders of these systems in an attempt to elicit more history and to build a symptom complex that is characteristic of a specific disorder.

After a detailed assessment of the chief complaint and the present history, the physician then usually asks about past history. What significant medical events have already occurred (for example, accidents, childbirth, surgery, medications, allergic reactions, and so forth)? A review of systems follows: the physician asks a standard series of questions designed to elicit any symptoms not volunteered by the patient. To facilitate a complete review, the physician usually begins with the head and works downwards (Do you have headaches? Any problems with loss of balance? Any visual impairment? and so on).

Information elicited from comprehensive history-taking forms the basis for drawing up a problem list for the patient. The physician follows history-taking by performing a medical examination. He or she can usually make a preliminary diagnosis based on the history alone and frequently can predict the physical findings before the examination. Nevertheless, an internist usually performs a complete medical examination, even if the history-taking has already pointed to a specific disorder limited to one part of the body. This is done because physical abnormalities may be found that have not yet become symptomatic. Also, a complete physical examination demonstrates to the patient that the physician is conducting a thorough evaluation; this is usually highly reassuring.

After a detailed history and complete physical examination, the internist now has a considerable data base and a well-defined problem list. However, he or she will wish to pursue or to confirm the diagnosis by performing further studies. These are usually a combination of screening tests that are appropriate for the person's age and health background and more specific studies aimed at further defining the symptom complexes and perhaps physical abnormalities that have been elicited.

Often a physician will make a diagnosis and formulate an initial treatment plan with a more limited data base. However, the diagnosis and treatment plan may be modified as the data base is expanded. The physician will plan on monitoring the patient's progress. A conscientious physician will review selected portions of the history and perhaps repeat certain parts of the physical examination every time the patient is seen for a follow-up visit. Selected tests or studies may also be repeated at intervals. In others words, continuous monitoring and updating the data base at intervals are likely to be an integral part of the treatment plan. Also, the problem list will be expanded or reduced, depending on the patient's progress.

The foregoing approach to medical case management is a model which has been developed over the past century and has definitely stood the test of time. The recent modifications orienting the practitioner to problems rather than symptoms are particularly pertinent. A problem-oriented model can be readily applied to management of child-sexual-abuse cases. At minimum, a child-protection agency should obtain a comprehensive history from the child before taking any action. The history should include a detailed description of the sexual behavior and a complete past history of personal and family functioning. After encouraging the child to supply as much information as possible in his or her own words, the investigator should review the common features of sexually abusive behavior and family dysfunction with the child to elicit data that may not have been volunteered.

In some cases, an immediate intervention plan must be initiated on the spot if a comprehensive history from the child validates the allegation and the interviewer believes that the child may be in danger. In other cases, it will be possible to obtain collateral interviews and a physical examination first, thereby adding to the data base and completing the validation process before an initial intervention plan is formulated and implemented. As the data base expands, a problem list can be compiled and become the basis for the intervention plan. If the intervention plan calls for some type of treatment, the data base should be expanded with further studies: for example, an arts therapy diagnostic assessment or psychological testing or perhaps a psychiatric evaluation. Such information will help to define the problems more precisely and to make the treatment plan more realistic. Lastly, as treatment proceeds, the child-protection agency must conduct periodic follow-up reviews to monitor the progress of the case.

Whether applied to medicine or to child sexual abuse, this case management model embodies five basic principles

Intervention Based on Comprehensive Assessment. Effective intervention depends on *collection of a comprehensive data base* as a basis for planning. It matters little if the complaint is "I feel tired all of the time" or "My father makes me have sex with him." It is not acceptable medical practice to respond to a complaint of "feeling tired" by concluding that the patient is not sleeping well and immediately prescribing a sleeping pill. Instead the complaint must be thoroughly assessed. Is fatigue really the problem? Does it mask an underlying illness or disorder? What has happened to precipitate the patient's decision to seek help now? And so forth. Likewise, a child-protection agency must obtain detailed information before prescribing remedies in a child-sexual-abuse case. Failure to do so and precipitous intervention based on insufficient data can produce disastrous results.

Emergency Response to Crisis. In both medicine and child protection, there must be a *capacity for emergency response to crisis based on signs of immediate risk to life or well-being.* Examples of emergency medical situations abound. Medical personnel are trained to assess emergencies and to respond immediately with life-support measures if necessary. Likewise, child-protection agency staff should be prepared to make an emergency child-protection assessment and to respond with immediate measures to protect the child victim of sexual abuse (up to obtaining a temporary order of custody and removing him or her from a dangerous home situation) if necessary. Emergency response to crisis can never be haphazard, either in medicine or in child-protective services. Both disciplines depend on personnel who are trained to recognize the signs which indicate risk to life or well-being and who have access to life-support systems and the capacity to employ them when necessary.

The Patient as a Primary Data Source. In validating a complaint, *the primary source of data should be the patient (or client).* A competent physician is unlikely to turn to collateral sources of information before first interviewing a patient who is able to articulate a history. Who would think of turning to a patient's spouse for information ("Have you noticed that he or she seems tired all of the time?") before obtaining complete information from the patient? Yet this practice of turning to collateral sources first for verification occurs frequently in child-sexual-abuse cases. For example, a child-protective-services worker is very likely to question a victim's mother first in an incest case, even if the child is fully capable of verbalizing the situation ("Mrs. Jones, we understand that your thirteen-year-old daughter, Lizzie, has complained to the school guidance counselor that her father is having intercourse with her. Do you think that is true?") Instead, the investigator should first use collateral sources only to the extent necessary to gain access to the child for investigative interviewing. Validation of child sexual abuse in large measure depends on obtaining information from the child before he or she can be pressured to withhold information or to recant the allegation.

Identification of All Pertinent Problems. Helping a patient with a serious medical problem or helping a child who has been sexually abused both depend on identifying all of the problems which are likely to impact upon either situation. *Compiling a complete problem list* can only be accomplished by collection of a comprehensive data base. Identifying and listing all of the problems helps, in turn, to focus the intervention and treatment plan. Even when it is decided to decline to treat some of the identified problems, nevertheless it may be helpful to acknowledge their existence and to structure the intervention plan around them. Both medical intervention and child-sexual-abuse intervention must consider the family and environment of the patient (client) while compiling the problem list. It is extremely helpful to utilize a preformulated list of problem cateogories in order to make the problem list as complete as possible.

Flexible Intervention and Treatment Planning. An intervention or treatment plan, whether aimed at a medical problem or at a child-sexual-abuse situation, must always be *flexible enough to accommodate a change in the data base.* Whenever possible, a comprehensive data base should be collected and a complete problem list should be compiled before an intervention or treatment plan is formulated and implemented. Often this will not be possible and the intervention or treatment plan will be predicated upon limited data and an incomplete identification of the problems which are present. However, collection of data and identification of problems should always be continued thereafter. A flexible intervention or treatment plan can thus be modified as a more complete understanding of the situation is achieved. Regardless of how complete the data base at the time of its implementation, the intervention or treatment plan should always include a method of ongoing monitoring and have the capacity to be modified over time if the data collected through the monitoring process so indicate.

Active versus Reactive Response

A philosophy of case management of child sexual abuse cannot fail to consider the posture of the intervenors. It is not possible to intervene passively in a situation which, by its very nature, involves misuse of power. The intervenor has three choices: Active intervention, ignoring the situation entirely, or assuming a reactive posture which invites manipulation by the more active protagonists. Active intervention involves the legitimate exercise of authority—encouraging and sometimes ordering people to do certain things, setting limits on some types of behavior, defining and enforcing sanctions when necessary. This posture requires the intervenor to identify and utilize whatever leverage is available to prevent people who are in a power position from abusing others who are less powerful than themselves.

    Inducing people who have abused power to redirect their behavior in a less harmful (hopefully more positive) fashion is frequently viewed as being manipulative. The alternatives, however, are to decline to intervene at all (by ignoring the situation) or else to adopt a reactive stance. Unfortunately, the factors which enabled the child sexual abuse to occur in the first place (misuse of power, massive denial, active suppression) are not likely to disappear. A passive approach by intervenors who choose to react rather than to initiate action eventually invites the perpetrator to ward off all intervention by continuing to misuse power and to deny and suppress the allegation. However distasteful to one's self-image as a gratuitous and benign "helper," an active response to child sexual abuse is the only viable response.

Creative Use of Crisis

This last element of my philosophy of case management of child sexual abuse also tends to be very threatening for helping professionals. We are trained to respond to crisis by taking whatever steps are required to reduce tension and to alleviate anxiety. Most professional practice looks askance at precipitating crisis. Creative use of crisis is considered only slightly less reprehensible. Nevertheless, a crisis is inevitably precipitated when a disclosure of child sexual abuse is made. Intervenors do not really have a choice about precipitating crisis at the time of disclosure; a crisis will occur regardless. The challenge is to use that time of crisis most effectively on behalf of the child victim—careful planning and timing can enable the crisis to be used very creatively in some cases.

Again, the task at hand is to intervene in a situation which involves misuse of power. To change this state of affairs will require disruption, confrontation, and an infusion of outside support and strength on behalf of the weaker party. The sexual abuse of a child within that power system was, in part, aimed at reducing tension. Disclosure of the sexual abuse with all its consequences will undoubtedly increase tension while removing one adaptive mechanism to cope with tension. An effective intervenor will utilize the crisis period following disclosure as an opening wedge to try to change the balance of power and to redirect behavior. Creative use of crisis recognizes that the crisis will occur anyway and tries to make the net effect positive. It is a waste of time, energy and effort to try to avoid the crisis altogether. By the same token, moving to reduce tension without recognizing that some disruption is necessary to redirect the power situation is to encourage the status quo to be resumed without delay or alteration.

To summarize, my philosophy of case management is underlaid by the premises that child sexual abuse is a societal disorder as well as a personal tragedy for all the participants and that society has both the right and the responsibility to intervene when cases are discovered. Although there are acknowledged risks to intervention, I further believe that the involvement of competent and responsible professionals is preferable to ignoring the situation. Although the application of medical models is not currently popular in some social work circles (Miller, 1980), the problem-oriented case mangaement model currently used in medical practice is particularly well suited to child-sexual-abuse intervention. This does not imply that child sexual abuse is an illness nor that it should be treated as such. It is rather an interpersonal social problem that is multidetermined and with multiple variables. Accordingly, case management must include comprehensive data collection, a capacity for emergency response to crisis, the use of the client as a primary data source, and identification of all the problems which are present. Intervention and treatment planning must draw upon an ever-expanding data base and must be flexible enough to be changed as new information is derived through continuous monitoring.

Although distasteful to some, I strongly believe that active intervention in child-sexual-abuse cases is the only truly helpful response for the child victim. Active intervention should be neither hasty nor precipitous; however, the active intervenor is clearly taking direct charge of events rather than waiting for the perpetrator of child sexual abuse to take charge and responding to his or her defensive and evasive manuvers. Since a crisis in inevitably precipitated when we take official notice of child sexual abuse, it behooves the intervenor to anticipate the crisis and, with careful planning based on readiness to act, utilize the disruption as creatively as possible to improve the position of the child victim.

Methodology

Successful preparation for case management demands that the intervenor ask three basic questions. They are: What do I need to know? What do I need to do? When do I need to do it? This section will strive to answer each of these three basic questions as fully as possible. Readers are encouraged to apply these categories of response to their own professional practice situations and seek additional answers within their own communities.

What Do I Need to Know?

There are five categories of response to this question. An intervenor in a child-sexual-abuse case must know the following.

Dynamics and Mechanics of Child Sexual Abuse. It is impossible to intervene intelligently in a child-sexual-abuse case without first being familiar with the usual dynamics and mechanics of the phenomenon. Child sexual abuse nearly always involves a known perpetrator who uses nonviolent means (pressure, persuasion, bribery) based on his or her position of power or authority to engage a child in sexual behavior. The sexual activity will probably begin with less intimate behavior (exposure, masturbation, fondling) and progress to various types of sexual penetration. This behavior nearly always represents an attempt by the perpetrator to gratify nonsexual needs. There will probably be multiple episodes of sexual activity between the perpetrator and the child over time. The perpetrator is likely to pressure or persuade the child to keep their sexual activity a secret from others. The child is likely to maintain the secrecy over a long period of time (months to years).

The secret of child sexual abuse may be disclosed accidentally or purposefully. Accidental disclosure (due perhaps to injury, observation by others, sexually transmitted disease, or pregnancy) implies that none of the participants decided to tell anyone else about the secret. Purposeful disclosure, in contrast, is the result of a conscious decision by a participant to break the secret. After the child sexual abuse is disclosed, the perpetrator and others who occupy power positions and who are threatened by the disclosure will characteristically try to suppress the allegation by pressuring anyone (especially the child victim) who appears to be cooperating with outside authority figures to withhold information or recant the story of the sexual abuse. Evasiveness, denial, hostility, righteous indignation, and undermining the credibility of the child are the tactics most frequently employed by perpetrators after a disclosure of child sexual abuse has occurred.

The foregoing dynamics and mechanics and an analysis of the behavior of the participants are explained in detail in chapter 1. Any professional person who becomes an intervenor should be cognizant of this behavior and be able to assess the information elicited from the case at hand within an overall conceptual framework of behavior related to childhood sexual victimization. Professionals who do not understand the dynamics and mechanics of child sexual abuse are seriously handicapped when they become involved in a case and are very likely to overlook or fail to elicit pertinent information as well as to misinterpret or fail to appreciate the significance of that which is learned.

Civil and Criminal Statutes Related to Child Sexual Abuse. All communities have laws which address sexual behavior between adults and children. In most jurisdictions there will be both criminal and civil statutes that address this issue. It behooves intervenors to know exactly how their own state and local statutes deal with child sexual abuse. Sexual activity with children is undoubtedly covered by the local child-abuse reporting statute (usually a type of civil legislation). In addition, the behavior is probably prohibited by the sections of the criminal statutes or penal code which deal with sexual assault, physical assault, risk of injury to a minor or indecent exposure. Chapter 11 discusses these issues in detail and offers a methodology for assessing the sexual behavior to identify elements of crimes. Readers are encouraged to look up the appropriate statutes for their own jurisdictions and become thoroughly conversant with them.

Why should a professional person bother to learn the laws which deal with the sexual victimization of children in his or her community? The answer is simple. Perpetrators of child sexual abuse fear exposure for many reasons, but their fear of being charged, convicted, and punished for a criminal offense is likely to be paramount. After disclosure of child sexual abuse, the perpetrator is going to be engaging in evasive and defensive activity regardless of the posture of the intervenor. Accordingly, the intervenor must be fully apprised of the legal implications of the sexually abusive behavior. Further, he or she should be aware that the legal justice system, however imperfect, probably represents the only authoritative leverage which can be brought to bear upn the disorder of power that sexual victimization of a child represents. The intervenor who overlooks this harsh reality and proceeds without knowledge of the legal implications of child sexual abuse chooses to make his or her case management efforts ineffective and risks further injury to the child victim. Lastly, the intervenor must be cognizant of his or her responsibilities for reporting and information gathering and fulfill these responsibilities as the law requires.

Elements of Validation. An intervenor who does not know how to validate a case of child sexual abuse is in an untenable position. Chapter 2 includes a detailed analysis of the validation process and strives to present a comprehensive step-by-step plan to be followed by the beginner. Validation of child sexual abuse is almost totally dependent upon information elicited by a skilled and knowledgeable interviewer, primarily from the child victim. The interviewer must be able first to establish a relationship with the child, both to facilitate communication and to develop trust. Only then is it possible to interview for facts and elicit information which can reliably be used to validate the case.

A skilled and knowledgeable interviewer will be able to validate most cases after making a credibility assessment of the child's story (see chapter 2). A credible history of sexual abuse from the child is strengthened by the presence of behavioral indicators of sexual abuse, physical indicators of sexual abuse, or corroborating information from others. Physical indicators of sexual abuse are regarded with the highest credibility by law enforcement and legal justice system personnel. Although a physical examination should always be performed, it is, however, unlikely to produce evidence which proves that a child has been sexually abused. Corroborating information from others is most likely to be elicited by interviewers who convey belief in the child.

Understanding the elements of validation (behavioral and physical indicators of sexual abuse, investigative interviewing, and credibility assessment) is an essential first step for intervenors. It is not necessary for the intervenor to be able to perform all of the elements of validation himself or herself (it is, however, highly desirable). Nevertheless, the intervenor must grasp the essentials of the validation process in order to participate effectively. It is impossible for an intervenor to proceed with a case if he or she does not understand and have confidence in the process by which it is validated.

Child-Protection Assessment. Every intervenor in a sexual abuse case must know how to make a child-protection assessment. Disclosure of sexual abuse cases nearly always places the child in a more vulnerable position. Cases involving unknown perpetrators without access to the child following disclosure are rare indeed. Most cases involve a known perpetrator who will be in a position of continued access to the victim. Following disclosure, the child will almost certainly be subjected to great pressure to recant or deny the allegation. This pressure will be brought by the perpetrator and by others who occupy power positions and stand to lose something (prestige, community standing, a job, or the like) if child sexual abuse is validated. In some cases, the pressure will be verbal and nonviolent; in other cases, the child may be threatened with force or violence; in still other cases, the child may be physically abused in an effort to suppress the allegation. It is necessary to weigh the relative risk of all of the above, with obvious emphasis on the child's physical safety but also with attention to the need for protection from emotional abuse as well. A child-protection assessment should be based upon information elicited from investigative interviewing as well as observation of the behavior after disclosure of the child, the perpetrator, the child's family and other protagonists in the sexual abuse situation. If the intervenor believes that the child will be significantly at risk, based on this assessment, he or she is obligated to take steps to insure the youngster's safety.

What are the factors to be considered in making a child-protection assessment when sexual victimization has been disclosed? They are as follows.

The Child's Assessment. A child who is old enough to be interviewed about sexual abuse should always be asked if he or she feels safe after the disclosure. Children should also be asked how they expect the perpetrator and their family members to react after the secret of sexual abuse is broken and outsiders learn about it. Most of the time, children can anticipate these reactions with a high degree of accuracy. When a child expresses fears about these reactions, a careful exploration of the fears should be made. Why is he or she afraid? What does he or she think will occur? What past experiences form a basis for the child's fears?

A child's request to be separated or protected from the perpetrator or his or her family should be considered very seriously indeed. When in doubt, it is preferable to accede to the request and arrange separation if necessary rather than to risk the child's safety.

History of Threats or Use of Force or Violence. It is important to determine if there is any previous history of threats or use of force or violence. Did the sexual activity involve either? If threats of force or violence against the child or a third party were made, were they ever carried out? In an incest case, do family interactions of any kind involve use of force or violence? If so, what occurred? Do any of the participants keep firearms or dangerous weapons at home? Do they ever threaten to use these weapons? Were such threats ever carried out?

A history of use of, or threats of force or violence should increase concern for the child's safety after disclosure of sexual abuse. Absence of such history does not insure that force or violence will not be employed in the future. On the other hand, the probability that force or violence will be used against the child after disclosure is greater if such behavior was a part of the sexual relationship or characterized other family interactions in the past.

Presence of Functioning Adult Ally. Child victims are virtually always weaker than the perpetrators of sexual abuse. A key factor in making a child-protection assessment is to determine if there will be a functioning adult ally for the child in his or her own home. This is a particularly important issue in intrafamily child sexual abuse. It is folly to make an automatic assumption that one or more of the parents, grandparents, or siblings will necessarily ally themselves with the child victim. Oftentimes they are not willing to serve as allies for the child, especially when the disruption following disclosure of sexual abuse threatens *their* security or interferes with *their* sense of well-being. In particular, one should not assume that a mother will necessarily be willing to support and protect her child if the perpetrator is her spouse or boyfriend or a male sibling (the victim's uncle) or father (the victim's grandfather). In any of these sets of circumstances, the mother may instead ally herself with the perpetrator and against the child.

How to determine if a parent, grandparent, sibling, or perhaps an aunt or uncle might serve as a functioning adult ally for a child? The following questions should be asked.

1. How did this individual react at the time of disclosure? Did he or she react with hostility and denial or with openness and a willingness to believe that sexual abuse may have occurred? Was the response rational and controlled or unrealistic and uncontrolled? Was hostility expressed toward the child or the perpetrator or the intervenor?

2. What has been the individual's past history regarding the child? Has he or she been supportive and reliable or undermining and unreliable?

3. What is the individual's present attitude toward the child? Does he or she find the allegation of child sexual abuse credible or is there an attempt to undermine the youngster's credibility? Is spontaneous concern expressed to the child's well-being or is there more focus on the disruption following disclosure? Has the individual volunteered his or her support for the child? Has he or she

accepted any responsibility for the child's future well-being? Has there been a rejection or denial of such responsibility? Does he or she behave as if the child is to blame for the sexual activity or for the disruption following disclosure? Does he or she express hostility toward the child, reject him or her, or wish that the child would leave?

4. What is the individual's present attitude toward the perpetrator? Does he or she believe that the perpetrator should be held accountable for the sexual behavior or not? Does he or she believe that the perpetrator is being victimized rather than the child? Is the potential ally fearful of the perpetrator? Does he or she express inability or unwillingness to confront that person or to withstand the response?

To serve as a functioning adult ally for a sexually victimized child, a person must be willing to believe that sexual abuse did occur and must not blame the victim for its occurrence. This person should respond realistically and with adequate concern for the child's well-being. Beware of the hysterical reaction or the person who responds with great hostility or disbelief. Likewise to serve as an ally, the person should readily accept responsibility for assisting the child after disclosure. Persons with a past history of failing to support the child at a time of crisis are unlikely to be supportive after a disclosure of sexual abuse. Persons who express fear of the perpetrator or who share misgivings about supporting or protecting the child are probably, in effect, saying that they cannot be allies for the youngster.

To summarize, intervenors must make a child-protection assessment for all victims of sexual abuse regardless of the identity of the perpetrator. The key factors to be considered are the child's assessment of his or her own safety and the response of significant others to disclosure. A child's request for separation or protection should never be disregarded. A past history of use of force or violence or threat of the same is definitely an indicator of increased risk to the victim after disclosure. Lastly, the presence of a functioning adult ally for the child in his or her own home is highly desirable. However, the intervenor cannot assume that a child's family will necessarily be supportive or protective. Instead, the capacity for key family members to serve as allies to the child is an integral part of the child-protection assessment.

Local Resources and Response. An intervenor needs to be familiar with the strengths and weaknesses of the four systems which deal with child sexual abuse in any community. They are the child-protection agency, the legal justice system, health/mental health providers, and the amalgam of essential life-support services. It is impossible to deal with a child-sexual-abuse case effectively without input from all of these groups.

Child-Protection Agency. This agency has the statutory authority to investigate and validate cases of reported child maltreatment. Sexual abuse of children definitely comes within the jurisdiction of child-protective services. Intervenors must understand their responsibilities for reporting, information gathering, and validation. If the child-protection agency is doing its job properly, it will either provide treatment for validated cases or exercise an oversight function for treatment as part of its overall case-management role in child sexual abuse. Intervenors should be familiar with the child-protection agency's intake system, investigative procedures, criteria for validation, methodology for child-protection assessment, and philosophy of intervention and case management. The agency's relationship with local law enforcement personnel and policy regarding the reporting of validated cases to the police must be determined. In addition, the child-protection agency should be able to delineate overall case management procedures with special attention to authoritative intervention, use of the legal justice system to obtain leverage, goals for intervention and treatment, and parameters for monitoring child victims in validated cases.

Legal Justice System. This system includes law enforcement personnel (both state and local police in some jurisdictions), and personnel of both the civil and criminal courts (including probation officers and parole officers). In some communities, correction personnel should also be included for they may well be involved in rehabilitation programs for convicted offenders. Intervenors need to be familiar with police procedures to investigate child sexual abuse as well as the way that prosecutors and judges view this behavior. Chapter 11 discusses many of the issues related to police investigation, decisions for arrest, setting of bond, preparation for court, and so forth. The strength (or weakness) of any approach to child sexual abuse today is directly related to the intervenor's capacity to use the authority of the legal justice system to the child's advantage in case management.

Health and Mental Health Providers. Nearly all disclosed cases of child sexual abuse come to the attention of health or mental health providers. Unfortunately, health and mental health professionals have traditionally been reluctant to provide the services required by the victims and their families. Successful case management depends on the availability of good health and mental health services. Intervenors must not only know the local service providers but have established liaisons and enlisted their cooperation. It is not acceptable for health and mental health providers to plead ignorance of the essential diagnostic and treatment skills required. They must rather be held accountable to develop the necessary clinical competence.

Essential Family Life-Support Services. We are blasé about medicine's capacity to provide total life-support for victims of cardiac arrest or serious trauma. No one questions the advisability of providing an array of expensive life-sustaining machinery in hospital recovery rooms or intensive-care units. Yet families in crisis are also often in need of essential life-support services: for example, emergency shelter care, money, food, clothing, and day-to-day guidance in carrying out activities of daily living. Immediate availability of these services can assist bewildered family members to accept temporary dependency during a period of striving toward greater independence and minimize the negative effects of family disruption following a disclosure of child sexual abuse. Strategic deployment of these services when needed can influence family members to support the child victim (rather than to reject him or her) and permit the youngster to remain with the nuclear family rather than be separated from them.

Intervenors in child-sexual-abuse cases need to know the full extent of family life-support services available in their communities. Locating emergency shelters and establishing liaisons with the providers of public assistance and food stamps are obviously indicated. However, intervenors also need to identify women's support groups, shelter homes for runaways, and individuals and institutions who may be willing to "adopt" a family in crisis. Most communities have potential resources of this type which need to be identified, encouraged, and developed.

The intervenor who has been able to develop fully a response to the question, "What do I need to know?" is ready for the next step in preparation for case management. Having identified the necessary knowledge base, he or she may then ask the following question:

What Do I Need to Do?

This question invites a breakdown of the ten essential tasks in case management of child sexual abuse. Most have already been discussed earlier in this chapter and in chapter 2. The essential case management tasks for child sexual abuse are

Reporting

Investigation

Validation

Child-Protection Assessment

Initial Management Planning

Diagnostic Assessment

Developing a Problem List

Formulating a Treatment Plan

Treatment Intervention

Monitoring and Reassessment

In listing these tasks, I will also try to explain why they need to be done. While explaining what needs to be done and why, I will also try to respond to the third question "When do I need to do it?" Although a listing implies an exact order of precedence, some of the tasks should be approached simultaneously and the circumstances of each case will ultimately determine when each task is accomplished.

Reporting

Whenever child sexual abuse is suspected, the case must be reported immediately to child-protective services. Intervenors should not delay reporting to child-protective services in order to conduct preliminary investigations and attempt to validate the case. Likewise, the child-protection agency should not delay its own investigative procedure. It is essential for the statutory child-protection agency to be involved at the outset in all cases of suspected child abuse to insure adequate child protection.

Cases involving violence or threat of violence should be reported immediately to the police as well. The statutory child-protection agency should have a policy regarding its own timing of reports to local law enforcement officials. All validated cases should be reported to the police even when no violence was involved (see "Initial Management Planning").

Investigation

Case investigation can be separated into two types of tasks—interviewing for facts and collection of physical evidence. In cases involving recent trauma to the victim, these tasks must be pursued simultaneously. For example, the case of a seven-year-old girl who has been assaulted by a stranger in an alley and who stumbles home bleeding from vaginal lacerations will require simultaneous attention to interviewing for facts and collection of physical evidence. In addition to medical examination of the victim, collection of physical evidence may also include examination of clothing for tears, dirt, bloodstains, and semen, taking photographs of the scene of the sexual activity, and so forth (see also chapter 11). On the other hand, the case of a seven-year-old girl who tells her mother that her grandfather has been fondling her genitals on weekend visits for the past three years should first be approached with investigative interviewing. Collection of physical evidence in the latter situation will probably be confined to performing a medical examination after the investigative interviewing has been accomplished.

When approaching a case involving sexual abuse of a child by a family member or by someone who has continuous access to the child, I recommend that investigative interviewing proceed as follows.

1. *Interview with the complainant face-to-face.* This will probably be someone whom the child has told about the sexual abuse—a school guidance counselor perhaps, a friend of the family, or maybe a relative. In all likelihood, this person will already have called child-protective services and made a report via a telephone intake system. Whenever possible, the intervenor should begin the investigation by contacting the complainant and sitting down and talking face-to-face with him or her before talking to anyone else. (Ask him or her not to discuss the case with others, especially the family involved, until after the meeting has taken place.) Why? An initial face-to-face interview with the complainant has these advantages.

a.   The intervenor will elicit far more detailed information about the sexual activity, background information about the child, the perpetrator, and the family in this fashion than can ever be accomplished via a telephone interview. The more that the intervenor can learn about the situation from the complainant first, the better.

b.   The intervenor can assess the credibility of the complainant to a far greater degree in a face-to-face encounter. Does the complainant appear trustworthy and reliable? What is his or her attitude toward the child? Toward the complaint? Does he or she have something to gain or lose by making this complaint? Did the child confide voluntarily in the complainant or did the complainant learn about the sexual activity via accidental disclosure? Does the complainant appear worthy of the child's trust? And so forth.

c.   The complainant can assess the intervenor's credibility as they meet together. So often we forget how difficult it is for a person to report suspected child abuse and with what misgivings the reporter awaits the action following the report. Conscious use of self can be the intervenor's most powerful tool in investigating a case of child sexual abuse. If the intervenor is able to convey to the complainant that he or she is a competent and knowledgeable person who is capable of handling a case of child sexual abuse, the further cooperation of the complainant is virtually assured.

d.   The intervenor can decide if the complainant can be used as a bridge to the child. It is of great strategic importance to be able to interview a child who has been sexually victimized by someone within the family circle without family pressure. Practically speaking, this can usually only be accomplished by interviewing the child before other family members are aware that the complaint has been made. The easiest way to effect such privacy is to use the complainant as a bridge to the child: that is, ask the complainant to introduce the intervenor and the child within some neutral setting so that investigative interviewing can take place. Sometimes more than one investigative interview will be required to validate a case. Again, the cooperation of the complainant may be enlisted to arrange more than one private interview with the child. Most of the time, the complainant *can* be used effectively as a bridge to the child. However, a face-to-face interview is the best way for the intervenor to determine the complainant's credibility and trustworthiness as well as to convince the complainant that he or she should cooperate in this way.

2. *Interview the child.* The methodology of investigative interviewing with children is described in detail in chapter 2. Investigative interviewing should take place in a neutral setting under circumstances which help the child to relax as much as possible. If the situation involves sexual abuse by a family member, it is highly preferable to interview the child alone before family members can exert pressure upon him or her to suppress the allegation. Hence the foregoing recommendation to use the complainant as a bridge whenever possible to arrange a private interview.

It will first be necessary for the interviewer to establish a relationship with the child. The use of media (drawings, dolls, puppets) may be particularly helpful with young children, both in establishing a relationship and in facilitating communication about the sexual behavior. A skilled and knowledgeable interviewer will use a variety of techniques (see chapter 2) to assist the child to recall as much information as precisely as possible. In addition to collecting and recording facts, the interviewer is simultaneously addressing the tasks of validation, child-protection assessment, and intitial intervention planning. The intervenor is reminded that laws which limit the police in interviewing (or interrogating) a child who has been charged with an offense are not applicable to the child victim of an offense. The presence of a parent or guardian is required to interview a juvenile offender, but not a child victim.

3. *Interview other family members.* Who first? The identity of the perpetrator, the total number of child victims, and the complainant's and child's assessment of the probable reaction of other family members to disclosure of the sexual abuse all will influence the intervenor's decision. If there is more than one child victim involved, the other victims should be interviewed next if possible. However, the intervenor may not be able to obtain access to younger child victims without interviewing a parent first. In general, in cases of child sexual abuse by a family member, it is preferable to interview the mother next after interviewing the child. If a skilled and knowledgeable interviewer believes that a child's account of sexual abuse is credible, the person who interviews the mother should convey belief in the child. It is important to remember that much of the validation process will already be completed (see ''Validation'' below) and that the interview with the child's mother is an important part of the child-protection assessment (see below). The mother's response to the disclosure of child sexual abuse will also be a major factor in the intitial management planning (below).

Other family members who live at home (excluding the perpetrator) should be interviewed next if possible. These interviews may elicit additional information about the sexual activity and may corroborate the victim's story directly or indirectly. For example, a young sibling of the child victim may confirm that he or she was diverted with another pastime or sent out of the room by the perpetrator while the sexual abuse was taking place. Siblings may have nevertheless observed part of the sexual activity or be aware of elements of the secrecy phase or even have been part of the secrecy phase. It is not unusual when interviewing siblings of the child victim to learn that they also had been approached sexually or even sexually victimized in the past. In addition to gathering additional facts, interviews with other family members help to determine if they will be supportive of the victim. Thus these interviews address the tasks of validation and child-protection assessments as well.

4. *Interview the perpetrator.* The perpetrator should not be interviewed until the intervenor has decided to believe the child (or not) and has made a preliminary child-protection assessment. Disclosure of the sexual abuse places the child in a position of great risk from the perpetrator. He or she can be expected to deny that the sexual abuse occurred and to try to undermine the credibility of the child. If the perpetrator admits that the sexual abuse did occur, he or she is still likely to deny that the behavior was harmful or inappropriate and can be expected to try to shift responsibility and blame to others. (especially the victim). Interviewing the perpetrator will contribute little to validation but may be an important factor in child-protection assessment and intervention planning.

5. *Collateral interviews.* Information elicited from the complainant, the child, and other family members may indicate the need for collateral interviews with persons who know the family or perhaps with family members now living away from home. Collateral interviews with older siblings who have left home may be particularly helpful in supplying information about previous sexual abuse of other children by the perpetrator. It may well be appropriate to interview other members of the extended family (for example, cousins) as well as unrelated children to whom the perpetrator had access and opportunity for sexual abuse. Such interviews often provide additional information about sexually abusive activity by the perpetrator.

Validation

The process of validation of child sexual abuse is explained in detail in chapter 2. Validation will depend in large measure on investigative interviewing of the child by a skilled and knowledgeable interviewer. In a small proportion of cases, there will be corroborating physical evidence of some type or the child's story will be corroborated by others who were participants in the sexual activity or observers. The likelihood that the perpetrator will admit to the child sexual abuse is much greater when he or she perceives that others believe the child's story. In my experience, false allegations by children regarding sexual abuse by an adult are exceedingly rare. Validation of cases depends to a large extent on the intervenor's willingness to believe that child sexual abuse can and does occur as well as the capacity to obtain an investigative interview with the child victim before the perpetrator and family members have been able to pressure him or her to recant or deny the allegation.

Child-Protection Assessment

This process was described in detail earlier in this chapter. The purpose is to decide when a child may need to be protected from abuse (physical, emotional, or sexual) by someone who occupies a power position and has continued access to him or her. The intervenor should begin the child-protection assessment as soon as he or she starts to interview the complainant, the child, other family members, and the perpetrator. A past history of force or violence, the absence of a functioning adult ally in the home or the child's fears or request for protection are all indicators that a separation should be made.

Initial Management Planning

After a preliminary investigation has taken place, it is the responsibility of the intervenor to decide if the complaint of child sexual abuse is valid. If a case is validated, a child-protection assessment must be made. Initial intervention planning cannot proceed in an intelligent fashion until the aforementioned tasks have been accomplished. Nevertheless, the groundwork for initial management planning is laid as interviews with the protagonists take place. An intervenor must, after all, convey his or her intentions and responsibilities to the child and to family members as the interviews proceed. The final shape of the initial intervention plan will, of course, depend on the information that is elicited and the reponses of the protagonists. Here are the essential steps.

  1. *Report to the police.*   All validated cases of child sexual abuse must be reported to the police. Sexually abusive behavior toward children is a crime. At the present time, the authority of the legal justice system is the only incentive for perpetrators to stop their sexually abusive behavior and, hopefully, to adopt less destructive ways to gratify basic human needs.

  Intervenors should urge child victims and adult family members to make a formal complaint to the police regarding the sexually abusive behavior. This implies a responsibility to support these individuals throughout their entire involvement with the legal justice system. Intervenors in child-sexual-abuse cases also have a responsibility to improve the legal justice system's response to child sexual abuse within their communities. Punishment which is not allied to treatment or rehabilitation for this disorder of power is a totally inadequate response.

Some victims and families will refuse to make a complaint to the police. In these cases, the intervenor should inform the family that the police will be notified, nonetheless, in a so-called blotter report that (in the intervenor's opinion) the situation represents a validated case of child sexual abuse. These blotter reports usually result in an improved cooperative relationship with the police and may turn up additional information about the case which will assist in devising an intervention plan. Also, a blotter report to the police will convince the family of the gravity of the situation and may serve as a deterrent to the perpetrator in the future (this is speculative).

2. *Medical examination* The initial intervention plan should include a medical examination for the child victim(s) if the circumstances of the case did not require that this be done on an emergency basis when the case was reported. The intervenor should not expect that the medical examination will validate the case; the physical findings will rarely be conclusive. Nevertheless, the medical examination should be performed by a knowledgeable and competent examiner who follows a protocol for identification and collection of evidence. Chapter 2 includes a description of the essential elements of a medical examination for child sexual abuse as well as the types of physical evidence which may be obtained from this procedure. It is important to remember that a complete medical examination by a competent examiner can be enormously reassuring to the child victim and his or her family and is an essential part of the treatment process (see chapter 4).

The timing of the medical examination may be very important. It will usually be necessary to obtain parental permission for the examination to be performed. This will, of course, require a disclosure of the complaint to the child's parent(s). It is preferable to defer this disclosure (and the medical examination) until after investigative interviewing of the child by a skilled and knowledgeable interviewer has taken place. Validation of the case based on information obtained by investigative interviewing thus will usually precede the medical examination. Unless the circumstances of the case require emergency medical examination (for example, a history of recent forceful penetration or the child's complaint of pain or trauma), it is far better to schedule the examination as part of the initial intervention planning.

Little is achieved by requiring an exhausted and frightened child to sit in an emergency room for several hours in order to undergo an examination by an intern or resident (often at 2:00 A.M.). Such experiences are usually unsatisfactory and may well be traumatic. Emergency-room examinations for child sexual abuse are never justified unless a true medical emergency, as previously described, exists. Emergency-room personnel will not be permitted to send the child away without performing an examination. It is up to the intervenor to avoid this scenario by scheduling the medical examination on a nonemergency basis, preferably in the office of a competent and knowledgeable physician, whenever possible. Thus an atmosphere of crisis can be avoided, the child and parent(s) can be adequately prepared ahead of time, and the examination process can be therapeutic as well as diagnostic (instead of an ordeal).

3. *Decisions regarding separation.* If the intervenor believes that he or she is dealing with a valid case of child sexual abuse, it is essential that the child and the perpetrator be separated during the intitial intervention phase. This separation is important for the following reasons:

a. The physical safety of the child is assured
b. The child will not be subjected to direct pressure from the perpetrator to deny or recant the allegation.
c. The perpetrator will be more likely to perceive that the intervenors believe that child sexual abuse has occurred and consider the situation to be serious even if he or she denies the allegation.

If the perpetrator is a family member, the disruption caused by separation should be viewed as a constructive tool for changing those power relationships which allowed child sexual abuse to occur in the first place. Who should be separated? How should separation take place? For how long? The answers to these questions obviously depend on the circumstances of the case. The following types of separation may occur.

Perpetrator from child and family members. This type of separation is most desirable but sometimes difficult to achieve. It has the advantage of shifting most of the inconvenience of separation to be experienced by the person who was responsible for the child sexual abuse. Additionally, the child remains in his or her home with his or her nuclear family and is less likely to be ostracized and forced to assume the burden of the "guilty party." If the perpetrator is someone outside the family circle or if he or she is someone who does not reside in the same household as the child, it is usually easy to effect a separation of the perpetrator from the child and family members. Under these circumstances, there will be little, if any, household disruption and hence little retaliatory pressure on the child.

However, if the perpetrator is a family member or if he or she ordinarily resides in the same household as the child, it will be more difficult to separate him or her from the child and family members. The greater the perpetrator's power position within the family or household, the harder it will be to enforce a separation. If a complaint has been made to the police, the perpetrator may be charged with a criminal offense and be arrested. This does not necessarily mean that he or she be imprisoned awaiting trial; instead the likelihood is very great that the perpetrator will be free on bond pending trial. If the latter circumstance occurs, it is advisable to seek a restraining order from the court which requires the perpetrator to leave the household and stay away. Even a restraining order will not be effective if the victim's family is afraid to report infractions to the police.

Whenever possible, it is preferable for the perpetrator to leave the household on a voluntary basis. If the intervenors and the adult family members are firm, some perpetrators will move out of the home temporarily. In some jurisdictions, a police agency may negotiate with the perpetrator to leave the home pending action on a complaint of child sexual abuse.

Child and family members from perpetrator. If the perpetrator is a family member or resides in the household and refuses to leave, it may be preferable for the child and the other family members to leave instead. This option hinges on the willingness of the child's adult ally within the household to take responsibility for moving the family out of the home. Usually this scenario involves a mother who must choose to remove herself and her children from the home of her spouse or boyfriend. This choice will require a significant degree of independence to be exercised by a person who is probably very dependent upon the perpetrator. Undoubtedly, the intervenor must be prepared to offer essential family life-support services (see item 4 below) in order to make this viable.

Child from perpetrator and family members. Although this type of separation may be the easiest to arrange, it is usually least desirable for the child victim. In addition to the usual trauma of separation, the child victim of sexual abuse who is removed from his or her family and home is at great risk of becoming identified as the person who caused the family problem. The parents may agree to a voluntary separation or the intervenor may need to arrange for a temporary order of custody for the child. In some cases, children will run away from home and refuse to return. Despite all the drawbacks of separation, it is still preferable to remove the child from a living situation which is either physically dangerous to him or her or else is characterized by enormous pressure by the perpetrator and other family members to withdraw the complaint of sexual abuse.

4. *Total life-support services.* Families which are in a state of disruption following disclosure frequently need total life supports, especially if the perpetrator was the head of the household and the family breadwinner. Earlier in this chapter I emphasized the need to be familiar with the essential family life-supprt services available in the community. In some cases, emergency shelter services will be required. Other families will not require shelter but will require emergency financial assistance. Some may require both. Almost invariably, the functioning adult ally for the child(ren) will require a great deal of direction and support to accomplish necessary activities of daily living. For example, mothers are often bewildered by the tasks of money management and family decision making. They will be able to maintain their new positions as decision-makers

and heads of household only if they receive generous amounts of guidance and one-on-one support. The initial intervention plan should anticipate the need for total life-support services and provide them as required.

5. *Anticipatory guidance.*   In cases of child sexual abuse, the disruption following disclosure usually follows a predictable pattern. Family members usually react with shock and disbelief. Initially they may express anger toward the perpetrator and support for the child victim. Very early, they begin to feel shame and embarrassment and wish to minimize publicity about the sexual abuse and keep it a secret from friends, relatives, business colleagues, school-mates, and the like. The disruption following disclosure is quickly reassessed by each family member in terms of "What will this mean to me?" Frequently, there is a backlash of anger against the victim.

If family members were in part responsible for the sexual abuse itself or for some of the circumstances that allowed the sexual abuse to happen, they may also feel guilty for their behavior. In turn, the guilty feelings may be rechanneled into anger and hostility—against the perpetrator or against the child victim or against supporters of either. Child victims themselves may feel very guilty for their past behavior and for the disruption following disclosure. Depression and suicidal feelings are frequently experienced. Anger and hostility may also be present and the child may act out his or her anger in a variety of ways. Mothers of sexually abused children may initially react to disclosure with great anger toward the perpetrator. If the perpetrator is a spouse or boyfriend, they may initially separate from him and plan a permanent separation. Later they may regret these actions and desire a reconciliation.

Anticipatory guidance regarding all of the common family reactions after disclosure is an essential part of initial management planning. The intervenors must forecast all of the probable reactions of each family member and assist him or her to recognize these reactions and prepare to cope with them. It is unrealistic to expect that anticipatory guidance will prevent negative reactions from occurring; clearly that will not be so. However, use of anticipatory guidance can help clients to work through their reactions more constructively. Also, the credibility of the intervenor is enhanced when the anticipatory guidance proves to be on target.

6. *Preparation for court.*   The majority of child-sexual-abuse cases will have some type of court involvement. Initial intervention planning should include assisting families through the court process. If criminal proceedings are involved, the family should be told what to expect regarding the setting of bond, hearings for probable cause, continuances, and so forth. Accompanying them to the police station to swear out a complaint is only the first step. Children, in particular, should receive adequate preparation for court. This may include a visit to an empty courtroom, role playing to prepare for a hearing or a trial,

accompanying family members to court, and so forth. Intervenors may be able to enlist the services of personnel in victim/witness assistance units, rape crisis centers, spouse abuse support groups, and the like. In any event, supporting the client through the court process is an integral part of child-sexual-abuse intervention. It is unrealistic to expect people to participate in "treatment" unless—or until—they receive this support.

Diagnostic Assessment

During implementation of the initial management plan, intervenors should make a diagnostic assessment of the victim and his or her family. The diagnostic assessment of the victim should address the ten major impact issues for child sexual abuse (see chapter 4, "Treatment of the Sexually Abused Child") and determine the degree of the child's emotional trauma and treatment needs. A diagnostic assessment of the family should be made in both extrafamily and intrafamily cases. This assessment will help to determine the degree of family contribution to the child sexual abuse as well as the family treatment needs (see chapter 9, "Family Treatment").

The purpose of conducting a comprehensive diagnostic assessment is to gather data for developing a problem list on which to base a treatment plan. A significant proportion of this data base will be collected during the investigation, validation, and child-protection assessment. However, the diagnostic assessment should also include a complete individual and family social history, mental status examinations, diagnostic art therapy sessions, observation of family functioning (especially with respect to abuse of power in family interactions), evaluation of school performance in many cases, psychological testing. This diagnostic assessment should proceed methodically rather than haphazardly with the goal of obtaining as complete a data base as possible on the victim, family and perpetrator.

Developing a Problem List

Why develop a problem list? This is a useful tool for treatment planning. It is particularly helpful in working with large numbers of cases to have developed a set of problem categories against which family functioning can be measured. Chapter 13, "Evaluation of Child Sexual Abuse Programs," offers a rationale for using a set of predetermined problem categories to assess the family in each case. The problem categories enable more rigorous and methodical case assessment and encourage collection of a comprehensive data base. Evaluating family functioning with the help of a predetermined list of problem categories is a good way to be certain that all pertinent problem areas are addressed. It helps to identify and document that problems exist in certain problem categories (for example, environmental problems or substance abuse) even when it is decided not to try to treat some of the problems which have been identified.

Formulating a Treatment Plan

After a case of child sexual abuse has been validated, a treatment plan will clearly be required. Depending on the circumstances of the case, the treatment plan may address the victim's needs only, involve key family members only, or it may involve the entire family. Some intervenors may wish to consider the initial management plan as part of the treatment plan. This is entirely acceptable so long as the treatment plan is not limited to immediate needs of a family in crisis without addressing the longer-term needs for treatment of emotional trauma and restructuring of intrafamily relationships.

Intelligent treatment planning requires comprehensive diagnostic assessment, collection of a data base, and development of a problem list (see above). The treatment plan should be based directly upon this information. As previously mentioned, those who are formulating the treatment plan may choose not to treat certain identified family problems. This is acceptable so long as it involves a clear decision-making process versus failing to address a problem by default. Multidisciplinary team review of cases may be particularly helpful in formulating the treatment plan, especially in deciding what problems to treat and how therapy should proceed. (See also chapter 12, "Multidisciplinary Team Review of Child-Sexual-Abuse Cases.")

Treatment Intervention

This task may be broad or limited, long term or short term. Treatment intervention may be focused solely upon the victim or upon the perpetrator or upon key family members. Ideally, the entire family will be involved in some type of family treatment, even in cases of extrafamily child sexual abuse (see chapter 9, "Family Treatment"). At minimum, treatment intervention should always take place with the child victim (see chapter 4, "Treatment of the Sexually Abused Child"). Depending on the degree of physical or emotional trauma, treatment intervention may be limited to short-term counseling or extended to long-term therapy.

Treatment intervention should follow an established treatment plan which, in turn, should be based on a family problem list compiled through comprehensive diagnostic assessment. The progress of treatment intervention should be assessed at intervals—the treatment plan should have identifiable and measureable goals and include reassessment at intervals.

Monitoring and Reassessment

Ongoing monitoring and reassessment of treatment intervention constitute the last essential case-management task for child sexual abuse. This task requires that the data base be expanded at intervals. In other words, intervenors never stop collecting data about the case situation so long as they continue to be involved with the victim and the family. Why bother to do this at all? One of the greatest failings in case management of child sexual abuse is the inability or unwillingness to accurately assess the impact of intervention long enough or carefully enough. Until we begin to do this, we can only speculate about the effectiveness of our intervention.

What about recidivism? Monitoring should, of course, address the issue of repeated sexual abuse. As the case is reassessed at intervals, therapists must be assured that the child has not been sexually abused again. But there should also be a commitment to reassess for therapeutic progress. Are family patterns of interaction less destructive? Have key family members become more assertive and less dependent? Has the victim's self-image improved? Does depression persist? Do the family members have clearer role boundaries? Have the children completed age-appropriate developmental tasks? Do they have better developed social skills? Are they less isolated? Are they using their new social skills to good advantage? Treatment issues and criteria for improvement for key family members are addressed in greater detail in chapters 4 through 10.

Summary

This chapter has presented a philosophy of case management for child sexual abuse followed by a response to the questions, "What do I need to know?"; "What do I need to do?"; "When do I need to do it?" The basic knowledge required for adequate intervention and the ten essential case management tasks have been discussed and described in turn. Lastly, an approach for ordering a step-by-step case management process has been presented. Chapter 14 "How to Start a Child Sexual Abuse Program," addresses the staffing and organizational requirements for effective community-based case management.

4

Treatment of the Sexually Abused Child

Frances Sarnacki Porter,
Linda Canfield Blick,
and *Suzanne M. Sgroi*

Effective treatment of the sexually abused child requires an understanding of the significant impact issues for the victim. Helping a child to overcome the effects of sexual victimization is not easy; however, it is not impossible, either. Unless the child victim is psychotic (fortunately a rare occurrence), the treatment goals will usually be a reflection of the impact issues. This chapter will examine all of the common child-sexual-abuse impact issues and discuss the treatment implications of each. It is meant to be read in conjunction with chapter 5, "Group Therapy with Female Adolescent Incest Victims," and chapter 1, "A Conceptual Framework for Child Sexual Abuse."

The following ten impact and treatment issues for victims of child sexual abuse will be addressed:

1. "Damaged Goods" syndrome
2. Guilt
3. Fear
4. Depression
5. Low self-esteem and poor social skills
6. Repressed anger and hostility
7. Impaired ability to trust
8. Blurred role boundaries and role confusion
9. Pseudomaturity coupled with failure to accomplish developmental tasks
10. Self-mastery and control

The first five impact issues (1–5) are likely to affect all children who have been sexually abused, regardless of the identity of the perpetrator. In other words, sexual abuse by anyone—known or unknown, family member or non-relative—can be expected to have these effects upon the child to some degree. The last five impact issues (6–10) are much more likely to affect intrafamily child-sexual-abuse victims. However, sexual abuse by a significant other who, although not a family member, is a known and valued person for the child can trigger many of the responses (and treatment issues) described in 6–10 as well.

We have intentionally described the impact and treatment issues in functional terms whenever possible. For the nonpsychotic victim who does not fit a specific diagnostic category (for example, anorexia nervosa), little is gained by affixing labels. Instead, most child-sexual-abuse victims need informed and practical assistance in overcoming the traumatic effects of their experiences. Immediate treatment can prevent the emergence of some destructive and dysfunctional behavior patterns and redirect others in a less destructive and more functional fashion. Instead of being forced to "live crippled," most victims can be helped to live happy and productive lives despite residual emotional scars.

For cases of intrafamily child sexual abuse, some combination of individual, group, dyad, and family therapy will be the treatment of choice. Unfortunately this is often not possible because participation in treatment requires the parents of victims to assume responsibility and be accountable for their actions. Many such parents prefer to react to the disclosure of intrafamily child sexual abuse with denial and hostility and by rejecting the child. The logical consequence of this response is to identify the child victim as the " problem." Sometimes parents permit or encourage the "problem" child victim to live outside the home; other times, the child remains at home but family participation in treatment is nil. If the child is placed outside the home, treatment can usually proceed without significant interference by the family. If the child victim of intrafamily sexual abuse remains at home with family members who vigorously deny that the sexual abuse ever took place, he or she may not be accessible to treatment. If therapy for the child is permitted under these circumstances, many obstacles can be anticipated. Sometimes hostile family members will actively sabotage treatment efforts. More often, a passive resistance to the child's treatment program (and, indeed, to the premise that anything is amiss) will be encountered.

Although treatment of the child victim of intrafamily sexual abuse is best accomplished when therapeutic efforts are directed toward the entire family, the harsh reality is that therapists must often choose to focus only on the child or not to treat at all. Although it is not an optimal approach, much can be achieved by working with the child alone, either individually or in a group therapy milieu. Parental resistance to family treatment or parental denial of the child's treatment needs is an unacceptable reason to decline or neglect to treat a sexually abused child. At minimum, every case of intrafamily child sexual abuse which is identified and validated by a child-protective services agency should remain open until a reasonable treatment plan for the child victim has been implemented and monitored for at least six months. This is the only way for the statutory child-protection agency to insure that its obligation to provide or arrange for the treatment of child victims is being met.

When a child is sexually abused by someone outside the family, his or her treatment needs (beyond the narrow consideration of medical management) are frequently overlooked. It seems that we are so absorbed by intrafamily situations that the impact of sexual abuse by an outsider upon a child victim receives little attention. These children are often severely emotionally traumatized by their sexually abusive experiences and may need treatment badly. Unfortunately, parents of children who have been sexually abused by someone outside the family are likely to resist therapeutic intervention as well. We speculate that such parents prefer to deal with their own guilt and embarrassment by denying the significance of the sexual abuse and its impact upon their children. If this is true, the tendency of such parents to ignore blatant signs of trauma to the child (for example, withdrawal, depression, school phobias, bedwetting, fear of being left alone, fear of the dark, fear of strangers) and to refuse treatment is understandable. Frequently, therapists will be told, "We want him or her to forget about it. You just keep raking up the past and making it seem worse." The underlying message from the parents is very clear—*they* wish to forget, *they* are also traumatized, *they* feel responsible or guilty to some degree for their children's problems. To acknowledge that treatment for the child is required will reinforce their own negative responses to the situation and seems too painful to be endured.

We believe that all child victims of sexual abuse need some level of therapeutic intervention, regardless of the identity of the perpetrator. We further believe that with respect to the child victim and the family's response to disclosure and intervention, there are more similarities and parallels between intrafamily and extrafamily child-sexual-abuse cases than have previously been recognized. Most statutory child-protection agencies focus almost exclusively on cases of intrafamily child sexual abuse. Extrafamily child-sexual-abuse cases tend to occupy a low priority level if it appears that the perpetrator is "out of the picture" and no longer has access to the child. We have found a similar level of resistance to acknowledging the trauma to the child and permitting significant therapeutic intervention in *both* intrafamily *and* extrafamily child-sexual-abuse cases. It seems to require nearly as much energy and effort to engage the family of a child who has been sexually abused by an outsider as is demanded for the intrafamily child-sexual-abuse case. We have found that it is first necessary to address the needs and emotional trauma of the parents and siblings of the child who has been sexually abused by an outsider in order to be able to implement a treatment plan which addresses the therapeutic needs of the victim.

Accordingly, we recommend that the intervention and treatment plan for *all* child-sexual-abuse victims include a treatment approach for the family. It is certainly true that some cases (both of the intrafamily and extrafamily types), after diagnostic assessment, will appear to be amenable to short-term intervention which may even be limited to "counseling" rather than "therapy." Other cases of both types will require a long-term treatment plan which will optimally include more than one treatment modality and will be characterized by a focus on the entire family. Of course, each case presents a unique set of circumstances, and intervention and treatment plans should reflect this fact.

As previously mentioned, in many cases of both types, intervenors will be permitted to work only with the child victim, despite their recognition that it would be preferable and more effective to implement a treatment plan that includes the entire family. We strongly recommend that such children receive treatment, nevertheless, and that the statutory child-protection agency insist that a treatment plan for the child be designed and carried out. When the treatment focus is solely upon a child victim who continues to live at home, therapists should be aware that, in all likelihood, the child's behavior will change if the treatment plan is successful. Regardless of the type of sexual abuse (intrafamily versus extrafamily), a child who becomes more confident, more self-assertive, and whose behavior becomes more appropriate for his or her age and developmental level will almost certainly "make waves" and upset the status quo at home. Accordingly, at minimum, the treatment plan should include an approach to the family's response (which may well be negative) to these changes in the behavior of the child victim.

The next part of this chapter will discuss all of the major impact issues for the child victim of sexual abuse and comment on the treatment implications for each. (Readers are also referred to the "Behavioral Indicators" section of chapter 2). The last part of the chapter will present an approach for diagnosis and formulation of a treatment plan while emphasizing the most important therapeutic considerations.

Impact Issues and Treatment Implications

"Damaged Goods" Syndrome

Almost invariably, a child victim of sexual abuse feels damaged by his or her experiences, even if no force was used and even when no physical trauma occurred as a result. The "damaged goods" syndrome is an amalgam of reactions.

1. *Physical injury or fear of physical damage.* If physical injury or pain indeed occurred, the child has a concrete reason to believe that he or she was damaged. Usually there is no physical impairment resulting from child sexual abuse. However, if the victim experienced pain as a part of the sexually abusive activity, it is easy to understand why he or she is likely then to believe that an injury must have occurred. Even if the pain or discomfort was transient, the presumption of injury leading to permanent damage may remain if definite steps are not taken to correct this misperception. For example, a seven-year-old girl whose uncle had explored her vaginal and rectal openings with his finger said to her therapist, "I think something is broken inside of me. He hurt me, you know."

Older children also experience intense concern about physical impairment resulting from sexual abuse. Adolescent girls who have been sexually victimized often ask questions which reflect their fears about damage to themselves: "Will I be normal when I grow up? If I have a baby, will it be all right? When I have sex with someone else, will he know I had sex with my dad first?" These concerns are intensified for those victims who become impregnated as a result of sexual abuse. The experiences of pregnancy, abortion, or carrying a fetus to term and undergoing delivery of the baby all provide a concrete focus for the victims' fear of body damage. Even if no permanent physical impairment *did* occur, these girls will require intense support and reassurance to help integrate these experiences.

Occasionally, permanent physical damage *does* result from child sexual abuse.

> Thirteen-year-old Mary was sexually abused by her mother's paramour for several years. At age eleven, Mary contracted a symptomatic gonorrhea infection of the cervix which was treated. The sexual abuse continued and Mary was reinfected with gonorrhea within a year. This time, she was not brought back to the clinic for adequate treatment and followup. Unfortunately, the infection spread into Mary's Fallopean tubes and ovaries. By age 13 years, the damage resulting from inadequately treated infection and reinfection was so great that a complete hysterectomy (removal of the uterus), as well as removal of the tubes and ovaries was required.

Needless to say, any child whose sexual victimization leads to such drastic impairment is, in fact, damaged for life. Fortunately, such cases are rarely encountered.

2. *Societal response.* Societal response to the child victim after the sexual abuse has been disclosed is also a major component of the "damaged goods" syndrome. As Burgess and Holmstrom (1979) have previously reported, the family's and community's response to learning that a child has been prematurely introduced to sexuality often contributes to the victim's perception that he or she has been damaged or mysteriously altered by the sexually abusive experiences. Our society places profound emphasis on the individual's introduction to sexual behavior with others; a person's first interpersonal sexual encounter is viewed as an important rite of passage and as a sign of maturity. In this context, the sexually experienced child is an uncomfortable and troublesome paradox. The fact of the child's premature and inappropriate sexual experience, if acknowledged, becomes a trigger for the conflicts, ambivalence, guilt, and fear regarding human sexuality which are harbored by members of his or her family and community. The youngster is likely to be viewed with intense curiosity, pity, disgust, or hostility, depending upon the perceptions and hangups of the people who learn about the sexual abuse. The following case example is illustrative.

> Judy told her therapist that many of her classmates at school had read about

her dad's arrest for sexual assault in the newspapers and had identified her as the victim. She said, "Lots of kids started asking me about it. They didn't care about me. They just wanted to know about what happened." Judy began to withdraw at school and her grades began to decline.

Because sexual experience is regarded by society as the prerogative of adults, it may be extremely difficult even for family members and professionals to continue to view the sexually victimized child *as a child*. Instead the boy or girl may be viewed more as an adult and be treated more as an adult than as a child.

Five-year-old Sandy had been sexually abused by her father. Her mother made a complaint to the police and her husband was arrested and forced to separate from the family. Although she seemed sincere in her desire to help her child, Sandy's mother found it difficult to cope with her own reactions to the reality that Sandy had been involved in sexual behavior. She began to treat her five-year-old daughter as if she were fifteen. This distorted perception was clearly demonstrated during an art therapy session when Sandy's mother drew a picture of her young daughter wearing seductive clothes, high-heeled shoes, earrings and makeup.

In the following case example, the fact of Sandy's chronological age was sharply at odds with her sexual experiences. Unable to cope with this paradox, the mother began to perceive her child as an older, more sophisticated rival for her husband's affections. Although such a distorted perception may help the mother to cope with her own feelings of inadequacy, it cannot fail to undermine the mother-child relationship and to be destructive for the victim.

Sometimes societal response to the child victim can be even more inappropriate. The sexually victimized child may be viewed neither as a child nor as an adult but rather as a piece of "damaged goods" lacking the attributes of both childhood or adulthood. When viewed in this way, children are particularly vulnerable. If they are perceived as so altered and damaged that the usual constraints and restrictions about sexual behavior do not hold, sexually victimized children may become "walking invitations" to others who wish to act out.

Lisa, age 17 years, had been sexually abused by both parents since she was twelve. Her story was publicized in the newspaper for weeks. Lisa was placed with relatives who lived in another town because both her parents were in jail. Although she wished to keep her past experiences a secret, her new classmates discovered that she was the victim described in the newspaper articles because a car belonging to her family was recognizable from a photograph. A number of boys in the school began to proposition her, saying they were sure she wished to be sexually active because of her "background." The pressure became so great that Lisa began to fear that she would be sexually assaulted and asked to be moved again to another location.

Treatment Implications. Treatment of the "damaged goods" syndrome should begin in a concrete fashion with a comprehensive physical examination of the victim, performed by a physician who is knowledgeable about child sexual abuse and aware of the psychosocial issues. If physical damage did occur, it should be identified and treated medically as soon as possible. If physical damage is absent (the usual finding), the process of conveying this fact emphatically to the child and the family should begin immediately.

In previous years, physical examinations of asymptomatic children who had been sexually abused were often discouraged on the grounds that examination would "further traumatize the child." For this spurious reason, parents and children would thus be left with a lingering suspicion that "something might be wrong." Instead, it is far preferable to confront the child's and parent's fears directly and provide a reality basis for the assertion that the child is all right.

The ability to state authoritatively that physical damage is absent or has been treated is a stepping stone to convincing the child, the family, and significant others that the victim has not been otherwise damaged by the sexual victimization. It helps the child and family to anticipate the possibility that they and others may perceive the child in a different light. Adults should be helped to understand the basis for a distorted perception of the sexually experienced child. Avoiding or overcoming such a distorted perception can only be accomplished by refuting it directly and utilizing every opportunity to convince all participants that the child is *not* damaged, physically or emotionally. In particular, parents, siblings, teachers, and others should be made aware of the importance of behaving toward the victim *as a child* of appropriate age and experience—not as an adult or as a piece of "damaged goods."

Guilt

Some sexually abused children do not feel guilty about their behavior prior to the disclosure of the secret of sexual activity. However, intense guilt feelings following disclosure of sexual abuse are practically a universal victim response. Children who have been sexually victimized usually experience guilt on three levels.

1. Responsibility for the sexual behavior. Many child victims feel as if they are responsible for the sexual activity which took place. By definition, the sexual abuse was initiated by an adult or by someone who occupied a power position over the child. Nevertheless, the children tend to feel guilty about their participation as soon as they perceive the societal response to their sexual activity. Unfortunately, as Burgess and Holmstrom (1974) have described, society tends to blame sexual abuse victims of any age and children are no exceptions to this response. Amazingly, the perpetrator's assertion that a seductive child is responsible for the sexual behavior is often given credence by judges, attorneys, police officers, physicians, social workers, and the like. The

rationalization seems to be that adult-child sexual behavior is so far removed from societal norms that, when it does occur, a perverted *child* must have been the causative factor. This attitude is conveyed to the child in multiple verbal and nonverbal ways and reinforces the youngster's tendency to assume guilty responsibility for the inappropriate sexual behavior.

2. Responsibility for disclosure. Almost invariably, as described by Burgess and Holmstrom (1975), child sexual abuse is treated as a secret by both the perpetrator and the victim. When the secret is disclosed by the child victim, he or she is obviously responsible for the disclosure. However, children may assume responsibility for disclosure under other circumstances—for example, purposeful disclosure by someone else or accidental disclosure. In all of these instances, the child may feel that he or she has betrayed the perpetrator or has somehow violated a trust relationship. Needless to say, this response is intensified when and if the perpetrator ascribes responsibility for disclosure to the child and conveys hostility or reproach at the same time.

3. Responsibility for disruption. Disclosure of child sexual abuse can be expected to cause profound disruption for the victim, the victim's family, and the perpetrator. In intrafamily child sexual abuse, the disruption is even greater. If the child was directly responsible for the disclosure, he or she can be expected to feel guilty about the disruption that follows which (in all likelihood) will be greater than anticipated by the youngster. However, as children accept guilty responsibility for accidental disclosure or for disclosure by others, so also do they accept blame for the disruption which ensues in the latter circumstances. Since the disruption is likely to be painful, the victim's family and significant others are likely to perceive him or her as responsible for any discomfort which they must suffer. Again, this type of feedback intensifies the victim's feeling that he or she is guilty for the disruption experienced by all.

Treatment Implications. First, the victim must be helped to identify his or her guilty feelings and to sort them out. It will be important to determine the age of the child at the time the sexual abuse began, and to learn as much as possible about the child's behavior and the position which he or she occupied with respect to the perpetrator and other family members thereafter. Distinctions must be made about ascribing responsibility for the sexual abuse. Therapists can and should consistently convey to the child, family members, and the perpetrator that a child can *never* be held responsible for initiating sexual activity with an adult or an older person. Likewise, a child cannot be held responsible for the disruption following disclosure. The therapist's message to all must be that the child had a right to expect protection, not abuse, from the perpetrator, and that he or she had a right to disclose the secret of the inappropriate sexual activity. Contrariwise, the perpetrator alone is responsible for initiating the sexual activity and for any and all negative consequences which may result, including the disruption following disclosure.

Care must be taken to help the older child identify those elements of behavior for which he or she should bear responsibility. Frequently a child victim comes to occupy a favored position with respect to the perpetrator and other family members. Some child victims have been very manipulative as a result of this position of advantage and may have behaved very inappropriately toward others. Such youngsters may be experiencing some appropriately guilty feelings and the therapist's task is to help them to make such distinctions. It is no more helpful to absolve a youngster of appropriate guilt feelings than it is to ascribe guilty responsibility inappropriately. Instead, responsibility for behavior should be appropriately ascribed. Then the task of the therapist is to help to relieve the child of inappropriate guilt or blame while at the same time to assist him or her to expiate legitimate guilt and to redirect future behavior.

Fear

All child victims of sexual abuse can be expected to be fearful of the consequences of the sexual activity as well as the disclosure. The child's concrete fear of physical damage as well as his or her more diffuse fears of future disability in interpersonal or sexual relationships due to societal response is thoroughly discussed above ("'Damaged Goods' Syndrome'').

Child victims also may fear subsequent episodes of sexual abuse both before and after disclosure as well as reprisals from the perpetrator after disclosure. These fears may be expressed on a conscious level. Often they are manifested by sleep disturbance, especially in the form of nightmares. Some of the nightmares are very generalized as the following example illustrates:

> Carol, a 14-year-old sexual abuse victim of several years' duration, reported to her therapist that every night she had nightmares which would cause her to awake in terror. She said she always dreamed that she was falling into blackness, alone and frightened. Sometimes in the nightmares, a huge shape like a bowling ball was trying to crush her.

Other victims may have dreams that seem to focus more closely on the sexual abuse and their fears of physical reprisals.

> Seven-year-old Tom suffered severe sexual abuse by his mother which resulted in significant trauma to his penis before he was placed in foster care. Tom told his therapist, "I have three dreams," and went on to explain that there were monsters in all of the dreams. In one type of dream, he and the monsters would fight and no one would win. In the second type, the monsters would win the fight and he would be killed. The third type of dream involved Tom winning a fight with monsters, and he would kill them. Tom's foster parents described him as an extremely frightened child when he first came to live with them. They confirmed his story of nightmares and reported that he awakened almost

every night screaming and clinging to his genitals.

Still other child victims may have dreams which reflect their fears of separation.

> After physical and sexual abuse by her stepfather, 12-year-old Meg requested placement away from her family. Meg's therapist met often with the foster family to find out how her adjustment to the new home was progressing. They reported that Meg experienced nightmares repeatedly. She screamed and cried in her sleep and would have to be awakened and held and reassured that she was safe and that no harm would come to her. When the content of the nightmares was explored, Meg described faceless and unknown people who were trying to kidnap her. She said that in the dream, she would be walking to or from school and they would "get me and take me away."

Treatment Implications. Therapists must assist child victims to identify their fears, many of which are realistically based. Additionally, victims should be encouraged to express their fears and to ventilate their feelings. Fear of physical damage resulting from the sexual abuse should be approached very concretely, as previously described. Realistic fears of reprisal and separation can only be dispelled or worked through if concrete assistance is available. The child's home or living situation should be made to feel as safe as possible—sometimes a difficult task in intrafamily child sexual abuse when the child has no functioning adult ally at home. It is sometimes helpful to "build in" new trust relationships for the victims as well as to strengthen and reinforce existing relationships (see also, "Impaired Ability to Trust," below).

Depression

Nearly all child victims will exhibit some symptoms or signs of depression after the disclosure of sexual abuse. Children who are victims of ongoing sexual abuse may appear depressed prior to disclosure as well. There may be overt signs of depression with the child appearing sad, subdued, or withdrawn. Or the depression may be masked and expressed as complaints of fatigue or physical illness. Some children may act out their despair with self-mutilation or suicide attempts. For example, nine-year-old Craig explained to his therapist about trying to kill himself.

> My uncle kept doing it to me and to my brothers. He would make us lick him [on his penis] and touch us. I didn't like it—I tried to hang myself with my belt. I put it up in my bedroom and then put the belt around my neck. My mom came in and took me down. I didn't really hurt myself.

Other children will go to greater lengths to try to injure or kill themselves:

After finding out that she was pregnant by her father, Pam tried killing herself and the baby by punching herself in the stomach. She did have a miscarriage but only after her father, upon hearing the news, hit her and caused her to fall onto a coffee table. The self-destructive feelings did not stop with the miscarriage. Pam tried to kill herself many times with pills and alcohol. On one occasion she took off all of her clothes in the middle of winter and plunged herself into the freezing waters of a lake. Fortunately she survived and was hospitalized.

Treatment Implications. Therapists for children who have been sexually victimized should anticipate that their clients will be depressed to some degree and be alert for signs as they appear. Suicidal feelings should be anticipated as well as suicide attempts. Many victims can be helped through opportunities to ventilate their feelings and as they perceive that they are believed and supported. More severely disturbed victims may require hospitalization and psychotropic medication for their own safety.

Low Self-Esteem and Poor Social Skills

Fear of physical damage, societal response to the sexually experienced child, experiencing guilt and blame for participating in sexual behavior, for disclosure and the disruption following disclosure—all these feelings tend to undermine the child-sexual-abuse victim's self-esteem. In addition, society tends to reward winners and to be contemptuous of losers and victims. Low self-esteem combined with a feeling of being somehow spoiled or damaged in turn tend to undermine the victim's self-confidence.

Many victims of intrafamily child sexual abuse have been pressured by their parents to limit outside relationships and to depend only upon interaction with other family members to meet their social needs. As a result these children often have limited social skills. The frequently unsatisfactory experiences which may result when victims attempt to make friends among agemates and to initiate outside social relationships further tend to decrease self-esteem. Victims often feel helpless and are rarely assertive on their own behalf. They also feel unworthy and undeserving of anything.

One 17-year-old sexual abuse victim told her therapist, "I feel this big." She demonstrated by placing her finger one-inch above the ground. After this girl had been in an adolescent therapy group for several months, she announced to the others, "Before I came here, I thought incest victims all had two heads and were green. I'm glad to see we are like everybody else."

Negative feelings can extend beyond victims' thoughts about themselves to visual images of themselves. It is not unusual for victims of child sexual abuse, especially incest victims, to describe themselves in derogatory terms. Many slender and attractive girls who have been sexually victimized will describe themselves as fat and ugly. Some find themselves so unappealing that they will initiate a series of sexual relationships (often with disastrous results) to prove to themselves that they are "desirable." Possessing inadequate social skills, they tend to act out sexually and thus reinforce society's image of them as seductive and promiscuous creatures who are themselves to blame for the sexual abuse by an adult.

Treatment Implications. Low self-esteem and acting out behavior to test that perception are so commonly seen among child-sexual-abuse victims that therapists should anticipate their occurrence. Individual therapy should be used initially to help victims identify and express negative feelings about themselves. Group therapy is probably the most effective treatment modality for this impact issue. Victims derive intense support from a positive group experience, and opportunities to enhance self-esteem abound. See chapter 5 for a more detailed description of this process.

Repressed Anger and Hostility

Although they may appear outwardly passive and compliant, most child-sexual-abuse victims are inwardly seething with anger and hostility. First, victims are angry at the perpetrators who abused and exploited them. They are also angry with parents or family members who failed to protect them from the sexual abuse or, in some cases, may have set them up to be abused. The rage and hostility felt by victims may extend to neighbors, friends, school personnel, classmates, and others in the community, depending on their responses to the disclosure of sexual abuse. Most often, the victims' anger is repressed rather than expressed or acted out. Sometimes the repressed rage is manifested by depression or withdrawal, sometimes by physical symptomatology ("feeling bad"), sometimes by aggressive fantasies or behavior, and occasionally as psychotic symptomatology.

> Linda was sexually abused by her stepfather when she was 10 years old. The abuse occurred while her mother was at work, and later the child tried to tell her mother what had occurred. Linda's mother responded to the disclosure with anger and disbelief and blurted out for the first time, the information that Linda's father was really a stepfather. Feeling thus betrayed, Linda began to act out aggressively at school. At age 13 years Linda attempted to strangle one of the boys in her class and was referred to a therapist.
>
> Early in the course of therapy, Linda revealed that she was an incest victim. Her negative feelings toward her stepfather intensified as she described the sexual abuse. Linda described voices that she heard telling her to kill her stepfather. She explained how she would "stab him and watch the blood run

down and then cover him with a sheet and put a cross on him." After immediate psychiatric evaluation, Linda's need for a structured and specialized therapeutic environment was confirmed, and she was placed in a residential psychiatric center.

The foregoing case example illustrates severe psychiatric disturbance with rage and hostility expressed as homicidal ideation and psychosis. Most victims are not psychotic, and their anger is repressed and transmuted.

Treatment Implications. Victims must be helped to get in touch with their repressed rage and to express anger in a healthy and non-destructive fashion. Many victims say little initially because they are afraid to confront their own anger and unsure of their ability to handle their feelings. They compensate by being unassertive and by saying as little as possible. A typical conversation with such a child in the early stages of treatment might proceed as follows:

Therapist: How are you today?
Child: OK, I guess.
Therapist: How about last week?
Child: OK.
Therapist: How are things with your family?
Child: OK, I guess.
Therapist: Did anything good happen to you in the past week?
Child: No.
Therapist: How about anything bad?
Child: I guess not.

This type of conversation could and frequently does go on for weeks. Eventually, as they become stronger and more assertive, the children come in with a prepared agenda. A teenager might say, "My mother promised me she would take me to the store and then she didn't because she was doing something for my brother. That makes me mad. I'm important too." A month before, this same teenager might have said, "I guess my mother was busy. It's OK that she couldn't take me." As previously discussed, the group therapy modality is well-suited to provide opportunities for victims to learn to express anger in a safe setting and to assist them to find nondestructive ways to express anger.

Inability to Trust

A child who has been sexually victimized by a known and trusted person can be expected to have difficulty in developing trust relationships thereafter. The degree of impairment will, of course, be dependent upon many factors: the identity of the perpetrator, the type of relationship between the perpetrator and the child, the degree of pain or discomfort or, conversely, pleasure, satisfaction, or advantages experienced as a result of the sexual abuse, the amount of disruption following disclosure, the response to disclosure by others, and so forth. Often, the child's inability to trust is a direct consequence of broken promises by the perpetrator or significant others. Thus the child's inability to trust often has a concrete reality basis.

> Cheryl said to her therapist, "Every time my father did it, he would say that if it hurt me, I should just tell him and he would stop." The child explained that her father would put vaseline on her and then would try to insert his penis into her "butthole." When asked if she told him to stop, Cheryl replied, "Yeah, I kept telling him it hurt and asked him to stop, but he didn't. I guess he just didn't hear me."

Cheryl's father managed to convey directly to his child that her reactions or needs were irrelevant while he was sexually abusing her. Some victims are ultimately rejected by their entire families as well as by the legal system as the following case example illustrates.

> Darlene, age 15 years, ran away from home to the local police station and initially reported physical abuse by her father. When the Youth Services Officer asked if she had also been sexually abused, Darlene responded affirmatively. Both the police officer and the child-protective-services worker believed that Darlene was an incest victim. When confronted by authorities, Darlene's father denied the allegations entirely. He refused to permit Darlene to return home and was supported by his wife and the other children in this decision. Darlene's sister, Ann, became so angry that she slapped Darlene's face for "telling lies about our dad."
> As the investigation proceeded, it was learned that the sexual abuse had occurred in another jurisdiction. Thus the local police were powerless to arrest Darlene's father while the police in the jurisdiction where the sexual abuse *had* occurred declined to pursue the complaint. Rejected by her parents, sister, and the legal justice system, Darlene was unable to return home and was placed with a friend of the family. Prior to the disclosure of incest, she had performed well at school. Afterwards, she began to be absent from school often because of numerous asthma attacks and stomach aches. Her academic performance suffered correspondingly.

In Darlene's case, inability to trust became a major therapeutic issue. Rejection by her entire family led to a feeling of alienation which had a concrete basis since, in fact, she was not permitted to return to her home. For Darlene, extensive support and treatment will be required in order for her to feel able to trust anyone again.

Treatment Implications. Inability to trust is directly linked to the victim's low self-esteem and past experiences of betrayal. Therapists must recognize that the recovery process will be slow and will probably correlate well with the degree to which the victim's self-esteem improves. Feelings of alienation can only be overcome through experiencing more satisfying interpersonal relationships with others. Again, a combination of individual and group therapy is likely to be more successful than individual therapy alone.

Blurred Role Boundaries and Role Confusion

Child sexual abuse is disorienting because the victims frequently experience role confusion due to the inevitable blurring of role boundaries between the perpetrator and the child. For an adult who occupies a power position to turn to a relatively powerless child for a sexual relationship implies a profound disregard for the usual societal role boundaries. Although the sexual activity is primarily in the service of nonsexual needs, the premature and inappropriate sexual experience with an adult generates a great deal of role confusion for the child victim. If the adult occupies a familial relationship with the child, role confusion is greatly magnified. Distressingly, the child's role confusion is shared by other family members as the following case example illustrates.

> One mother had her husband arrested when she learned that he had sexually abused her five-year-old daughter. This mother later said, "I know she is only five but she realizes she has a special relationship with her daddy. I bet she wishes I wasn't here and he was. . . . I don't like the way she looks at me sometimes, like she's better than me." As competitive feelings with her daughter intensified, this mother began to resent the child more and more. Treating her daughter as a peer and as a rival rather than as a child increased the alienation between them. Ironically, this growing alienation between mother and daughter also increased the bond between the child and her father.

Blurred boundaries in incestuous families also tends to increase the likelihood that sexual abuse will occur since more opportunities for sexual abuse are thereby created and the stage is set for incest.

> Twelve-year-old Sylvia was aware that whenever she took a bath, her father would find an excuse to walk into the bathroom. He would linger a long time while she was in the bathtub, looking at her out of the corner of his eye. When she would ask him to leave, he would refuse, suggesting it was all right for him to be there with her because he was her parent. A few months later, he began entering her bedroom at night, crawling into her bed and sexually abusing her.

Treatment Implications. The therapist's task is clearly to help the child victim to resolve role confusion, despite his or her past experiences. It is especially important for at least one adult family member to confirm the therapist's assertion regarding appropriate role boundaries. Under ideal circumstances, the perpetrator will explain to the child that he or she is responsible for the sexual behavior and that the sexual activity was inappropriate and should not be repeated. In the absence of family participation, the treatment process should include role-playing and role-modeling appropriate behavior in an effort to reduce role confusion.

Pseudomaturity and Failure to Complete
Developmental Tasks

Child sexual abuse is disruptive because the extensive stimulation and preoccupation with the sexual relationship tends to interfere with accomplishment of age-appropriate developmental tasks of childhood and adolescence. In addition, role confusion often leads to the child's premature assumption of an adult-like role in an incestuous family. In a father-daughter incest case, the mother may relinquish her role as spouse, parent, and family caretaker to her daughter. The following case example illustrates the results:

> Marjorie is the second eldest of five children. Although a personable 11-year-old girl, she had no friends and did not participate in any extracurricular activities. Instead Marjorie was responsible for coming home directly from school to care for her younger siblings, ages two, four, and five. Marjorie's child-care responsibilities continued on weekends, holidays, and vacations. Marjorie was expected to clean the house every day. Whenever her mother was dissatisfied with Marjorie's performance, she slapped or beat her daughter. At night, Marjorie never knew when her stepfather would be coming to her bedroom to molest her. In eleven years, Marjorie went from being a child, to a "parent" (for her siblings), a housekeeper for the entire family and finally to a wife and lover for her stepfather. She appears mature and competent. She is eleven going on thirty.

As sexually victimized children assume more adult responsibilities, the gap widens ever further between them and their peers. Once identified by peers, the isolation usually becomes permanent. The victims are left with no appropriate social outlets and are therefore alone and more vulnerable than ever.

Treatment Implications. Needless to say, treatment cannot proceed until the sexual abuse has stopped and until the victim's caretakers acknowledge his or her right to behave as a child. Pseudomature victims must be allowed to relinquish inappropriate responsibilities and assume a more child-like role and act as a child. Only by this means can unaccomplished developmental tasks be addressed. If the child's home situation does not permit him or her to relinquish the inappropriate role which was a significant dynamic of the sexual abuse, it will not be possible to treat this impact issue.

Self-Mastery and Control

The bottom line is that child sexual abuse involves a violation of the victim's body, privacy, and rights of self-mastery and control. This particular type of violation has subtle and long-lasting effects. All of the aforementioned impact issues are components of self-mastery and control. The issues of low self-esteem, repressed anger and hostility, blurred role boundaries and role confusion, pseudomaturity and failure to accomplish developmental tasks are all particularly significant. Unless the victim receives treatment, prospects for avoiding the destructive consequences of failure to achieve self-mastery and control are extremely poor.

Treatment Implications. Despite the previous message from the perpetrator and sometimes from family members to the victim that he or she has no rights, is entitled to no privacy, and exists merely to be used by a more powerful person, the therapist must convey a different message. Self-mastery and control imply accountability, behaving responsibly toward oneself and others, development of independence from one's family and background, and freedom to make one's own choices. Achieving this level of self-mastery and control is virtually impossible in the repressive atmosphere which characterizes most incestuous homes. In the absence of participation in a family treatment program, it will be difficult if not impossible for most incest victims to accomplish these treatment goals while still living at home.

Once again, role modeling, role playing, peer-group support, and positive peer pressure are the treatment modalities of choice. Victims must be permitted opportunities to test their capacity for self-mastery and control and indeed to make some mistakes. Effective decision making and good judgment are only achieved through practice when individuals are permitted appropriate opportunities to make choices and to be responsible for their own actions without fear of harsh reprisals. A responsive treatment plan for the child will include these structured opportunities. The parents or care-takers as well as other family members should be prepared for the impact which the victim's progression toward self mastery and control can reasonably be expected to have upon them and upon family interaction. If family members are prepared to encourage and reinforce responsible independent behavior from the victim, the net effect of such behavior is more likely to be positive.

Case Management Issues

Chapter 3, "An Approach to Case Management," describes the case management issues which must be addressed whenever a disclosure of child sexual abuse occurs within a community. It is not possible to discuss "treatment" of the child victim intelligently except within the context of an overall plan of case management which also addresses *reporting, investigation, validation, child-protection assessment* and *initial management planning*. Chapter 2 also describes the "how to" of investigation and validation in detail. Chapter 3 also discusses the child-protection assessment in detail and describes initial management planning.

When the foregoing initial tasks of case management have been completed, there remain the following five tasks which are the essential components of longer term intervention in cases of child sexual abuse: *diagnostic assessment, formulation of a problem list, formulation of a treatment plan, treatment intervention,* and *monitoring*. Those who wish to address the treatment needs of the child victim must be prepared to do so within the overall context of a comprehensive diagnostic assessment of the child and all accessible family members. Even if the child victim alone is accessible for treatment, it will be important to obtain as much data as possible about the family. (Diagnostic assessment of the child victim will be addressed later in this chapter). Formulation of a problem list for the entire family should likewise be accomplished. It is useful to employ previously established problem categories as described in chapter 13. All problems which affect family functioning must be identified by those who would treat the child victim by employing any treatment modality (individual or group or dyad therapy, family therapy, or the like).

Formulation of a treatment plan should be based upon the family problem list. Ideally, a treatment plan for the child victim should be incorporated into a broader treatment plan for the entire family. When circumstances make this impossible, the treatment plan for the child victim should nevertheless be based upon the family problem list and take cognizance of the effect that successful treatment intervention for the victim may have on other family members. (Treatment intervention for the child victim will be addressed in detail in the last section on this chapter.)

The sine qua non for implementation of any treatment plan will, of course, be the capacity for continued access to the child victim of intrafamily sexual abuse who continues to live at home. The logical agency to assume responsibility for treatment intervention is, of course, the statutory child-protection agency. It may require stringent monitoring to be assured that those who are responsible for treatment intervention have continuous access to the child victim and vice versa. Cooperation with school officials is important, since the school is a neutral setting wherein the child victim's progress can be monitored. If the family is hostile and uncooperative, it is helpful also to be in touch with at least one other member of the nuclear or extended family who accepts the importance of treatment intervention and is supportive of the child victim (when such a person can be found or encouraged).

Diagnostic Assessment of the Child

A careful diagnostic assessment of the child is essential for effective treatment planning and intervention. In every case, four major sources of information should be tapped.

Direct Interviewing of the Child

The most significant information source will be the child victim. Skilled interviewing should elicit the following.

1. *Validation data.* All of the details of the sexual abuse and the child's reaction to this activity have profound implications for treatment. The therapist for the child should review validation data elicited by others before discussing this material with the child. It will not be surprising if additional information about the sexual victimization is subsequently elicited by a therapist who has established a trust relationship with the child.

2. *Impact issues.* All ten impact issues should be carefully explored with the child victim. The information elicited will be extremely important in formulating a treatment plan.

3. *Mental status examination.* The person who will become the therapist for the child must perform a mental status examination early in the diagnostic assessment if this has not been done already. Although few victims will be psychotic, a careful mental status examination will quickly identify those children who should receive immediate psychiatric evaluation (youngsters who are profoundly depressed or suicidal, psychotic victims, children with borderline reality testing, and the like).

4. *Social history.* Likewise, a careful and detailed social history from the child is an essential part of the diagnostic assessment. Too often, a social history is obtained from adults only. Treatment planning and intervention for child victims of sexual abuse will be facilitated by social data which may be obtainable *only* from the child, especially when other family members are hostile and uncooperative. This information may also assist in determining family contribution to the sexual abuse and have important implications for planning family treatment. (See also chapter 9, "Family Treatment.")

Psychological Testing

This will be very important for some children and less so for others. Careful testing by an experienced examiner will yield valuable information and assist in treatment planning for the more severely traumatized victims. For children who are generally withdrawn and noncommunicative, projective testing may be especially helpful.

Arts Therapy Diagnostic Assessment

A skilled arts therapist can contribute invaluable data, especially with young victims or with severely traumatized or nonverbal children. Chapter 10, "Art Therapy with Sexually Abused Children," describes the use of the arts therapies in diagnosis and treatment.

School Performance and Behavior

The child's school performance and behavior can yield information crucial to treatment planning and intervention. It is worthwhile for the therapist to make a special effort to obtain data from the victim's teachers, school social workers, or guidance counselors. Sometimes access to school records will be limited by hostile parents who refuse to give permission for their release. Nevertheless, a determined therapist usually can still obtain verbal impressions of the child's school performance and behavior from school personnel. This will contribute to treatment planning and is also extremely important in monitoring treatment intervention.

Treatment Intervention

Treatment of a child-sexual-abuse victim may involve a lengthy, emotional process. The key issue is not simply the sexual violation. Psychodynamically, the major thrust of treatment involves strengthening the child's ego to help improve self-image, to learn to trust others, and to begin to feel secure.

To begin this strengthening process, the victim needs permission to accept the feelings of anger and hurt, so that these feelings may be expressed without experiencing further guilt. Victims often blame themselves for the sexual abuse, thus inhibiting the healthy attitude that they have a right to be angry and feel hurt because their parents have "let them down." The children fear both the acceptance and expression of these feelings, believing also that their parents or families will further reject them. The therapist should help victims to understand that the sexual abuse was not their fault and that they have a right to their own feelings.

Each child must ventilate his or her feelings about the sexual trauma in relation to:

Guilt and shame;

Positive and negative feelings toward the perpetrator;

Positive and negative feelings toward the nonoffending parent;

Feelings about the reaction of siblings;

Feelings about the reaction of peers and people in the community.

Once this sharing process begins, the children can simultaneously start to focus on issues of:

Effects of the criminal or juvenile justice systems on their lives;

Parent-child relationships and intrafamilial roles;

Communication patterns within their families;

Boy-girl relationships;

Sex education and birth control.

The sharing process should occur in individual and peer-group therapy initially. When the victims and their family members are strong enough to express their *real* feelings toward each other, then mother and daughter, father and daughter dyad sessions can be utilized as a therapeutic tool.

Guilt and Shame

The children feel guilty and shameful about the sexual abuse, for having disclosed the secret; for the after effects of the disclosure (for example, dad's arrest, the parents' separation or divorce, a family breakup, or mom's nervous breakdown), and for possibly having enjoyed the sexual stimulation or the secondary gains they received from the relationship (such as rewards of money or material goods, a powerful position in the family, or special attention of some type). The shame permeates the children's attitudes about themselves and causes them to feel dirty and unworthy of anything positive. As they begin to vent their negative feelings one by one, their therapists and peers can correct the victims' inappropriate perceptions. When the children blame themselves for the sexual abuse, the therapist must reinforce society's rule and stress that adults are responsible for protecting children. Not only did the perpetrators violate this rule, but they clearly had a choice between right and wrong behavior and chose to harm children for the purpose of self-gratification.

Helping the children to focus on the abuse in a healthy perspective begins to relieve some of their emotional burden. If they can begin to grasp the reality of an adult's responsibility, they will realize that the consequences of the sexual abuse are not their fault. The more extensive the trauma, the greater difficulty the child is likely to have in accepting his or her position as a victim. Often, acceptance is hampered by pressure from family members. The family blames others for their trouble and will try to convince the child to recant the story so that the family can return to ''normal.''

> Lisa, 14 years old, had been molested by her father for over six months. After intervention by child-protective services, the child, her mother and father began treatment. Although the polilce had been involved, they decided not to arrest the father if he would go for treatment. He did, but stopped going after only six weeks. In the meantime, Lisa and her mother were participating in an adolescent group and in a mothers group. Initially, they were doing well but after the father stopped treatment, he began pressuring Lisa and her mother to stop also. Eventually, Lisa quit, saying that the treatment was not helping her. The therapist knew of the pressure because Lisa's mother reported it. Upon leaving the group, Lisa was told that she was welcome back anytime and that everyone was concerned about the pressure from her father. Within four months Lisa called, in tears, revealing that her father had again molested her and requesting help.

Lisa's situation is not unusual. Without an improvement in the child's ability to be assertive, sexual abuse can reoccur. Assertive behavior is unlikely unless an effort is made to eliminate the child's guilty and shameful feelings.

Positive and Negative Feelings toward the Perpetrator

The children need help in sorting out and venting their feelings about the perpetrator. In most cases the child has both positive and negative feelings for the perpetrator, both in extrafamily and intrafamily sexual abuse. Many incestuous fathers are the more nurturing of the two parents. Other rewards received by the child may have added to the positive feelings about the perpetrator.

> Eighteen-year-old Carol told the group that, ''I loved my stepfather. For two years, I considered him my lover. He bought me beautiful things like a diamond ring and a car.'' She went on to explain that he had cared very much for her, but when she wanted to break away from and be with peers, he began physically abusing her.

Other perpetrators are violent and nonnurturing. Their victims have few if any good feelings toward them.

> Meg's stepfather was a vicious person. There were no positive feelings toward

him by Meg, even though they had lived in the same house for eight years. He had never been kind to her. When the sexual abuse began, he hurt Meg, causing her to bleed. He would have sexual intercourse with her and if she resisted, he would beat her.

Meg had every right to hate this man and to express her honest feelings. Whatever the child's feelings, the therapist should be careful to avoid projecting his or her own angry or negative feeling about the perpetrator.

The therapist needs to help the child with the love-hate relationship in both an emotional and physical sense. Emotionally, the sharing of feelings will serve to reduce guilt and allow an expression of anger, while physically the children need to learn the difference between physical contact and love. The sexual contact is often accompanied by affection and the children confuse this physical act with love. If this issue is not clarified, it can lead the children to sexually promiscuous behavior in their search for love.

Positive and Negative Feelings toward the
Nonoffending Parent

Dealing with feelings toward the nonoffending parent in incest cases is equally significant. Surprisingly, the children are often angrier at this parent than at the perpetrator of incest. Whether the nonoffending parent consciously knew about the sexual abuse or not is insignificant. The children blame this parent for not protecting them, even if this parent was absent from the home while the sexual abuse was taking place.

> Fourteen-year-old Nekisha was involved sexually with her father for seven years. The sexual abuse began after her mother "deserted" the family. Nekisha blamed her mother for the sexual abuse, feeling that if she had been in the home it would not have occurred.

This anger may be more intense if the child told the nonoffending parent about the sexual abuse and was not believed. Many victims have said, "I told my mother when it first started. She asked my dad if it was true and he denied it so she didn't do anything. I guess she just didn't believe me."

It is usually harder for the children to express their anger toward the nonoffending parent particularly if they are still living with that person. The children fear retaliation through further rejection, feeling, "this person is the only parent I have left and I want to hang on". The children are usually unaware of the fear and anger they feel toward the nonoffending parent. Therefore, the therapist must be aware of this issue and help them to work through these feelings.

Feelings about the Reaction of Siblings

Feelings about siblings depend on the closeness and nature of the sibling relationships and the siblings' reactions once the secret is disclosed. In cases where the siblings were also victimized by the perpetrator, their response is usually supportive.

> Chrissie, 13, and Suzanne, 11, were victims of sexual abuse by their natural father. Chrissie was 13 when the secret was disclosed because she was pregnant. Dad's relationship began with Chrissie two years earlier. A year later he began to fondle Suzanne's breasts. Neither sister shared the secret—fearful of their father who had threatened physical harm if they told anyone. Upon learning of her sister's pregnancy, Suzanne (although younger) felt very responsible and said, "I should have told mom he was doing it to me, then Chrissie would have never gotten pregnant. It's all my fault." Chrissie and Suzanne continued to be very supportive of one another thereafter.

Often the reaction to disclosure is more painful for male siblings of female victims. They generally take one of two positions: either sharing the sadness of their sister(s) victimization and feeling as though they had let their sister(s) down by not protecting them (even when they were unaware of the abuse), or conversely blaming the victim for causing the abuse.

> Chrissie and Suzanne's 15-year-old brother, Larry, felt terrible when he learned what their father had done. Larry was angry at his father for abusing the girls and angry at himself for not protecting his sisters even though he was unaware of what was happening. Larry had a very hard time sharing his feelings and withdrew from his sisters. They, in turn, felt that he was really angry at them and somehow blamed them for the abuse. The family therapist explored his feelings on an individual basis and then helped him to tell his sisters how he really felt. The girls felt much better upon learning of their brother's concern.

Patty and Lisa's brothers had different reactions.

> Patty, 19, and Lisa, 17, had been sexually abused by their natural father. Patty had been impregnated by her father but had miscarried. Lisa had been fondled. When the sexual abuse was revealed to the police and their father was arrested, their four brothers, ages 11 to 15 became very angry at the sisters. They blamed them for initiating the abuse and called the girls derogatory names. The girls wondered how the boys could support their father because he had severely physically abused *them*. The boys felt the two types of abuse were different and that it was still the girls' fault. After six months of family therapy, the oldest brother admitted feeling devastated upon hearing of his sisters' sexual abuse by their father. He felt his world shattered. The man he had looked up to had destroyed his image of a man. Later, this boy tried to molest Lisa and several of his younger brothers.

Whatever the siblings are feeling, it's important to find out how the *victim* perceives their feelings, and, eventually, try to sort them out face to face.

Feelings about the Reaction of Peers

Reactions of the victims' peers and others in the community vary. The victims need to talk about this also. When friends and neighbors learned of the sexual abuse, did they withdraw or did they remain supportive? Peer alienation is difficult to cope with, particularly at a time when more support is needed. If the children are being teased and harrassed, they must express their hurt and anger at such negative behavior from people who are supposed to care. Other friends and neighbors may be very helpful. Some neighbors offer their homes as a temporary place for the victim to stay while decisions for their continued safety are made.

After victims have vented their feelings about themselves and all of the significant people in their lives, they can begin to examine their present situation, the difficult decisions which need to be made, and proceed with the restructuring of healthy relationships.

Effects of the Criminal or Juvenile Justice Systems
on Their Lives

Criminal or juvenile court involvement is difficult to cope with, but it is often a necessity. If an arrest was made, the child needs support for having made the statement to the police which led to the perpetrator's arrest. All of the possible legal alternatives facing the perpetrator should be explained to the victim (unless he or she is very young) before the arrest is even made. The victim should know that the perpetrator may go to jail while awaiting trial or be convicted and incarcerated or placed on probation with or without an order for treatment. He or she also must understand that the case could be dismissed with no penalty for the perpetrator. Again, the child needs to be reminded of the perpetrator's choice to commit a crime and that criminal court is a consequence of that choice.

Victims who must testify in court should be properly prepared for testimony. They should have a chance to express their feelings to the therapist, supportive family members, and their therapy peers. A child's feelings can range from being glad to have a chance to tell "my side," to feeling anxious, to questioning if this is the best way to proceed, to feeling frightened of the perpetrator and possible retaliation.

> Carol, 18 had just been notified that her criminal court hearing date was finally approaching. Her stepfather had been arrested while she was 17 and the case was continued many times. Carol had been nervous about the trial the entire year. Her stepfather was a dangerous, manipulative man, and she feared the consequences of testifying. Just a few weeks before the hearing, Carol, who lived away from her family, received a phone call from her mother telling her not to testify or her father would kill her.

As the court date approaches, victims will need increased support from the individual therapist, supportive family members, group members, and friends. Arrangements should be made for the child to meet with the attorney to review the child's questions, and to have the attorney prepare the child for court testimony. If possible, the child should be brought to the court room to familiarize him or her with the surroundings. On the day of appearance a separate waiting area should be made available to the victim so that he or she does not have to sit and face the perpetrator prior to the hearing. When possible a closed courtroom should be requested.

After the court appearance, the child will need time to share feelings about the experience and its outcome.

> After Carol's testimony, she came out of the courtroom and collapsed in hysterics. The defense attorney had been very intimidating during most of the hearing. He talked in a loud voice and used a line of questioning which made Carol appear to be a promiscuous seductress leading her stepfather into the sexual abuse. In reality, it had been just the reverse. Carol was 11 when the relationship started, a frightened child. The court hearing was a "probable cause" hearing to decide whether the case was serious enough to be bound over to the circuit court. Even though the ruling was in Carol's favor, it took her weeks to strengthen herself emotionally after this experience.

Juvenile court or family court can be just as difficult for the child as the criminal court, although the civil court experience is usually less intense. Badgering or intimidating a child witness in juvenile or family court is usually forbidden and the case is heard in a closed court room. Even with these supports, the emotions experienced by the child are no less draining. Juvenile court proceedings in sexual abuse cases generally result in separation of a child from either or both parents. This can be a time of rejection for the child or a time of security.

> Meg, 12 years old, had been physically and sexually abused by her stepfather. Even though he was arrested, Meg's mother put so much pressure on her that she perjured herself on the witness stand. The criminal charges against the stepfather were then dismissed. Meg felt rejected and unprotected by her mother and could not tolerate the continued abuse by her stepfather. She told her therapist about the continued abuse and begged for help. Meg was able to tell the juvenile judge what had really happened and she was removed from her unsafe home.

The same procedures should be followed for emotional support and preparation for testimony in civil court as for the criminal court. Afterward, a great deal of time will be required for the victim to work through all of the court experiences and their implications.

Parent-Child Relationships and Intrafamilial Roles

Parent-child relationships and intrafamilial roles are two of the most critical areas requiring restructure. The roles within the family become confused before incest occurs. After father-daughter incest, the role reversal between the mother and daughter establishes a situation in which the daughter takes over mother's role in the home to some degree (for example, by caring for her siblings, preparing the meals, becoming dad's confidant and his sexual partner.) Without clear definitions of each person's role within the family, the boundaries become confused for the entire household. Often, there is no privacy or private space for any of the members. Anyone in the household may barge into another's private space. One 14-year-old girl's bedroom was used as a route to the bathroom as she had one of two connecting doors. It did not matter whether she was dressed or undressed or even if she refused her four adolescent brothers and parents permission to come through her bedroom (they did it anyway). Often one bedroom in the house is designated as the "entertainment room." A television set may be in this bedroom and everyone congregates there.

> Lori and Lynn, two adolescent sisters, told the police and protective-services worker that their sexual abuse by father occurred in their parents' bedroom. They said, "we always would go in there to watch T.V. and he would give us back rubs. One day he rolled me (Lori) onto my front and started rubbing me all over. I was afraid to tell him to stop."

The blurred boundaries include extensive use of someone else's clothes, without permission. The 14-year-old girl (described above), with four brothers, would have to fight for clothes to wear as her brothers felt free to take and wear her clothing.

Many parents lose control over their children's behavior as they become adolescents. The adolescents begin to break their curfews, curse and talk back to their parents, skip school, and act out in other ways. In incestuous families, this acting-out behavior seems to stem from the double messages the parents have given the children. The adults demand respect from the children and give them rules to follow. However, the parents do not follow rules themselves and convey to their children that getting older and acquiring power confers ability to break rules.

> In one family, the father was physically abusive to all of his seven children and sexually abused two of his daughters. He was incarcerated and the mother was left to run the house. All of the children were involved in some kind of negative behavior—drugs, alcohol, skipping school, disobeying rules at home, and so forth. In family sessions, the children were very angry at their mother for not protecting them from their father's abuse and for playing the role of "goodie-two-shoes." To the therapists and outsiders, the mother tried to project a saintly image, but at home she yelled and screamed at the children and

threatened to punish them if they didn't behave. However, she could not enforce her threats because her children had lost their respect for her and knew that she did not follow rules or set effective limits upon herself.

In an emotional sense, because of the role reversal, the mother and daughter in father-daughter incest begin to behave like siblings. The daughter is angry at her mother for not protecting her and for forcing her to take on too much responsibility so that she cannot enjoy the freedom her peers have. The mother is angry at her daughter for taking over her position within the home and is jealous because her husband's attentions are directed toward the daughter.

Communication Patterns within the Family

Role reversal and blurred boundaries are directly linked to poor communication patterns within the family. The ultimate question which must be asked is: Why didn't the victim feel comfortable to trust the nonoffending parent and tell about the sexual abuse? If the child did tell, why didn't the nonoffending parent believe the child? If the parent did believe the child, why did the incest continue?

Misperceptions based on poor communication abound with the incestuous family. For example, one parent may report that husband-wife sexual relations are very satifying and frequent, while the other parent will say that relations are infrequent and unsatisfactory. The victim and family members need to learn to face one another and communicate their true feelings rather than assuming what a given member thinks. This behavior should be practiced in a structured therapeutic setting.

> In a family therapy session, the cotherapists asked each member to share how he or she felt about one another. The response was to look at the therapist and say "my sister knows I care about her." The therapist would then direct this brother to "tell her." He would look at his sister and say, "you know I care." The therapist would have to intervene again and say, "talk directly to your sister and tell her that you care." The brother would finally say, "I care about you," while looking at his sister.

It is often a painful process to begin to trust another person enough to be able to share your inner thoughts with him or her. The sister's response could have been, "I care about you, too" or "I'm angry at you. You've hurt me." It is hard to accept negative statements of feelings in return. In the incestuous family there are many hurts and angry feelings to share. Learning to communicate with someone for the first time can be scary and painful and thus should be a required therapeutic exercise, initially with the support of a therapist.

Boy-Girl Relationships

Boy-girl relationships are difficult for victims. Following any type of sexual abuse (especially incestuous), the victim may question his or her sexual identity.

Also, they may harbor feelings of mistrust and anger toward others of the same sex as the perpetrator.

> Tommy, age 7, was seriously sexually abused by his mother. When he started therapy with a female therapist, he was angry and mistrustful toward her. During play therapy, in a particular game, he would make it a point to state her player was a "girl" and then he would "beat the girl player up." This went on for weeks until one day, Tommy said, "I'm not really mad at you, I'm mad at my mother because of the bad things she did."

Female victims may become fearful or seductive toward men. Victims who are fearful have a difficult time engaging in male-female relationships due to their lack of trust. Victims who become seductive may be setting themselves up for further sexual assaults, which, in turn, may cause them to regard men as untrustworthy. Others may become involved in a series of sexual relationships in order to prove to themselves that they are desirable or undamaged. Ultimately this causes them to feel "dirty."

> Fifteen-year-old Samantha said, "After my father molested me I slept with a lot of guys. I didn't think anyone would want me so I tried to prove they did. In the end it just made me feel worse about myself; they didn't really care about me."

These victims need help in appreciating themselves and in realizing their own self-worth. Effective therapy will reinforce their positive feelings about themselves and create opportunities for them to enhance their self-esteem more safely.

Victims may be handicapped by their precocious sexual experience which is not comparable to their peers'. One thirteen-year-old said, "How can I talk to my friends about their first kiss when I've already had sex with my dad? I'm not like they are." This is a reality which must be acknowledged. Again, victims must be helped to believe that they are not damaged and that their previous experiences do not "spoil" them for life. They need encouragement and positive relationships with therapists, peers, and (hopefully) their families to be persuaded that they can enjoy age-appropriate experiences.

Sex Education and Birth Control

Despite their precocious sexual experience, many victims are woefully ignorant about their own bodies. Good sex education and information about birth control can help the victims understand how their bodies function and what, if any, physical changes occurred because of the sexual abuse. A discussion on sex education with a knowledgeable person in a supportive atmosphere can help to elicit questions and fears and provide reassurance. If the victims continue to have sexual intercourse, for whatever reason, making them aware of birth control and contraceptives is equally important. Premature pregnancy can lead to additional problems for the victim and may create a cycle of physical or sexual abuse. If the victims' self-esteem is low, they may become involved in destructive marriages and place their own children at risk. If the pregnancies end in abortion or the baby is given up for adoption, victims may experience further guilt.

Victims' parents are often opposed to sex education and the sharing of information on birth control. These parents view themselves as "moral people," and believe it is wrong to educate their children in this way. The parents will need help in accepting the necessity to provide the victims with education that can prevent further trauma.

Treatment Phases

The treatment of a child-sexual-abuse victim can be divided into three main phases: (1) crisis intervention; (2) short-term therapy (lasting six months to one year); and (3) long-term therapy (lasting up to two years or more). Each victim is automatically involved in the crisis intervention phase of treatment which begins at the point of disclosure.

Crisis Intervention

The crisis intervention phase is emotionally stressful for the intervenors as well as for the client. This phase is complex, requiring skilled intervention and close networking of community resources. Ideally, the therapist for the victim will become involved with the case early in the crisis intervention phase.

During this stage, victim and family often require "total life support"—a mixture of concrete environmental services and intensive day-to-day support and guidance. This concept is described in greater detail in chapter 9, "Family Treatment." Briefly, the therapist must be prepared to assist the victim and family to cope with investigative interviews, medical examinations, visits to and from child-protective services and law-enforcement personnel, interviews with attorneys, court appearances, publicity following disclosure, and the like. If the nuclear family has been gravely disrupted and separation of family members must occur, such mundane matters as food, clothing, shelter, money, and transportation will be uppermost in their minds. These immediate needs must be addressed by someone. A therapist who is willing to get his or her "hands dirty" and participate in providing "total life support" will have a much greater chance of establishing a relationship of trust with the victim which will be invaluable in short-term or long-term therapy.

During the crisis intervention phase, the tasks of reporting, investigation, validation, child-protection assessment and initial management planning must all be accomplished. (See also chapter 3, "An Approach to Case Management.") In one sense, it is accurate to say that the situation will remain in crisis unless all of these case management tasks are addressed and until an initial management plan is implemented. The initial management plan must include methods of providing whatever concrete environmental services are required by the victim and the family. The following case example is illustrative.

> Thirteen-year-old Karen had skipped several menstrual periods. Medical examination revealed that she was 14 weeks pregnant. When questioned, Karen admitted that the baby's father was *her* father. Shocked at the news, Karen's mother called the police and child-protective services. Within a few hours, a therapist from the child-sexual-abuse unit met with Karen and her mother and helped them to plan their next moves. The mother was fearful of her husband and decided to move herself and her children to her sister's home until after he had been arrested. The therapist supported this decision and provided transportation for them to make the move.

> Next, it was necessary to deal with Karen's pregnancy. Both Karen and her mother agreed that she should have an abortion. The therapist helped to make the arrangements (including financial arrangements) and to cope with the frustration of waiting another five weeks until a second trimester abortion was feasible. Much additional support was extended to Karen, her mother, and siblings around this event. The therapist accompanied Karen and her mother to the hospital and stayed until the procedure was finished. By this time, Karen's mother felt safe enough to move the family back into their own home. Since her husband was incarcerated and since she had quit her job in order to be closer to the children during the crisis, the family needed help in obtaining public assistance to live on until the mother obtained another job.

In the above case description, "therapy" was confined to individual support during the crisis intervention phase. After their environmental needs had been addressed, the family members were ready for individual and group therapy. Without the concrete services that they required, conventional therapy would have been useless. Treatment of this child-sexual-abuse victim had to occur within the context of meeting the immediate needs of her mother and siblings as well.

In contrast, the principal focus during the crisis intervention phase must be on meeting the victim's physical and emotional needs if he or she is to be removed from the home. The child will need help in dealing with the parental rejection which must underlie the separation. Separated victims will need to depend on the therapist as an ally as they cope with the disruption to their lives following disclosure.

> Seventeen-year-old Chrissie summoned the police to her parent's home after

learning of her fifteen-year-old sister Carol's pregnancy by their stepfather. Both Chrissie and Carol had been sexually abused by Mr. G. for five years. He had coerced Chrissie through lavish gifts of jewelry and a car. Carol had spent ten years of her life in an institution for the retarded. She was pressured into the sexual relationship with Mr. G. When the police arrived, Mr. G. was arrested. Mrs. G. did not believe the girls and refused to take them home. Both girls were placed in a shelter facility.

In the following months, the therapist helped Chrissie to get adjusted to independent living, enroll in night school, prepare for court, receive medical care for the syphilis she had contracted from Mr. G., and emotionally begin to put her life in order. Carol required a great deal of time to have explained what was happening to her life. The therapists helped Carol with medical appointments for her pregnancy, all hospital arrangements, support in the hospital while the baby was being delivered, adoption proceedings (Carol's choice), foster placement, court preparation, placement in a special school, and psychological testing. Both girls needed concrete services for months, coupled with individual and group therapy.

Carol's and Chrissie's needs were greater than Karen's due to the lack of parental support, complications of Chrissie's age, Carol's pregnancy and functional retardation, and the extensive emotional trauma sustained by both. Conventional therapy was initially impossible for either girl. Chrissie was concerned with her physical survival, while Carol needed help to accept her mother's rejection and with her pregnancy.

In chapter 1, "A Conceptual Framework for Child Sexual Abuse," the concept of a *suppression phase* as part of the dynamics following disclosure was discussed. During the suppression phase, various family members or others may pressure the child victim to deny or to recant the allegation of sexual abuse. The suppression phase of child sexual abuse may extend throughout the crisis intervention phase of treatment and into the short-term or long-term therapy phases. Nevertheless, the therapist should anticipate that emotional pressure upon the child to recant or to deny the allegation of sexual abuse will be greatest during the crisis intervention phase.

For the therapist, one of the most important tasks will be to prevent the suppressive forces exerted upon the child from harming him or her or from building to a crisis point. Success will depend in large measure upon the extent to which a trust relationship has been established between the therapist and the child. The ability to prevent threats, recriminations, badgering and retaliatory measures by others against the child is also very important. Anticipatory guidance, helping the child to anticipate events (for example, saying, "Other youngsters in your position are sometimes threatened by their families if they decide to go through with testifying.") can be helpful.

If a victim *does* recant his or her allegation, the therapist must immediately begin to determine why the child has changed the story. As chapters 2 and 3 both emphasize, careful *validation* of child sexual abuse is an essential early step in case management. If a victim begins to deny that sexual abuse ever did take place in a previously validated case, the therapist should immediately examine the child's recent activities and experiences. In all likelihood, someone who had access to the child managed to frighten or otherwise pressure the youngster to recant the story; needless to say, this represents a case management emergency. If the therapist cannot give the child enough support to determine the true facts of the case, the youngster may well sustain a lie (that the sexual abuse did *not* occur) which could permit sexual abuse to reoccur and prevent therapeutic intervention.

Short-Term Therapy

Short-term therapy follows the crisis intervention phase and will suffice for some victims depending upon several factors. Children who have not been subjected to severe physical and emotional trauma may require only short-term therapy (up to six months). The level of emotional support by significant others is also important. In general, the greater degree of support for the child in his or her family circle or community, the more likelihood that short-term therapy will be able to resolve the treatment issues. The perpetrator's relationship to the victim is also a key factor. If, for example, the perpetrator does not reside in the victim's home and the parents' response is supportive, short-term therapy may be indicated. The first five impact issues described earlier in this chapter will certainly need to be addressed: "damaged goods" syndrome, fear, low self-esteem, guilt, and depression.

Long-Term Therapy

Victims who have been subjected to severe physical and emotional trauma will undoubtedly be candidates for therapy lasting up to two years or more. Likewise, children who receive little emotional support from significant others will probably require long-term therapy. Obviously, a punitive and uncooperative parent or caretaker cannot facilitate the strengthening of the victim's ego. Again, the child's relationship to the perpetrator will be an important determining factor. If the perpetrator is a parent or parent-figure who resides with the victim, long-term therapy is usually necessary to work through the problems of violation of trust, security issues, role confusion, pseudomaturity, and so forth. Children who are candidates for long-term therapy are likely to require treatment for all ten of the impact issues that were discussed earlier in this chapter.

Treatment Modalities

Individual Therapy
Individual therapy with the victim should begin in the crisis intervention phase and continue until the child is strong enough to be sustained by another treatment

modality. Most children will require a transition period of participating in both individual therapy and an additional treatment modality before the individual therapy can be stopped.

A comprehensive diagnostic assessment should be done in the first three months of individual therapy. An identification of the child's strengths and weaknesses is essential. The critical psychodynamic goal between the therapist and the child during this period is the establishment of a trust relationship. A child who has felt powerless, insecure, and afraid to trust others for years must develop trust in his or her therapist before other issues can be resolved. Trust develops with time and stems from the therapist's emotional support and stated belief that the child was telling the truth and that sexual abuse *did* occur.

The therapist must be consistent with the child and keep any contract agreements which are made. This can be as simple as being on time for the client's appointment. One eight-year-old child named Jennie developed trust through the therapist's demonstrated consistency with her. Often the child and therapist would play outdoors for half of the session, and talk for the other half. Frequently, the secretary would forget that they were in session while outdoors and notify the therapist for a phone call. The therapist would remind the secretary that she was with Jennie, that Jennie was *important* and that they were not to be disturbed. After this scenario had occurred several times, Jennie said to the secretary, "She [the therapist] isn't going to take that call because she's with me and I'm important." The child felt a true sense of importance, began to trust her therapist and share her feelings.

Individual therapy provides a time for the children to begin to express their feelings about the sexual abuse, about their families, and about the events which have occurred since disclosure. Individual therapy allows victims a safe time and place to "put the pieces together" and to begin rebuilding their self-esteem. For many adolescents this phase lasts from four to six weeks, and then integration into group therapy can begin. For some children, the emotional trauma is too great to participate in a group. They become confused and disoriented by the intimacy of sharing such emotionally packed issues with peers and therefore require long-term individual therapy.

Group Therapy

Group therapy is the preferred eventual treatment for most adolescent victims. The individual support received during the crisis intervention phase and in individual therapy allows formation of some initial strengths. In a group, adolescents can see that they are strong enough to accept criticism and praise from their peers. Adolescence is a developmental stage when peer influence has great impact. Open group membership (where individuals begin and end at different times) enables veteran members to act as role models for newcomers. Some will be emotionally stronger than others and can share these strengths. Other adolescents have been through experiences involving criminal or juvenile court or foster-home placements and can help members who are facing these same situations.

Group influence can be a powerful, supportive, and persuasive tool if it is guided by trained group therapists. The group should meet at a safe place where the adolescents feel free to discuss anything, (sexual abuse, family attitudes, sex education, boy-girl relationships). They need to be able to express their feelings without incurring further guilt, and to receive answers to questions. The therapists are present as a resource, to answer questions, to provide guidance, and to demonstrate appropriate behavioral interactions. Group therapy generally lasts from one to one-and-a-half years. Chapter 5, "Group Therapy with Female Adolescent Incest Victims," describes this modality in greater detail.

Arts Therapy

For the younger child, arts therapy is always a useful approach. Often young children (preschool through latency age) have not reached the level of cognitive development to be able to resolve their problems verbally. Play therapy might be used with a child who is afraid to be angry with one or both parents but can be angry at a puppet family instead. As a puppet figure, the child may be able to say, "I hate you" or "I want to kill you" without feeling guilty. This is a healthy process of venting negative feelings and then learning appropriate behavior by setting up a "good" family interaction as a demonstration.

Other arts therapies can help traumatized children of all ages. Drawing pictures of monsters and stabbing them allows for the same release of anger. By drawing an outlined body image and helping the child color in his or her own form, the child can integrate a "whole self." Arts therapy is particularly helpful to the young nonverbal child or to an older child who is depressed and withdrawn or hostile. Chapter 10 extensively describes use of the arts therapies in diagnosis and treatment of child sexual abuse.

Mother-Daughter Dyad Therapy

In cases of father-daughter incest, it is important to have some sessions with the mother and the child together to discuss their relationship. This modality usually follows individual therapy and may occur simultaneously with group therapy. Mother-daughter dyad therapy is important so both can understand why there was a communication breakdown between them and why the mother was not a viable resource for the child when the sexual abuse first began. Both mother and daughter need to be aware of role reversal and how and why it needs to be corrected. Each participant must share her hurt, anger, and jealousy concerning the sexual abuse. The child needs to hear clearly from her mother that she will be protected now and that the incest was not the child's fault. It must be reinforced to the child that both parents were supposed to protect her and that both failed.

This is a very difficult and painful process for both mother and daughter. Mother should also be in a mother's group during this treatment phase in order to receive peer support. In some cases, the interaction between mother and daughter will not change significantly. However, the critical change which must occur is for the mother to assume responsibility to protect the child from further sexual abuse or, if the abuse occurs again, to take immediate action to halt the behavior and protect the child.

Parent-child dyad therapy would seem to be indicated in any incest case involving a perpetrator who is older than and in a power position over the child, regardless of the sex of the participants.

Family Therapy

Family therapy can only occur in incest cases when the parents are honestly willing to take total responsibility for the sexual abuse of the child. The perpetrator must admit responsibility for the abuse, apologize to the child, and reassure the child that it will not happen again. The nonoffending parent must take responsibility for not protecting the child. This is a time when siblings should be included in therapy (many would have received individual therapy prior to this). The family needs to discuss as a whole, the emotional pain associated with the sexual abuse, the role reversal which took place, the need for children to be permitted to engage in age-appropriate behavior, the blurred boundaries, the poor communication patterns, the need to learn good parenting skills, and the need for expansion of social and support systems for all members.

Chapter 9, "Family Treatment," discusses this treatment modality in greater detail. Family therapy must be preceded by individual therapy and, in some cases, group therapy for all of the key actors in the incest drama. The therapist must understand that the incestuous family represents a disordered power system. Conducting family therapy with these clients requires the therapist to be both skilled and strong enough to avoid being manipulated and to prevent the more powerful family members from further victimizing their weaker relatives.

Summary

Sexually victimized children tend to react to their abusive experiences in a largely predictable fashion. It is impossible to assess the degree of impact and to formulate a treatment plan until a case of child sexual abuse has been validated and access to the victim assured. The ten most commonly encountered impact issues for child victims of sexual abuse were identified and the treatment implications of each impact issue were described. A careful diagnostic assessment is essential to successful treatment intervention. Each phase of treatment for the child should reinforce the others. Most child victims of sexual abuse will benefit from multiple treatment modalities carefully implemented as part of a comprehensive treatment plan.

References

Burgess, Ann W., and Holmstrom, Lynda L. *Rape: Crisis and Recovery*. Bowie, Maryland: Robert T. Brady Company, 1979, p. 60.
————. "Sexual Assault of Children and Adolescents." *Nursing Clinics of North America* (September 1975):551–63.
————. *Rape: Victims of Crisis*. Bowie, Maryland: Robert T. Brady Company, 1974.

5

Group Therapy with Female Adolescent Incest Victims

Linda Canfield Blick
and *Frances Sarnacki Porter*

During the summer of 1977, the staff of Connecticut's Sexual Trauma Treatment Program (STTP) formulated a multiple-impact approach to the intervention and treatment of the incestuous family. The program was funded by the National Center for Child Abuse and Neglect,[a] under the auspices of the Connecticut Department of Children and Youth Services (DCYS), Division of Child Protective Services. As a public agency, DCYS is under a statutory mandate to investigate cases of reported child abuse, neglect, or abandonment and to provide services to families when child maltreatment is validated.

Operating as a specialized pilot program, the role of STTP was to validate these cases and provide therapy to families where there was either intrafamilial or extrafamilial sexual abuse. Initially, the program's intervention was crisis-oriented, with a tendency toward short-term treatment of extrafamilial sexual abuse, and long-term treatment of intrafamilial sexual abuse. The primary objectives of STTP were to: (1) protect the child; (2) stop the sexually abusive behavior; (3) minimize and treat the sexual trauma; and (4) stabilize the family.

The various treatment modalities employed were individual, group, marital, and family therapy, as well as art therapy and a family weekend retreat program. The focus of this chapter will be the formation of a therapy group for adolescent incest victims and the techniques that were developed for use with this group.

Rationale for Adolescent Group Therapy

In assessing Connecticut's early child-sexual-abuse statistics, we realized that many of the victims would be adolescents. Table 5–1 shows a breakdown of cases of suspected child sexual abuse reported to the Connecticut Department of Children and Youth Services in fiscal year 1976 by type of report. It should be noted that adolescent girls (over 12 years and under 18 years of age) constitute 48 percent of the female population reported. When the small percentage of venereal disease cases reported for the 12 to 18 years age group are excluded, the proportion of adolescent females rises to 54 percent.

---

[a]National Center for Child Abuse and Neglect, DHEW, Grant No. 90–C–399.

Table 5–1
Reports of Suspected Sexual Abuse of Children in Connecticut[a]

	Incest and Rape	Sexual Molestation	Venereal Disease	Total Cases of Suspected Sexual Abuse
FY 1976[b]	35	118	34	187
Females over 12 yrs. [c]	22 66.7%	53 50.5%	4 14.8%	79 48.0%

[a]Connecticut Department of Children and Youth Services.
[b]FY 1976 (7/1/75–6/30/76) includes males and females, birth to age 18.
[c]These figures are comprised of females only.

These statistics provided the rationale for the development of a group of female adolescent incest victims in August 1977. The group was formed for the primary purpose of helping the girls deal with the emotional trauma resulting from their incestuous relationships. Trauma was manifested by symptoms of psychosomatic illness, depression, loss of appetite, nightmares, poor sleeping habits, anxiety, fear of going outdoors, and fear of men. The adolescent therapy group provided the victims with an opportunity to share their experiences with other girls like themselves. Their common incestuous experiences helped to minimize the girls' sense of isolation and the social stigma inherent in the breaking of the incest taboo. Ruth expressed these sentiments when she said, "I didn't know it happened to anyone else. It's nice to know others have the same problem. Not that I'm happy it happened to you, too, but . . . well . . . you know what I mean. It kind of helps that I'm not the only one."

The adolescent therapy group also provided an opportunity for the participants to relate to other girls in a socially acceptable environment. Victims of an incestuous relationship usually have a history of alienation and isolation from peers and community systems. With the exception of a few girls who had outgoing personalities, the victims tended to have few friends outside the family. The majority of their leisure time was spent at home with their siblings and parents.

When questioned about her peer relationships, Jill replied that she had "tons of friends," and proceeded to rattle off the names of half a dozen school mates. Questions revealed that Jill saw all of these girls at school only. One girl (a friend since age seven) visited her at home once or twice a week. Otherwise, Jill spent her leisure time staying at home watching television and playing with her stuffed animals. The adolescent therapy group provided 14-year-old Jill with her first extended opportunity to socialize with girls of her own age.

A trend toward group affiliation is a normal developmental stage of adolescence. Group treatment of adolescents thus becomes part of a natural process. The adolescent's need for peer identity, acceptance and approval is normally met within the framework of conformity and sharing with agemates. Many of the therapeutic needs of traumatized adolescents can readily be addressed in a group therapy setting.

Victims of an incestuous relationship typically undergo a period of confusion and feelings of powerlessness, lasting from a few days to a lifetime. Entering the group, they experience feelings of shame, guilt, embarrassment, and inadequacy. As they become more trusting and comfortable with the group members, they unconsciously (or perhaps consciously) strive to regain and develop some sense of self-worth, a partial separation from their parents, and the formation of a separate identity. They attempt to clarify role relationships and understand their own evolving sexuality. In addition, the group can provide a safe social milieu where the girls can clarify and express their feelings about the incestuous relationship and the family disruption following disclosure. Marcia's description to new members summarized her perception of the group: "Everybody sits around and says what they're feeling and talks about what happened, how they feel about it, their reactions; people give suggestions and sometimes it gets awfully silly."

Although there is accuracy in Marcia's comments, she neglected to mention the unsettling subjects the girls often talk about, and the many intense, tearful, and sad meetings. Several other girls when asked, "Why the group?" have said:

"We talk about our fathers."
"Problems we have at home."
"Like when you have intercourse."
"Touching."
"How we feel about other people and what they think about what happened to us."
"How we can face up to our fathers."
"Mothers—how they feel. Do we talk to them about it?"
"Important to trust people."

Preliminary Considerations

Prior to the formation of a therapy group for adolescent incest victims, attention should be directed to eight different issues which require staff input and planning. The areas of preliminary consideration are:

1. Place for meetings
2. Time and scheduling of meetings

3. Participant's time commitment to the group
4. Transportation to and from group meetings
5. Group membership
6. Refreshments
7. Agency support system
8. Use of cotherapists

Place for Meetings

To begin, a decision must be made regarding the place that the adolescent group will meet. Although this may not be a problem for private agencies with adequate space, public agencies may lack an available and appropriate room for group meetings. The best place for the group to meet is usually within an agency so that a neutral setting is offered. It is important for the participants to be able to feel relaxed and comfortable in the meeting site. Holding the group meetings at the agency also allows the therapists to maintain better control of the therapeutic process since it affords them the greatest control of the environment for the group meeting.

If an agency lacks the space for a group, other sites may be explored in community facilities, schools, hospitals, or churches. Alliance with community resources can be a crucial part of intervention for the sexually abused child. Providing space for group meetings may initiate involvement by a community resource in a cooperative effort to help victims and their families.

We do not recommend that group treatment of incest victims be conducted in the homes of the participants. Even if no other family members are present, the atmosphere is likely to be highly charged, emotionally, and not conducive to relaxing, sharing, or objectivity. Holding group meetings in victims' homes also eliminates the opportunity for the girls to work toward building a separate identity. Lastly, the home setting for group meetings would tend to increase the girls' feelings of helplessness and encourage other family members to put them under pressure.

We observed the growth of a sense of pride and belonging as the adolescents begin to regard the group-room as their "own special place." Although this room was used for other functions of the Sexual Trauma Treatment Program, they were permitted to decorate the walls with their own posters and pictures. One of the most positive events was the creation of a group mural which was encouraged by the art therapist during a group session. The members were then given the choice of taking their pictures home or leaving them to decorate the walls. All of the adolescents chose to have their artwork remain in the group-room. During subsequent sessions, many of the members would comment about the mural and sometimes add to their own picture. The mural seemed to be a focal point for discussion among the girls, particularly before the meetings began.

During a group meeting, one of the girls became upset when she noticed that her picture was missing. It had fallen down during the week and had not yet been rehung. It was placed back on the wall by the next group meeting. This girl's first comment upon entering the room was, "Oh, good! My picture is back where it belongs. . . . I feel better."

Time and Scheduling of Meetings

Once a decision has been reached about a place for the group meeting, the next issue is when it will convene. If the group members live close to the site, it is feasible to meet in the late afternoon, immediately after school. However, if they live at a distance (necessitating transportation by car, and therefore reliance upon parental convenience) evening meetings will probably be preferable.

The adolescents who attended group meetings at Connecticut's Sexual Trauma Treatment Program lived anywhere from two miles to forty miles from the agency. The travel time required ranged from ten minutes to one hour. The significant proportion of girls who required transportation assistance necessitated group meetings that were held in the early evening, after supper.

Initially, the adolescent therapy group meetings were held from 7:00 P.M. to 8:00 P.M. which worked out well until the population was expanded from three members to five. Since more time was needed to accommodate the increased membership, the girls agreed to meet for one-and-a-half hours from 6:30 P.M. to 8:00 P.M.

If at all possible, the group meeting should be scheduled in the beginning of the week, no later than Wednesday. Frequently, issues are brought up by various members who then request some follow-up help with these problems later in the week. The STTP adolescent therapy meetings were held once a week, on Mondays.

The following case example illustrates the importance of holding group meetings early in the week.

Two days after an adolescent group meeting, Gerry contacted her therapist to report that her stepfather had again been sexually abusing her for the last two months. The sexual activity was escalating. She was afraid of him and needed help. Gerry was embarrassed to raise the problem in the group meeting, since she had recently been coerced by her mother to drop her complaint and invalidate the criminal charges against her stepfather. Gerry confided in her therapist on Wednesday because of the discussion at an adolescent group meeting on Monday. The meeting had focused on the problem of incestuous sexual abuse of children reoccurring after a period of time has elapsed and the perpetrator once again feels safe. Gerry was a quiet and withdrawn child who had difficulty in requesting help. If the group had met later in the week and she had had the weekend to repress her "stirred-up" feelings, she might not have sought assistance.

Participant's Time Commitment to the Group

In the initial stages of planning, the therapists need to determine approximately how long the participants will attend group meetings. During the formation of the STTP adolescent therapy group, the therapists suggested a time-limited contract of eight weeks. As the group evolved, it became apparent that a longer term of participation was needed to accomplish the agreed-upon goals. In general, the group's goals were: a resolution or significant reduction of the trauma; improved communication with the family; and the development of some assertive behavior. To accomplish these goals, the individual's contract was eventually extended from eight weeks to an open-ended contract.

Each member's withdrawal from the group was decided by group consensus and was judged on the basis of fulfillment of her individual contract. The group members designed individual contracts for each participant, consisting of areas that needed improvement or modification. In this way, each individual was cognizant of every other member's behavior and progress. Due to individual differences in emotional trauma, progress and growth, open-ended contracts lasted from six to eighteen months.

Consideration should be given to holding group meetings during the summer months. Child sexual abuse, with its resultant trauma, is a persistent problem, unrelated to the seasons of the year. This concept mandated STTP's decision to meet during the summer months. Some resistance was encountered from group members who felt that a vacation from school also meant a vacation from the group. This resistance was overcome by: (1) taking a "group summer vacation," that is, not meeting for two weeks at the end of the school year; and (2) by planning special events during the summer months such as picnics, swimming, and trips to the movies.

Transportation to and from Group Meetings

The success or failure of an adolescent group depends on whether or not the members can obtain consistent transportation. Some members may live within walking distance of the agency or may have access to public transportation. In the absence of either situation, the adolescent must rely upon some adult (usually a parent) for transportation by car. Reliance upon parents for transportation encourages the adolescent's dependent position and provides the parents with the power to interfere with their daughter's attendance at group meetings without directly appearing to do so.

For example, Chris's parents give her permission to attend adolescent group meetings. Yet, each time she was ready to leave home, she was without transportation. Either her parent felt ill, had "too much work to do tonight," or "forgot" and did not come home on time to transport her to the group. When the therapist offered to pick her up, Chris said that she "was needed at home that night." After five weeks of unsuccessful resolution of the problem, Chris reluctantly acknowledged that she would never attend the group meetings.

Sometimes a parent is cooperative about providing transportation for his or her daughter in the early stages of group therapy, but, as the daughter begins to mature and develop some self-assertion, the parent may become ambivalent about the daughter's participation. This ambivalence may materialize as a member's sporadic attendance, as with Anita.

> Initially, Anita's parents were supportive of her attendance in the adolescent group and her mother agreed to transport her regularly. Over a period of time, Anita became aware of her feelings, worked out various issues, and began to accept her own self-worth. At home, she attempted to improve her relationship with her family by becoming more assertive. With Anita's increasing assertiveness and emotional growth, her mother became more hostile and rejecting of her. Mother's anger at her daughter's independence was manifested by bringing her to the group meetings late or not at all.

Resistance to their daughter's involvement in the group, was the underlying issue for both Chris's and Anita's parents. They merely used transportation as a means of sabotaging their daughter's participation.

Therapists who wish to develop an adolescent group must be sensitive to parental resistance, often reflected in a refusal to provide transportation. This parental opposition usually surfaces when the adolescent identity-conflict is blossoming, intensifying the already existing parent-child conflict. The therapist should discuss the possible development of this situation with the family early in the course of treatment. In this way, if and when the problem develops, there is some preceding awareness by the family. The therapist's credibility is thereby enhanced and successful resolution of the issue becomes more likely.

In Connecticut's Sexual Trauma Treatment Program, some adolescents were transported to group meetings by a case aide. Usually, agency transportation was used for girls from inner-city marginal income families, who had no car. For a period of several months, the agency did not have access to a case aide. To insure the continuity of the group, the two therapists travelled from half an hour to an hour, before and after the group, to transport some of the members.

Attendance in the adolescent therapy group was more consistent when transportation was provided by the agency. However, this action clearly removes the parents from responsibility for their daughter's treatment. Whenever there is an option, the best practice (as followed by STTP) is to have the parents be accountable for their daughter's group attendance by providing transportation. If this fails, then the agency should provide transportation, if possible.

Group Membership

Consideration should be given to the common features between the prospective members. The type of sexually abusive experience, the family's reaction, and the victim's reaction all are primary considerations. Ancillary considerations are the age and developmental stages of the prospective members.

During the planning stage of Connecticut's Sexual Trauma Treatment Program, a decision was made to form a therapy group of adolescent girls from ages 11 to 18 years. All of the girls would be victims of sexual abuse, where the perpetrator was either a father or father figure (intrafamilial), or an outside perpetrator (extrafamilial). The one common bond to be shared by the girls would be that of sexual victimization by an older, more powerful person. In spite of the seven-year variance, it was believed that the sexual abuse, combined with common adolescent issues of identification, separation, and emerging sexuality, would be the bond between the members.

Although the group was initially open to victims of sexual abuse by an outside perpetrator, there was little participation by these girls as compared to the father and father-figure victims. It seemed that the adolescent's decision to join or not to join the group was based upon the degree of the agency's involvement with the family. In general, we worked with the nonincestuous families on a crisis intervention basis, which meant that the involvement with them was short term, anywhere from two-to-six weeks. The functional supportive family system for these girls may have minimized their trauma and influenced their decision to avoid longer-term treatment. On the other hand, the agency staff probably placed less emphasis on their participation since their cases had a lower priority status. Over a period of time, it became apparent that the group would be composed of adolescent *incest* victims. To insure a membership of girls who would be appropriate candidates, the two therapists decided to interview all of the prospective members and screen those who were interested in joining the group.

One girl, age 11, was thought to be appropriate for the group, while another girl, also age 11, was considered to be a poor candidate for membership. Leigh was highly motivated to join the group because she knew several of the members. She wanted help with her fear of her brother who was about to be released from prison after having served a sentence for raping her. The therapists were reluctant to have her join the group due to her immaturity and low level of intelligence. It was agreed that Leigh would attend three sessions, after which she and the therapists would review her participation. During the group sessions, Leigh exhibited a variety of inappropriate behaviors. This included interrupting whoever was talking, talking secretly to the girl next to her, talking to herself out loud, and laughing when another member related a devastating experience. Whenever Leigh spoke, she would perseverate about her own experiences by repeating verbatim her fear of her brother. This occurred as often as three times in one group session. Due to her disruptions and her apparent inability to benefit from the group, Leigh was asked to withdraw after three sessions, and was seen instead in individual therapy.

As Leigh's case demonstrates, discretion must be used in deciding which girls join the group. Due to individual differences, the therapists of STTP did not always strictly adhere to the age range of 11 through 18. Experience showed that one 11-year-old was too immature for the group. However, some 11-year-olds close to their twelfth birthday were admitted. A 19-year-old mother of one child was also a successful member of the group. Her capacity both to benefit from and give to the group was based upon her unresolved sexual trauma resulting from an incestuous sexual relationship with her father between the ages of 11 and 16 and resultant delay in emotional development.

The size of the adolescent therapy group fluctuated, depending upon new referrals and terminations. Initially, the girls were informed that membership would be open and would increase in size as the agency received new referrals. Three members constituted the smallest population, while the largest population was thirteen members.

In starting an adolescent group, consideration must be given to the size of the group and whether membership will be open or closed. Some variables contributing to this decision may be: (1) the age of the girls; (2) the number of therapists; (3) the length of time the group will meet and therefore the intensity of the sessions; and (4) the anticipated need in the community for a group.

Membership in the STTP adolescent therapy group was open for the purpose of accepting new referrals and offered long-term treatment to the members (six months or more). The shared responsibility of two cotherapists allowed new members to be accepted as referred until the group size reached thirteen girls. The decision to limit the group at this number was based upon the need to involve all of the members in the group process. The cotherapists agreed that it would not be possible to keep more than thirteen members involved and actively participating.

Refreshments

In planning an adolescent group, consideration should be given to providing refreshments for the meetings. This responsibility should be given to the group members if they are receptive to the idea and have enough money for the snacks. Otherwise, the allocation of program money should be explored. In the adolescent therapy group run by the Sexual Trauma Treatment Program, refreshments consisting of beverages and cookies were usually provided by the therapists for weekly group meetings. There was also a group celebration of everyone's birthday, as well as holiday parties. The purpose of these activities was to improve group cohesiveness and give some special attention to the group member who was celebrating a birthday.

Whenever possible, the therapists would have the girls contribute to the refreshments, especially for a party. This was not always feasible, as some of the girls were from marginal income families. Rather than acknowledge any possible difficulties, some girls would either not attend the group the following week or would "forget" to bring the food as agreed. The adolescents were permitted to bring in what they wished. However, the overzealous girl from a family with a limited income, was advised to bring in napkins or candles, rather than the cake she originally volunteered to make.

The obvious benefit of refreshments is the symbolic nurturance of the group members. This can be a powerful, subtle, therapeutic tool as is seen in the following case:

> In the early sessions, Marlene would leave her coat on, not eat any of the refreshments, and remain quiet and withdrawn. It was extremely difficult for her to talk about her relationship with her father, and she would cry and admit to feelings of unhappiness. As the group meetings progressed, she was able to make a statement about what had happened to her. Once this was accomplished, she felt more relaxed and began to communicate with the members about other areas of her life. A noticeable difference (as expressed by several members) was Marlene's acceptance of refreshments for the first time, two months after joining the group.

Apparently Marlene could not accept or enjoy any refreshments until her own experiences were revealed to the group. Debby, on the other hand, used food to help her through her story.

> It was the first time that Debby related the details about her stepfather's sexual abuse. During the course of her emotionally laden description, she nervously fingered a cookie. As she revealed the details about being impregnated by him, she would pause, look at the cookie, then proceed again. The visual image was of a child using a cookie as a tranquilizing agent; it allowed her to become distracted, pull her resources together, and then resume her story.

In addition to having refreshments for the adolescent group members, it is helpful to make coffee or other beverages available to the parents. Many of the STTP parents traveled half an hour or longer to bring the girls to the meeting and would wait the one-and-a-half hours until the session was over. Refreshments not only served to occupy the evening, but served as a relaxing mechanism, allowing them to spend some time talking to each other.

Agency Support System

A general understanding of the purposes of an adolescent therapy group and the consensus of the staff members regarding its need is important for the individual group members. Adolescents are sensitive to staff members who are unfriendly toward them. This behavior may occur in the agency waiting room or while talking on the telephone. Any aloofness displayed by the staff makes the adolescent feel unimportant or rejected and may result in withdrawal.

Members of the STTP staff make a point to introduce themselves to the girls and to maintain a casual relationship with them. The girls enjoyed this special attention and reciprocated with friendliness. Occasionally, the members would inquire about other staff members and would even share some group refreshments with them.

> Judy's apprehension about men was related to sexual abuse at age 7 by a stranger, and again at age 13 by her father. In the agency, a male clinician was friendly to her, in a casual, nonthreatening way. As Judy felt increasingly comfortable with his behavior, she would stop by his office and say hello. After a while, she would even give him a piece of leftover cake after the meeting was over. This man provided a positive male-role model for Judy.

Judy's single gesture of giving was an indication of her willingness to trust at least one man.

Due to the atmosphere of friendliness and support from the entire staff, the group members felt relaxed and accepted. If an adolescent needed some help with a problem, and her own therapist was unavailable, she would often ask to speak to another therapist. Whenever a girl who sounded anxious or depressed was too shy to ask for assistance, the agency's astute secretaries would suggest that another therapist was available.

> Doreen was seen in individual therapy by one of the group therapists. However, she felt comfortable with the other group therapist through her sporadic group attendance. One day, she telephoned for help but her therapist was in court and unavailable. Recognizing the depressed tone of Doreen's voice, the secretary indicated that the other group therapist was in the office and could speak to her. After a short conversation, Doreen revealed her father's threats to kill her unless she dropped the criminal charges. The therapist scheduled an appointment to see her that day.

Group Therapist(s)

The final consideration in starting an adolescent group concerns the sex of the therapist(s), and the number of therapists. Since this topic is more fully discussed later in the chapter, only a few brief statements will be made at this time.

Connecticut's Sexual Trauma Treatment Program used two female cotherapists for the adolescent group. It was felt that the girls needed to work through their feelings about men in a nonthreatening environment. The inclusion of a male therapist in the early stages of group therapy would have undoubtedly caused inhibition and possibly other problems. This hypothesis was demonstrated whenever a new girl joined the group. In general, she related in a withdrawn or seductive fashion towards the male clinicians at the agency.

There are several advantages to assigning two therapists to an adolescent therapy group. Cotherapists can share the responsibility of facilitating such an intense group. Another advantage is the therapists' increased perception of the group process and its members. A third advantage is that the group can meet even if one therapist is absent. And finally, the group members benefit from the combined input of two therapists.

Intervention Issues

After preliminary considerations for group formation have been explored, therapists must address significant intervention issues of the group therapy process. These include the following:

1. Individual versus group therapy
2. Group expansion
3. Psychodynamics amenable to group intervention
4. Treatment issues

Individual versus Group Therapy

Coordination between individual and group therapy of the same client is very important. In Connecticut's Sexual Trauma Treatment Program, one of the two cotherapists for the adolescent therapy group was usually assigned to work with the adolescent victim(s) as new cases were acquired. This assignment facilitates coordination of individual and group therapy. In several cases when individual treatment was provided by another therapist, a significant complication was observed. As the adolescent became increasingly involved with the group, she experienced conflicting loyalty between the group and her individual therapist.

> In the beginning stages of individual therapy, Claudette had a good relationship with her therapist whom she saw weekly. Several weeks later, she joined the adolescent group, while continuing with her individual therapy. Over a period of time, Claudette began to trust the group members, which was manifested by her risk-taking behavior. She discovered that she could openly discuss her suicidal feelings, experimentation with drugs, and feelings of rejection and abandonment by mother. Some of the girls in the group had shared these experiences, while other girls understood and gave her a lot of support.
>
> As Claudette relied more and more on the adolescent group, she revealed less and less to her individual therapist. She began to question why she was one of

the few girls in the group whose individual therapist was not her group therapist. Also, during this time, she was aloof and unreliable in keeping her appointments with her individual therapist. This behavior persisted until she accepted the fact that a change in therapists would not occur.

It appears that the cohesiveness of the group, coupled with its intensity, trust, and basic nurturance creates a bonding between the members and the group therapists. While it is not always possible for the same clinician to serve as individual and group therapist, there needs to be an awareness of this issue and some sensitivity to its dynamics.

Individual therapy is utilized to deal with the initial crisis stage, develop trust between the adolescent and her therapist, and build upon the adolescent's ego strengths. This intervention serves as a framework for her initiation into the adolescent group.

Group therapy is an adjunct to individual therapy which should still continue on an intensive level for approximately three months. As the member becomes more involved in the group, she regards it as the primary therapeutic tool. This generally results in a reduction of individual therapy except when needed, requested or during crisis periods.

Group Expansion

It was the experience of the STTP therapists that the "start-up" time for an adolescent therapy group was three months. Initially, there were three members, all victims of an incestuous relationship with their fathers. During the first meeting, the three members (two sisters and one other girl) were told that membership would be open, and the population would increase in size as the agency received new referrals. The group's progress during the first couple of months was rather slow, as the girls cautiously dealt with the issue of trust.

Two months later, a fourth girl joined the group. The response to her was very positive. In expressing their feelings about the new member, some comments were: "You're a talker and you like to let out your feelings" and "Glad you're here 'cause we kept talking about the same thing."

After six months, the adolescent therapy group had expanded to six members. Each time a new girl joined the group, the members successfully concerned themselves with the issue of trust and openness. Experience showed that the purposes of the group could be achieved with open membership and with a varying group population of between three and thirteen members. Over 22 months, a total of 21 girls participated in the STTP adolescent therapy group, with a maximum population of 13 members at one time. The cotherapists felt that they could effectively conduct a group of approximately 8 to 10 girls between the ages of approximately 12 and 18.

Initially, the therapists decided that one criterion for group membership would be regular attendance. There were many sensitive and crucial issues that the group would be discussing, and it was important that the members learn to trust each other by making a commitment to attend. Rose had a particularly difficult time in accepting new members, because she felt her position as indigenous leader would be threatened. On the night that two new girls attended the group, she hid her face in a book and admitted to being "scared to talk. . . . How do I know they won't blab their mouths?" Although the new girls had joined the group two weeks earlier, Rose's unnecessary absences magnified the trust issue. Further problems with fragmented attendance resulted in the decision that, if a girl missed the group meetings for more than two consecutive sessions without an important reason, she could not return to the group.

As mentioned earlier, the contract with the members was open-ended, rather than time-limited. During the first year, significant progress was observed in girls who attended this adolescent therapy group for at least six months. Thereafter, a six-month commitment was requested of the members. This resulted in overlapping time commitments for individual members and enabled excellent role modeling by the "older members" which aids in the integration of the newer members.

> During a slow moving group session, consisting of several new members, Christine stated, "I think it would help them if I told my story. . . . He would touch my breasts and lower area while he thought I was asleep."
>
> She then indicated that she was sleeping in her mother's bed when father came home from working the second shift. When Christine woke up, she discovered that father had hands inside her pants. She said to him, "You can forget it, you're not turning me on." She got up from the bed, went to another room, and said she was moving out. Father replied, "Think of my marriage." Christine retorted angrily, "Think of my life!"

Depending upon their own sexual-abuse experiences, the details and issues discussed by Christine were relevant to all of the girls on many different levels. Christine's story started some group exchange and helped the new members to realize the possible benefits of the group process.

STTP demographics indicate that the adolescent group members were approximately 50 percent urban and 50 percent suburban residents. The group was composed of Caucasians, Blacks, Hispanics, and several foreign language speaking members. The socioeconomic backgrounds were from lower to upper middle class. Despite profound socioeconomic and ethnic differences, an atmosphere of friendliness and acceptance resulted in an absence of racism and interpersonal value conflicts.

The common denominator creating this cohesion was the sexual abuse. Upon joining the adolescent therapy group, the girls universally expressed feelings of isolation. Sharing their experiences with other victims helped to break down their feelings of ostracism and laid a preliminary foundation for the beginning stages of camaraderie.

As Beth explained, "I wanted to tell someone and even tried to tell my mother once before, but she just changed the subject. I felt that no one would believe me. I was different from other girls and I was the only one it happened to."

Psychodynamics Amenable to Group Intervention

We have observed several important psychodynamic issues which characterize most incest victims. The impact of these issues has played a major role in designing group intervention techniques.

To begin with, the one common bond the adolescents share is that of being a victim of a universal taboo. There is no positive status to this type of victimization. People react with shock, horror, disbelief, and anger once the secret is disclosed. They tend to succumb to society's sense of helplessness leading to subsequent withdrawal from or rejection of the victim. This alienation is confusing to the victim who experiences an intensification of guilt.

Frequently, the victim will act nonchalant about the reaction of peers and the community. One group member (who was impregnated by her father and had an abortion) said that several of her peers were circulating the rumor that she had had a baby. When asked how she felt about this, she replied in a high-pitched, angry-sounding voice, "I don't care!"

Another girl indicated that the newspaper article describing her father's arrest for incest sensitized the community to the father-daughter relationship. She ignored the teasing and taunting until the stories calmed down, but lost a few friends during the process. Now she distrusts "having close friends who will turn on you. Better to have several friends."

The responses of these two adolescents are defense mechanisms against the guilt they really feel. The foundation for this guilt is already laid, as a result of the stress and familial disruption which ensues once the secret is disclosed. The victim of father-daughter incest suffers from various types of guilt resulting from: (1) reporting the incestuous relationship; (2) disloyalty and disruption to the family; (3) being different from peers; (4) pleasure derived from the sexual relationship; and (5) vengeful angry feelings toward both parents, especially her mother.

Although initially the family may be supportive of the victim, the support tends to be withheld once the reality sets in about father's absence from the home and loss of income. This reaction was clearly demonstrated in the case history of Meg, who was impregnated by her stepfather. During the initial crisis stage, Meg's mother believed her story and was supportive of her. About a month later, she began to feel that Meg was impregnated by someone else.

Eventually, she pressured Meg to drop the charges against her stepfather. Meg was removed from her mother's home and placed in foster care after the mother repeatedly exposed her to the stepfather's continuing sexual abuse.

The adolescent victim has experienced historical alienation from the nuclear family which, as indicated above, may continue after the disclosure of the secret. Her anger and resentment toward her parents are oppressive because she is generally unable to express her feelings. This is related to the intimacy-dependence conflict of the parent-child relationship.

Long before the disclosure of incest, mother had relinquished her responsibility to her daughter, thus creating internal confusion over roles and identities. An atmosphere of chaotic uncertainty about family roles and one's own identity do not afford the development of trust. This lack of trust adversely affects peer relationships, school performance, and a child's normal dependence on community support systems.

Over a period of time, the mother-daughter role reversal becomes complete with father's attraction to daughter as a sexual partner. The child keeps the sexual relationship a secret because of rewards and favors, fear of punishment, fear of abandonment or rejection, or fear of repercussions from telling (Burgess and Holmstrom, 1975). In some instances, the victim will tell mother who either ignores her or does not believe her. One girl's feelings about this disbelief were, "I thought she didn't care about me and didn't want me to be her daughter anymore." In any event, the child is alone with the secret between herself and her father.

After the relationship is exposed, the victim experiences a variety of confusing and distressing feelings. Due to her relationship with father and her sense of alienation, she has been compliant and either not in touch with her feelings or using all of her energy to suppress their emergence. In general, she is afraid to look at her anger—at father for violating her body and trust; and at mother for not protecting her. When she enters the group, she finds it easy to talk about *everything but* these pertinent issues.

The adolescent victim's feelings of guilt mark the rage and hostility she feels toward family members and significant others. Acknowledgment of these emotions is so frightening that they are often repressed and manifested in psychosomatic complaints and initial outward complacency. It is therefore understandable when she reveals a poor body image and low self-esteem. We have observed slender, pretty girls who describe themselves as "fat and ugly." Many of them feel damaged and believe that permanent change has occurred to their bodies. They also fear that they will be unable to have children.

Other manifestations of low self-esteem and feelings of worthlessness are suicidal ideation or actual attempts at suicide. Adolescent victims of incest sometimes use drugs and alcohol as a way of running away from their feelings of despair.

Another way of handling an incestuous relationship is simply to run away from home or marry at an early age. What may be perceived as adolescent rebellion and acting out, may actually be the youngster's only way of escaping an intolerable home situation characterized by an incestuous relationship.

Treatment Issues

Ventilation of Anger. During the group process, it is vitally important for each member to vent her feelings about the sexual trauma. She will need to discuss feelings about herself, the perpetrator, the reaction of family members, peers, and the community. A diversity of attitudes will evolve in the group, and these must be dealt with in a sensitive, diplomatic fashion. As an illustration, we could see that two girls felt quite differently about their fathers. Jodi stated, "My father said he did this to me out of love—I don't hate him. I just feel sorry for him now." At the same time, Holly expressed, "I don't want you for my father no more. . . . I can't trust you . . . because you might try it again. You have a wife and should have done it to her, not me, your daughter."

Socialization. The fragmented communication patterns which exist within the incestuous family have laid the basis for a chronically dysfunctional system. Once this situation is combined with blurred generational boundaries, there is the development of unhealthy parent-child relationships and confused intrafamilial roles. The poor quality of intrafamilial relationships is frequently reflected in the girls' inadequate community and peer relationships. This situation was described in detail in the case history of Julia. The blurred generational boundaries between father and herself created a sibling-sibling relationship, rather than a father-daughter relationship. In addition, Julia was a lonely child with few friends, who sought daily companionship in the fantasy world of her deceased dog and stuffed animals.

Many of the victims, like Julia, have poorly developed social skills and experience real difficulty in developing meaningful and gratifying relationships with their peers. Much of the group therapy process can focus on improving the girls' social skills, encouraging healthy interaction with their peers, and forcing them to respect the rights of others. For some, the adolescent therapy group provided them with their first sustained experience of maintaining appropriate boundaries with others, and vice versa.

Preparation for Court. Since legal intervention is an integral part of the community response to child sexual abuse, it is imperative to discuss the procedures and ramifications of the criminal justice system. Group members can provide intense support to the girl who must appear in court—before, during, and after the experience. Role playing for the court appearance is a favorite activity and, provides valuable preparation for testifying.

Sex Education. In the adolescent group, it is crucially important to explore boy-girl relationships, sex education, and birth control. The confusion which arises from being treated as a lover-daughter can hamper the adolescent's normal puberty. Several girls expressed difficulty in relating to their boyfriends. As Karen stated, "Whenever I kiss my boyfriend, I just see my father's face." This may throw the adolescent into turmoil and be manifested by sexual acting-out as an attempt to become "normal" like her peers. Or, she may act out to prove that others, besides Dad, care about her. Clearly, sex education and birth control information are required to minimize further trauma to the adolescent victim.

Intervention Techniques

In developing the techniques for positive group interaction with adolescent incest victims, an eclectic approach affords flexibility when eliciting difficult, painful feelings, or developing healthy relationships. It is important to remember that the members' victimization and dysfunctional family patterns are common bonds. However, each girl still brings to the group various strengths and weaknesses, degrees of trauma, and family-community support systems or lack thereof. These require individual treatment planning and coordination by the group therapists.

We developed or adapted some of the following intervention techniques for use with adolescent incest victims:

1. *Group Ice Breaker.* This is a word game to promote a common shared experience.
2. *Group-Go-Around.* A brief weekly synopsis from each member about her week's experiences, which helps develop responsibility and provides a monitoring method for the therapists.
3. *Individual Contracts.* Provides identification of each member's strengths and "things to work on."
4. *Role Playing.* Prepares the child for a given situation, for example, court, confrontation with a family member.
5. *Arts Therapy.* May assist in improving body image.
6. *Sex Education.* Provides correct information regarding human sexuality and birth control, as well as reassurance to victims that their incestuous sexual experiences did not result in physical damage.
7. *Awareness of Body Language and Movement.* The observation and discussion of each member's nonverbal expressions.
8. *Symbolic Nurturance.* Provides weekly refreshments and birthday cakes.

9. *Fun Days*. Provide opportunities to practice social skills through planned trips such as movies, camping, picnics, and so forth.
10. *Role Modeling*. Cotherapists model appropriate interactions between mature people and demonstrate positive authority and peer relationships.
11. *Immediate Verbal Praise for Positive Behavior*. Promotes positive behavioral changes and increased self-esteem.
12. *Reinforcement for Expression of Feelings*. Encourages further self-expression.
13. *Concepts of Responsibility and Independence*. Helps members to achieve autonomy.

When first establishing a group, or whenever a new member joins the group, there is a period of mutual peer apprehension which is related to trust. The use of a word game exercise has been a very effective *"ice breaker"* for new members. The girls are divided into groups of two, three, or four (depending upon the size of the group) and are assigned the task of engaging in a 20-minute exercise. The word game should be simple, noncompetitive, and possessing neither right nor wrong responses. One game is based upon a sentence completion format where the members exchange mutual feelings, aspirations, and so forth. By focusing on a shared, nonthreatening experience, there is an expeditious enhancement of the initiation process. Any similar ice breakers can be utilized.

This technique is useful to continue during the first few months of a newly established group. Psychodynamically, these adolescents have learned not to trust others, and it takes time for them to feel comfortable in the group and ultimately to begin sharing painful experiences. Other nonthreatening exercises can be as simple as having each member share her nickname, drawing a family tree, or working on a group mural.

A good technique for promoting ongoing discussions and developing individual responsibility is the *group-go-around*. This should be utilized as the opening topic each week once the group has had its first few meetings. The group-go-around consists of each member presenting a brief synopsis of her experiences during the preceding week. This format not only permits member participation, but it also informs the members of each other's current situation. The exercise places responsibility upon the adolescent to request group or "air time" during a given session. For example, one adolescent may have had a fight with her boyfriend or parents during the week and wish to share the incident with the group. In a group with 8 to 12 members, it is important to request time to focus on a given member's problem, as it would be impossible to talk in depth with everyone in an hour-and-one-half. The other members benefit by the discussion of almost any topic because it usually pertains to their own situation in some way. As a unit, the group then plans the amount of time that will be devoted to the respective members. Usually this approach is quite successful, although on occasion the therapists must intervene with those members who are unusually quiet or withdrawn and who do not request time for themselves for a period of a few meetings. This is a good way for the therapist to monitor an adolescent's progress and hopefully identify any protection issues—recurrent sexual abuse.

Individual contracts are individual lists made by each member identifying her own strengths and "things to work on" or problem areas. This technique helps individuals focus on their own strengths and weaknesses and gives them a benchmark to refer back to as their behavior improves. Each member reads her contract aloud to the group and asks for comments and additions or deletions. Often adolescents with poor self-esteem will put nothing under the "strength" column. It is important for them to hear from group members that: "You're really pretty" or "I find you easy to talk to." Conversely, some adolescents will list only positives and nothing "to work on" as it is too threatening to look at their own problems. Again, it is helpful for them to hear: "You help everyone else with their problems but you never talk about yourself" or "Whenever anyone asks you a question you say 'I don't know.' I don't think you are trying hard enough—that's just a cop out."

Role playing is a favorite technique with the adolescents. This is a drama staged with members playing specific persons in a described scene. The scene may be anything from confronting mom for not protecting her child; or "What will I say to my father when I see him again?" to a courtroom scene. Any scene may be played out several times, each ending with a different outcome.

> One adolescent who had been severely physically and sexually abused by her father was facing her first visit with him in three years, as he had been incarcerated for the abuse. She had not wanted to see him previously, but in three months he was to be paroled and Louise feared he would kill her for having him arrested. In the group she role-played this first meeting three times. The first time, the scene ended with her stealing a gun from a guard and killing her father. The second ended with her telling him she never wanted to see him again, and the third ended with him being changed and Louise wishing to see him again. In reality, Louise was accompanied to the jail by one of the group therapists for support. This meeting lasted for an hour and included emotional sharing. Louise's father apologized for his behavior and said he was glad he had gone to jail or he would not have stopped the abuse. He asked to see her again, but Louise said that she never wanted to see him again as she still felt she did not trust him. The next week at the group she reported her decision and said it had helped first to run through all the possibilities, as it helped her to be prepared for the actual meeting and decreased some of her anxiety.

Arts Therapy can be used in four specific ways: for fun, to provide distraction from premature intimacy that threatens future involvement in the group; for diagnostic purposes; and for treatment purposes to work on problem areas such as poor body image. Arts therapy is an identified professional discipline and should be done by or under the supervision of a trained and certified arts therapist (see chapter 10).

Adolescents enjoy art and often use it as a means of expressing their feelings. It is a fun exercise that can be as simple or elaborate as the group members choose—from newsprint and crayons to marionettes. This type of exercise often provides relief from continuously intense discussions week after week. The skilled group therapist must recognize the importance of not allowing the group or a specific member to share too much too soon. Such sharing can cause feelings of "I told them too much, they [the group members] probably won't like me now. How will I ever face them again?" True interpersonal intimacy is something these adolescents have not experienced, and they become frightened at the level of trust necessary to build such a relationship.

Body image is a serious problem for the sexual abuse victim. As we have learned, the victim's guilt and shame is often expressed in negative self-esteem and poor body images. The adolescents will describe themselves as "fat and ugly" even though they are slender and very attractive young ladies. A useful art-therapy technique for body imaging is to have the members lie on cardboard and draw the outline of their body and then cut out their figure. Each person may decorate the figure in any way he or she pleases. Some individuals will design themselves while others will do "made-up or fantasy" people. Adolescents with a particularly poor body image find this a difficult exercise to do and either cannot complete the project (usually only drawing in the head and omitting the body completely) or draw only a fragmented person. If the member is emotionally able or receptive to such a project, it can promote a discussion of her own self-image.

Sex education is another way to correct the "damaged body" perception. Each victim of child sexual abuse should have a complete physical examination which contributes to "treatment" as well as to diagnosis and evidence collection. The examining physician, the supportive family members, and the therapist should allow the victim to discuss fears of bodily damages sustained and correct any false impressions. For victims to understand that "everything is O.K.," they need to know what "everything" is.

Traditionally, sex education is taught in school through the study of animals and plant pollination. Little emphasis is placed on the human reproductive system and its functioning either at school or at home. This lack of knowledge often reinforces the perception of damage. Therefore, in addition to the individual sharing, it may be helpful to invite a physician or a nurse (preferably female to a female group) to provide the members with the correct information. In this session, it is important to allow the members to ask questions of the health professional. This is usually more successful if the questions are written down prior to the meeting, as the adolescents are often too embarrassed to verbalize them. Distributing simple diagrams of the reproductive system helps the members to follow the discussion.

Other important components of sex education are information about birth control and venereal disease. Many adolescents will become involved in a series of sexual relationships to counteract their feeling that "no one would want me because I've had sex with Dad." This behavior reinforces poor self-esteem and may lead to unwanted pregnancies or sexually transmitted diseases which can create obvious additional problems for the immature, emotionally traumatized victim. Written reference information, such as the book, *Our Bodies Our Selves,* may also prove helpful.

Psychodynamically, many incestuous parents view themselves as very moral people and deny the child's sexuality. Therefore, the group leaders may run into interference from the parents when the group topic turns to sex education. To counteract, or at least minimize, parental resistance, the parents should be prepared in advance for this session. At STTP's first adolescent therapy group meeting concerned with sex education, many children were unable to attend because their parents telephoned and said their children were "sick." Before the next sex education session the parents were prepared in advance and group attendance was greatly improved.

Awareness of body language and movement is a technique available to both group members and group leaders. It is a nonverbal cue which helps in assessing an individual's mood. Group members who feel uncomfortable may sit outside of the group circle, may hold their heads down with their hair covering their eyes, or may refuse to make eye contact with anyone during a conversation. All of these nonverbal signals tell the other group members and the group leaders that the withdrawn individual is having a difficult time. Some members speak loudly and attempt to take over the group. By trying to gain control of their environment, they avoid close relationships. Meg was withdrawn initially, and when she was asked to share difficult and painful feelings she would look at her cookie and pick it apart as she talked. If she was feeling particularly angry, she would crush it. Often Meg's anger was expressed nonverbally through the crushing of the cookie. The therapists or group members should bring this behavior to the attention of the others in the group and try to help elicit a more appropriate form of expression.

Refreshments often proved to be a distraction from difficult topics for some members and a shared treat for others. This *symbolic nurturance* (or act of giving something nice to one another) proved to be an important treatment technique. In addition to the usual refreshments, the group leaders would provide a cake in celebration of each member's birthday. One sixteen-year-old girl cried and said, "this is the first time I have celebrated my birthday." These cakes are a recognition of each member's importance, uniqueness, and individuality. As the group becomes more cohesive the other members may wish to share the responsibility of bringing refreshments. It is a positive socialization process that they can actively share with one another.

Fun days—trips to the movies, picnicking, or camping—help in the socialization process and to reinforce self-esteem. In Connecticut's Sexual Trauma Treatment Program, the adolescent therapy group traveled to a YMCA camp for several weekends. Activities were planned so the girls might explore new opportunities. The girls helped one another in winter backpacking, cross-country skiing, meal preparation, and at night shared dancing and singing. Meg, having grown up in the ghetto, had never been cross-country skiing. At the camp, she attempted this activity for the first time and proved to be an excellent skier. Other weekend campers who did not know the group's origin praised Meg for her great skiing ability. Meg beamed with delight at her accomplishment, and laughed along with her group leader who continually fell into the snow. The camping experience allowed the group members to see that they could succeed at new things and that the therapists were human too.

If camping is not available, having a picnic, going to the movies, or roller skating are alternatives. If money is a problem, each member can contribute to an activity, a specially assigned job or task can help from further feelings of inadequacy. Fun days need not require money, just organization and creativity!

Role modeling is an ongoing process as the therapists demonstrate positive adult interaction. It is important for the group members to observe the therapists working together in a cooperative, consistent manner, demonstrating appropriate parental behavior. It is important to demonstrate interactions even when there is a disagreement between the leaders. One therapist may make a point which the other disagrees with. This should be handled by saying, "I have a different opinion about that: I might handle it this way." Open disagreement of this type shows the girls that it is acceptable to express another opinion without being critical or rejecting. Conversely, any type of open, honest communication establishes a forum for trust.

Immediate verbal praise for positive behavior and *reinforcement for expression of feelings* promote positive behavioral changes. The therapists should initiate such praise and encourage group members to praise one another. Often it is necessary to begin with the smallest improvements such as sharing of an honest feeling: "I (group member) would like to tell you (group) what's happened to me but I'm afraid. It hurts too much." Such a statement is difficult to make, requiring much courage by the traumatized member. The therapist may respond in several positive ways: "I'm glad you shared that with us. Everyone here has felt the same way you have at one time or another. If you think you can go on, we'd like to hear what you have to say. You may feel better once you've gotten it out."

For some victims, to be able to look another person in the eye as they are talking is a great accomplishment.

Some group members may be physically aggressive and punch others to show affection or anger. This behavior needs to be brought to the individual's attention. The adolescent needs to be told that if she needs a hug or some tenderness she should say so; she should learn to express anger verbally rather than by hitting and physically hurting someone.

Building self-esteem is a slow and arduous process. It can take months of continuous encouragement, reinforcement, and praise before any significant behavioral changes are seen. These techniques are successful, however, if used repeatedly and consistently over time.

The *concepts of responsibility and independence* promote autonomy giving these formerly powerless individuals the opportunity to have self-control. Every member should be encouraged to make her own decisions after exploring all viable alternatives, for example, to continue being seductive and risk further assault and reinforcement of poor self-image or to learn to relate to both males and females on a sincere level. Each member is asked to take responsibility by honestly expressing her feelings and encouraging one another to do the same. As each member becomes more responsible, she will begin to have a sense of independence. This can even happen for members who live with nonnurturing parents as they realize that their parents' behavior is not their fault, and that they can develop a different personality that is more appealing to them. Given permission to free themselves of their guilt, they can blossom into healthier persons.

All of these techniques help to promote group cohesiveness. An atmosphere which is safe, trusting, and nurturing provides a traumatized individual with the security to sort out questions of identity and future goals; an opportunity to learn new methods of healthy communication, and to grow as, and into, a person who likes herself and can live a satisfying life.

Assessment of the Group Process

Throughout the twenty months of STTP's adolescent therapy group, modifications were made, successful techniques were developed and expanded, and unsuccessful techniques were discarded.

The adolescent therapy group began with a nucleus of three members and grew to a maximum of thirteen. As the overall Sexual Trauma Treatment Program developed and the adolescent therapy group became an established treatment modality, its membership increased gradually and continuously. Enrollment was closed when the size reached thirteen, as the larger size decreased the amount of individual attention any one member could receive. This created some dissatisfaction on the part of the members. Eight to ten members appeared to be the optimum functioning size for two therapists with one-and-one-half-hour group sessions.

Each member was asked to make an initial commitment of six months to the adolescent therapy group. At this stage significant improvement began to occur for most members. Optimum benefit from group treatment occurred from between one-and-a-half to two years. Since the group was open-ended, "older" members proved to be good role models for newer members. Taking on leadership roles helped established members develop responsibility and greatly increased their self-esteem.

Whether a member remained in the adolescent therapy group for the minimum recommended period of time was contingent upon her ego strengths, willingness to trust group members and, most importantly, upon her family support systems. Frequently, the parents were skeptical about their daughter's involvement in the adolescent therapy group for a variety of reasons. Some parents incorrectly assumed that the therapists would share with them information about the group process and content of the discussions. Some parents were concerned about the disclosure of their identity, while other parents were concerned about the "gory" stories. When the girls displayed emotional pain by crying after an intense meeting, the parents would become disturbed and viewed the process as traumatic or regressive. Finally, parental resistance and anger often emerged whenever the therapists discussed sexuality or engaged in a formal process of sex education. Sensitivity to these issues can determine the success or failure of an effective adolescent group therapy program.

Extending the concept of individual worth was done by consistently reinforcing positive behavior with praise. With increased self-esteem, the girls began to lower their defenses, thereby facilitating the development of trust and intimacy. The members would then voluntarily contact one another outside of group meetings. Once these relationships were experienced as mutually satisfying, the members felt safe enough to reach out to their peer community, including involvement with boys of their own age or at least the formation of more comfortable relationships with males. In addition, school performance improved, daydreaming lessened, and an interest in extracurricular activities developed.

When a member first entered the group, she often exhibited a false sense of maturity. Over a period of time this would diminish and the adolescent would begin to display age-appropriate behavior.

The therapists also measured improved self-esteem through the members' ability to be assertive. Usually, upon entering the group, the majority of girls were passive, unquestioning, and unassertive. Their effect was one of total compliance. Growth was noted in their ability to challenge the therapists' statements on appropriate issues.

A valuable indicator of growth was a member's willingness to seek help in the event of repeated sexual abuse. Depending upon the circumstances, she would seek help from the group, her individual therapist, or her mother. Going to her mother was viewed as a reflection of improvement in the mother-daughter relationship.

Unfortunately, for most of STTP's population, the mother-daughter relationship remained fragmented by poor communication and by mutual feelings of rejection. Although the daughters were angry with their mothers for not protecting them and for being emotionally unavailable at the time of the sexual abuse, they would not express such feelings for fear of suffering further rejection. Many of the mothers regarded their daughters as competitors, which further inhibited the establishment of healthier mother-daughter relationships. A larger cross-section of group members may have produced more successful results.

In certain cases, the therapists were unable to engage an adolescent in the group process for a multitude of reasons. These included the severity of trauma experienced or pressure from family members. For whatever reason, the therapists found that these individuals would misdirect their anger and blame to the therapists or group for their lack of progress. Within a short period of time they began to discuss termination. Since these girls were at high risk for recurrent sexual and even physical abuse, the therapists and group members attempted to predict the negative scenario which might result if the girls left the group. After leaving the group, a number of girls returned several months later requesting help because these predictions had been accurate. These predictions, in turn, increased the therapists' credibility with the clients.

Another indicator of improvement was a member's ability openly to express feelings of love, hate, fear, or sympathy for their fathers. Some of the members shared both the positive and negative aspects of their sexual relationship with their fathers. The sexual relationship afforded them special attention, emotional intimacy, and power within the family. Working through their angry feelings at their fathers for the violation and control of their bodies and their own guilt for participation in the incestuous relationship enabled a redefinition of the relationship. For some, the redefinition resulted in a superficial relationship; for others, a deeper involvement with some degree of understanding and acceptance; for still others, the termination of further contact with their father.

Through this resolution process, the therapists often observed a decrease in the sexual and intimacy problems which have historically characterized the incest victim.

In spite of these progressive changes, several complications arose in the group. Many of the members experienced suicidal ideation. Individuals who had suicidal ideation showed a reluctance to introduce these feelings in group meetings. Although we are unclear about this reticence, we know that the individual members were extremely embarrassed to share this information. It may be related to their feelings that they had created enough "problems" already by disclosing the incest secret. They may have feared further rejection or perhaps suicide is viewed as another "taboo topic." This phenomenon required that the cotherapists be constantly aware of each member's situation and sensitive to minute changes in behavior and attitude which might indicate suicidal thoughts.

The therapists' first experience with suicidal ideation in the group, occurred

when Diane, age 16, arrived for a session. Unlike her usual talkative, bubbly
self, she was quiet, thoughtful, and withdrawn. In spite of her apparent sadness,
she denied any problems. Due to the group's concern, support, and persistence
about her changed demeanor, she finally stated she had attempted suicide
several days earlier. Diane related this information with much shame, embarrassment, and initial reluctance. As she opened-up further, it became obvious
that she was still suicidal. After the group session was over, Diane expressed
a desire to return home. By emphasizing the seriousness of her situation, the
therapists convinced her to be seen by a physician. Fortunately, through an
established relationship with a physician consultant at a nearby community
hospital, the therapists were able to have her evaluated immediately. On the
basis of the collateral evaluation, it was decided that Diane could return home,
but needed close monitoring.

The action of the therapists was therapeutic by providing her with support,
interest and guidance during her crisis. This initial experience stimulated the
therapists to explore suicidal ideation in the other group members. The response
was overwhelming. *Every* member talked of suicidal feelings and the various
ways she had coped with these feelings. The suicidal ideation ranged from
taking a few aspirins and just becoming sick, to one member who threw herself
naked into an ice-filled river.

One area where the group was particularly helpful was in the preparation
for criminal and juvenile court hearings. Role playing a courtroom scene appeared to be a valuable technique, not only to improve performance but in
decreasing the individual's anxiety.

However, this is an area where the therapists were less successful in predicting the outcome as the criminal court process is arduous, intimidating, and
demeaning for the victim. Cases may be continued for a year or more, and then
the child frequently faces a belligerent defense attorney. Through an interrogation of her sexual relationships with other males, he ultimately may imply that
she is a whore, responsible for seducing her father.

As the therapists who accompanied Melissa and her sisters to the courtroom,
we found ourselves totally unprepared for her demoralizing cross-examination.
Up until that moment, Melissa, age 17, was overtly a strong person manifesting
little emotion. The sexual abuse began with intercourse at age 11 with her
stepfather. Soon afterwards, he involved her in prostitution and drugs which
led to heroin addiction. For the next five years of her life, her only survival
was to live off the streets. Upon referral to STTP, Melissa exhibited a façade
of callousness and emotional indifference and yet the badgering of the defense
attorney penetrated her hardened exterior. After her testimony, Melissa left the
courtroom and literally collapsed on the floor in hysterics. Her rejecting mother,
who overlooked the scene, stated, "you got what you deserved for causing us
all this trouble."

In view of this kind of experience, it is understandable that many of the
members were appropriately disillusioned with the criminal justice system.

Fortunately, until Melissa's case, the other hearings had been much more humane. This demeaning and intimidating attorney had taken the therapists by surprise. It had been a painful initiation process for the therapists as well as Melissa. Once armed with this unfortunate knowledge, the therapists and group members were able to prepare other victims who were to testify for any circumstance. As the therapists and group better prepared the members, the hearings became less traumatic. One fourteen-year-old who had role played both the positive and negative court experience, expressed her disappointment when her father pleaded guilty and she was not needed to testify. She said, "I wanted them [the court] to hear what happened to me, what I had to say." When any difficult circumstance faces the victims, honesty in discussing all possible alternatives is the only way to minimize the risks of further trauma.

Our present criminal justice system is, at this time, the only viable course for ordering manipulative perpetrators into treatment and ultimately deterring or eliminating further sexual molestation of the victim, the victims' siblings, or other outside children. In addition to the victim's preparation, it is the therapist-advocate's obligation to communicate with the prosecutors, defense attorneys, and judges regarding these difficulties in an attempt to minimize further trauma to the victim.

Regardless of the topics discussed, the key components to establishing a successful group were having a core group of committed members and therapists. Therapists need to be actively involved with the group, providing transportation if needed, extending time before and after sessions and during the week to individuals who need extra attention, and possessing a willingness to be flexible in their approach to the adolescents—confronting and direct when necessary, and quiet and passive at times when members emerged as positive, appropriate group leaders.

Finally, one member beautifully summed up the adolescent therapy group's purpose when she said:

> The group has given me a place to go, to be able to talk, to say what I felt, be angry if I wanted, be happy if I wanted, by myself. Instead of at . . . where I felt like I was acting a part to keep my family together, to make everybody happy; here it helped a lot to be able to talk to somebody.

Running a group of this nature is a difficult and emotionally draining task which requires a high energy level and spontaneous flexibility from the cotherapists. There are several advantages for utilizing two therapists for this modality.

First, the shared responsibility allows for diffusion of anger and hostility expressed by the members who regard the therapists as surrogate parents. When one therapist is engaged with an individual member, it allows the other therapist to be sensitive to the nonverbal messages conveyed by the other members. The cotherapist dyad affords role-modeling of adult behavior, including conflicts resolved in an accepting manner.

Since all of the members have experienced maternal rejection, it is strongly felt that two female cotherapists can facilitate working through hostility-abandonment feelings. Afterwards, group members can begin to develop a positive relationship with a woman who has been consistently supportive and nurturant while simultaneously maintaining appropriate limits and boundaries. In addition, since there is a general discomfort culturally with females discussing intimate issues in the presence of males (which is further compounded by the sexual abuse), the program staff was concerned that the presence of a male therapist in this initial group would inhibit the girls from talking. It is important at some stage that the girls interact with an appropriate adult male for role-modeling purposes.

Due to programmatic constraints, the therapists discussed but were not able to implement an additional group. Ideally, certain "advanced" members would move into this group coled by a male and female therapist. This would provide them with role-modeling of parental figures as well as help them deal with their feelings about men and their method of relating to them.

The therapists should bring to the group a strong base of knowledge in group treatment and adolescent behavior. Each therapist must define her role with the other therapist and constantly communicate any personal feelings or factual information they have about the group. Mutual support during the program is important to help maintain the therapist through stressful periods.

References

Burgess, Ann W., and Holmstrom, Lynda L. "Sexual Assault of Children and Adolescents: Pressure, Sex and Secrecy." *Nursing Clinics of North America* (September 1975).

6 Sibling Incest

Carlos M. Loredo

Although the most frequently reported type of incest is parental, usually involving father and daughter, the most common form of incest may be sexual activity among siblings, typically between brother and sister. Sibling incest describes a sexual interaction between individuals who have one or both parents in common. Sibling incest may take the form of brother-sister, brother-brother, or sister-sister interactions.

Historically, much has been written about sibling incest (Santiago, 1973). In ancient Egypt, sibling incest and marriage were openly sanctioned. Other societies in pre-Columbian America and in certain areas of Polynesia permitted and often compelled males of royal families to wed their sisters (Haeberle, 1979). Clinically, however, it is agreed that relatively little is known about sibling incest (Poznanski and Blos, 1975; Sagarin, 1977).

Research Literature

Brother-sister incest is the most common type of sibling incest reported, although some references allude to the other two types of interactions (Benward and Densen-Gerber, 1975; Rhinehart, 1962; Wathey and Densen-Gerber, 1976). It has been suggested that although the most frequently reported type of incest is typically father-daughter (Justice and Justice, 1979; Lester, 1972; Lukianowicz, 1972; Meiselman, 1978), the most common form of incest that occurs is between brother and sister (Weeks, 1976; Weiner, 1962). Other research indicates that girls are equally as likely to participate in sibling incest as in parent-child incest (Benward and Densen-Gerber, 1975): In this study sister-sister was the most common form of sibling incest. It has also been reported that boys are as likely to participate in incestuous relationships with brothers as with their step-fathers (Wathey and Densen-Gerber, 1976).

Carlos M. Laredo, Ph.D., received the bachelor's, master's, and Ph.D. degrees in counseling psychology from the University of Texas. He specializes in the areas of child psychology, victim and offender treatment for physical and sexual abuse, and divorce/separation mediation. He has published several chapters and articles on physical and sexual abuse. Dr. Laredo currently teaches at the Austin Community College, serves as a consultant for several agencies in Austin, Texas, and has a private practice in psychology.

Some investigators suggest that sibling incest does not involve the stressful ties that are apparent in parent-child incest, so that sibling incest may go unnoticed and undetected (Poznanski and Blos, 1975). The effects of sibling incest have been attributed to the age discrepancy of the participants (Justice and Justice, 1979), age of the victim and anxiety of the parents (Lester, 1972), and consent of the victim (Benward and Densen-Gerber, 1975). Some studies suggest that brother-sister incest is the least damaging of all sexual interactions between siblings (Arndt and Ladd, 1976; Weeks, 1976) and produces few or no ill psychiatric effects (Lukianowicz, 1972b).

Clinical Observations

Sibling incest occurs for numerous and multiple reasons. It may be a result of sexual curiosity and experimentation among siblings and may evolve out of sex play that has "gone too far." Sibling incest may exist due to situational pressures, personality disorders and dysfunctions within a family system, or assumptions of inappropriate roles within the family system. Sometimes, the sexual interaction(s) may be encouraged or forced by a third party, perhaps the parents.

Sibling incest may not always be a situation involving one victim and one aggressor. Both may willingly engage in the behavior as an attempt to cope with unmet needs. Such needs may include a desire for affiliation and affection; a combating of loneliness, depression, and a sense of isolation; and a discharging of anxiety and tension due to stress. Other more violent forms of sibling incest occur, involving a clear aggressor who acts out sexually with a weaker sibling to gratify needs for retaliation, retribution, power, or control.

Assessment

A thorough assessment of both immediate and long-range effects of sibling incest requires a careful and in-depth evaluation, as evidenced by the following case example:

> Sally, an attractive 35 year-old woman, was referred by a friend for symptoms of depression. Sally and Bruce are married and have two children, Teddie (2½) and Cindy (9 months). Since Cindy's birth, Sally has run away from home and left the children unattended and has overdisciplined Teddie on several occasions. Further inquiry revealed that Sally had attempted suicide while in her early 20s, but had been apprehended as she tried to jump off the bridge. She blamed her state of mind at that time to depression. She indicated that she had gone to a therapist and had discussed a 10-year-old incestuous relationship involving her brother.

During Sally's evaluation, it became apparent that (1) the incestuous relationship had barely been discussed with the previous therapist; (2) her depression and anxiety were directly related to the birth of her daughter, whom she perceived as another sex victim; (3) Teddie was projected by Sally into the role of Cindy's (future) sex abuser; and (4) her flights and depression pertained to her anxiety over an upcoming family reunion involving the sexually abusive brother and their parents, who had knowingly allowed the behavior to continue despite Sally's pleas. After making initial rapid progress, Sally discontinued therapy, against the therapist's recommendations. She returned several months later after experiencing a fugue state. Sally maintained feelings of anger toward her brother and parents and had personal feelings of worthlessness. Because of the victimization, she had assumed that (1) one must cope with all problems by one's self and (2) expression of feelings and needs were signs of weakness. So even though Sally had been a quiet, obedient, and studious person throughout high school and college, she experienced as a result of the victimization severe (and unrecognized) trauma culminating in attempted suicide, physical child abuse, and a fugue state.

In order to differentiate sexual behavior among siblings that is harmless curiosity and experimentation from interactions that are potentially detrimental and symptomatic of unresolved psychological concerns, a number of issues must be addressed:

Normal Sexual Behavior. The task of identifying what is "typical or normal" sexual behavior and exploration between siblings is a difficult one. Due to cultural, ethnic, geographic, and individual differences, the notion of typical sexual behavior among siblings becomes a relative issue. The clinician, however, must determine the likelihood of both short- and long-term effects. As such, one must assess whether the incest involves (1) some aspect of victimization, or (2) two or more willing participants, exhibiting some form of psychopathology. One must also recognize that even in cases involving no victims or psychopathology, long-term effects should not be overlooked: for example, prepubertal sibling incest can produce adjustment difficulties as participants begin dating, sexually interacting with peers, or becoming sexual partners with a mate in their later adult life.

Nature and Duration of Incest. What type of sexual activity is occurring and how long has it lasted? Is it consistent with the developmental level of the participants (for example, looking, exposing, fondling, and so forth) or is it age-inappropriate and reflecting more advanced sexual knowledge and experience than would be expected from a child of the given age (for example, sodomy, fellatio, intercourse)?

The literature indicates that the nature and duration of sexual victimization are related to traumatic effects on the victim. Although the nature and duration of the behavior may contribute to feelings of victimization in some cases, the emotional impact of sibling incest does not appear to be highly correlated to these two factors alone.

Six-year-old Gina had engaged in intercourse with the family dog, her 11-year old brother, and multiple incest with her father and brother for the past two years. Apparently little trauma seemed to be generated by the sibling incest and bestiality (her brother had masturbated the dog) for the two children. The main difficulty centered about a physically and sexually abusive father who had manipulated the three oldest children to perform in the "circus." He had bribed them with gifts and allowed them to miss school. The children were also physically beaten by him (belt buckles, fists, and boards) to remind them of what would occur to them should they disclose the sexual activity. The mother worked for long hours to maintain a steady income and was unaware of the sexual activity. She responded appropriately to the disclosure, filing charges, and offering unconditional support to the children. The children were both terrified that the father would abuse them following disclosure, were glad he was gone, and missed his "kind" attentions. They were curiously nonchalant about the sibling incest and bestiality. Some incestuous behavior continued during the early phases of individual and family therapy (father absent), but was discontinued. Neither child demonstrated adverse effects during the two-year follow up. Their most difficult adjustments were to the new limits imposed by their mother. The determinant factor in this case was the quick, empathic, and supportive responses of the mother. The long-term effects may not be evident, however, until the children reach puberty.

Access to Victim. How did participants become involved? Did it occur through mutual agreement and negotiation, or did one sibling gain sexual access to the other through deception, intimidation, or force?

Consensual. Did both agree to the interaction, or was there an initial consent to exploration and sex play but an unwillingness to proceed any further? At times, participants may have agreed to invitations of "fooling around," even though a younger sibling may not have been aware of the sexual implications. It is important to note that even though a sibling may have cooperated, it does not follow that consent was given, or that the sexual nature of the interactions was completely understood. As the previous case example would indicate, some consensual sexual interactions might occur as a result of other prior sexual experiences. Although consensual sibling sexual interactions may not produce immediate deleterious effects, the significance of such actions may not be apparent until much later in adult life.

Enticement. Was a person's naïveté exploited? With younger brothers and sisters, candy, money, or special privileges may be granted to obtain sexual participation from the child. As the child matures and becomes aware of the duplicity, the enticing behavior fails to have the desired effect. At this juncture, other more aggressive means would have to be employed by the perpetrator unless he or she did not want to hurt the victim. To continue the incest, the offender would proceed only as "far as she wanted to go"; provide bigger and better rewards for the "victim"; or result to intimidation or force.

> Glenda, age 14, had first agreed to holding hands and sitting in her brother's lap. This progressed to back rubbing and massages. In talking with her peers, Glenda discovered that her brother had not been honest with her. When approached again, Glenda told her brother to stop or she would tell her parents. Her brother complied and never again approached her sexually.

Intimidation. Were threats, curses, and other aggressive verbal expressions used to obtain compliance? Some may threaten to tell parents or friends intimate details of sexual involvements that the victim has sought out and enjoyed. These are usually fabricated by the perpetrator. With this mode, guilt and shame are typically used to gain the sexual interaction.

> Connie is 42 years old, self-referred for interpersonal difficulties. During the course of therapy, she noted that her brother had first enticed her into masturbation. Her brother took pictures and then threatened to send copies to her teachers and friends unless she complied. When Connie refused, her brother mailed her a print to their home address. Thereafter, Connie had regular intercourse with her brother for three more years, until she told her boyfriend who "pounded him to a pulp."

At times, the abuser may insinuate that lack of cooperation will invite further, more violent and degrading abuse.

Physical Force. To what extent was force necessary to obtain compliance? Physical force may be utilized to overcome a resistant or unwilling participant. For some abusers, however, excessive and violent force, not sex, becomes eroticized and serves as the source of pleasure or gratification from the behavior. Sibling incest of this nature may involve objects introduced into the orifices of the victim; physical abuse; bondage; and forced sexual contact with animals. Use of physical force is not common in sibling incest. Evidence of such behaviors, however, is indicative of pathology and perhaps severe dysfunction.

Intent of Participants. What were their motivations? How persistent is the activity? Does it occur as one part of broader interests and interactions, or does it appear to be an excessive preoccupation activity that predominates in the sibling relationship?

Exploration. Sibling incest of this type is probably the most common, least reported, and least traumatic of all types of sibling incest. It is important to recognize that infants and children derive pleasure from stimulation of erogenous zones, yet they are "sexually inarticulate" (Haeberle, 1979). It is only through social conditioning and development that children learn to interpret certain actions, activities, and social encounters as erotic and having sexual connotations. Such activities as playing "doctor" and "spin the bottle" provide children an opportunity to explore each other and themselves in the company of others. Such behaviors need not have a sexual motivation nor do they necessarily serve to gratify sexual needs at that time. Sexual exploration can occur as part of normal social development, or as a result of social contacts with others. Since siblings frequently spend a great deal of time with each other, some degree of sexual exploration between them can be anticipated. Where consensual exploration takes place, little trauma will be generated, although some guilt and embarrassment may occur during adolescence for fear of being "found out."

Retribution. The aim of the abuser is to get even for past injustices. Incestuous behavior is used to degrade and humiliate the victim. The ultimate goal of the incestuous offender is to express anger. The victim and the sexual act are the means used to achieve that goal.

Power-Control. Although similar to incidents involving retribution, the underlying intent is to manipulate, overpower, and control the victim. Fear, intimidation, threat, and force can all be employed to obtain the desired outcome.

Sadism. By far the most life-threatening of all types of sibling incest are those perpetrated by the sadist. Excessive force and violence are used to obtain submission, but it is the degree of force and pain experienced by the victim that become the arousing stimuli for the perpetrator. These kinds of attacks may have serious physical and psychological long-term effects on the victim.

> Genie is a 21-year-old college student who is extremely shy and withdrawn and rarely leaves her dorm room. She indicated that her 13-year-old brother began fondling her at age 4. This was followed by manual masturbation, which progressed to masturbation using sticks, bottles, and vegetables. He would gag and beat Genie until she began sobbing and shaking. It was at this point that he would introduce some foreign object(s) into Genie's vagina or anus. As the abuse would become excruciatingly painful to Genie, her brother would go to the corner of the room and masturbate to orgasm. The attacks became more and more violent, leading to fireplace pokers rammed into her vagina until she passed out from the pain. "Toward the end, he didn't seem satisfied unless I bled or had welts."

Age of Siblings. What is the age relationship between the siblings involved? Are they peers, or is one sibling significantly older than the other?

Although age and age discrepancy of participants are not directly related to severity of trauma, several factors must be understood. Where participants are peers, two distinctions must be made. With younger children, both participants would be more likely to engage in sexual behavior solely for exploratory, non-agressive reasons, as compared to older counterparts. Older participants would be more likely to understand sexual connotations. As such, sibling incest by adolescents is more likely to involve pathologically disturbed individuals.

Where there is a large age difference between the siblings, one must investigate cues that perhaps the older sibling is beginning to develop a fixation for younger children. Large age discrepancies also lend themselves to abuse, control, and exploitation of younger, more naïve siblings.

Predisposition of Siblings. The effects of sibling incest will be influenced by the personality characteristics of the siblings. Different types of victims will react to the same type of assault in a variety of ways. An offense committed against a confident, self-assured sibling would not be likely to be as debilitating as one perpetrated upon a sibling who is shy, depressed, passive, and withdrawn.

The more severely disturbed individuals will be more likely to commit the forced-sadistic offenses. Upon investigation, the clinician is likely to discover that many of the aggressive offenders are themselves the victims of sexual abuse.

Family Dynamics. Is there something occurring within the family to activate sibling incest? Are children being sexually stimulated by witnessing sexual behavior on the part of the parents? (See second case example.) Are they exposed to pornography or sexually explicit material? In all cases of sibling incest the possibility of other types of incestuous behavior within the family needs to be investigated. Are circumstances such that roles have been reassigned within the family?

It is important to determine sources of strength and support within the family. What alliances, if any, will be formed with the victim and offender? Will these alliances perpetuate or interrupt the incestuous activity? Do parents have an investment in keeping the entire matter quiet? If so, what appear to be their overriding concerns?

Disclosure of Activity. In the majority of clinical cases parents and other persons in a position of authority within the home were aware that incestuous behavior was taking place within the home. In some instances parental figures had witnessed the interaction. Sometimes, parents were told by a caretaker or another relative that they had witnessed such an incident. At times, parents were told by the victim that he or she was being molested.

I didn't think anything of the screams. I thought it was someone else—it's real noisy around here. . . . No, I was not bothered by her bloody underwear,

'cause I thought she was just having a lot of problems with her period. . . .
I never thought about why her underclothes and bras were torn.

When parents first become aware of the incest, victims expressed a sense
of relief because they believed that parents would intervene in their behalf and
the abuse would stop. In the majority of cases the parents disregarded the
allegations, asked the victim to keep quiet, or tried to disassociate themselves
from any additional awareness that sibling incest was continuing. In most instances incest activity resumed several weeks following the disclosure, accompanied by threats or demonstrations of drastic retaliations, because the parents
had been told. At this point, many victims resigned themselves to passive
resistance, until such time as they were assured of escape or protection. Others
simply gave in and lived for the day that they got married, or their brother left
the house.

Parents have a variety of reactions to public disclosure ranging from incre-
dulity and rage to apparent disinterest. Often times parents only express concern
over what neighbors might think or say.

> I could see them from my bed while he was doing it. I was afraid to yell out,
> because if I did, I knew he would hurt me worse. And my folks knew what
> was going on. I had told them several times, but they told me to keep quiet
> since I would disgrace the family if anybody found out. I think my brother left
> the door open on purpose. They could have seen what was going on, but they
> acted like nothing was going on.

It is a sad and true commentary that not all parents care about their children.
Other parents do not think about the best interest of children. In fact many adult
clients often relate that lack of parental responsibility (denial, complicity, failure
to protect) was more traumatic than the effects of the sibling incest.

Case Management Issues

Denial of Impact. An interesting clinical note is that once sibling incest was
uncovered or revealed, many clients indicated no difficulties resulting from the
incest. This outcome was belied by underlying dynamics of conflict, confusion,
or guilt that were identified by the clinician. Denial of ill effects was particularly
characteristic of adult clients who typically noted that the incest was a thing of
the past and of no further concern to them. For many of these same adult clients,
unresolved conflicts resulting from sibling incest were major therapeutic issues,
nevertheless.

Family Focus. All interventions must have a child and family focus. The needs
of the victim are the primary concerns, yet interventions must address the family

system whenever the victim is still a child and often when the victim is an adult. To be able to function effectively within that system, the clinician must try to form an alliance with the parent(s) so they are reassured that their needs will also be addressed. For the victim who is now an adult, unresolved issues of secrecy, parental denial or compliance, or parental response to disclosure may all be business that must be addressed with still living parents.

Response to Disclosure. It is a well-known fact that the responses of parents and other persons involved with the family can compound the trauma and the victim's recovery. Facilitative responses would be those that reassured the victim, showed interest in the victim's needs, and allowed all parties included to express feelings and emotions related to the incident. An important point is not to overreact. Do not reveal feelings of revulsion or disgust or convey a condescending or judgmental attitude about the victim, offender, family, or incident.

Initial Contact. The initial contact with the siblings, family, or client is of *utmost* importance. Where initial involvement began with the initial crisis intervention, ''success'' was greatly facilitated. In cases where crisis intervention did not occur, or was conducted by someone else, participants were much more difficult to engage.

Remember that during the initial contact, complaints may be vague and the explanations of incidents unclear and puzzling. It may be that your presence is not appreciated. A flexible, understanding, and firm approach is necessary.

Approach. Be calm and reassuring. Make your purposes clear and invite questions. *Avoid* threats: A firm and assertive posture obviates the need for threat. Be sure to interview family members separately. This will provide the clinician with valuable information and will allow all interested parties to disclose without having to worry about being overheard. Insure them that as few people as possible will be involved, and that their rights to privacy will be insured. Do not forget to address and clarify the issue of confidentiality. Parents and children must understand that their case and their difficulties will be handled with care and sensitivity. They must also understand that the proper agency, authority, or individual will be notified, and there are conditions which might warrant breaking the confidentiality agreement (continued physical-sexual abuse; coercion; evidence of severe pathology).

Therapeutic Context. Initially, issues of incestuous activity and dynamics may dominate the therapeutic discussion. As the incest is dealt with, however, the true, underlying problems will then surface. The incest is a symptom, not the problem. Prevention of further difficulties necessitate that these problems are dealt with and resolved in the therapeutic intervention.

Many of these case management issues are illustrated by the following example. The ensuing discussion is a personal account of my own intervention approach to sibling incest.

> A referral of suspected sibling incest was made by a child welfare worker from an outlying county. The family lived in a small (under 300 persons) farming community and had been visited by the social worker. The family was very resistant, and the social worker was somewhat intimidated by the issue of incest. The visit ended in threats of termination of parental rights. I agreed to visit their family in their home (100 miles away), since they refused to come to the clinic. Numerous phone calls were made and the appointment finally scheduled. I arrived at their home and knocked for about five minutes. After I had been sitting on the porch for one hour, Mrs. White came out to the porch, and I introduced myself. She said that the children were with her parents and her husband did not want me there. I empathized with their position, and her feelings of being intruded upon and resentment to having been told that her children would be taken away. I talked to her about incest; its effects; my methods of interaction; and the need for intervention. I waited for her husband and had a similar conversation with him. We agreed to have the children talk to me during the following week.
>
> The following week, the parents informed me that they had talked with the principal, who decided that I would have to speak with him before I could talk to the children. I again discussed my need (and their interest) for privacy and confidentiality. They agreed to have the children present for my next visit, and I came the following week and spoke with the children. It was very difficult to obtain any information from them. Anytime I tried to speak with one of them, the other two would crowd around the house, bushes, or climb the trees to overhear our conversation. I finally took the victim to the middle of a plowed field and asked her brothers to leave us alone for a few minutes. We sat on the ground and talked about her horses and pigs. As Pattie relaxed, it was evident that she wanted to discuss what had happened but was ashamed to say certain words because her mother had instilled very religious values. So we drew stick figures and enacted stories on our dirt ''blackboard.'' In this manner Pattie was able to relate her story of incest with her two older brothers. Pattie wanted to tell her mother, so I assisted her in doing so. She also told her father of the events. We discussed ways for all of us to approach the incident and the situation. Five additional visits were made. Once the parents were allied with the therapy, the intervention proceeded very quickly.

The crucial elements in this case were maintaining a firm stance about my sincere desire to help, as well as my insistence that I would not make a judgment as to what had occurred, because regardless of *what* had happened, there had to be some difficulty with the school, the children, or both. I was very careful to be as inobtrusive as possible, and not invade their life, even though I was obviously intruding, and initially not welcome. My emphasis was to demonstrate that I was on their side. They cared about their children, did not want to lose parental rights, and wanted to raise good children. I persisted, in spite of their initial efforts to discourage therapy: keeping the children away from home; failure to respond; their stated inconvenience of going to the physical location where therapy was being offered; use of authority figure to dissuade my talking to the children; and missed phone calls and appointments. Once I earned the family's trust, we explored the dynamics of the reported incest. Apparently it was a one-time incident, where one brother attempted to carry out his friend's instructions, while his other brother watched. Once the dynamics were uncovered, the parents held a family meeting, where all was aired and discussed with the support and encouragement of the parents.

Therapeutic Considerations: How I Do Therapy

1. *Determination.* Therapists must be willing to persist with both the client and family. At least half of the cases I have encountered could have been dismissed as client "resistance." As I later discovered, my persistence often was the key in establishing family trust.

2. *Flexibility.* Closely related is the therapist's ability to meet client needs. If you are unable or unwilling to make crisis intervention calls, personally interact with involved agencies, make home visits, offer family therapy, extend the "50-minute hour," or become an advocate for the client, your "success" rate will be relatively low.

3. *Confrontation.* I am continually surprised and chagrined by the number of child and adult clients who have previously received therapy for sibling incest and have *never* discussed *any* aspects of the sexual activities with their therapist. The majority of the therapists, however, were told of the incestuous activity. One must assess and treat the incestuous behavior by discussing the facts, exploring the causes, and examining the effects of the behavior on the *entire* family system. Many therapists, because of discomfort with their own sexuality or childhood sexual experiences, refuse to discuss sexual issues with the client and family. Therapists must be willing to confront client and family denial of *any* adverse effect resulting from the sibling incest. It is much too easy, and detrimental, to believe the typical response that "OK, it's just something that happened once."

4. *Advocacy.* Children's welfare is often overlooked by many "concerned" individuals, including parents, the courts, and helping professionals. We helping professionals understand the need for child advocacy and often suggest that this advocacy is not within our therapeutic purview. Therapists must get out from behind their desks, out of their offices, and into the courts, the homes, and the political system. We must become socially and ethically responsible.

5. *Family secrets.* All family members must be interviewed separately during the early stages of therapy. Interviews where privacy and confidentiality cannot be assured may not provide much relevant information, because family members may be afraid of retribution and punishment. Where individuals are

provided a supportive and nonjudgmental environment, it is much more likely that the therapists will discover individual-family dynamics that are critical to the treatment process.

6. *Milieu treatment*. Therapists must address the role of family, society, and environment on the client. As such, a family focus is necessary. Issues of security, protection, and emotional support must be examined. Therapists must explore peer influence and peer pressure. Social environment must be assessed to determine its contributing factors, if any. Religious, cultural, and ethnic mores must be explored with the family to determine how these values would be likely to affect the family. Any detrimental attitudes or behaviors need to be discussed and the family must be prepared to deal with them.

References

Arndt, W.G., and Ladd, B. "Brother-Sister Incest Aversion, Guilt, and Neurosis." Unpublished paper, University of Missouri Psychology Department, 1976.

Benward, J., and Densen-Gerber, J. "Incest as a Causative Factor in Anti-Social Behavior: An Exploratory Study." *Contemporary Drug Problems* 4 (1975):322–40.

Haeberle, E.J. *The Sex Atlas: A New Illustrated Guide*. New York: The Seabury Press, 1978.

Justice, B., and Justice, R. *The Broken Taboo: Sex in the Family*. New York: Human Sciences Press, 1979.

Lester, D. "Incest." *Journal of Sex Research* 8(1972):268–85.

Lukianowicz, N. "Incest—I: Paternal Incest." *British Journal of Psychiatry* 120(1972):301–308(a).

Lukianowicz, N. "Incest—II: Other Types of Incest." *British Journal of Psychiatry* 120 (1972):308–313b.

Meiselman, K.C. *Incest: A Psychological Study of Causes and Effects with Treatment Recommendations*. San Francisco: Jossey-Bass, Inc., 1978.

Poznanski, E., Blos, P., Jr. "Incest." *Medical Aspects of Human Sexuality* 9, 10(1975):461–63.

Rhinehart, J.W. Genesis of Overt Incest. *Comprehensive Psychiatry* 2 (1962):338–49.

Sagarin, E. "Incest: Problems of Definition and Frequency." *The Journal of Sex Research* 13, 2(1977):126–35.

Santiago, L.P.R. *The Children of Oedipus: Brother-Sister incest in Psychiatry, Literature, History, and Mythology*. New York: Libra Publishers, Inc., 1973.

Wathey, R., and Densen-Gerber, J. "Incest: An Analysis of the Victim and the

Aggressor." Paper presented at the 3rd Annual National Drug Abuse Conference. New York: March 1976.

Weeks, R.B. "The Sexually Exploited Child." *Southern Medical Journal* 69, 7(1976):848–50.

Weiner, I.B. "Father-Daughter Incest: A Clinical Report." *The Psychiatric Quarterly* 36, 1962:607–32.

Individual and Group Treatment of Mothers of Incest Victims

Suzanne M. Sgroi and
Natalie T. Dana

Any program which deals with incest must emphasize therapeutic intervention with mothers of incest victims and develop treatment modalities aimed at these women. Since the needs of individual clients differ, it is preferable to have a variety of treatment modalities for mothers. These women tend to be so needy that most will require multiple treatment modalities either successively or in concert: individual therapy, mothers group therapy, couples therapy, family therapy, parent group therapy, and the like. It is of course, very difficult and often counterproductive to treat the incest victim who remains at home without also providing treatment for other family members. The victim's mother, in particular, should be a focus for therapeutic intervention.

Vigorous outreach and concrete support are the sine qua non for treatment of mothers in incestuous families. Most of these women do not seek out treatment for themselves; those who do are likely to be under pressure by others, especially other family members, to withdraw from treatment. All need to receive outreach efforts by those who would treat them. At the same time, the outreach efforts must "feel like help"—that is, concrete assistance with the mundane everyday problems that often seem so overwhelming to the mother who may, for the first time in her life, be grappling with the problem-solving required.

We found it impossible to reach out effectively and engage mothers of incest victims in treatment without using the modality of individual therapy. In other words, we were not able to work successfully with mothers via other treatment modalities unless individual therapy was also used. On the other hand, the individual therapist who decided that a mother should also receive one of the other treatment modalities had to present the additional therapeutic intervention in the early stages of their relationship. Otherwise, the mothers almost uniformly resisted participation in other treatment modalities. We speculate that their low self-esteem, lack of trust, isolation, and fear of developing new

Natalie T. Dana, M.S.W., is presently a clinical supervisor for the Connecticut Child Welfare Association Child Abuse CAREline. She was a child-welfare worker for ten years in the Connecticut Department of Children and Youth Services, serving the last two years as a staff member in the Sexual Trauma Treatment Program. Mrs. Dana worked primarily with mothers whose children were victims of sexual abuse and served as coleader of a mothers treatment group.

relationships were powerful factors mitigating against their participation in anything other than a one-on-one relationship. Accordingly, simultaneous participation in other treatment modalities had to be introduced as soon as possible as a "therapeutic package" in concert with individual therapy.

Dynamics

In our experience, most of the mothers of incest victims exhibited behavior patterns that were consistent with the two modes of husband-wife interaction described by Dr. A. Nicholas Groth: dominant husband or dependent husband (see chapter 8). Wives of dominant husbands tended to be women with very low self-esteem and limited social skills who, in general, acceded to the extremely dependent and passive position relegated to them. In contrast, wives of dependent husbands tended to be stronger and more self-assertive women with greater capabilities and better developed social skills. Wives of dependent husbands seemed more capable of "making it" on their own without their husbands' support.

Wives of both types of husbands tended to be dissatisfied with their roles vis-à-vis their spouses. In particular, wives of dependent husbands often had made conscious decisions to turn away from the spousal relationship and to seek gratification of their needs in diversions or occupations outside of the home. This was less often the case for wives of dominant husbands—their extreme dependency and fear of the outside world with its demands and challenges reinforced their isolation and tendency to remain within the family circle. Both groups expressed great dissatisfaction with their relationships with their husbands. Wives of dominant husbands complained "He always makes me feel more like a child than a wife." In contrast, wives of dependent husbands would say, "He expects me to behave like his mother all the time." Nevertheless, firmly fixed patterns of family interaction usually resulted in behavior "like one of the kids" from wives of dominant husbands. For their part, wives of dependent husbands, in general, accepted their husbands' dependent and often child-like behavior and acted "more like mothers" than as spouses with their husbands.

Husbands, in their turn, frequently expressed dissatisfaction with their spouses' performance as wives, as mothers, and as homemakers. Dominant husbands were very critical, often describing their wives as "dumb" or "silly." In general, these men were exceedingly contemptuous of their wives' ability to act independently; at the same time they themselves were aggressively relegating the women to subservient postures. Dependent husbands were more likely to describe their wives as "cold" and "unforgiving." In addition to the marked interpersonal dysfunction between husbands and wives, sexual dysfunction was frequently present. In some cases the marital sexual relationship was entirely absent. In other cases, husbands and wives had intercourse, but very infrequently. Both husbands and wives tended to express dissatisfaction with the quality of their sexual relationship. In only a few cases, husbands and wives had sexual intercourse frequently. It is noteworthy that some incestuous fathers carried on simultaneous sexual relationships with their children *and* their wives.

For their part, the women often tended to be "psychologically absent" in their relationships with both their husbands *and* their children. They seemed to exhibit a lack of psychological investment in the interpersonal aspect of their marriages and family lives. We speculate that this posture was the end result of multiple unsuccessful attempts at psychological investment that were either rebuffed or ignored by their mates. Lest we convey the impression of total victimization, however, one should note that the wives *chose* and, to a certain extent, "set up" their responses and modes of interaction. "Psychological absence" is an excellent defense mechanism and at the same time an effective method of escaping responsibility. The extreme blurring of role boundaries in incestuous families is a condition for which all adults within the family circle must be held accountable. Poznanski and Blos (1975) note that the wives of incestuous husbands choose to ignore or do not respond to their husbands' open and inappropriate behavior with the incest victims. Movements outside established role boundaries are perceived and limited by responsible spouses and parents. For whatever combination of reasons, one of the characteristics of the "psychologically absent" mothers of incest victims is to fail to protect by failing· to limit inappropriate behavior between their husbands and their children.

In many cases, psychological absence of mothers is concretely experienced as physical absence. Again and again, mothers are predictably not present for extended time periods. Wives of both dominant and dependent husbands escape the frustration, unpleasantness and boredom of their roles by seeking companionship, distraction, or employment outside of the home. Because the wives of dominant husbands tend to be more dependent and socially isolated, they are more likely to justify physical absence from the home in the form of a job. Whatever the justification for physical absence, however, the effect is the same with respect to the incestuous relationship: mother manages to avoid setting limits for others and fails to fulfill her own role responsibilities by being elsewhere.

Many mothers of incest victims seemed to have more of a sibling relationship with their children than a maternal relationship. In particular, wives of dominant husbands in general behaved like "one of the kids." The children, in turn, perceived their mother's relatively impotent position and tended to treat her more as a peer than as a mother. It is interesting to note that some of these mothers seemed capable of managing the physical functions of mothering and homemaking (preparing meals, washing clothes, cleaning the house, bringing the children to the doctor for checkups, and so forth), but could not adequately fulfill the attendant psychological functions (psychological nurturance, guidance, limit setting, role modeling, and so forth).

As incestuous relationships between the husbands and the children were initiated and progressed, rivalry and competition between mothers and children likewise flourished. The perquisites and enhanced status accorded the children with incestuous relationships were perceived with jealousy by all other family members, including the mothers. Although much psychological energy was often invested in denying the overt aspects of the family's altered relationships, the mothers' tension and frustration were often expressed as rivalry and anger toward the children. The more assertive wives were likely to have more direct confrontations with the children, usually channeled toward the "safer" areas of contention such as household chores, allowance, sibling interaction, and so forth. Sometimes these confrontations would be expressed as "family fights" with the husband often lining up on the side of the child or against his wife. Less assertive mothers were more likely to harbor secret feelings of jealousy and rivalry toward the children, especially the adolescent daughters.

Role reversal between mothers and children was sometimes present. This was especially evident when mothers worked outside the home, delegating many domestic responsibilities to the children. Sometimes mothers would assign domestic tasks to very young children which are usually considered to be responsibilities of adults: preparation of food, shopping, cleaning the house, and so forth. Mothers would return home and be unreasonably angry and often punitive if these tasks were not completed in a satisfactory fashion. Their anger sometimes was a verbalized expression of the role reversal phenomenon: "You knew I would be too tired to do this!" or "I'm hungry, why isn't supper ready?" The mother's demand that a child fulfill adult responsibilities sometimes took the form of requiring the child to be the negotiator or "go between" with the husband. The mother might say "Find out what Daddy wants me to do about this," or "You talk to him; you always seem to know what he wants!"

Impaired communication between family members characterized nearly all of our cases. The mothers were usually largely responsible for the poor communication since they themselves often served as noncommunicative role models in their interactions with husbands that were observed by the children. Psychological absence, denial, dependency, and energy invested in "keeping the incest secret," all tended to reinforce poor communication patterns. Dependency needs magnified to a sense of entitlement were often reflected in poor communication or absent communication between family members. For example, family members often behaved as if the following unspoken dictum had actually been verbalized: "You *know* that I expect this of you (for example, behavior, task accomplishment, understanding), so I should not have to tell you to do it!"

Since, in our society, mothers more commonly assist children in practicing communications skills and take the leadership role in role-modeling communication patterns within the family, the failure of mothers to do so in incestuous families is all the more symptomatic of the dysfunctional patterns within the family circle.

Low self-esteem, poor self-image, and diminished body awareness were characteristic of many of the mothers. These negative self-perceptions all probably antedated their marriages but could hardly fail to have been reinforced by the husband-wife relationships. Isolation and alienation from more positive and supportive interpersonal relationships tended further to diminish self-esteem. The less assertive women tended to have poorer social skills, greater isolation, and a past history of more failures, both large and small. Low self-esteem and the expectation of failure are probably the most significant ongoing psychodynamic components of the depression that is so often seen in mothers of incest victims.

Treatment Issues

Treatment of mothers of incest victims can be conceptualized on several levels. We chose to approach the treatment issues on a functional basis. Our goal was to help the women recognize those treatment issues that were related to their capacity to function on a day-to-day basis as whole human beings who were wives and mothers. Always we sought to assist the women to see how psychodynamic issues were related to their ability to behave and function as they wished (and were expected) to act and perform. Over time and with increasing experience, we formulated the following treatment issues for dealing with mothers of incest victims.

Inability to Trust

Most of the mothers had a past history of betrayal by their own parents and caretakers. Failure of nurturance, both psychological and physical, verbal and physical abuse, and in some instances sexual abuse, were common features in their background history. This betrayal, too often, was reinacted in their marriages. These women tended to seek out mates who had some of the same characteristics as their nonnurturing and absent caretakers. The cycle of betrayal was completed, unfortunately, by their own children when the father-child or sibling incest relationship was revealed or brought to consciousness.

Inability to trust another human being was thus a major therapeutic issue for the mothers. Their relationships with others were characterized by suspiciousness, hostility, frequent withdrawal, and ambivalence (pulling back and extending oneself simultaneously). All these characteristics tended to anticipate betrayal by the other person. Outreach, warmth, genuine friendliness, respect and absolute consistency had to be conveyed simultaneously by the therapist. Testing behavior and requests for limit setting were frequently seen. Therapists need to anticipate such behavior and set limits and respond appropriately in a supportive and nonthreatening fashion. Time is a great ally for this treatment issue. The longer the client can be exposed to other supportive, helpful, non-punitive and totally consistent adults, the greater chance there is to build trusting and therapeutic relationships. Contrariwise, short-term treatment of inability to trust is practically a contradiction in terms. This is not to say that it is absolutely essential for a single therapist to be involved for many years with a single mother in order to develop trust. Rather, the trust relationships that are built into the treatment plan must be absolutely consistent and without overt elements of betrayal. The character and duration of each trust relationship should be anticipated, defined, and implemented with the client's participation. The therapist should be careful to insist that there be mutuality in all trust relationships initiated as part of the treatment plan: that is, the client must agree to both initiation and termination of all new relationships.

Impaired Self-Image

Low self-esteem and poor self-image will frequently be important treatment issues for the clients. These women "feel bad" in a literal sense and often have many physical complaints and illnesses. It is interesting to note that low self-esteem and poor self-image can be identified in carefully dressed, well-groomed, and physically attractive women just as often as these qualities are found in poorly turned out and unattractive individuals. There seem to be multiple dimensions to this treatment issue.

Past History. Many of these women have a past history of abuse or neglect in their own childhoods. For them, feeling ugly, unattractive, and unsuccessful is a lifelong problem and a self-fulfilling prophecy with past, present, and future implications.

Marriage. These clients, in general, have marriages characterized by limited or no success or gratification. Their interpersonal relationships with their husbands have tended to reinforce their feelings of low self-worth, unattractiveness, and failure. Women who faithfully fulfill the dependent or dominant roles determined and demanded by their husbands nevertheless experience little satisfaction as a result of their compliance.

Body Awareness. We found that mothers of incest victims expressed very limited knowledge of their own bodies that, in a sense, reflected their limited knowledge of their emotional states. Some of these women had minimal awareness of the physical and physiological aspects of their own sexuality. This limited body awareness may have been related to negative self-image and denial of themselves as sexual beings. At any rate, it probably reinforced sexual dysfunction, frigidity, reluctance to have sexual intercourse with their husbands and, perhaps, was a limiting factor in affectional relationships with their husbands and their children. There were certainly a variety of strategies practiced to avoid sexual relationships with husbands. Consciously or unconsciously, many women pushed their daughters into positions which placed them at risk of being required to fill a marital sexual role vacated by their mothers.

Failure. A pervasive sense of past and present failure and anticipation of future failure is a significant component of low self-esteem and impaired self-image. These women find it difficult to achieve success, especially in the home. Many find that adequate performance on their part is met with indifference or even scorn by their husbands and even their children. There is little incentive for these women to perform well and, again, anticipation of failure becomes a self-fulfilling prophecy.

Depression. Impaired self-image is nearly always a component of depression. Many mothers of incest victims are clinically depressed at the time of disclosure. Helplessness, hopelessness, anticipation of failure, and low self-esteem all are likly to be evident.

Treatment of impaired self-image must take into account all of these dimensions, although it may not be practical or even possible to address them all simultaneously. Identifying a personal past history of victimization and ventilating angry and hurt feelings about the past that have probably been suppressed are important first steps. Assisting wives to identify aspects of their relationship with their husbands which are linked to childhood victimization is also helpful. Women who have low self-esteem and a poor self-image need to be helped to identify their own strengths and to receive consistent positive feedback from others regarding elements of their behavior which are praiseworthy. They should be helped to identify tasks and goals that are within their reach and should be assisted to plan and execute projects which will be successes rather than failures. Depression should be addressed in a reality-ordered fashion. All of the above strategies may be helpful. Some clinically depressed mothers will require intensive psychotherapy or antidepressant medication or both.

Denial

Denial of feelings and denial of the reality of the sexually abusive relationship are closely related. Many mothers initially react with denial when the incestuous relationship is disclosed to and by outsiders. The initial reaction of disbelief is sometimes influenced by the mother's own previous awareness of the incestuous relationship. In some cases, the mothers have received previous complaints about the incestuous relationship from their children. The mothers' response to disclosure by the child usually has been disbelieving and largely ineffective. Some mothers pay lip service to the validity of the complaint by promising the child, "I'll never leave you alone with Daddy again." This patently impossible promise is then followed up most often by ignoring or overlooking overt evidence of a continued incestuous relationship between the father and the child. Other mothers learn about the incestuous relationship by observation or inference. In either instance, the mothers subsequently invest enormous amounts of energy into submerging conscious awareness of the incest relationship. They often are nonverbal participants in the "incest secret."

Treatment of denial begins by encouraging the mother to verbalize the reality of the sexual abuse. The simple exercise of hearing the story from the child is an important first step. Thereafter, it is helpful for mothers to verbalize the story of the sexual abuse on repeated occasions to trusted listeners. The exercise of repeated verbalization serves to bring this extremely threatening material to consciousness and help it to remain there. It is an important part of the expiatory process for the mother to verbalize her feelings about the previously denied behavior to the child victim and request his or her pardon.

Mothers must be helped to see that denial of the incestuous behavior, in all likelihood, is part of a larger framework of coping with unpleasant reality by denial. It will probably be impossible for most mothers to move beyond major use of denial as a defense mechanism unless or until they have been able to develop secure trust relationships so that the frightening and unpleasant reality does not have to be faced alone. Denial must also be minimized before the "incest secret" can be dealt with by mother and children.

Unreasonable Expectations of Husband and Children

Many mothers have extremely unrealistic expectations of their husbands and children that antedate the marriage. These unrealistic expectations often coexist with the anger felt by the women toward their husbands for the dysfunctional marriage and the sense of betrayal felt after the incest secret has been disclosed. Many women entered marriage in the hope that their spouses would provide them with the nurturance and security that was lacking in their families of origin. These women often expressed an idealized fantasy of the bliss of the "perfect" marriage, illustrating that their unrealistic expectations continued in the face of their own dysfunctional marriages. When questioned about their expectations of a spouse, most women described a combination of positive attributes that was inconsistent with human experience. Alongside their unrealistic expectations of their husbands was little awareness of their own failings and limited contributions to the marital relationship. In particular, the women initially found it difficult to be accountable for their own mistakes, instead tending to project all responsibility for marital failures upon their husbands.

Many mothers of incest victims had equally unrealistic expectations of their children. Role reversal between mothers and children was common, especially displayed by the wives of dominant husbands. Some mothers perpetuated a multigenerational cycle of role reversal that had begun with their *own* mothers' unrealistic expectations of them.

Therapeutic intervention for this treatment issue is almost totally dependent on building up the mothers' low esteem. It is necessary to build in legitimate access to nurturance and support that "feels like help" for the client before she can be expected to alter her unrealistic expectations of her husband and children. The therapist must help the client to substitute functional and appropriate methods of gratification of basic needs for dysfunctional behavior patterns. To instruct a mother to stop demanding nurturance from her children when she has no legitimate way to meet her needs is useless effort. Group reinforcement of the premise that adults should not look to children to gratify needs while the group itself offers suport and nuturance to the mother can be particularly effective.

Failure to Establish and Enforce Limits

Establishing and enforcing limits and role boundaries are major tasks of parenting. Most mothers of incest victims have failed in their responsibility to maintain appropriate limits between themselves, their husbands, and their children. This is not to say that mothers must accept responsibility for their husband's incestuous behavior. However, the women must acknowledge their own failure to prevent the incestuous behavior by contributing to and permitting the blurring of role boundaries among family members. It will be difficult for most women to be held accountable in this fashion. For the mother, it is far more palatable to blame the husband entirely for the incestuous behavior and to perceive herself totally as an additional victim.

Therapeutic intervention for this treatment issue is dependent on establishing trust and helping the mother perceive herself as an autonomous and responsible human being who is capable of success and who can be held accountable for her actions. It is difficult to achieve true accountability for past inability to establish and enforce limits and boundaries. In our experience mothers tended to intellectualize this issue to a great degree; they could verbalize their share of responsibility for failing to prevent the incestuous behavior but displayed little or no emotional investment in the exercise. Again, group therapy can be helpful in bringing this issue to consciousness. We found that mothers could confront each other on this issue and be held accountable by their peers to a much greater degree than by their therapists.

Anger

Many mothers of incest victims are smoldering with pent-up rage. They are angry with their own families of origin for betraying them and failing to protect them. The women are angry with their husbands for failing to satisfy their needs and for carrying on an incestuous relationship with their children. In addition, mothers are angry with their children for participating in the incestuous relationship and also for failing to meet their needs, however unrealistic was the latter expectation. Elements of rivalry, competition, and jealousy contribute to the anger felt toward the children. Further, the women are angry at the mandated agencies which entered the picture after the incest secret was disclosed and began to insist upon accountability. Last, mothers of incest victims are profoundly angry at themselves—anger born of frustration, sense of betrayal, inadequacy, dissatisfaction, and feelings of impotence.

Treatment of suppressed anger depends upon identifying it and helping the client to ventilate it. Getting "in touch" with suppressed anger is extremely frightening for most of the mothers. They can ventilate the anger only if they feel safe and secure enough to do so. Therapists should use great caution when encouraging the mothers to express anger or in creating opportunities for them to ventilate. Some mothers are justifiably fearful of the consequences of such exercises. Their therapists would be well advised to proceed slowly with this issue and to concentrate on building up and supporting other areas of ego functioning first.

Impaired Communication

Incestuous families, in general, have poor intrafamily communication patterns that are fostered by the parents. There is often little direct verbal communication between husband and wife, between parents and children and among the children themselves. The mother's pivotal position in the family makes her a logical focus for skill-building to enhance communication among all family members.

Treatment of impaired communication by mothers should emphasize two major problem areas: failure to send messages altogether and the sending of mixed or ambivalent messages. Communication is a skill which must be exercised responsibly. Isolated, withdrawn, hostile, inadequate mothers have little desire to communicate with their husbands and children. They must be encouraged to do so and helped to understand that clear communication is a responsibility and a necessity within families, not a luxury or an elective option. Group therapy, with its opportunities for communication exercises, is especially effective for this treatment issue. Through individual or group therapy, mothers must also be helped to understand how important it is for them to send clear messages rather than mixed messages. Many mothers send messages which convey their own ambivalence, especially to their children. Confrontation by one's peers in a group therapy session can be helpful in illustrating the difference. Role playing and role modeling are valuable tools for the therapist as well.

Assertiveness

Wives of dominant husbands are more likely to need assertiveness training than wives of dependent husbands. Mothers of incest victims in general tend to be passive and nonassertive when it comes to meeting their own needs within the family circle. Again, part of their unrealistic expectations of their husbands and children is the belief that other family members should somehow anticipate *their* needs and desires and move to satisfy them without being notified or asked.

Assertiveness training is also best done in a group therapy milieu. Exercises should include indentification of needs or desires, formulation of realistic expectations of oneself or others, development of an adequate plan to accomplish one's goal and implementation of that plan (including clear and direct communication of the plan to others). Once again, role playing and role modeling are effective tools for the therapist who is working in this area.

Impaired Socialization

Many mothers of incest victims have very limited social skills and little aptitude for developing interpersonal relationships with others. Although social isolation has often been fostered and enforced by their husbands, the wives often contribute to their own isolation as well. It is common for these women to express a desire to have more friends and to engage in more social interaction outside the family circle. However, their almost reclusive behavior and limited social skills when they are in a social situation tend to belie their protestations. Although discontented, lonely, bored, and often feeling alienated, these women nonetheless frequently avoid the unfamiliar and hostile-appearing outside world. Avoidance and shunning of social relationships is an attitude that is likely to be assimilated and mimicked by their children as well.

Massive support and outreach combined with structured group social and recreational functions are one approach to this treatment issue. Encouraging these mothers to develop new relationships with other adults not only provides gratification and decreases isolation, it is a positive first step toward substituting functional and satisfying behavior patterns for dysfunctional ones. Mothers can, in turn, role model their newly developed social skills for their children. The previously closed family system must be opened if family members are to substitute more functional patterns of interaction between themselves and with outsiders. Treatment of impaired socialization is a sine qua non for the treatment of mothers of incest victims.

Concrete Environmental Help

It is useless to attempt to treat any client's emotional dysfunction in a milieu of environmental problems that clamor for attention. Mothers of incest victims often come to treatment while the family is in crisis and undergoing profound disruption. Husbands may be temporarily or permanently absent and wives and mothers are faced, often for the first time, with sole responsibility for family finances, housing, and behaving as the head of the household. This is more often an issue for wives of dominant husbands; however, even the more assertive and dominant wives may be bewildered and frightened when they suddenly find themselves facing these responsibilities alone.

Offering concrete help for coping with one's environment is an essential therapeutic first step for these women. Indeed, a concrete service freely offered is often the first treatment initiative that "feels like help." In addition to guidance with housing and family finances, many mothers need direct advice on how to run the household since assigning tasks and responsibilities was formerly done by their husbands. In addition, these women often need assistance in coping with the demands of the legal justice system, often for the first time in their lives.

Group Treatment

As our treatment of incestuous families began, we recognized that many of the mothers had certain needs that could not fully be met in individual therapy. We saw that their feelings of guilt, coupled with their own isolation in the community and the struggle to deal with large impersonal agencies, immobilized many women who had never before assumed a supportive protective role in the family. Most of these women did not have a support system of their own in the community. We hoped that the group would provide another network besides the family that would be geared just for them. Getting out once a week to share with other women can in itself be therapeutic.

We further recognized that feelings of shame and social stigmatization could be minimized by the group experience. Further, we believed that many of the women could face the realities of their own contribution toward the incestuous behavior and family dysfunction more fully when simultaneously confronted and supported by their peers. Lastly, the group therapy situation offered opportunities for developing social skills, role modeling, and role playing to a much greater degree than individual therapy.

Referral

When an incest case was accepted for treatment by Connecticut's Sexual Trauma Treatment Program,[a] the mother was assigned an individual therapist. Each mother was told about the Mothers Group by her individual therapist, who in making an assessment determined if the group could be helpful to that client. If appropriate, the therapist made a referral to either of the group leaders, and a personal interview was arranged for the new member. This served to acquaint the member with the function of the group and also familiarized her with one of the leaders, so the initial entry would be made easier. One of the authors (N.T.D.) served as a coleader for the Mothers Group.

The easiest point of entry into the Mothers Group is during the initial disclosure phase when the family is in crisis and in a state of disequilibrium. Group therapy must be presented to the mother as a "package deal" in conjunction with individual therapy and she must buy into the program. Group participation must be presented to her in a nonthreatening way with the expectation that the group experience will help her to see how others have dealt with the same problems and how they have survived. If the mother cannot be engaged at this time, later entry into the group is almost nonexistent. Once the initial crisis begins to be resolved, the family finds its own equilibrium, and the mother no longer feels the incentive to participate in a therapy group, particularly if she has established an ongoing relationship with an individual therapist.

If the group coleaders also serve as individual therapists for mothers, the "package deal" is easier to sell. Also, if a mother initially resists group participation, the coleader who is also her individual therapist can, at strategic intervals, notify the client when the group is struggling with a problem that she is trying to face alone. This may facilitate her entry into the Mothers Group at a time when participation is most likely to "feel like help" to her.

Ongoing contact with the individual therapist is essential, particularly during the initial crisis period (this crisis phase lasts approximately four to six weeks). As the mother is able to develop a trusting relationship with her therapist during this period and is able to ventilate the turmoil in her life, the group experience can then sustain, support, and strengthen her. Individual therapy time is usually decreased as the member becomes more integrated in the group. Continued individual therapy should always be available, however, if the mother requires it or if other crises occur.

[a]Sponsored by National Center for Child Abusive and Neglect, DHEW, Grant No. 90-C-399.

Group Formation

The Mother's Group began in November 1977 with three members and one therapist. All three members had daughters who had been sexually abused by a family member. One member dropped out after four meetings. It was not until February 1978 that three new members joined and an additional therapist was added. The plan was to have two therapists from the start, but because of the low enrollment it was decided to wait to increase enrollment first.

One of the obstacles with a group of this nature is that the population consists of women who are characteristically dependent and isolated. Participation in the group, therefore, largely depended on someone transporting them to the meetings and back. This was done by a case-aide employed by the program. Several members were driven to the group by their husbands, who waited discreetly in their cars. At the designated hour of termination, the sound of car horns reminded those who watched a mother stand to attention, coat in hand, that the power she ascribed to her mate would not be easily overcome.

With few exceptions, the group provided for its members the only break in an otherwise routine week where adult companionship was minimal. The reasons are fully entrenched in the family dynamic of the wife's dependency on her spouse, thereby weakening her position in the family and her own self-esteem.

The lack of transportation or driving skills seemed to be a prime tool for keeping a wife dependent, particularly in the suburbs. Inner-city women had less difficulty with this issue, since they were accustomed to taking the bus and the use of a car was not a necessity by mere fact of their location.

The dependency of these women on their husbands was acutely visible if the spouse was out of the home, and the wife had to manage the family finances for the first time. Public assistance money was substandard for the majority, who found themselves in an economic bind and without the necessary skills to cope with it. The group helped these mothers by establishing priorities of what should be paid first, what could wait, how to shop for clothing, and the efficient way to shop with food stamps. Group members offered each other solutions from their own experiences.

The Mothers Group thus served as an opportunity for participants to meet other people, thereby increasing their social skills and decreasing their isolation. It also established a supportive network for the participants so that later, as their self-esteem was heightened, they could reach out to each other independent of the group. We saw examples of this many times when members were going through conflicts at home and would reach out to one another by telephone. Also common babysitters were shared so members could attend meetings, and finally some car pooling occurred—members would bring others to the group themselves.

The group met weekly from 7 P.M. to 8:30 P.M. and was led by two female cotherapists. All of the members had children who were victims of either intrafamilial or extrafamilial sexual abuse. The demographic composition of the members was one-third Black and two-thirds Caucasian; however, the percentages varied slightly at different times. There were no Hispanic members in the group. The socioeconomic composition ranged from lower to middle class. Friction or uneasiness due to ethnic or socioeconomic differences were absent. The mothers were aware that membership was open and new members would join in as the agency accepted new cases. Some of the original members could be relied upon to reach out to new members when they joined.

Treatment Issues

Establishing Trust. Trust, which is essential to any group process, is enhanced as members share their experiences with the realization that they are not alone.

> Joanne came into the group with a long kept secret of sexual abuse at the age of 9 years by her 18 year old brother. She only told her priest and her therapist in the program. She witnessed sexual behavior between this same brother and her own daughter two years ago and this incident was causing traumatic reprecussions in her handling of this child and in her marriage. Joanne was not prepared to talk in the Mothers Group.

> As each member shared her story, Joanne relived some agonizing moment in her past. When her turn came, she composed herself momentarily, blurted her story and wept uncontrollably.

> Many weeks later Joanne shared with the group that if she had known she would have to tell her story to the group, she never would have come. She said she decided to tell her story when she realized that the other members were trusting her with their much guarded secrets and she did want to unburden to those who understood. It became clear that the issue of trust was very important for Joanne because, as new members came in to the group, she would selectively share with those she felt she could trust.

Many of the members mentioned the reality that incest is not something you can share with your family or friends, since most people are very uncomfortable when they hear of such problems. The group affords an opportunity for members to ventilate their feelings to others who are "in the same boat" in a nonthreatening, nonjudgmental atmosphere.

Sharing Past History of Abuse. Many of the Mothers Group had been physically or emotionally abused in their families of orgin. One woman had spent eight years in an orphanage where she was brutally beaten as well as sexually abused. Another fled her home at age 15 years and never returned after her alcoholic father brandished a loaded gun at her and threatened to kill her. Still another woman was forced to take on heavy household chores at a very early age by a cold and unloving mother. When her mother became ill, this woman was forced to leave school at age 14 years to care for the rest of the family. All of the group members described poor relationships with their own mothers. The following case examples are typical in their history of early victimization.

Case Example I

Lana was raised by her mother and a series of mother's boyfriends. She described her mother as physically abusive and emotionally neglecting. Lana was hospitalized for one month after an incident when her mother threw hot oil at her. She recalled that her mother never visited her in the hospital. Upon her release she went to live with her grandmother. When Lana was 12 years old her mother's boyfriend raped her.

Case Example II

Mary Alice was the youngest of two children in a middle income family. When she was 2½ years old her mother tried to kill her and her father with a knife. Her mother was hospitalized in a mental institution and Mary Alice was raised by her paternal grandparents who were described as cold, unloving, and physically abusive.

When Mary Alice was 11 years old, her brother made her undress and he then proceeded to fondle her.

At age 16, she attempted suicide by taking an overdose of pills. She married at age 20 and had three psychotic breakdowns which required hospitalization.

In her marriage, Mary Alice assumed a dependent or passive role and was treated no differently than one of the children by her domineering husband. Eight-year-old Frances surpassed her as the mother and became a victim of sexual abuse.

The mothers that we have seen have suffered such severe deprivation that they have never had their own needs for nurturance realized. They have had no appropriate role models and were left emotionally immature with poor self-images. Their own need for nurturance carried through to their adult relationships and influenced their choice of spouse. Generally speaking, they are attracted to a man who will dominate them and foster their need to be dependent and passive. They are further victimized by their husbands in these relationships, as they were by their own parents. In general, past experiences have left them poorly equipped to deal constructively with their husbands and their children and help to set the stage for current family pathology. In particular, their fractured self-images and low self-esteem made it difficult for them to provide proper nurturance for their children.

Dealing with Denial. The group allows the mother the opportunity to focus on certain areas that they may normally block or deny. In talking about incest the mothers are encouraged to ventilate their feelings surrounding the conflicting loyalties between husband and daughter. Often mothers describe their feelings of being "put in the middle" of the family disruption with both sides pulling at them. Sometimes the women will send out clear signals to other group members and the therapists that the material being addressed represents so painful an issue that they cannot yet relinquish the defense mechanism of denial. Although respecting the validity of such feelings, the group is nevertheless more likely to be successful in encouraging the mother to face the issue rather than to continue to evade it.

Identifying Unreasonable Expectations. After the initial crisis for a new member subsides, topics in Mothers Group meetings may become quite divergent. There tends to be a tremendous amount of blaming directed by the women at their spouses, very often universalized to all men. As individual members share their frustration and disappointment, the stage is set to explore the often unreasonable expectations of men in general, spouses in particular, and marriage as an idealized escape from problems and entry into bliss. Unreasonable expectations of children may also be identified in this setting. Group members are quick to identify unrealistic expectations by others (although less likely quickly to identify their own). "Well, what did you expect?" is a commonly asked question. In the group milieu, mothers can sometimes even tolerate gentle teasing as their peers help them to identify reality.

Practicing Limit Setting. Since they have had poor or inappropriate role models for themselves, group members found it difficult to provide structure and maintain role boundaries within the family. Blurring of role boundaries encourages role reversal, especially between weak, dependent, inadequate mothers and their daughters. The daughter tends to "mother her mother" and assume many maternal responsibilities. This, in turn, further weakens the mother's position and increases her impotence and dependency. Thus the stage is set for incest to occur.

A Mothers Group provides an ideal opportunity to discuss and practice limit setting in a "safe' environment. The members can discuss problem situations encountered by each in turn and identify the appropriate role boundaries and role functions. Role playing then provides an opportunity to act out limit-setting in a variety of situations.

Part of family limit setting involves the mother's own responsibility to set limits for herself. Some of the blurring of boundaries extends to a feeling of hostility or jealousy toward their children. The "special" relationship that one father held for his daughter most certainly left out the mother. This mother described a typical morning greeting with her husband. She said he would barely utter a response to her, but when 13-year-old Cindy entered the room father's response would always be "Good morning, sweetheart"; "How did you sleep, dear?" This blatant display fed into the mother's feeling of rejection and worthlessness. The group response to such an example would be to help mother explore her participation in the daily morning scene and through role playing, act out appropriate responses and limit setting.

Dealing with Anger. In an effort to refocus on the issues of the sexual abuse, there have been mothers who state very clearly that they do not wish to think about it, much less talk about it. With these mothers, we have learned that it is the pent-up anger that frightens them and their rage within that they are not able to deal with effectively. They have learned no constructive way to handle this anger, and it is the therapists' responsibility to give recognition and validation to those feelings and to suggest appropriate outlets. Some mothers have left the group because they have not been ready to confront the anger which festers inside. On one occasion, art therapy was used as a treatment modality to release some of their feelings. With the help of a trained art therapist, the mothers found the simple exercises illuminating and cathartic.

Competition and rivalry are exacerbated by the mother's low self-esteem. The group effort is to help the mother to establish her own identity as a woman, wife, and mother. Without a basic sense of self, the feelings of rivalry are too frightening and she feels guilty for the anger towards her daughter. She must learn how to meet her own needs and those of her daughter in more appropriate ways, and then learn that she does indeed have choices and the ability to act on them. Thereafter, she can begin to gain insight into her feelings.

> Anita initially came to the group expressing contempt for her 16-year-old [victim] daughter who she termed a "slut." Allison had been acting-out sexually with multiple partners. She quit school, drank, took drugs and was totally beyond control by Anita. As Anita began to establish her own identity, her self-esteem heightened and she was able to come to the realization that Allison's anger was directed towards her for her failure to protect her and that the acting-out behavior was a reaction to the sexual abuse by her father. This in turn helped Anita to be less angry with Allison and more supportive and helpful to her daughter.

Improving Communication. Dysfunctional intrafamily communication patterns were common to all group members. Group pressure enabled individual members to accept more responsibility for improving family communication. Particular emphasis was placed upon the mother's responsibility to take a leadership role in improving communication with her children, especially those who were victims of sexual abuse. The Mothers Group used role-playing techniques to help the members to improve their communications skills.

> Becky initially felt self-conscious and giddy in the role-playing exercises, but when Mona assumed the role of her rebellious teenage daughter, expressing

the feelings that she had come to understand from the group, Becky's posture changed. As if the script had been written for her, she told her "daughter" how sorry she was that she failed to protect her from her father and how it would not happen again. Speechless, Mona smiled. Becky wept.

Much effort was made by the group leaders to help the members become aware of the feelings identified by role-playing exercises and to link the expression of such feelings to barriers in communication.

Assertiveness Training. The effort to break out of the patterns of submission was difficult when the spouse remained in the home. Very often the mother who participated in the group would feel torn between the input from the group and the new feelings she had, and her spouse at home who was unwilling to relinquish his power. The changes he saw were threatening to him and he would place tremendous pressure on her to withdraw from the group, often placing so many obstacles in her way as to make full participation impossible. Some common obstacles were for the spouse suddenly to become physically ill or even to threaten suicide, and the age old promise that "things would be different" this time.

We have seen an inherent problem in members of the Mothers Group. These women have such low self-esteem that they need to have demonstrated that they deserve to have their needs met and that they are capable of meeting them. A group focus on assertiveness training helps the member begin to assert herself in her rightful role of mother and protector of her daughter rather than of child-woman and competitor.

Laura had made the decision that she would begin to handle all the decision making which pertained to her daughter, as she could see that Jennifer was playing one parent off the other. She reminded her husband that he had been in charge in the past and had failed to act as a responsible parent towards her. It was now her turn. Change was very gradual as both Jennifer and her father were adept manipulators.

Weekly the group applauded her efforts whether successful or not. The members would arm her with new tasks to try out in the following week. Laura began to become more verbal about her feelings, but it was not until another crisis at home presented itself that Laura could fully assert herself. This time she stayed in charge.

Improving Social Skills. At the outset, we hoped that a Mothers Group would decrease isolation and help the members to improve social skills. The group appeared to fill this function well for all the mothers who became permanent members.

The loyalties within the group flourished into sustained friendships. With few exceptions, the group members were truly interested in one another, and would rally if one was sick or absent for some time, with cards, flowers, and phone calls. We saw a lot of nurturing between the women for each other, and a supportive arm or a hand held were visible reminders that someone cared. We recognized that the mothers in the group needed a great deal of nurturing from the leaders. One way we felt we could be nurturing was by providing snacks and coffee at the meetings. Coffee and soda were always provided and, initially, we did supply food. Interestingly, as the members in the group began to feel better about themselves, they began to take an interest in their appearance, and voted against having food at the meetings because they were dieting.

Assisting with Concrete Services. The Mothers Group enables members to deal appropriately with concrete issues of housing and finances. For people who have been so dependent, assuming adult responsibilities is extremely difficult, and often they will put up with the abuse because taking more assertive action is so painful and anxiety provoking. Sixty-six percent of the women in the group separated from their mates and signed up for Public Assistance. For these women, the total weight of the financial responsibilities for the family was imposed upon them for the first time. They looked to the group for support and direction.

> After disclosure of the sexual abuse of eight-year-old Carla, father was incarcerated, mother was hospitalized for a psychotic breakdown, and the three children were placed in foster care. Upon her discharge from the hospital, Joan (who had lost her employment) resumed care of her children and was forced to rely on Public Assistance for the first time in her life.

> Joan's childlike demeanor convinced us she was truthful when she said her husband made all the decisions. She was indeed incapable of making an independent decision. She asked for directions from everyone and went about implementing sometimes opposing viewpoints. After much individual work with Joan, she was able to rely on the group process for support and to accept responsibility for making changes. The group was helpful in assisting Joan in working through the state bureaucracy, telling her what she was entitled to, and how to go about making requests. Group members brought her clothing which their children had outgrown.

> When Joan finally made the decision to divorce her husband, the group was instrumental in helping her through yet another bureaucratic system, by telling her of their experiences in terms of visitation and child support.

Improving Body Awareness. Many women in the group had limited knowledge of their own bodies and reported that their sexual experiences have not been satisfying. They saw the sexual aspects of their marital relationship as duty bound. Several women stated that they kept track of their sexual relations with their husbands, using this to gauge how many times they could refuse him before once again acceding to his sexual demands, without causing further problems for them. For most women in the group sexual intercourse became nothing more than something to be tolerated.

Donna cringed and her body stiffened when she spoke of the Sunday midday sexual interlude which had become a regular pattern in her marriage. Donna was primitive in her understanding of her body and claimed not to know what orgasm meant, much less having experienced one. She spoke of relief that his leaving the home put an end to this Sunday charade for her, rather than a cessation to the sexual abuse of her daughter. Donna told the group, amongst knowing nods, how she would busy herself Sunday morning outside the home in an effort to circumvent the act of sexual union with her husband.

To help members to deal with issues of sexuality, copies of *Our Bodies, Ourselves* were distributed to members and eagerly read by them. One group member revealed that her knowledge of body function and masturbation in her own youth had been so limited that, when she began to menstruate at age 18 years, her father had to explain to her that she was not injured. Although they acknowledged responsibility for sex education of their own children, the members expressed great discomfort and feelings of inadequacy in discussing such topics as puberty, menstrution, and birth control. One of the authors of this chapter, a woman physician (S.M.S.) was invited to lead two informal group sessions to address these concerns. The instruction was enthusiastically received and the mothers raised many questions and discussed ways of presenting information to their children.

Support through Legal Justice System Involvement. Another issue addressed by the Mothers Group was the effects of the criminal justice system on their families. The commonly held feeling of these women is that the very system that is designed to protect them and their children actually victimizes them. It is a major hurdle for these women to report their mates to the police. After a complaint of sexual abuse has been made and the man is arrested, too often he is released immediately, thus putting tremendous pressure on these women, who are woefully unable to handle this stress. Most of the women perceived the procedures of the criminal justice system as punitive toward them and their children. Multiple interrogations and appearances in police stations and court and frequent continuances of the cases were confusing, tiresome, and stressful. Perceiving the negative effects upon themselves, they were also worried about negative effects upon the children.

In some cases, women were genuinely fearful of physical retribution by their husbands. The police were not always responsive to their fears, although the states attorney's office assisted by requesting the judge to issue restraining orders upon the husbands in a few cases.

The Mothers Group was able to provide much support to the members whose families were involved with the criminal justice system. Procedures were reviewed and explained and more experienced members shared their coping techniques with newer members. When children were required to testify, other therapists within the Sexual Trauma Treatment Program helped the children to prepare for their court appearance by role-playing techniques. Likewise, the Mothers Group assisted members who needed to testify by providing role-playing experiences to help them prepare to appear in court.

Assimilation of New Members

The introduction of a new member is difficult because she usually entered at the period of crisis or disclosure and was uncertain how much to let herself go. New members were often embarrassed and felt certain that they would not be able to open up. The group members are asked to share what brought them into the group, and one by one they briefly described the nature of the sexual assault upon their daughters. The new member was then asked to share with the group her situation. Once done, this quickly broke down any barriers that might have existed and established a feeling of a camaraderie. The new member knew that she was not alone and saw that others had gone through the same trauma. It allowed for peer support and enabled the mother in crisis to see how others have coped, and how the group members have handled similar challenges and problems.

Once persuaded to join the Mothers Group, most of the women became permanent members. A few women came to only one or two sessions. Without question, the group had the greatest appeal to women who had a limited support system in place. Group therapy has little appeal for extremely suspicious women who find it almost impossible to trust others and who find it too uncomfortable to share their experiences with others. The same is true for women who are extremely shy and withdrawn. Also, it is difficult for women with limited intellectual capacity to remain within the group because so much of the group process depends on verbalization and conceptualization.

Leader's Role

We have found it extremely necessary that a Mothers Group be run by two coleaders. This type of therapy is so emotionally laden that one therapist would find it difficult to be able to perceive all the verbal and nonverbal messages of all the participants. It would be far too emotionally draining for one person, and it is doubtful that one leader could consistently attend to the group's needs with the necessary energy that is required.

The leaders act not only as facilitators to the group process, but also act as appropriate role models. They try to meet some of the members' dependency needs by being nurturing and supportive. This also requires a great deal of energy input by the leaders.

Additionally, use of coleaders enables a greater degree of group continuity.

It is extremely important for therapy groups with incestuous families to meet consistently and to maintain continuity week after week. Coleaders enable the group to be "covered" through illness, vacations, and the like.

Transportation and Child Care

Two major obstacles to mothers' participation in the group were transportation and child care. We would have preferred to have the mothers be responsible for their own transportation, but we knew that for this population that was not feasible. For the most part, these women were socially isolated and did not have a support system in the community. Without a case aide or volunteer, the leaders could not manage to transport the group members.

We tried allowing the women with child-care problems to bring their children to the meetings and we would arrange babysitting. This became unmanageable due to our office space and also the time of the meetings. As we exceeded their bedtime the noise level and manageability of the children made it unworkable. This plan was also discarded because most of these women never went anywhere without their children and we felt it would be therapeutic in itself to have one night a week exclusively theirs.

We did try on several occasions to have the meetings in different members' homes. The women enjoyed this and the atmosphere enhanced discussion. We could not continue because the catchment area covered such a large area that the case aide would have to begin picking up the members at unreasonable hours and getting them back home too late for babysitters. The office location was central and more convenient.

Transportation remained a problem throughout the program; however, child care did not. For the most part the mothers could arrange for someone to watch their children. We found it did offer a ready-made excuse if a member did not feel like attending.

Assessment

A Mothers Group has a definite and vital role in the treatment of incest. We recognized that group therapy is not the treatment of choice for every woman in the program, and therefore did not extract a time commitment for their attendance at the onset. (This is not to say that we did not address ourselves to resistance and to termination issues).

All of the mothers in the group were engaged in either individual, couples, or family therapy, simultaneously with Mothers Group attendance. This was helpful in that there was feedback between therapists so we could help deal with the residue of emotional reactions that were generated. Many times the mothers would be worried about a pending family session and would find the added support of the group very helpful.

We found it most important in the initial phases of therapy for group and individual therapy to be coordinated closely. The group could not possibly sustain the needs of these women at the time of disclosure. It is only after they began to grow in self-esteem that individual therapy could be lessened while they continued to attend the Mothers Group.

At the end of the program there were no mothers in the group who were only receiving group therapy. This was a goal that was not met due to time restraints and the severity of the cases. All of these families are multiproblem families and incest is one problem among many. Communication patterns have long been short-circuited and the family behaves in a fragmented and inappropriate way.

As these mothers gathered support and strength from the group, they saw that they could be different and made attempts to gain control in their lives and in their families. They increased in confidence and self-esteem. Several mothers started in weight reduction clinics, and we saw this as a positive step in regaining their sense of self. As they began to take hold of their own lives, they also began to assert themselves at home. We see the mother asserting her rightful role in the family as being a clear indicator of success for her, as well as an indicator of her heightened self-esteem.

Summary

Treatment of mothers of incest victims must address their special needs in a vigorous outreach effort. It is advantageous to use multiple treatment modalities, but all must be combined initially with individual therapy. The dynamics of the mother's position in and contribution to the incestuous family form the basis for treatment issues. One functional approach to dependent women with dominant husbands is to combine individual therapy with Mothers Group therapy. Although not a panacea, this combination of treatment modalities proved highly effective for some mothers whose children had been sexually abused by family members.

Reference

Poznanski, E., and Blos, P., Jr. "Incest." *Medical Aspects of Human Sexuality* 9, 10(1975):461–63.

The Incest Offender

A. Nicholas Groth

Incest refers to overt sexual activity between persons whose kinship pattern prohibits marriage. Such illegal sexual contact may be cross-generational, involving an adult and a child, or it may occur between agemates. There are many types of sexual combinations among relatives that may occur, but this chapter will address the most prominent pattern of pathological intrafamilial sexuality: parent-child incest.

The type of incest which most commonly comes to the attention of clinicians, social service workers, and law-enforcement officers involves a sexual relationship between a parent and a child. In most identified cases the offending parent is a male adult and the victim is a female child. For this reason the emphasis in this chapter will be on father-daughter sexual involvements. Such incestuous offenses are not confined to sexual activity between a biological father and daughter, but encompass any sexual relationship in which the male adult occupies a parental authority role in relation to the child. Incest, then, also includes sexual activity between an adoptive parent, or a stepparent, or a common-law parent, or a foster parent and his ward.

Those persons who commit incest cannot be distinguished from those who do not—at least in regard to any major demographic characteristics. Such offenders do not differ significantly from the rest of the population in regard to level of education, occupation, race, religion, intelligence, mental status, or the like. They are found within all socioeconomic classes. However, they do differ from nonoffenders obviously in that, when faced with life-demands they cannot cope with, they seek relief from the resulting stress through sexual activity with children.

Fixated Offenders

Sexual offenders against children may be divided into two basic types with regard to their primary sexual orientation and level of sociosexual development.

A. Nicholas Groth, Ph.D., is director of the Sex Offender Program, Department of Correction, Connecticut Correctional Institution, Somers, Connecticut. Dr. Groth, a clinical psychologist, received the Ph.D. from Boston University. He has specialized in working with offenders and victims of sexual assault both in institutional and community settings. He has held teaching appointments at Wheelock College, Simmons College, and Northeastern University, and is currently the codirector of the Saint Joseph College Institute for the Treatment and Control of Child Sexual Abuse in West Hartford, Connecticut. Dr. Groth is author of *Men Who Rape: The Psychology of the Offender* and coauthor of *Sexual Assault of Children and Adolescents* (Lexington Books, 1978).

There are some males who at the onset of their sexual maturation develop a primary or exclusive attraction to children. Children become the preferred subjects of their sexual interests, and although these men may also engage in sexual encounters with agemates and may, in some cases, even marry, such relationships are usually initiated by the other partner and result from social pressures or constitute a means of access to children. Psychologically their sexual preference remains predominently cross-generational; their sexual orientation is fixed on children. Men who show such an arrest in their psychosexual development are technically described as pedophiles if they are sexually attracted to preadolescent children or as hebephiles if they are sexually attracted to young teenage or adolescent children.

Regressed Offenders

There are other men who do not display an early sexual predisposition toward children, but who exhibit a more conventional, peer-oriented sociosexual development. Their sexual interest and activities focus primarily on agemates. As they enter adulthood, however, these adult relationships become conflictual. Increasing responsibilities and demands (marital, vocational, financial, parental, and the like) are sometimes compounded by unanticipated misfortunes (for example, illness, infidelity, loss of income). The sum of these responsibilities, demands, and misfortunes prove more than these men can cope with, and they find themselves becoming sexually attracted to children. Such sexual interest in children appears to be a departure from their more customary and conventional sexual orientation toward agemates activated by some precipitating stress or combination of stresses.

The sexual attraction to a child, then, may constitute a fixation on the part of the adult offender: a sexual orientation toward children as the result of arrested sociosexual development. Or it may constitute a regression, the result of progressive or sudden deterioration of emotionally meaningful or gratifying adult relationships. In general, fixated child molesters are drawn to children sexually in that they identify with the child and appear in some ways to want to remain children themselves. They tend to adapt their behavior and interests to the level of the child in an effort to have the child accept them as an equal. As one such offender observed, "When I'm with a child, I act more like a child." On the other hand the regressed child molesters are drawn to children sexually in an attempt to replace their adult relationships which have become unfulfilling or conflictual. Such offenders select a child as a substitute and tend to relate to the child as if the child were their peer or agemate. In reference to his sexual involvement with his 14-year-old stepdaughter, one such offender said, "She told me that she loved me and said she should be my wife. I told her whatever she wants I'll do. My daughter was a great deal more a wife to

Table 8–1
Typology of Pedophilia

Fixated	Regressed
1. Primary sexual orientation is to children	1. Primary sexual orientation is to agemates
2. Pedophilic interests begin at adolescence	2. Pedophilic interests emerge in adulthood
3. No precipitating stress/no subjective distress	3. Precipitating stress usually evident
4. Persistent interest—compulsive behavior	4. Involvements may be more episodic
5. Pre-planned, premeditated offense	5. Initial offense may be impulsive, not premeditated
6. Identification: offender identifies closely with the victim and equalizes his behavior to the level of the child; and/or may adopt a pseudo-parental role to the victim	6. Substitution: offender replaces conflictual adult relationship with involvement with the child; victim is a pseudoadult substitute and in incest situations the offender abandons his parental role
7. Male victims are primary targets	7. Female victims are primary targets
8. Little or no sexual contact with agemates; offender is usually single or in a marriage of "convenience"	8. Sexual contact with child co-exists with sexual contact with agemates; offender is usually married/common-law
9. Usually no history of alcohol or drug abuse	9. In more cases the offense may be alcohol related
10. Characterological immaturity/poor sociosexual peer relationships	10. More traditional lifestyle but under-developed peer relationships
11. Offense—maladaptive resolution of life issues	11. Offense—maladaptive attempt to cope with specific life stresses.

me than my wife was. She was with me all the time." Both relate to the child as a peer. Psychologically the fixated offender becomes like the child, whereas the regressed offender experiences the child as a pseudoadult. When an incest offender is referred for assessment, it is important to differentiate whether he is a fixated or regressed offender, since this will have important implications with regard to the meaning of his offense, what risk he represents to the community, the treatment of choice, and prognosis for recovery or rehabilitation. In cases of incest involving a fixated offender, the dynamics of the individual offender are of paramount importance and the family dynamics, relatively speaking, are nonessential or extraneous. You are dealing with a person who happens to be married and who therefore has easy and constant sexual access to his own children but who is in fact sexually oriented to youngsters, and this attraction is not confined to his own children nor is it activated by his marital relationship. It is a product of his development and a characteristic of his psychological makeup. It has been our observation that fixated child offenders are more likely to target boys as their victims and regressed child offenders are more likely to select girl victims.[1] This is not always or exclusively the case, but it does appear to be a significant and prominent trend. In the face of this trend, in cases of father-son incest, there may be a greater probability that the offender is a fixated pedophile.

In cases of incest involving a regressed offender the family dynamics play a key role. The interrelationships among all members of the nuclear family, the structure of the family network, the dynamics of the participants, the environmental context and the situational events affecting the family all have more relevance. In our clinical experience we have found that in fact the majority—an estimated 90 percent—of incest offenders fall into this category. For the most part they tend to be regressed child offenders who have not exhibited any chronic or persistent sexual interests in children prior to their incestuous activity and whose sexual involvement with their own child has occurred in the context of a deteriorating marital relationship or a traumatizing event or life crisis. Most incest appears to be, in part, the result of family dysfunction. We have yet to encounter a case in which the incestuous activity was an exception to what otherwise was a stable, harmonious, well-functioning family. Instead the incest always constituted only one issue in a multiproblem family. However, although it is important to recognize and address the dynamics of family dysfunction in such cases, it is even more important to avoid being distracted from the responsibility that the offender must bear for creating and contributing to the family dysfunction. Attention to family dysfunction should not permit the pathology of the incestuous offender to be masked or minimized. Although the family dynamics may have contributed to the activation of his incestuous behavior, they did not create his predisposition to react to stress in this fashion nor does overall family dysfunction, however severe, detract from the seriousness of the incest offense.

Family Patterns

Although there are a wide variety of individual differences among incest offenders and no two cases are ever identical, there do appear to be two prominent patterns of incest-prone families with respect to the role relationship between husband and wife.

Passive-Dependent Type

In one pattern the husband relates to his wife psychologically more as a dependent child than as a competent partner and looks to her to fulfill his emotional needs. Over time she comes to feel emotionally unsupported, neglected, or even deserted by her husband and may turn elsewhere for emotional support and fulfillment. As she becomes increasingly self-sufficient and no longer is constantly attentive to his needs he turns to his daughter as a substitute or surrogate companion-wife-mother, who is then expected to take care of him, prepare his meals, do his laundry, get him up for work, spend leisure time with him.

Eventually his emotional dependency and intimacy with her evolves into a sexual relationship which may progress and continue until the daughter reaches adolescence, becomes interested in peer relationships and starts dating—all of which becomes anxiety-producing to the offender since it again raises the threat of being abandoned by his caretaker, unless there is another child to replace this one.

Case Example 1

Jack is the oldest of four children. He has two younger brothers and one younger sister. His father worked as a union bricklayer and dairy farmer to support the family and his mother worked occasionally as a registered nurse. The family experienced some hard times financially but was never on welfare. Jack reports being closer to his father than his mother and although the family was intact during his early years, his parents divorced when he was about 16. His parents fought and, being the oldest child, he felt caught in the middle. After the divorce Jack initially remained with his mother but following an argument he was thrown out of the house and went to live with his father. There was no evidence of child abuse or neglect on the part of his parents, nor any history of sexual abuse, criminality, or mental illness. His mother has since remarried and Jack remains in touch with both his parents.

His medical history appears unremarkable with two possible exceptions. He was enuretic to about age 9 or 10 suggesting some persistent psychological stresses during his formative years, and at age 19 he was kicked in the head by a cow and suffered a state of confusion for four hours during which he could not determine the day or the time or where he had parked his car. He suffered a brain concussion but was not given medical treatment at the time. Currently he reports momentary episodes, lasting 5 to 10 seconds, in which his mind goes blank. He evidences no gross organic symptoms, however. His general health appears good and Jack does not abuse alcohol or drugs. He does drink beer in moderation but has never gotten involved with any drugs.

He began school with kindergarten and repeated the third grade because he was ill (tonsils and ear infections) and missed classes. He completed 10th grade in high school but flunked out in the 11th grade. Jack states that school never interested him and he would rather work. After leaving school he enrolled in an agriculture course for two years but quit in his second year when he impregnated and had to marry his girlfriend.

Jack received no formal sex education at home or at school, but he grew up on a farm and learned the facts of life from observing the animals. He himself was never the victim of a sexual assault nor did he experience any sexual traumas during his development. At the beginning of adolescence he became involved in some sexual activities with farm animals. His first experience with intercourse occurred around age 16 or 17 with a girl his same age named Rita who later became his wife. He states that Rita was also a virgin prior to their relationship. Jack did not play the field as a young man. His sexual activity was confined pretty much to Rita and when she became pregnant he married her and left school to support his wife and family.

Jack and Rita have been married eight years. They have three children. The oldest is a girl, Beverly age 8, the victim in the instant offense; the next is a girl age 7; and the youngest is a boy age 4. Jack suspects that the youngest child may not be his. Jack states that although he and Rita had gone together for about two years prior to their marriage he had not planned to marry her. When she became pregnant she demanded they marry and he felt that this was the right thing to do and that things might work out. Jack expected Rita to run the household and look after his needs and those of the children. However, he described his wife as a spendthrift who put herself before the children and who shared none of his goals. This led to increasing arguments. The marriage became conflictual and unstable and Rita separated from and reunited with Jack on six different occasions. He complained about her housekeeping and felt she did not take proper care of the children. In turn he was criticized by her for not paying enough attention to the children and for not going out enough. Jack believes that after the birth of their first child his wife began seeing other men and states that for the last year and a half he knows she has been sexually involved with other men which is why he doubts the paternity of his son. He states that their sexual relationship steadily deteriorated. She was not sexually attentive to his needs and he felt impotent with her. He admits to a couple of extramarital one-night stands involving underage adolescent girls but feels he has not really been unfaithful to his wife while they were living together.

Apart from the incestuous involvement with his oldest daughter, Jack denies any unconventional sexual interests or experiences. He does seem more comfortable with younger women as sexual partners and is currently living in a common-law relationship with a 19-year-old woman whom he met at his place of work.

Jack works as a dairy farmer. He has been self-sufficient since age 13 and enjoys farmwork. He has a stable work history and hopes someday to operate his own farm. He is a dependable worker who has been with his employer in one capacity or another for almost 15 years.

Jack states that he did not have any difficulty making friends as a child and his current friendships date back to his childhood. He does admit to being quick-tempered as a youngster but explains that this ran in his family. He is not a fighter and states that he did not beat his wife or children. He has no psychiatric or criminal record, apart from the instant offense. Jack also has no military history since he was given a 1-H deferment because of being married, having a family, being in school, and being a farmer.

Jack admits to being incestuously involved with his 8-year-old daughter, Beverly. He states that this sexual activity began this past year and extended over a 6-to-8 month period. It originally occurred in the context of bathing his daughter. He found himself attracted to her. "I tried to stop myself but I just couldn't." Jack would intimately touch and fondle his daughter and on four occasions inserted various objects (Q-tip, a pen cap, a .22 caliber bullet) into her vagina. He would not expose himself but felt sexually aroused and would masturbate privately following these incidents. Jack can offer no explanation for these offenses. He states they were more impulsive than premeditated and denies any sexual fantasies about this daughter. Jack states that Beverly was the only child he felt attracted to. He denies any similar sexual interest in his other daughter or toward prepubertal girls in general. He feels Beverly paid more attention to him than his other children did and although he did not explain what he was doing to her he told her to tell him if it hurt—if so, he would stop—and to keep this secret.

His wife found out about this activity at one point prior to their final separation but when she confronted Jack with it, he denied it. Jack began to recognize that his daughter was becoming increasingly afraid of him, and although he had become sexually active with his current girlfriend he found he could not stop the activity with his daughter. His wife finally pressed charges and he has no contact of any kind currently with any of his children. Since the termination of all contact with his wife and children, Jack reports feeling no longer affected by incestuous urges.

Although depressed by what has happened, Jack feels that in general his life has become a lot happier since his marriage to Rita has, in effect, ended. He states that his relationship to his current girlfriend is excellent in every way and they plan someday to marry.

Because of his wife's spending habits and the expenses involved in the current legal proceedings, his financial resources have been seriously depleted and his plans to go into business for himself set back. Currently he is paying Welfare for the support of his children.

As frequently is the case in incest, the inappropriate sexual activity appears to be in part the result of and a symptom of family dysfunction. It is a reaction to the stesses and frustrations encountered by Jack in his marital relationship. Jack's relationship to his wife was characterized by unspoken expectations which, when not met, led to feelings of rejection and deprivation. It would appear that both he and his wife were not really prepared for marriage and quickly found the demands of being married and raising three children exceeded their maturity and capability. Unable to cope with each other, both took out their problems on the children.

Jack is a regressed offender with a deeply ingrained and chronic personality maladjustment characterized by marked dependency, docility, depression, and underlying feelings of resentment and marked vulnerability. Under the impact of stress he does not draw upon realistic capacities to cope, but instead succumbs to apathy and exhaustion. His psychological defects are serious, and under stress his reality testing falters. Psychosocial stressors such as social inadequacies, family tensions, and work upsets create a risk of again acting out. This risk will wax and wane depending upon the quality of his adult (marital) relationships and the availability of a child over whom he has authority. Sexuality is more comfortable for him when his partner is inexperienced or nonpowerful, that is, unlikely to refuse, resist, or reject him, such as an animal, a "virgin," or a child. The sexual activity he exhibits in the offense has strong symbolic features: he approximates intercourse with an 8-year-old with phallic objects rather than his penis, and although at the point of disclosure he confined his actions to masturbating his daughter and then himself, had he not been stopped, over time he would most likely have progressed to intercourse.

Individual counseling will be a frustrating task for the clinician since Jack is removed at present from both the stimulating presence of his daughter and the threatening presence of his former wife. When faced with adult life demands he sought a sexual relationship with his daughter to fulfill unmet emotional needs and to cope with unresolved life issues. Now that this situation has changed, he is not experiencing any subjective distress. A treatment plan involving him in group therapy may therefore be more productive at least in the initial stages of treatment than individual counseling. His prognosis appears guarded. He does not yet fully appreciate the significance or the seriousness of his behavior. To some extent his likelihood of recidivism may depend on how successful he is in establishing a relationship with a woman whose needs are congruent with his, a relationship in which his passive-dependent longings will be fulfilled, and one which does not make demands on him he cannot meet. He needs to feel he is cared for and needs to be given to as evidence of this caring. Treatment directed toward helping him to assess the quality of his relationships and to recognize what type of involvements are suitable for him would be of help to Jack in guiding him along paths that avoid a repetition of his earlier mistakes.

Aggressive-Dominant Type

In the other pattern the husband occupies the dominant role in the family and maintains a position of power by keeping his wife and children financially dependent on him and socially isolated from extrafamily relationships. In selecting a spouse who is very insecure or immature, he achieves a feeling of strength, power, and control in the relationship. To this end he reinforces her helplessness and dependency on him. However, at the same time such a wife does not provide him with much emotional support and he turns to his daughter to fulfill his emotional needs and sexual demands. Sexual access to his daughter is experienced as part of his narcissistic entitlement as the head of the family.

Case Example 2

Phil was the second oldest of nine children. Although his family was intact during his developmental years, his father was a heavy drinker who would physically abuse his wife and children. His father worked as a mechanic to support the family but spent most of his time in a barroom. The family never received any welfare or public assistance funds. Phil was brought up in the Catholic faith and attended parochial schools. He repeated the first and second grade because he was ''slow'' and left school in the eight grade at age 16. He tried to get into the Army Reserves at this time but his father would not sign a permission slip, so Phil went to work in a factory and later began doing roofing, which is his current trade.

Phil suffered no serious illnesses or injuries during his development, but he was enuretic to age 14. He was not a behavior problem at home or at school. Just prior to adolescence he was sexually victimized by two adult males for a period of about a month. In exchange for some money, Phil would perform oral sex on them. This was his first sexual experience of any kind. He reports being uninformed and inexperienced in regard to sexuality prior to marriage: "I never got around before I got married." He had his first experience with heterosexual intercourse just before meeting his wife, Lorraine. She had been married before and Phil reports having "scrambles" with her ex-husband on a few occasions when he began dating Lorraine.

They have been married for 14 years and have two children of their own, in addition to Lorraine's two children from her prior marriage.

The marriage has been a conflictual one. Lorraine states that Phil has struck her on occasion. She states that he has been sexually inattentive to her and objects to his association with one of his brothers who she believes is sexually involved with his widowed mother-in-law. Lorraine also reports that Phil does not treat his children right, yells at them, and shows them no love or affection. He also has a drinking problem. Phil, in turn, accuses his wife of not disciplining the children, wanting more than he can provide the family, and being unfaithful to him. He has kept tight rein on his family, requiring that his children come directly home immediately after school, and objecting to his wife socializing with neighbors or even talking on the telephone. Phil realized he has driven his wife away because of his attitude that "in my house there is only one way to do things: my way." He feels his wife doesn't sufficiently love or care for him and has been of no help to him, yet he states he'd "take her back in two seconds."

Phil blames his incestuous behavior on his drinking. He reports that he began drinking around age 12 and that this reached serious proportions about six years ago. Phil's sexual involvement with his stepdaughter has been going on for at least two years and was discovered when he objected to her boyfriend and forbid her seeing him. Phil finds it hard to explain his sexual involvement with his stepdaughter except to say, "If my wife had given me the proper attention and loving, none of this would have happened. I couldn't have my wife in her youth, when she was first married. I figured I might have lost my wife's love and the only way I could have any part of her love would be from the stepdaughter, which we always got along good."

Phil is considerably remorseful and depressed. His life has been disrupted by his arrest, and he has come to realize that he needs help. The loss of his wife and family creates much anguish, and he agonized over his wife's refusal to sit down and talk over with him what has transpired. Although he admits his neglect and harsh treatment of his wife, he denies that she really wants to divorce him and believes she is being influenced in this decision by her family. In spite of what appears to have been a conflictual relationship, Phil appears to be highly dependent emotionally on his wife. He is angry at her for what he perceives as her unfaithfulness and treachery and yet is unable to relinquish his needing her. He does not appreciate how he has contributed to destroying their relationship.

Phil is a psychologically immature person in regard to human relationships. His ability to appreciate the needs and feelings of others and how his actions impact on them is quite limited. He functions at a very concrete, immediate level and has very little insight into his own behavior. His offense, then, appears more symptomatic of emotional immaturity, poor judgment, and self-centeredness than of malicious intent. Apart from the instant offense he has no criminal history.

His involvement with his stepdaughter appears exploitative and opportunistic in nature. He used his position of authority to gain access to her. There does not appear to be any violence associated with the assault; instead Phil enticed, bribed, and misled his stepdaughter into the sexual behavior and rewarded her with special privileges in return for her participation. There was no physical abuse.

His psychological testing indicates that Phil is handicapped by intellectual defects which limit his ability to cope with life-demands in a mature and adaptive fashion. His difficulties involve issues of dependency and anger. He is troubled by chronic tension (for which he has used alcohol as a source of relief) and he is agitated, depressed, and anxious. There is a self-centered quality to his functioning, and he appears to be a hypersensitive person who is overly responsive to criticism and quick to project the blame for his difficulties on others. He has a tendency to misunderstand and misinterpret the actions of others which has led to a life-long history of troubled interpersonal relationships. Phil feels angry and resentful toward persons who do not fulfill his demands and, at another level, helpless and overwhelmed by the demands placed on him. These characteristics appear to be long-standing personality traits. There is no evidence of insanity or incompetency.

Although faced with many of the same issues as Jack, Phil attempted to maintain a position of strength and control over his family rather than to adopt a passive-submissive posture. No matter how much power and authority he assumed, his life still confronted him with demands he found overwhelming, leaving his psychological needs for security and comfort unmet. He tried to compensate through incest with his stepdaughter for the experiences he could not achieve with his wife, but he fails to realize it is not control and authority over others that gains the respect, alliance, love, affection, caring, and support he needs for emotional fulfillment. In effect, then, he prevents from occurring that which he is seeking to find.

Phil too is a regressed offender. With the breakup of his family, the risk of further victimization is significantly reduced. Emotional support in working through his loss and in facing life on his own can be provided through individual counseling. In the early phases of treatment Phil may welcome the opportunity to depend on the strength, authority, and helpfulness of the therapist. By progressing slowly and supportively, independence and feelings of self-worth can develop. Phil can also gain support through participating in a self-help program such as Alcoholics Anonymous which will help him to address his alcohol abuse and provide socialization experiences.

Both Jack and Phil require a treatment plan that will address their parenting skills, their socialization skills, their ability to cope with stress and frustration, their communication skills, and the like. However, both these offenders, as in most cases of incest, need to be regarded as chronic risks. Although not curable, they are treatable, and if they are not motivated for treatment or if it turns out that they are not treatable, then prevention through imposed controls or incarceration must be the goal. With each case the clinician must ask: What needs to be done to reduce the risk of this offender repeating his offense? What alternatives are available to achieve this goal? Can the offender change? Can the situation be changed? To answer such questions some guidelines will be offered later in this chapter.

One of the basic components in the psychology of the incest offender is his deep-seated, core feeling of helplessness, vulnerability, and dependency. As he experiences the stresses of the adult life-demands of marriage and parenthood, his underlying insecurities and feelings of inadequacy become activated and increasingly prominent. He feels overwhelmed and not able to control or manage these life-demands. As a result he may exhibit one of two basic responses in an effort to cope with his crisis. He may either withdraw from adult responsibilities and adopt a passive-dependent role as a quasi child with respect to his family. Or he may overcompensate by adopting an excessively rigid, controlling, authoritarian position as "the boss in the family." In adopting a position of dependency the offender feels unable effectively to manage family operations, withdraws from the psychological demands and responsibilities of his adult marital relationship, and forms the incest relationship as a substitute or replacement. In adopting a position of dominance, the offender actively rules and controls the other family members to reassure himself of his adequacy and effectiveness. For both types of offenders, the passive-dependent-submissive type and the aggressive-controlling-dominant type, the incest behavior is a precarious and unsuccessful attempt to compensate for or replace a feeling of loss or deprivation. For this reason the formation of extended and meaningful extrafamilial relationships on the part of the spouse or offspring or the intervention attempts by external agencies or programs are very threatening to the offender. Such contacts pose the risk of family abandonment or of weakened control over the family.

In working with such offenders in treatment their characteristic modes of relating become similarly evident. The passive-dependent type of offender exhibits his sense of helplessness by looking to the therapist to cure him in some magical way. Although cooperative, he presents himself as the victim of external forces and events over which he has no control. The aggressive-dominant type of offender may be more blatantly resistant, denying the offense, failing to keep appointments, actively sabotaging the treatment plan, or even abandoning the family if all else fails.

Sexual Encounters between Adults and Children

The label "incest" does not refer to a diagnostic category; in regard to sexual behavior between an adult and a child it is a descriptive term identifying a family relationship between the offender and his victim. Incest is sexual behavior and in this context, then, is one category or subdivision of sexual offenses against children. Although it is not completely known what creates a sexual predisposition toward children on the part of an adult—what bio-psycho-social components, what developmental events, at what points, in what combinations, and in what intensities are critical in the etiology or such a sexual orientation— it is known that adults who are sexually attracted to children exhibit a wide variety of individual differences in this regard. Some are attracted only to girls; others, only to boys; some to both. Some are interested only in prepubertal children; others, in young adolescents; some in both. Some are drawn only to their own children; others, only to unrelated children; some to both. All these and other factors may combine in a variety of ways and differ from offender to offender.

Developmental traumas of all types need to be assessed in the life history of the sexual offender, especially sexual traumas. More so than nonoffenders, sexual offenders appear to have a higher incidence of having been sexually victimized when they themselves were children—a very conservative estimate is one out of every three. Very little is yet known about the long-range after-effects of sexual victimization on male children, but the clinician should be aware that one way of dealing with and combating the experience of being a helpless victim is to become the powerful victimizer;[2] the offender's offense may be in part a replication of his own victimization or other sexual trauma.

It must be kept in mind in addressing this complex and multidetermined issue that there is a wide spectrum of encounters between adults and children: (1) There are some adults whose sexual interests and activities are confined exclusively to children; (2) There are others who are predominantly interested in and sexually active with children and who prefer children but who may also under certain conditions engage in sexual activities with agemates; (3) There are some persons who initially appear to be oriented toward agemates but whose sexual interest in children emerges when their peer relationships become con-flictual and whose sexual involvements with children may then progress and coexist with or replace the sexual involvements with agemates; (4) There may be other persons whose sexual interests and activities are predominantly directed toward agemates and who may become sexually interested in and active with a child only under extraordinary situational circumstances, but such involvement is temporary and transitory and does not replace or continually coexist with sexual involvements with agemates.

Those adults who fall into categories 1 and 2 are described as fixated offenders, and those adults who fall into categories 3 and 4 are described as regressed offenders. Due to the ongoing and repetitive nature of their sexual contacts with children, adults who fall into the first three categories are those most likely to be identified, apprehended, and referred for evaluation and treatment. Although many offenders will allege that their offense is a single exception to an otherwise conventional sexual lifestyle prompted by extraordinary stresses, in fact it is rare that the clinician will be seeing someone who actually fits this fourth category, especially if the person is an incest offender. An example of the type of offender who will self-correct following a temporary encounter would be a serviceman who in a foreign country under wartime conditions might engage in sex with a child prostitute. Most incest offenders, however, find that they are unable spontaneously to abandon their emotional investment in and sexual involvement with their victim, sometimes even when the offense has been disclosed and efforts at clinical and legal intervention are being made. Their behavior thus takes on the character of a compulsion.

One of the basic tasks, then, in dealing with an adult who is predisposed sexually to molest children is to identify the various factors—offender, victim, and situational charcteristics—that will activate or inhibit such behavior on his part. In dealing with the incest offender a number of factors may relate to the commission of this offense by an adult who is prone to engage in sexual relations with a minor.

Motivations of the Offender

Parent-child incest behavior is equivalent to symptom formation in that it serves partially to gratify a need, to defend against anxiety, and to express an unresolved conflict. The incestuous offender becomes dependent on sexual activity to meet his emotional needs. He finds adult sexual relationships which require negotiation, mutuality, reciprocity, and shared commitment and investment either unsecurable or overtaxing, and he turns to his child for sexual gratification of his emotional needs without the demands of adult responsibility. Although it is a sexual offense, incest, like other forms of sexual assault, is not motivated primarily by sexual desire. The sexual offender is not committing his crimes to achieve sexual pleasure any more than the alcoholic is drinking to quench a thirst. Incest is sexual behavior in the service of nonsexual needs. It is the use of a sexual relationship to express a variety of unresolved problems or unmet needs in the psychology of the offender that have less to do with sensual pleasure and more to do with issues surrounding competency, adequacy, worth, recognition, validation, status, affiliation, and identity. It is the sexual misuse of power.

The incest behavior may serve a number of motivations simultaneously in the psychology of the offender. It may serve to validate his sense of worth and bolster his self-esteem:

> I liked the goofy attention I got from her. It was fun having her around and she made me feel good, like I was somebody again.

It may compensate for feeling abused or rejected by his wife or other women:

> When it came to being around women I always felt that in some way they were manipulating me or twisting me until they had me down and they'd keep me there. My wife used sex as a weapon against me to get her own way. When my daughter was born I was shoved aside.

It may serve to restore a sense of power and control to the offender:

> My wife was irresponsible so I took charge when it came to the kids. I was strict with them and they obeyed me. I guess that's why my daughter went along with it—she was obedient.

It may gratify a need for attention and recognition:

> I just couldn't seem to satisfy my wife. I tried everything. I just wanted her to want me—just for what I was, not for what I could give her. I try to buy attention if I can't get it any other way. I gave away all my money thinking maybe somebody would pay some attention to me or want me for that.

It may serve to meet a need for affiliation:

> I'm as lonely as hell. I have no one except my daughter. I think the world of that kid. I love her very, very much. It was a struggle. I wanted the sex to end and I wanted it to continue. My daughter and I were always close and we confided in each other. We could sit down and talk and just be good company.

It may temporarily strengthen his sense of identity:

> I guess I felt more like a man with someone younger that I was—there was nothing between me and my wife sexually. She'd tell me I wasn't any good in bed. I didn't have my wife as a virgin, so I guess having my stepdaughter made up for that. I was the first with her and she didn't have anyone to compare me against.

Although the incest offender may complain of a lack of sexual attention from his wife, it is significant that he turns to his daughter rather than to an unrelated adult as a substitute. An extramarital affair or a visit to a prostitute, are not typical outlets sought by the offender. Neither would be likely to provide him with a sense of being cared about although either might offer physical gratification. Sex in this fashion would be impersonal. It would confront him with the demands of negotiating an adult relationship—something which he feels exceeds his skills. And it would not provide the ongoing experience of intimacy and affection the offender is seeking. His daughter is more readily accessible, less demanding, more compliant. She is part of him, related, part of the family and therefore someone he feels closer to than an outsider. She is sexually inexperienced and if prepubertal, doesn't pose the risk of pregnancy. She can fulfill his sexual fantasies: the undemanding female who will be eagerly responsive to his every whim. As one offender crudely put it, "You know the saying: get them young and bring them up the way you like them." She is available upon demand. In addition, if the offender feels unappreciated, exploited, or betrayed by his spouse, the incest relationship not only compensates for what he feels he is being denied in his marriage, it also is a way to revenge himself, to get even, or retaliate against his wife for her failing or opposing him. In treating the incest offender, then, it will be important to identify the multiple and various motives underlying his offense in order to help him address these needs and issues in a more adaptive fashion. What motives are prominent in the offense, and what alternatives are available to the offender to resolve these needs?

Offender Characteristics

Although there is no set of unique personality features that distinguish incest offenders from other individuals, such offenders do tend to exhibit a number of pronounced traits or characteristics:

1. A general relating to life in which fantasy and passive dependency (submissiveness) replace active strivings (assertiveness), especially in interpersonal relationships, with the result that the offender experiences himself more as a helpless victim of external forces and events than as a person in control of himself and in charge of his life, producing

2. An intrinsic feeling of isolation, separateness, and apartness from others—the offender experiences himself psychologically as a loner, lacking any consistent sense of intimate attachment, belonging, or relatedness to others, which in turns results in

3. An underlying mood state of emptiness, fearfulness, and depression which combines with a sense of low self-esteem and poor self-confidence to make him oversensitive to what he interprets as criticisms, put-downs, exploitations, and rejections from a hostile and uncaring world; then

4. This lack of psychological comfort, security, and pleasure in life, and his deficient empathic skills, prompt him to regress from anxiety-producing adult relationships, to substitute fantasy for reality, and to replace adults with children who symbolize his own immaturity.

These unresolved issues that shape his incestuous involvement become reflected in his emotional overinvestment in his victim; his monopolization of her time; his restriction of her outside interests, activities, and relationships; his sexual preoccupation with her; the role-reversal in their relationship with her being regarded more as a peer than as a child; the identification he forms with his victim, his narcissistic sense of entitlement to her, and his projections of his own needs and desires on her; his preoccupation with fantasies about the victim; and the sense of pleasure, comfort, and safety he experiences in the relationship with her.

Mother-Child Incest

Although most identified cases of parental incest typically involve the father as the offending parent, there are situations in which the mother may be the offender or a co-offender, an active and participating accomplice in the sexual assault, or a passive bystander.

Case Example 3

> One 14-year-old victim reported that the first time her father performed sexual intercourse on her she cried out in pain and that her mother, who was lying next to her in bed, was holding her hand, trying to comfort her. On another occasion the victim's father had intercourse with her three times in one night as punishment for staying out too late, and the victim related that her mother was in the house at the time and witnessed what was going on. When the victim complained to her mother about her father's sexual behavior her mother said she could not do anything about it.

Typically such women are described as retarded or psychotic, but in fact our clinical research[3] would suggest that incest offenses by mothers may be more frequent than one would be led to believe from a review of the few cases documented in the literature. The socially accepted physical intimacy between a mother and her child may serve to mask incidents of sexual exploitation and abuse on the part of a mother. It may be that only sexually abusive mothers who are handicapped by serious mental illness or intellectual deficiency are detected since, by reason of their psychological impairment, they lack the skills to conceal successfully this behavior.

In the limited contact we have had with cases of mother-child incest, the same dynamics and motivations found in regard to the incestuous father are evident in regard to the incestuous mother. Where she is a co-offender or accomplice, her dependency on her spouse is a major contributing factor, and where she is an independent offender (especially if she is the only parent) her need for nurturance and control appear prominent. Some factors which may contribute to the evolution of mother-child incest may be the absence of this parent during the child's early years, relatively little discrepancy between the ages of the parent and child, sexual (especially incestuous) victimization of the mother as a young girl, the loss of spouse and the assuming of adult responsibilities (such as helping to support the family) on the part of the child, a history of indiscriminate or compulsive sexual activity on the part of the mother, and a history of alcohol or drug abuse.

Same-Sex Incest

Again, although most identified incest cases involve a parent with the child of the opposite sex, one may occasionally encounter a father-son sexual interaction, or, more rarely, one between a mother and daughter. It should not be assumed that such behaviors constitute a homosexual orientation on the part of the parent. Instead it may be that the child symbolizes the offender at a particular age, and it may be that the incest activity represents a recapitulation of the offender's own sexual victimization or trauma at that particular age. The same-sex factor may facilitate the symbolic identification with the victim and thus be more of a narcissistic victim choice than a homosexual one. In working with such cases, then, it is important to assess the offender's sexual interests, attitudes, and experiences with *agemates* of both the same and opposite sexes in order to determine the offender's actual sexual orientation and to interpret the incest behavior.

Case Example 4

> Peter is a 29-year-old white male with a good educational, military, and vocational background. He married a twice-divorced woman six years his senior who had two sons, ages 8 and 11, by a previous marriage. Peter describes his wife as "very domineering and promiscuous." She allegedly gave birth to an illegitimate child during their marriage. Peter's incestuous offenses followed the discovery of his wife's unfaithfulness. He forced his stepsons to perform fellatio on him and to submit to anal intercourse. These assaults extended over a two-year period until Peter, feeling remorseful, voluntarily confessed them to his wife. He has no criminal history apart from these offenses. His sexual interests are predominantly focused on adult women, and on several occasions he has had sexual affairs with other women, in one case with his wife's sister, but he has had no sexual interests or experiences with men.

Peter's sexual assault on his stepsons can be understood to constitute in part a retaliation against his wife by getting back at her through her boys, an acting out of his unexpressed feelings of anger and helplessness at being rejected by her; and in part an effort to compensate for what he feels is being denied him sexually. His choice of same-sex victims may reflect a projected identification with them, but also may simply be determined by the fact that his wife had only male offspring.

Offender Evaluation Issues

Incest offenders will come to the attention of the clinician in a variety of settings both community-based and institutional, such as outpatient mental health clinics or social service agencies, half-way houses and residential treatment facilities, mental hospitals and correctional institutions. Human service providers who work in such settings, then, need to have some specialized preparation and training in regard to dealing with this type of client.

The clinical evaluation of the incest offender needs to address the risk the offender constitutes of repeating his offense, the threat he poses to his victim, his need for and amenability to treatment, the modality of treatment that seems most appropriate for him, and the setting in which such treatment should take place. To accomplish this the clinician needs to assess the offender's general level of personality functioning, his overall ability to think rationally, act purposefully, communicate effectively, respond appropriately, and deal adaptively with his environment. Therefore, such issues as the offender's reality testing, frustration tolerance, characteristic mood state, impulse control, empathic ability, self-image and self-regard, and the like must be taken into consideration. Of major importance is the nature, intensity, and interrelationship of the offender's sexual and aggressive drives and his sexualization of nonsexual needs. Finally the clinician must consider the offender's prospective living arrangements and environment in regard to support or stress factors that will impact on him in that setting.

Since the offender typically operates from a position of power in regard to his victim, both in regard to age and social relationship, it is important then in confronting the offender that the clinician also operate from a power base. Knowledge is power and it is therefore necessary to obtain a dependable account of his incestuous behavior. It is essential to know the victim's version of the offense. These data permit the clinician to determine what the offender can acknowledge, what he minimizes or evades, what he distorts or misperceives, what he denies or justifies. All of this will have diagnostic and prognostic implications. Authority, too, is power and the clinician can capitalize on his role as an experienced worker in the area of sexual assault. The fact that the offender has victimized a child implies that adults are intimidating in some respect to him. The clinician's adulthood and professional position then provide an additional power factor. An affirmative approach that combines authority and support may prove most effective in working with the incest offender. In some ways, the approach that one would use with such an offender is the same as the approach one would use with a child: being direct, asking for cooperation in mutually examining the situation, being supportive but authoritative in exploring the known facts of the case. It is important never to lose sight of the offender's responsibility for his behavior nor to minimize its significance. Therefore, it is *essential* that clinicians who will be working with offenders have some knowledge of victimology and some experience in working with the victims of such offenders.

Once confronted with the victim's disclosure of his behavior, the offender may admit or deny his offense. If he denies it, he may adopt an openly hostile and antagonistic stance which can be countered by legal proceedings. Or he may adopt a more composed response where he presents himself as the victim of a false accusation. Such a position can be countered by suggesting that he undergo polygraph examination to substantiate his claim of innocence, pointing out to him that if he refuses there is the option of having his victim take the test. Or the clinician can point out that the veracity of the victim's allegations are not crucial. Instead, what are the unresolved family problems that prompt such allegedly "unfair" and "hostile" accusations on the part of his child toward him? The clinician can pose this question and emphasize that a concerned parent would want to participate in a treatment plan to resolve these problems.

If the offender admits to his offense he may qualify his admission by minimizing what he has done or projecting responsibility for it elsewhere. The most common type of minimization is to allege that the sexual activity occurred only once. Most probably it did not, and the clinician can point out that experience tells us such a single incident is extremely rare. More important, did the offender see this experience coming, did he anticipate becoming sexually active with a child? If so, then either he deliberately permitted the behavior to occur or he was unable to avoid it; if he did not see this experience coming, then there is nothing to prevent it from happening again in a similarly unanticipated fashion. In addition to or instead of minimizing the actual behavior, the offender may attempt to minimize his responsibility for his actions by putting the blame elsewhere. For the adult offender there are three frequent targets for such blame: alcohol, the victim, or the wife.

The offender may claim his sexual offense was the product of intoxication. Offense data can serve to substantiate or disprove a state of inebriation at the times of sexual involvement but actually this is beside the point. If drinking leads to incestuous behavior, why does he drink? What responsible course of action did he take in regard to his drinking when he discovered it resulted in incestuous activity? If in fact, the offender has a drinking problem it should be pointed out to him that this is not a cause of his incestuous behavior—drinking may instead serve to give him the courage to act on such impulses—and the incest and the drinking more likely are two separate and independent symptoms of the same underlying problem which he may not yet be aware of or know how to cope with.

Very often the offender will allege that the victim was at least partly to blame for his behavior, that she or he behaved in a provocative or seductive fashion and may have actually initiated the sexual activity. There are three possibilities: (1) the offender is lying, (2) the offender is misinterpreting the victim's behavior, (3) the offender is not lying. The major clinical issue in any case is not what the victim allegedly did but how the offender behaved. If the child behaved in a sexually inappropriate fashion why didn't the offender correct her or him? Some offenders may eroticize the normal behaviors of children and project their wishes and interests onto the child. In situations where the offender is telling the truth and the child is behaving in a sexually explicit fashion, it is essential for the clinician not to adopt the offender's perception of the child as seductive. The myth of the "seductive" child is one fostered by psychoanalytic practitioners as well as child molesters. Seduction refers to the deliberate and conscious manipulation of a person, without him or her fully realizing it, into a situation that will encourage that person to be receptive to sexual advances. This does not describe the activity of a child in relation to an adult. Any sexually inappropriate activity on the part of a child should be referred to as stylized— not seductive—behavior, and should be interpreted as indicating that the child may have been programmed to behave in this fashion, his or her behavior being symptomatic of the child's sexual trauma or victimization. If the child is in fact behaving in a sexually explicit fashion, a responsible adult will not encourage or promote such behavior but instead will correct it and try to determine why the child is behaving in this manner.

Generally the offender will report that his conflicted relationship with his wife is in some way responsible for his sexual intimacy with his child. Again, the offender must be confronted with his failure to address the marital problems in a responsible fashion (for example, seeking out marital counseling) and with his contribution to the creation and perpetuation of such problems in the marriage.

In those instances where the offender accepts full responsibility for his incestuous behavior, he may justify his actions as acceptable and as an indication of caring and commitment to his child. Sometimes the offenders will state that they see incest as less serious than adultery or that the incest was a form of sex education for their child. Usually such offenders have no appreciation of the negative impact of such behavior on the victim—seeing it instead as an expression of love and affection. In such cases, sensitizing and re-educating the offender is essential. Offenders need to hear that sexual abuse of a child usually leads to impaired psychosocial development with many life problems as a result: for example, sexual dysfunction, alcohol-drug abuse, prostitution, depression, difficulties in relating to others, and similar hardships. Confronting the offender with films such as "Childhood Sexual Abuse" (Motorola Teleprograms Inc.) which dramatize the plight of the victim or perhaps with audiotapes made by former victims may be helpful. The impact of seeing and hearing individuals recount how sexual victimization undermined their subsequent development and burdened their lives may help to dispell some of the offenders' attitudes and beliefs. There are some caveats for the clinician, however. If or when the offender admits his offense (or comes to appreciate his wrong doing) and experiences a sense of guilt and feelings of remorse for his behavior, he may in some cases experience a major depression which could in turn activate heavy drinking or suicidal urges or destructive behavior. The clinician needs to anticipate such reactions and be ready to provide crisis intervention and support for this client.

It would be erroneous to believe that an incest offender can be cured. Instead, it is perhaps more realistic to regard this problem in the same fashion as a drinking problem—rather than hoping to be cured, the offender must accept his own responsibility for maintaining a conscientious and lifelong effort to keep sexually abusive behavior under control. There is always the risk of recidivism. What treatment can do is to reduce the risk (1) by helping him to become in closer touch with the major unmet needs underlying this behavior and to find more adaptive ways of satisfying these needs, (2) by helping him to identify those life-demands he cannot successfully cope with and to find ways of avoiding stress related to those demands, and (3) by helping him become more sensitive to the life conditions and his characteristic behavior patterns that are antecedents of his incestuous activity so that he can detect early warning signals and interrupt the evolution of an incestuous offense. A treatment program encompassing re-education, resocialization, and counseling involving individual, marital, and family therapy supplemented by a peer or self-help support group is generally necessary, especially when the decision of the family is to remain intact or to reunite. Improving parenting skills, increasing social skills, enhancing communication skills, assertiveness training, sex therapy, and stress management may all be important components of the treatment program. In cases where the marriage terminates, the offender may either react with fear and depression, which requires helping him work through the loss, or with relief. In the latter case there may be no identified problems the offender feels any need to address and, therefore, assignment to a therapy group may be a more productive treatment plan than individual counseling. If the offender is institutionalized in a mental hospital or correctional institution, it is necessary, especially if the family plans to be reunited at some point, that the institutional treatment program for the offender and the community-based treatment program for the child, wife, and other significant family members be closely coordinated. For example, in Connecticut, a Sex Offender Program operated within the correctional system and a Sexual Trauma Treatment Program operated in the community. Prison staff who led a therapy group for incestuous fathers regularly attended case conferences at the Sexual Trauma Treatment Program, and staff from this community agency participated as cotherapists in the Sex Offender Program. Not only then were treatment plans and efforts for all family members synchronized, but also an ongoing treatment relationship and program was established in which the offender would continue following release from prison.

Treatment Considerations

Obviously not all incest offenders are alike. There is a wide variety of individual differences among such persons. Nevertheless, we have found in working with incest offenders that a number of issues present themselves with sufficient frequency to be regarded as common characteristics in regard to this client population. It may be helpful, then, to keep the following in mind in approaching and working with this type of referral:

1. You are dealing with an unmotivated client. He has not self-referred. It will therefore be important to insure his cooperation in a treatment program by having his participation mandated by an external authority such as a court.

2. His sexual offense is not only a symptom, it is also a crime and needs to be dealt with on both levels, requiring a combined mental health, social service, and criminal justice intervention.

3. He fears the adverse social and legal consequences of disclosure and will therefore tend to deny the offense or minimize his responsibility for his actions. He must not be allowed to deny his offense, minimize the seriousness of his behavior, or project responsibility for his actions elsewhere.

4. He has operated from a position of power in regard to his victim and has maintained his control by effecting secrecy in regard to his offense. The conventional therapeutic contract typically involves confidentiality. For this type of client confidentiality contributes to the dynamics of secrecy and reinforces the offender's position of power and control. It should be waived. Not only must any suspected or known incident of incestuous behavior be reported to the proper authorities but also if the offender's spouse is not aware of the situation, he must inform her of it, describing what has occurred. In the case of sibling incest, the parents must be similarly informed. The offender should be told from the outset that the worker may divulge information obtained in treatment to court, probation, parole, or other agencies upon request and whenever such disclosure seems warranted in the judgment of the worker. The clinician's primary responsibility is not the offender-client but the protection and well-being of the victim.

5. Although incest is a sexual offense, it is not predominantly motivated by sexual needs. It is the sexual expression of nonsexual needs. An incest offender does not commit a sexual offense primarily to satisfy a sexual need any more

than an alcoholic drinks to quench a thirst. It will, therefore, be necessary to help the offender uncover the underlying nonsexual needs and issues prompting his offense; and to discover why sexuality has become the mode of expression for these unmet needs or unresolved issues. Especially important in this respect will be a careful and detailed exploration of the offender's sexual offenses and his own sexual development, especially in regard to any history of his own (or his parents', sibling's, or wife's) sexual victimization or other sexual traumas.[4]

6. Although other family members may play a contributing role in the evolution of the incestuous relationship, the offender's responsibility for the offense cannot be mitigated by viewing incest as solely the product of family dysfunction. The offender must be held accountable, and therefore family therapy should not be the only, and especially not the initial, plan of action. It must be preceded by individual treatment

7. The offender generally feels himself to be overwhelmed by life-demands and to be the helpless victim of social forces and life events outside of his control. In addition, then, to conventional, insight-oriented psychotherapy, he needs to be provided with types of treatment that will help him develop skills and techniques to cope more adequately with life-demands, such as biofeedback and relaxation exercises to diminish anxiety, assertiveness training, parent effectiveness training, and the like.

Disposition Assessment

To the extent that the offender lacks the motivation or the ability to control his incestuous behavior, strict external limits and firm controls must be placed on him. Therefore, in considering appropriate disposition, a number of issues should be examined to determine whether the offender can be managed on an outpatient basis in a community-based program or whether he requires incarceration or institutionalization and residential treatment.

Outpatient care as a stipulation of a continuance of the case or as a condition of probation may appear to be a more appropriate disposition when:

1. The incest did not involve physical force or threat of physical harm to the victim.

2. The offense constituted a regression under stress, rather than a chronic sexual fixation on children, and occurred in response to identifiable and extraordinary precipitating stresses or events which have diminished or are no longer operative.

3. Apart from the incestuous behavior the offender does not have a criminal record and has not led a criminal lifestyle.

4. The offender acknowledges his responsibility for the offense, appreciates its inappropriateness, is concerned about the possible consequences of its impact on the victim, and is genuinely distressed about his behavior.

5. The offender has dependable social and occupational skills to manage most life-demands adequately, and he does not exhibit any evidence of major psychopathology such as psychosis, retardation, alcoholism, severe depression, organic brain dysfunction, and the like.

6. There are strong support services available in the community such as the availability of mental health services, employment opportunities, and an advocate for the victim if it is the wish of the family to remain united or an extended family placement for the offender should his marriage terminate or should it not be appropriate for him initially to reside in the same domicile with his victim.

Conversely, residential treatment within a security setting such as a correctional institution or a mental health facility would seem to be warranted when:

1. The threat of harm or actual physical abuse, injury, battering, or other violence played a part in the commission of the offense, or the offender used a weapon, alcohol or drugs to incapacitate the victim, or the sexual offense involved any bizarre or ritualistic acts (such as bondage or sadomasochistic practices), or the victim was forced into prostitution or pornographic activities, or there has been a progressive increase in aggression on the part of the offender over time.

2. The sexual offense is but one aspect of the offender's antisocial behavior, and he has had multiple and chronic difficulties with the law in both sexual and nonsexual areas.

3. The offender's psychological adjustment has always been tenuous or borderline, especially if his incestuous behavior is compounded by evidence of serious psychopathology such as psychosis, substance abuse, organic brain dysfunction, or the like which makes his conduct unpredictable.

4. The offense reflects a chronic and persistent sexual attraction to children (both related and unrelated) in general on the part of the offender and especially if it constitutes but one of multiple types of indiscriminate sexual activity evidenced by this offender (such as exposing, peeping, sexual contact with animals, fetishism, and the like).

5. The offender denies or minimizes his offenses or projects the responsibility for his behavior externally (such as blaming the victim or attributing the offense to a state of intoxication) and is more distressed by the consequences to himself of the disclosure than concerned about the impact his offense may have had on his victim, and thus is not genuinely motivated for treatment.

If the offender is to be treated on an outpatient basis, it has been our experience that such clinical intervention is more effective when it is mandated by the court as part of a disposition in a criminal proceeding. Initially the offender may make a serious effort to understand himself, his feelings, and the reasons for his offense. Family and marital problems which may have played a contributing role in the offense may be submerged as wife and children feel pressured to unite with the offender against the external threat of prosecution, conviction, incarceration, and disruption of the nuclear family. When these immediate threats and pressures subside, however, there may be a reemergence of the offender's pathological behavior.

If the offender is institutionalized, he will be relieved of many of the responsibilities, demands, and stresses of family life. His daily activities will be structured for him; other persons and agencies will assume his marital, parental, and financial obligations; treatment will be provided; and activating factors such as alcohol, the stimulating presence of a victim, and the like will be absent. Under such conditions his pathological behavior may subside or diminish only to reappear again upon release and reunion with his family.

Recidivism is a major concern when the untreated (or perhaps untreatable) offender has been released from a structured and protective setting and again becomes overwhelmed by intrafamily issues. The authority of the criminal justice system in the form of the court and the probation-parole department must provide back-up support for the clinician in such cases. Their help is crucial to insure continued participation in treatment by the offender until such issues are resolved or, failing that, to provide victim protection by again removing the offender from the community. Effective treatment intervention with such clients requires a multidisciplinary and interagency *team* approach.

Notes

1. A Nicholas Groth and H. Jean Birnbaum, "Adult Sexual Orientation and the Attraction to Underage Persons," *Archives of Sexual Behavior,* 7, no. 3 (1978), pp. 175–81.

2. A. Nicholas Groth with H. Jean Birnbaum, *Men who Rape: The Psychology of the Offender* (New York: Plenum, 1979), pp. 98–103.

3. Groth with Birnbaum, *Men Who Rape,* pp. 102–103.

4. For a protocol for assessing an offender's sexual development and offenses, see Groth with Birnbaum, *Men Who Rape,* chapter 5, pp. 207–214.

9 Family Treatment

Suzanne M. Sgroi

Family Treatment means *family therapy* to many helping services professionals. They further assume that family therapy is the treatment of choice for incest cases, that it should begin immediately whenever possible, and that family treatment is not indicated for other types of child sexual abuse. These are all misconceptions. Some degree of family treatment is nearly always indicated in both intrafamily and extrafamily cases. Instead of limiting therapeutic intervention to family therapy, a variety of treatment modalities should be employed with families of children who have been sexually victimized. When family therapy *is* utilized, it should be employed in conjunction with other treatment modalities and should not begin until individual therapeutic relationships have been established with the key family members.

This chapter first addresses the type and degree of family treatment required by the various categories of child sexual abuse. Then the characteristics and treatment needs of the parental incest family are described. Sections of the chapter are devoted to working with involuntary clients and to describing the psychosocial equivalent of total life support since an understanding of these key concepts and their application to family treatment of child sexual abuse is essential. Various family treatment modalities and the treatment needs they must address are then described. The concluding sections of this chapter discuss development of family treatment programs and treatment outcomes. It is meant to be read in conjunction with chapter 1, ''A Conceptual Framework for Child Sexual Abuse.''

Indications for Family Treatment

Assessment of Family Contribution

A family assessment should be conducted in every validated case of child sexual abuse regardless of the identity of the perpetrator. Although a lengthy assessment process may not be necessary, the strengths and weaknesses of *every* family member should be identified. The family's *contribution* to the sexual abuse must also be assessed. Was the child's victimization a capricious, one-time-only event with an unknown outside perpetrator whose access to the child was accidental, totally unforeseeable, and completely beyond the control of the parents or guardians? Although incidents of this type *do* occur, they are exceedingly rare. Instead, most cases of child sexual abuse involve perpetrators who are known to the child and interactions which are, in large measure, predictable and preventable. Assessing the type and degree of family contribution to the child's sexual victimization is key to determining indications for family treatment. The following issues should be examined for all cases.

Poor Supervision. Often children are sexually abused because of poor supervision by their parents or caretakers. In other words, the child is placed at risk for sexual abuse through the omission of a responsible adult. For example, a child who lives in a home where adults are frequently engaging in sexual activity with multiple caretakers is at great risk for sexual abuse, even if the caretakers have no intention of involving the child. The youngster's exposure to many adults who are engaging in casual sexual encounters with his or her parent or guardian is confusing at best, but may be downright dangerous since transient sexual partners are less likely to observe usual societal limits.

An example of poor supervision outside the home involves parents who permit young children to frequent public places such as restaurants or bars, especially at late hours and unaccompanied by a responsive caretaker. Parents who do not screen and set limits on their children's playtimes, playmates, and play areas are also exercising poor supervision. This is not to say that parents or guardians can or should exercise direct oversight of their school-age children on a 24-hour basis. However, many cases of child sexual abuse are occurring within a milieu of complete parental abdication of supervisory responsibility. Such children are likely to be perceived by their parents as "able to take care of themselves," even at ages five or six years.

Whenever poor supervision inside or outside the home has contributed to the sexual abuse of a child, parental assumption of appropriate supervisory responsibility becomes a family treatment issue. The odds are that a pattern of lack of parental supervision will be present rather than an isolated lapse. It is also likely that changing the pattern will require more than simply calling attention to the problem. Role modeling by the therapist and peer group reinforcement after discussion and demonstration of appropriate parental supervision will usually be required for significant change to take place. If it does not, the child may be sexually abused again.

Poor Choice of Surrogate Caretakers or Babysitters. Children are often sexually abused by surrogate caretakers or babysitters. Again, it is the responsibility of parents and guardians to select individuals who will be responsible for their children with great care. Complaints of sexual abuse of a child by mother's boyfriend who is left to care for the youngster while mother goes shopping or to work occur too frequently to be ignored. Adolescents are often used as babysitters for children with no thought given to the fact that adolescence is a stage of intense sexual curiosity and exploration. If appropriate limits are not set and enforced, adolescent babysitters often invite their friends to "keep them company" while they are ostensibly taking care of children. Sometimes a friend will instigate the sexual abuse of the child unbeknownst to the babysitter. Other times, the babysitter and friend(s) will jointly engage in sexual abuse of their charges. Of course, a related or unrelated babysitter may also sexually abuse a child by himself or herself. Adolescent males are generally inappropriate persons to be chosen as babysitters because, in addition to all the tendency toward sexual exploration associated with that developmental stage, society places fewer inhibitions on aggressive behavior in males than in females.

Child sexual abuse by a surrogate caretaker or babysitter also becomes a family treatment issue. The parent or guardian must accept responsibility for entrusting the child to this person. If inappropriate limit setting for visitors to the caretaker or babysitter was also involved, the treatment issue is compounded. If the caretaker or babysitter is a family member or occupies a parental or familial role for the child (for example, sibling or mother's boyfriend), this issue is further complicated by all the dynamics of intrafamily child sexual abuse.

Inappropriate Sleeping Arrangements. Sometimes the choice of sleeping arrangements for family members will be a contributing factor in child sexual abuse. The practice of "doubling up" children of the opposite sex to sleep together in the same bed or even in the same room also creates an unnecessary risk of inappropriate sexual activity. When there is a significant age disparity between them, sexual abuse of a younger child by an older silbing or cousin may also occur. As Laury (1978) points out, this practice is not limited to lower-class families who sleep under crowded conditions because of poverty. Middle-class parents may consolidate family sleeping arrangements in order to free a bedroom for use as a family room or den. Whatever the reason, when children of the opposite sex who are agemates regularly sleep together, a level of intimacy is fostered which places them at higher risk for sexual activity with each other. When a younger child sleeps with an adolescent sibling of the opposite sex, he or she is placed at risk for forced or pressured sexual victimization by the adolescent (see also chapter 6, "Sibling Incest").

Inappropriate sleeping arrangements are an obvious treatment issue which may be difficult to resolve because of associated dynamics. In all probability, the parents' choice to permit inappropriate sleeping arrangements is associated with blurring of role boundaries within the family.

Blurred Role Boundaries. Family interaction characterized by blurring of role boundaries can be both a predisposing factor for, as well as a result of, intra-family child sexual abuse. It is mentioned in this section because it is clearly a treatment issue for the family as a whole as well as for individual family members including the victim and the offender. Significant blurring of familial role boundaries can only take place when parents permit this to happen and fail to set appropriate expectations and limits for themselves as well as for the children. Inappropriate genital exposure, lack of privacy with respect to bathroom and sleeping arrangements, and permitting physically intimate behavior by parents and children to occur with children both as witnesses and participants—all are examples of blurring of familial role boundaries which may predispose to child sexual abuse.

Since parents or persons who occupy family power positions are clearly responsible for blurring of role boundaries, this treatment issue must be addressed to insure the future safety of the child. If treatment for this issue is limited to the victim and he or she must continue to live at home, the risk for reoccurrence of the sexual abuse is very great.

Sexual Abuse by a Family Member. This is an obvious family contribution to child sexual abuse as regards the actions of the perpetrator who is a family member. However, sexual abuse of a child by a single family member usually involves some degree of direct or indirect participation by other family members as well. For example, one family member may "set up" a child to be victimized by another family member. However, incest is more often a result of indirect contribution by every family member. As Poznanski and Blos (1975) point out, in cases of father-daughter incest, the mother has nearly always failed to set or enforce appropriate limits on the interactions between her husband and daughter which preceded the sexual activity.

Unless effective family treatment is provided for cases of intrafamily child sexual abuse, it can be predicted that every family member (father, mother, child victim(s) and siblings) is at risk to act out subsequent scenarios of sexual abuse. This could take the form of repeated sexual abuse of the original victim or sexual abuse of a sibling. If the parents separate, the offending parent may victimize another child (his or her own child or a stepchild) if an affiliation with another family takes place. If the nonoffending spouse remarries, there is great risk that he or she will select a partner who will sexually victimize *their* child(ren). Lastly, the child victim or siblings may themselves grow up to become sexual offenders. (This is also a possible outcome for child victims of sexual abuse by an outside perpetrator).

Family Treatment Issues, by Category of Sexual Abuse

Extrafamily. In this category of sexual abuse, perpetrators are likely to be known to the child and his or her family. Almost invariably, the victim's parent or guardian will have permitted the perpetrator to have access to the child as a visitor in the home or else will have entrusted the child's care to the perpetrator. Babysitters, friends of the family, neighbors, daycare or school personnel, or adults who work with children in groups are all included in this category. Whenever the child's parent exercised a degree of choice over the perpetrator's access to the child, the following may apply.

Family Contribution. In cases involving an outside perpetrator, the family contribution is usually limited to poor supervision or the appropriate choice of a surrogate caretaker of babysitter. The critical issue is *failure to protect.* Treatment of either variety of family contribution is usually best achieved by some combination of authoritative guidance and peer-group reinforcement. A comprehensive community child-sexual-abuse treatment program could provide a treatment modality that would be helpful (that is, a functioning parent group for parents to attend for a limited number of sessions in which issues of appropriate supervision and selection of babysitters would be discussed). An important exception should be noted here: sexual abuse by an unrelated surrogate caretaker who nevertheless occupies an important familial role for the child or a spousal relationship for a single parent (for example, mother's boyfriend). Family treatment issues for the latter are similar to those for child sexual abuse by a family member.

Impact on the Victim. This becomes a family treatment issue because of the perception by family members that a child who has been prematurely introduced to sexuality is somehow magically changed by his or her sexual experience (Burgess and Holmstrom, 1979). As explained in chapter 4, ''Treatment of the Sexually Abused Child,'' the family's perception nearly always reinforces the victim's belief that he or she has been damaged.

At minimum, there should be counseling of the child's parents which addresses all of the impact issues for the child as well as the associated treatment implications. In some families, short-term treatment (beyond counseling) will be required to resolve these issues. Siblings will also require counseling, and at least one session involving the entire family is indicated to set the tone for the future, to clear the air, and to bring any fears or concerns about the victim into the open. Some degree of family treatment is thus essential to the success of the treatment plan for the victim even in cases of extrafamily child sexual abuse.

Intrafamily (Nonparent Perpetrator). This category of child sexual abuse may involve older siblings, cousins, aunts, uncles, or members of the extended family as perpetrators. When a child has been sexually abused by a relative who is not a parent and who does not occupy a parental role with respect to the victim, the same types of treatment issues apply as with an extrafamily perpetrator, but in an expanded form.

Family Contribution. This may range from a major contribution to the sexual abuse to none at all. Poor supervision or poor choice of surrogate caretakers may underlie child sexual abuse by a relative who is not a parent. Sometimes an older sibling or cousin or aunt or uncle or some other member of the extended family may be permitted access to the target child with poor supervision or no supervision exercised. The large family picnic or other type of extended family gathering when there may be several hours of unsupervised activity for children ranging from older pre-school age straight through adolescence is a good illustration. Such gatherings may provide an opportunity for older children to pressure or force younger relatives to engage in a variety of sexual activities (including all types of sexual penetration) that go far beyond "acceptable" levels of sexual exploration by age mates. Although the parents or guardians of both the aggressors and the victims may be unaware of the character of the unsupervised activity, their lack of oversight and failure to anticipate the need for supervision become family treatment issues.

Likewise, child sexual abuse may occur when a relative who is not a parent is chosen to be a surrogate caretaker or babysitter. All of the same dynamics pertain as when the poor choice of surrogate caretaker is *not* a family member but with the additional problem of divided loyalty. As Burgess and Holmstrom (1977) aptly described, every family member must make a decision to ally himself or herself with either the perpetrator or victim whenever a child is sexually abused by a relative. Thus the divided loyalty itself becomes another treatment issue as well as the guilt experienced by each family member who must make such a difficult decision, regardless of his or her choice. For the parent or guardian who is responsible for the poor choice of surrogate caretaker, accepting responsibility and dealing with his or her guilt for *that* choice also become treatment issues. Lastly, avoiding future "mistakes" regarding appropriate supervision and choice of surrogate caretakers must be addressed.

Predictably, when the person who has sexually abused the child is a relative, the underlying dynamics will be complex. Therapists should be alerted to look for other types of family contribution to child sexual abuse such as, inappropriate sleeping arrangements and blurred role boundaries. Again, it should be noted that these are unlikely to be associated accidentally with child sexual abuse by a family member (the reverse is more likely to be true.)

Thus the critical issues regarding family contribution to this category of child sexual abuse are *failure to protect* (as in extrafamily cases) and *failure to set appropriate limits* (re sleeping arrangements and role boundaries). Treatment should again be provided for the parents since both of the above are clearly parental responsibilities and prerogatives. As before, a combination of authoritative guidance and peer-group reinforcement will probably be most effective. Therapists should anticipate that pressure will be required to engage these parents in an effective treatment program and that a longer period of participation in treatment will be required.

Impact on the Child. In addition to societal and cultural barriers to recognizing the actual impact of child sexual abuse by an extrafamily perpetrator upon a victim, there is an added dimension when the perpetrator is a relative. Chapter 4, "Treatment of the Sexually Abused Child," describes the phenomenon of "blaming the victim" for the sexual activity. Therapists must anticipate that divided loyalty (child versus perpetrator) will further complicate this issue. If a stranger or a person who is not a relative is the perpetrator, family members are probably less likely to blame the victim for instigating or failing to halt the sexual activity. However, the degree of blame placed upon the perpetrator and the victim when both are relatives may well be determined by the esteem in which they are held and by their relative value as perceived by other family members. Needless to say, this becomes a major treatment issue when the victim remains within the family after the sexual abuse has been disclosed. If powerful family members decide to hold the victim responsible for the sexually abusive behavior and cannot be swayed in this decision during early intervention, the prognosis for family treatment is poor.

Family Response to Treatment of the Child. Adequate treatment for the victim of child sexual abuse can never take place in a familial vacuum: even when the victim is separated from the rest of the family, their response to his or her treatment is profoundly important. If the treatment is effective, the child's behavior can be expected to change in a variety of ways which will inevitably affect the rest of the family. For example, a child who is fearful, withdrawn, and docile may become more assertive and demanding as he or she improves. Although these may be healthy behavior patterns, the child's changed behavior may be perceived as disruptive and unwelcome unless the family's response is anticipated and modified. The parents should be made aware of the impact of the sexual abuse upon the child and the treatment needs which will be addressed in therapy. They should be made a part of the treatment plan as much as possible and be helped to recognize and discourage inappropriate behavior and to reinforce healthy behavior as the child's treatment progresses. They should also be helped to see how their own behavior, especially with respect to blurring of role boundaries and inappropriate expectations of the child, has contributed to the sexual abuse. Unless the latter are modified, the family's response to the child's treatment is likely to be undermining and perhaps even destructive.

Intrafamily (Parent or Parent-Figure Perpetrator). First, all of the treatment issues described for intrafamily child sexual abuse by a nonparent perpetrator may also apply to this category. Perpetrators may be fathers or mothers of the child victim, stepparents, grandparents, or the boyfriend or girlfriend of the child's parent. Fathers and mothers of the child victim obviously belong in this category. Stepparents are included, despite the lack of a biological relationship, for the same reason as the boyfriend or girlfriend of the child's parent—they all occupy a familial role for the child. Grandparents are included in this category of perpetrators because they may also occupy a parental role for the victim. Cases of child sexual abuse by a grandparent may be especially complicated since this individual may also have sexually abused the child's parent in the past.

Family Contribution. Three critical issues pertain when a child is sexually abused by a parent or parent figure. They are *failure to protect, failure to set limits,* and *abuse of power.*

Failure to protect obviously applies when poor supervision and poor choice of surrogate caretaker are involved (when the perpetrator is a nonrelated boyfriend or girlfriend of the victim's parent). However, this critical issue applies to sexual abuse of a child by a parent, stepparent or grandparent as well. Almost invariably, the nonoffending parent(s) failed to protect the child victim in a variety of ways and these will be important treatment issues.

Failure to set limits is always a critical issue in this category of child sexual abuse. The perpetrator clearly failed to set limits on himself or herself; otherwise he or she would not have sexually abused the child. However, all parent figures failed to set limits with respect to blurring of role boundaries and role confusion as an additional family contribution.

Abuse of power is always a critical issue in family treatment of child sexual abuse by a parent or parent figure. Treatment of the victim must always address this issue, regardless of the identity of the perpetrator or the category of sexual abuse which pertains. However, *abuse of power* tends to be a way of life and a dominant aspect of family interaction in incestuous families. It is emphasized here because it will invariably be the key to family treatment. No significant family treatment will be permitted to take place unless this critical issue is addressed since powerful family members will either block participation by all or else will sabotage therapy for those who do participate.

No child victim of sexual abuse by a parent or parent figure who remains at home with the perpetrator will be safe unless there is family treatment which effectively addresses these three critical issues. It is unlikely that effective family treatment can or will occur in the absence of an authoritative incentive (the legal justice system). Some combination of individual, group, dyad, and family therapy will be required. Treatment efforts must be intensive and long-term for significant improvement to take place.

Impact on the Child. All of the family treatment issues described when the perpetrator is a family member who is not a parent pertain to this category as well. Therapists must anticipate that the victim's parent(s) will be less likely to acknowledge the impact of the sexual abuse upon the child and his or her need for treatment. Conflicts around divided loyalty will be very intense and the parents may choose to support each other and ignore the child's needs rather than make the significant changes in their own behavior that would otherwise be required. They may choose to blame the victim entirely both for the sexual activity and the disruption following disclosure. The parent(s) may also choose to reject the victim and to encourage his or her separation from the family. When this occurs, the child must be separated for his or her own safety, and there is little chance that family treatment offers any chance for the child to be reunited with the family. On the other hand, the parent(s) may choose to keep the child at home and further abuse power by exerting enormous pressure upon him or her to recant the allegation of sexual abuse and stop cooperating with outside authority figures. Again, when this occurs, the prognosis for family treatment is grave.

The minimum acceptable goal for family treatment with respect to impact upon the child is to "build in" at least one functioning adult ally for the child in the home. This person should be the nonoffending parent but could also be an older sibling, a grandparent, or other family member (with appropriate safeguards). If there is no person within the family circle who can serve as a functioning adult ally for the child, the therapist must reluctantly opt for the child to be removed from the home. This issue is also discussed under *child-protection assessment* in chapter 3, "An Approach to Case Management."

Finally, therapists should be aware that divided loyalty conflicts may be especially problemmatic when the perpetrator is the child's grandparent. The child's parent who is also the child of the offending grandparent has the additional burden of coping with a parental role occupied by the perpetrator. Therapists should anticipate that blaming the victim and rejecting the victim are at least as likely and perhaps even more likely to occur.

Family Response to Treatment of the Child. The family's response as the child victim progresses in treatment will probably be the most important determinant for success or failure. Strong family resistance or hostility can sabotage treatment efforts aimed at the sexually abused child. For example, a youngster who formerly was docile and passive and who performed age-inappropriate tasks without resistance may become much more assertive and unwilling to discharge inappropriate homemaking or child-care responsibilities. Although these changes may be healthy for the child victim, other family members are likely to react with alarm, hostility, and efforts to restore the status quo. Without some type of family treatment, it is unlikely that the child victim who continues to live at home can ever be "reprogrammed" to behave in an age-appropriate fashion or to occupy the role of a child appropriately. If blurred role boundaries were a prominent underlying factor, it is virtually impossible to restructure one without restructuring all. Even youngsters who live away from their families after disclosure of sexual abuse usually see or visit with family members thereafter. It is amazing how quickly a negative family response to the victim's new behaviors (even during a short visit) can undermine gains made over months of treatment. Accordingly, treating the child who has been sexually abused by a parent or a parent figure without family treatment will have limited success whenever the child continues to live at home with the perpetrator who still occupies a power position.

Characteristics and Treatment Needs of Parental Incest Families

Although the underlying premise of this chapter is that some level of family treatment is indicated for all categories of child sexual abuse, it is undeniable that the treatment needs of the incestuous family with a parent or parent figure who is the perpetrator are many and complex. Chapter 1, "A Conceptual Framework for Child Sexual Abuse," described the family dynamics of incest and profiles of each family member. Parental incest families have been appropriately described as character-disordered by Anderson and Shafer (1979) because they are comprised of individuals who exhibit many of the personality characteristics of character-disordered persons. The authors suggest that a treatment model for the character-disordered family should parallel the treatment model for an individual who is character-disordered.

Beavers's (1976) description of pathological families is highly applicable to families in which parental incest has taken place: isolated, closed, energy-draining systems with "little vital interaction with the outside world" and possessing limited adaptive mechanisms or capacity for interval change or growth of individual members. He further describes the most seriously disturbed families as "chaotic, clinging in a sticky lump (the amorphous family ego mass)"; in these families "dreams, fantasies, and a studied unawareness function in place of goal-directed, active negotiation among persons." For less seriously disturbed or "mid-range" families, Beavers (ibid) uses the analogy of a "primitive sea animal with one large muscle attached to a jaw" to illustrate their rigidity, limited coping mechanisms, and vulnerability. Therapists who have worked with numerous parental incest families are likely to recognize the applicability of Beavers's descriptions. The majority of parental incest families fall within the mid-range category; a smaller but highly memorable proportion are chaotic in type.

Assessing the degree and type of family pathology is certainly appropriate for those who would venture to treat parental incest families. The prognosis for treatment of chaotic families is extremely poor. The prognosis for treatment of "mid-range" families is more optimistic but should still retain the degree of caution usually employed when forecasting treatment outcomes for individuals who can be described as "character disordered." A careful assessment of family functioning and treatment needs should precede the decisions of whether to treat (or not to treat), who to treat, and how to treat. Invariably, the treatment needs described below will pertain for the parent who is the perpetrator of incestuous child sexual abuse; frequently they pertain to the family as a functioning unit and to the other family members as well. Since, by definition, child sexual abuse is perpetrated by someone who occupies a power position over the victim, it is not surprising that the perpetrator usually sets or exemplifies the overall style for the pathological family interaction as well.

Abuse of Power

In parental incest families more powerful individuals abuse their positions of power in order to gratify their own needs without regard for the harm to others which may result. This is, of course, exemplified by the parent's choice to engage his or her child in sexual activity in order to gratify nonsexual needs (see also chapter 1, "A Conceptual Framework for Child Sexual Abuse"). Child sexual abuse is always an aggressive act by the perpetrator, even when there is no force or violence employed. Aggressive rather than benevolent use of power by the strong against the weak becomes the modus operandi for all family interaction in parental incest families. Since perpetrator and other powerful family members can be expected to continue to abuse power until they are checked, this characteristic becomes the primary family treatment need. Until abuse of power is addressed effectively, there can be little attention to other family characteristics or to treatment needs of individual family members.

Fear of Authority

Members of parental incest families fear authority for the obvious reason: Authority figures are seen as hostile and threatening because exploitative, rather than benevolent, use of power is practiced and experienced within the family; hence the fear that authority (and power) wielded by others will be destructive to one's self. Beavers (ibid) commented:

> A strong determinant of family system capability is the assumption of members as to the probable nature of human encounter. Disturbed families behave as if encounters will be oppositional; competent families behave as if encounters will be affiliative. Indeed, it is the author's view that a clinical estimate of this underlying assumption will be of assistance in determining the degree of disturbance in family systems and individuals, without regard for diagnostic type or labels.

There tends also to be a guilty flavor to the fear of authority experienced by members of parental incest families—possibly in anticipation of discovery of the incest secret and fear of the consequences of its disclosure.

Fear of authority is largely dealt with by avoidance (see "Isolation" below). When encounters with authority are unavoidable, the member of a parental incest family (although assuming that the interaction will be oppositional) may exhibit a range of behavior from passive to aggressive. Anxiety, suspicion, evasiveness, denial, and hostility all may characterize behavior stemming from this family treatment need when a confrontation with authority is anticipated or actually does occur.

Isolation

The parental incest family tends to be isolated and withdrawn from society as a whole. Dr. C. Henry Kempe (1977) has described physically abusive parents as "without lifelines." This description is especially apt for parental incest families, even when a large extended family is available to the nuclear family unit. Fear of authority alone is an important reason for the isolation; it is easy to perceive the entire outside world as hostile and to cope by avoiding interaction with "outsiders" as much as possible. Powerful family members discourage weaker members from establishing alliances with persons who are outside the nuclear family. The children's friendships and opportunities for socialization away from home are strictly limited or forbidden entirely. Parents, especially incestuous fathers, may establish themselves as the sole linkage or communicator with persons who are outside the family. When strictly enforced, this practice enhances the parent's power position and increases his or her capacity for abuse of power. The heavy price paid for the isolation is, of course, the family's inability to replenish its energy through stimulation, support, nurturance and enjoyment derived from contacts with the outside world.

Denial

The parental incest family expends an enormous amount of energy upon denial. On the one hand, negative aspects of internal family functioning must be denied in order to be bearable (for example, the incestuous child sexual abuse, blurred role boundaries, abuse of power, unmet dependency needs, and the like). On the other hand, maintaining isolation requires that the outside world be perceived as hostile and threatening; this, in turn, requires denial of its positive and attractive aspects. Gutheil and Avery (1975) vividly describe an incestuous family whose members overused denial in an attempt to prevent the children from leaving the family circle and who portrayed temptations and allure of the outside world as "no bed of roses."

Although useful on a short-term basis, denial is not a very effective coping strategy because it requires increasingly greater amounts of energy to maintain denial in the face of multiple conflicting stimuli which somehow bridge the isolation gap. In addition, constant denial can be destructive to the individual who employs this defense mechanism because it diminishes one's capacity to empathize with others.

Lack of Empathy

Inability to empathize with others is a hallmark of the perpetrator of child sexual abuse. This characteristic includes unresponsiveness to another person's feelings at all levels—reactions, fears, needs, and the like. It is not unusual for offenders to report, "I told her to tell me if she wanted me to stop but she never said anything." At the same time, their victims report, "I told him he was hurting me, but he acted like he didn't hear me." Insensitivity to another person's feelings is rooted in denial and in failure or inability to communicate with others. It simplifies abuse of power because failure to perceive the negative consequences of exploitation of the victim diminishes or even eliminates guilt for the perpetrator. Accordingly, a callous disregard for others characterizes most family interactions and constitutes a major family treatment need.

Poor Communication Patterns

Members of parental incest families do not communicate well with each other or with outsiders. Poor communication patterns tend to be the rule rather than the exception. When weaker family members are exploited by more powerful relatives, they learn that power and control are all-important and greatly to be desired and sought after. Experiencing this harsh reality undermines the credibility of the parents' verbal communication of societal rules regarding interpersonal interaction. The family's isolation also tends to decrease opportunities for children to practice communication skills. Denial and lack of empathy both contribute to poor communication and failure to communicate. Refusal to communicate is also one way for individuals who occupy power positions to consolidate their power base by catching others off guard. Alternatively, less powerful family members may retaliate by refusal to communicate as well. The need to improve communication patterns must be addressed in effective family treatment for parental incest.

Inadequate Controls and Limit Setting

Persons who occupy power positions in parental incest families tend to have poor impulse control and to fail to set realistic limits upon themselves and others. They find it difficult to delay gratification of their own needs and desires and depend upon abuse of power to try to meet these needs. At the same time, they tend to fear their own impulsive tendencies and to project them upon others. Hence the inappropriate limit setting: sometimes the limits imposed by persons in power for themselves and others will be harsh and unrealistic. The setting of inappropriate limits invites the breaching of those limits. If imposed limits are breached with impunity, family members may feel both guilty and angry: guilty because of fear of authority; angry because a person in power abused power by failing to abide by established limits. This characteristic of parental incest families is closely related to blurred boundaries and extreme deprivation and neediness.

Blurred Boundaries

Inadequate controls and limit setting invite a blurring of role boundaries and role confusion in parental incest families. The boundaries that pertain are both physical and emotional. Physical boundaries are ignored whenever a powerful person abuses power by observing or touching a weaker person inappropriately. The blurring of physical boundaries can extend to demanding access to the victim's body, belongings, time in the bathroom and bedroom, and personal space. Such blurring of physical boundaries may coexist with rigid expressed limits for all family members—limits which are nevertheless breached by powerful persons whenever they wish.

Blurring of physical boundaries coexists with blurring of emotional boundaries in parental incest families. The parent or parent figure is not likely to breach physical boundaries unless he or she has an inadequate perception of the victim's role as well as his or her own role. By definition an adult's choice to turn to a child for gratification of the adult's needs constitutes role confusion. A resultant blurring of role boundaries and role confusion is inevitable for the child victim, and the youngster's behavior thereafter may well compound the problem. As the child's behavior in an inappropriate role persists, the problem of blurring of role boundaries and role confusion is increased for the entire family. All such behavior tends to be self-reinforcing and so the underlying problem becomes worse over time.

Extreme Emotional Deprivation and Neediness

All human beings have dependency needs which must be gratified in order for normal growth and development to occur. Infants are totally helpless and their obvious physical needs for food, warmth, and bodily care coexist with equally significant emotional needs. If the physical needs are not met satisfactorily, the

child will die or fail to develop normally in a physical sense. Inadequate gratification of the emotional need to be cared for consistently by nurturing humans
may also result in death in infancy. However, marginal gratification of essential
emotional needs in early childhood combined with adequate gratification of
physical needs tends to produce persons who experience extreme neediness and
deprivation throughout their lives. Under conditions which predispose to optimal
growth and development, children learn how to meet normal dependency needs
in ways that are constructive and healthy. These patterns of healthy need gratification persist into adulthood and are likely to be conveyed to one's own
children. Conversely, persons with exaggerated dependency needs tend to seek
gratification in ways that are pathological and destructive. In addition to a
lifelong pattern of failing to satisfy their own needs adequately, such persons
tend to reproduce themselves in a psychosocial sense: they teach these dysfunctional patterns to their own children as well as encourage dysfunctional patterns
of need gratification in their spouses and in others within their family and social
circles.

Magical Expectations

Individuals who are extremely needy and emotionally deprived tend to have
magical expectations of other people and the world in which they live. Extremely
needy persons look around them and perceive that at least some other people
around them appear satisfied with themselves and with their surroundings.
Presumably these satisfied people have appropriate sources of need gratification.
In contrast, the infantile level of emotional deprivation which characterized
parents or parent figures in the incestuous family encourages them to select
inappropriate choices for need gratification. Implicit in these choices is a magical
expectation that this time, in this way, by some unknown means or method, their
needs will finally be met. Repeated failures to meet basic needs via inappropriate
choices for need gratification simply reinforces the belief that somewhere an
elusive and magical solution exists; surely it *must* exist, for how else do others
manage to feel happy and fulfilled? The incestuous parent or parent figure
engages a child in sexual activity for the purpose of gratifying nonsexual needs.
(See also chapter 8, ''The Incest Offender.'') When parental incest is disclosed,
it may be inferred that the dysfunctional and destructive aspects of this form of
need gratification in some way outweighed whatever benefits or gains that were
derived for the offender, the victim, and the family.

Magical expectations tend to characterize all members of the incestuous
family, practically without exception. The offending parent exercises magical
expectations by selecting a child to gratify his or her nonsexual needs via sexual
expression. Other adult family members contribute to the pattern of magical
expectations either by directly encouraging the inappropriate sexual relationship

between the adult and the child or else by failing to perceive it while still tolerating a variety of infringements of role boundaries and permitting role confusion to take place. The victim, hampered by a lifelong indoctrination, has had ample opportunity to absorb a distorted perception of how the world really works. With constant reinforcement from authority figures at home that "rain falls up instead of down," small wonder that the child may eventually disclose the incest secret to an outsider, hoping for what is probably a totally unrealistic consequence of the disclosure.

Magical expectations cannot be overcome without addressing the extreme neediness and emotional deprivation of those who hold them. The latter becomes a primary treatment issue for the parental incest family, as described in the next section.

Treatment of Involuntary Clients

Members of parental incest families are usually involuntary clients for both extrinsic and intrinsic reasons. Society has such severe moral and legal sanctions upon incestuous behavior that both offenders and victims have much to lose if they acknowledge that incestuous sexual behavior *did* occur by virtue of participating in a treatment program. This dynamic also holds for any nuclear family members who were not directly involved with the sexually abusive activity as well as for members of the extended family. It follows that this extrinsic factor mitigates against voluntary participation in treatment for so long as persons who occupy power positions are able to deny that the incest took place or to resist efforts to force them to be held accountable for their actions. At the same time, the incestuous sexual activity becomes the "treatment handle" for incest offenders, victims, and families; it is generally the only legitimate reason for outside authorities to impose a treatment program upon the participants of parental incest.

The intrinsic reasons for members of parental incest families to assume the posture of involuntary clients are deeply rooted in the family pathology just described. Certain key family treatment issues also mitigate against voluntary participation in treatment. For example, *abuse of power* by powerful family members in order to satisfy their own needs at the expense of others is perceived by them to be a direct and satisfying method of achieving need gratification. It is highly unlikely that they will give up this aggressive behavior without fighting to maintain their powerful positions and all the associated benefits derived. Accordingly, those who treat parental incest families must be prepared to ward off attempts by the clients to abuse power within the treatment setting. Threatening, hostile, aggressive manipulative behavior (sometimes overt; sometimes practiced with great subtlety) should always be anticipated by the therapists.

The parental incest family's *fear of authority* also is unlikely to permit voluntary participation in treatment. Since family members are programmed to deal with outside authority by avoidance, it will probably be necessary to "back them into a corner" by imposition of the external authority of the legal justice system. Of course, a lifelong pattern of fear of authority does little to encourage family members to develop trust relationships with outsiders. As Beavers (ibid) pointed out, "disturbed families tend to behave as if encounters will be oppositional." The task of intervenors and therapists for parental incest families is to demonstrate the reverse: that encounters with outsiders *can* be affiliative. Unfortunately, it will be necessary to combat their opposition directly in order to accomplish this treatment goal.

Isolation of parental incest families also mitigates against voluntary participation in treatment. The habit of avoiding contact with outsiders for any reason is deeply ingrained in family members. In addition, *denial* of the incestuous sexual behavior itself, of the impact of the sexual abuse upon the victim, of dysfunctional behavior patterns inside the family, and of society's right and responsibility to hold the perpetrator(s) accountable—all tend to decrease the likelihood of voluntary participation in treatment. Although the *extreme emotional deprivation and neediness* which characterizes members of parental incest families might be expected to stimulate them to participate in treatment, their *magical expectations* tend to decrease the likelihood that they will voluntarily choose a child-sexual-abuse treatment program to assist them to gratify these needs. An accurate perception of the hard work and pain associated with discarding destructive behavior patterns which are familiar (albeit dysfunctional) and adopting constructive yet unfamiliar behavior patterns instead is totally inconsistent with the modus operandi of individuals who have entertained magical expectations all of their lives.

It follows that therapists for parental incest families must be individuals who are prepared to deal with involuntary clients. Good clinical skills are, of course, essential to recognize behavioral pathology, to identify treatment needs, to develop treatment plans which have a sound clinical basis, to intervene therapeutically, and to monitor the clients' progress (or lack thereof) in treatment. However, the therapist's clinical skills must be accompanied by a deep and abiding personal conviction that treating involuntary clients (although demanding and frustrating) is both appropriate and possible. Good clinical skills for working with disturbed clients can be learned in a variety of educational institutions and settings all over the country. A personal conviction of the appropriateness and value of adapting those skills to work with involuntary clients can only be acquired through working directly with others who are actively engaged in providing such services. The following unconventional strategies are essential to successful work with involuntary clients.

Therapeutic Use of Personal Authority

Intervenors and therapists must demonstrate willingness to use their personal authority with clients who abuse power. The therapist must convey by his or her own attitude and behavior that he or she understands how power is exercised and is able to use power in a responsible fashion. This involves confronting clients whenever *they* abuse power, interpreting the abusive and inappropriate aspects of their actions, and refusing to back down from a stance which insists that they stop their abusive behavior and acknowledge responsibility for their actions. It requires the therapist always to behave with absolute consistency, to be unflinching in the face of hostility and threats from the client, to refuse to be manipulated, to demonstrate that he or she is willing to be held accountable and to insist that others do likewise, and unfailingly to be honest in all dealings with clients. It requires courage and caring to be willing first to set appropriate limits for others, next to force them to abide by those limits, then, through demonstration, to encourage clients to set limits for themselves, and lastly to reinforce their efforts to behave responsibly and prevent them from escaping accountability. William Glasser (1965) presented a brilliant argument for authoritative therapeutic strategies in *Reality Therapy*.

Needless to say, it requires enormous energy for therapists to exercise personal use of authority in a responsible fashion. Individuals who have not worked out their own authority conflicts or who are personally so needy that they tend to abuse power themselves will not be able to work successfully with involuntary clients. A team approach to the clients and the direct support, affirmation, validation, and monitoring of one's colleagues are essential.

Use of Leverage to Induce Client Participation

The utilization and manipulation of external forces to induce clients to participate in treatment are anathema to many therapists. Once again, however, this will be required to treat involuntary clients. By definition, the involuntary client will choose to participate in treatment only as a forced alternative to something else. The "or else" will either be community sanction, penalties imposed by the legal justice system or, occasionally, fear of separation from a loved one who is strong enough to maintain the "or else" posture. Such inducements to begin must be maintained for months or perhaps years as treatment intervention proceeds; the moment that clients who abuse power, fear authority, and cope with stress by isolation and denial perceive that the pressure is off, they are likely to seize the opportunity to withdraw from treatment.

Therapists who use leverage to induce client participation in treatment must be knowledgeable about authoritative systems and willing to work closely with them (for example, the legal justice system, child protective services, and the like.) They must also be willing to use clients' anxiety about accountability as a therapeutic tool. These strategies are rarely if ever mentioned in conventional clinical training programs; yet certain client groups are never reached unless they are invoked. It "goes against the grain" of many well-intentioned therapists who see themselves as "helpers" of persons who want to be helped." However, it is characteristic of involuntary clients that although they desperately wish to be helped, they react with fear, hostility, and avoidance to conventional (voluntary) methods to help them.

Rosenfeld and Newberger (1977) illustrate the therapeutic community's conflict about involuntary clients. In an article entitled "Compassion versus Control," the authors describe five general categories of abusive parents who may require imposition of external controls because they are poor candidates for conventional therapy and thus can be expected to continue to endanger their children's lives and well being. The unfortunate implication is that an either-or treatment choice is required—*either* compassion *or* control. In fact, the use of leverage and imposition of both personal and external authority upon these persons can and should be extremely compassionate in nature. Therapeutic authority need not and should not be punitive but rather the reverse.

Inevitably, the individual therapist who uses leverage with involuntary clients will be accused by others of "playing God." One might ask, not very facetiously, is it not "playing the devil" to ignore desperately needy people who desire help but reject conventional therapeutic approaches? Is it more or less praiseworthy to decline or agree to develop and implement therapeutic strategies that utilize leverage to assist people who often are truly in emotional pain to learn slowly to employ more functional methods of meeting their own needs? If use of personal and external authority enables clients to behave in ways that are less destructive to themselves and their children, is society helped or hindered? Who is to say? Undeniably, the professional person who alone undertakes such challenges is at great risk of being overwhelmed. A group of professionals working together in a treatment program has, at least, a fighting chance to overcome the inevitable opposition from other colleagues which reverberates beneath all of the other factors operating against treatment.

Aggressive Outreach

Since involuntary clients will not, as a rule, "come" to treatment, helping strategies must be characterized by aggressive outreach. It will be necessary to pursue these clients with something that "feels like help." They will present initially with hostility, fear, isolation, avoidance, and denial. Treatment programs must be willing to "go after" these clients. It will often be necessary to pick them up bodily by providing transportation to and from therapy sessions and group meetings. A functioning peer group (fathers, mothers, parents, children) can serve as an outreach resource; assigning a "buddy" to a father or a mother or a child victim—someone who has "been there"—may be extremely effective. Role modeling by therapists and peers will be an important part of aggressive outreach. At the beginning, it may well be necessary to pick up these clients, transport them, and lead them by the hand (both figuratively and literally) into concrete individual and group exercises which give them, perhaps for the first time in their lives, the experience of "feeling good" as a direct result of some experience which illustrates and embodies an identifiable functional behavior pattern for them to adopt.

Once again, aggressive outreach is not currently in vogue as a high-status therapeutic strategy. Professional persons who are trained or work in the rarefied atmosphere of ivory tower treatment settings have a tendency to look down their noses at this approach. It involves getting your hands dirty with "hands on" contact with troubled people—driving cars, anticipating time and clothing needs, feeding people, manipulating the environment in a variety of ways. All this requires far more effort than sitting behind a polished desk in a quiet hospital or agency office with interference run by an efficient secretary-receptionist and with resultant shielding from the brutal facts of everyday life that are encountered by one's clients. Aggressive outreach requires hard work, long hours, careful planning, judicious use of volunteers, willingness to apply clinical skills in the real life arena, capacity to link the therapeutic insight with the concrete service which is being supplied in a stuffy car or a drafty corridor or perhaps in a hot kitchen, and so forth. Individuals who engage in aggressive outreach need to be strong enough that the office trappings of conventional therapy are not required to bolster ego or instill confidence. What is required, once again, is a team approach to share the burden, to develop and implement strategies, to monitor and validate the intervention.

Involuntary clients tend to require intervenors and therapists to provide some type of concrete services, especially in the beginning; nothing else is likely to "feel like help." A subtle but important corollary is the therapist's conscious use of self to convey to the client by providing some concrete service that benevolent use of power is possible, that authority need not be fearful, that isolation and denial are ineffective coping mechanisms because they cut the client off from much that is positive, that encounters with the outside world can be affiliative and that magical expectations can be replaced by realistic and appropriate ones. To demonstrate and convey this as an appropriate role, not as a Santa Claus or as a godlike figure nor yet as a "patsy" to be humored while the "gravy train" lasts, is perhaps the greatest challenge and realizable goal for the therapist who works with involuntary clients. It *is* possible to learn this clinical skill, but only in the context of a program which utilizes concrete services and aggressive outreach.

Provision of Total Life Support

This strategy was also described in chapter 3, "An Approach to Case Management." Involuntary clients from a parental incest family will require total life support when their pathological family system is disrupted by disclosure of incestuous sexual abuse of a child within the family circle. Therapists need to remember that societal sanctions against incest provide them with the right to disrupt pathological behavior patterns still further so that they may be replaced by constructive types of need gratification and modes of family interaction. The suppression phase (see also chapter 1, "A Conceptual Framework for Child Sexual Abuse") following disclosure will almost certainly serve to reinforce or reestablish dysfunctional family behavior patterns unless therapeutic intervention is swift and aimed at combating this drive toward homeostasis. Temporary separation of the perpetrator from the child victim is the optimal initial management plan (see also chapter 3, "An Approach to Case Management.") However, removal of a powerful family member and disruption of dysfunctional behavior patterns will not magically result in a "cure" or even improvement. Coping mechanisms in the form of dysfunctional behavior patterns, however maladaptive, must be replaced by something or they are likely to become reestablished. Removal of a family member who, although in some ways was abusive and destructive, creates an empty space. If the treatment goal is for the rehabilitated offender to be reunited with a healthier family, therapists and intervenors must somehow help family members to fill the empty space during the separation period. Hence the need for total life support. The components are as follows:

Environmental Services. Some parental incest families, bereft of their provider, may require the most elemental of concrete services: shelter, food, clothing, and money. Others will require guidance in obtaining these things instead. In the former instance, the "nonoffending" parent and children may need to be housed in a temporary shelter and given money for food and clothing. In the latter instance, the "nonoffending" parent may have enough financial resources to survive but will probably require guidance and encouragement to use them to pay the mortgage, to shop for groceries and clothing, to plan meals, to encourage the children to participate in school and afterschool activities, and so forth. Why so? Separation from the offending parent may force the spouse to perform tasks which are totally unfamiliar. In addition, the separation may induce a state of disorientation for the new "head of household" so that familiar tasks seem unmanageable without the support or demands or oversight of one's spouse. Direct guidance and encouragement will be required. A "therapy" session for the parent at this time should include a review by the therapist of the tasks to be done: Is the mortgage paid? Are the children going to school? Who does the shopping? Who prepares meals? Such mundane considerations and the client's near-paralytic state may well totally inhibit "therapy"; thus *treatment* will address such issues immediately.

One-on-One Support. A parental incest family which is in a state of disarray immediately following disclosure will require one-on-one support for each family member. A functioning child-sexual-abuse treatment program will anticipate this need and assign therapists, community resource persons, volunteers, reliable peers (from other parental incest families), and sometimes members of the extended family as supporters for each family member. No family member should be overlooked—even children who were presumably not directly involved—all need one-on-one support. Poor communication patterns and use of denial among family members may interfere with this strategy. It is not unusual for the remaining parent to refuse to discuss the reasons for the family disruption openly with all family members; instead he or she may try to insist that it is better for certain family members not to be told (as if they did not know already). Therapists should cut through this attempt to maintain dysfunctional behavior patterns by insisting that all family members be told about the incestuous child sexual abuse and by insisting that each family member receive one-on-one support. This strategy also tends to diminish isolation and loneliness and to begin to assist in developing trust.

Anticipatory Guidance. Total life support includes having the therapist anticipate problems for family members. Instead of assuming an oracle-like posture of predicting the future directly, the therapist should tell the client that other clients have discovered that a given course of action will have this or that likely result. The anticipatory guidance should address both concrete situations (for example, court appearances, medical examinations, and the like), but also the client's anticipated feelings or reactions to a given event. Anticipatory guidance based upon the therapist's experience and knowledge of behavioral pathology and the dynamics of child sexual abuse should be very effective. It will enhance the therapist's credibility when anticipated events or feelings are preceived by the client actually to occur.

Group Support. Total life support for a disrupted family will also include group support. Once again, there is no substitute for a functioning child-sexual-abuse treatment program with the modalities of treatment groups already in place. If it is possible to plug key family members into existing treatment groups early in treatment intervention, a significant part of total life support will have been achieved. The lonely, tired, frightened parent, victim, or sibling will learn that he or she is not alone, not unique, not a social outcast, not beyond help or improvement—all by meeting others who have had the same experiences and survived.

Capacity to Focus on Child Sexual Abuse

All of the preceding strategies to treat involuntary clients could be used with equal facility with many types of client populations. Capacity to focus on the child sexual abuse and to use it as a "handle" is unique to working with the parental incest family. It is nevertheless true that every population of involuntary clients must have its own "handle" to serve as the *raison d'être* for insisting upon treatment. However, therapists are often reluctant to employ the child-sexual-abuse "handle" in working with parental incest families. It is, of course, axiomatic that the therapist must be comfortable with his or her own feelings regarding child sexual abuse in order to address the topic effectively.

Again and again, one encounters incest cases "in treatment" in agencies where therapists decline to address the incestuous child sexual abuse. When asked why this has occurred, the therapists invariably reply, "They [the family] have consistently denied it." When asked why they have permitted denial to persist, these hapless therapists are likely to reply, "I'm not sure myself if it ever happened." When asked what *is* being addressed in therapy, the reply will be, "they have so many other problems; we are working on them."

What is really occurring in this scenario? A therapist who is uncomfortable and reluctant to deal with child sexual abuse has elected to identify with the aggressor (the perpetrator and more powerful family members) and to join the pattern of denial that the sexual abuse has ever occurred. The therapist is unwilling or unable to validate the case by using methodology to help him or her to decide if the sexual abuse complaint is bona fide (see also chapter 2, "Validation of Child Sexual Abuse"). Unwilling or unable to confront powerful family members, the therapist instead unwittingly negotiates a contract with the family: that is, the family stays "in treatment" so long as the therapist agrees to support their denial and avoidance of accountability for child sexual abuse. The family tolerates the therapist's usually inadequate attempts to deal with other family pathology as the price they must pay to avoid dealing with the actual underlying family treatment needs. Despite the investment of their time and money, the powerful family members stay in this futile treatment program because it meets the goals of avoiding accountability and keeps outside authority "off their backs." Encouraged by their superficial compliance (by attending enough scheduled sessions to maintain the façade), the therapist feels satisfied that he or she is helping the family and feels bolstered by the role of interposing himself or herself in a friendly manner between the clients and "hostile" outside authority. What is really happening? The "handle" of the incestuous child sexual abuse is being ignored, the impact upon the victim is not addressed, the real family treatment needs are also not addressed, time and money are being wasted. Worse still, the therapist is reinforcing the victim's, offender's and family's pathological and cynical view of how the world really works. A shameful scenario? Yes. A travesty of treatment? Yes. The current mode of "treatment" for many incestuous families? Alas, yes.

Treatment Approaches in Parental Incest

Needless to say, those who would treat parental incest families must employ strategies for working with involuntary clients, be prepared to offer total life support, and be willing to use the incestuous child sexual abuse to force powerful family members to address their actual treatment needs. As previously stated, individual and group treatment modalities must be used in conjunction with family therapy. If not, family therapy with an individual therapist is liable to have one of two results. Either the powerful family members will attempt to enlist the unwitting aid of the therapist to deny the sexual abuse, to avoid accountability, to maintain their positions of power which enable them to abuse power, and to maintain all of the internal family pathology or else they will drop out of treatment when confronted by the therapist who insists upon holding them accountable and addressing the real treatment issues. The former result reinforces family pathology and manipulates the family therapy sessions into a reenactment of the pathological interrelationships already present. The latter result effectively ends family treatment and sometimes also either ends or subverts victim treatment. Sometimes, powerful family members who drop out of treatment will compromise by allowing the child to remain in treatment, thereby identifying him or her as the problem. Unfortunately, unless the therapist is vigilant, they may still undermine and sabotage treatment for the child who remains at home.

What will work for these families? Several treatment modalities must be employed simultaneously. Individual, dyad, group, couples, and family therapy can all be used in some combination. Group therapy (for example, fathers group, mothers group, parents group, adolescent group) permits both peer support and confrontation—essential elements of treatment that are difficult to reproduce in individual therapy. Arts therapies (including play therapy) will be invaluable, especially for the more damaged and less expressive family members.

All family treatment must address the underlying family treatment needs. Appropriate use of power, reconciliation of authority conflicts, affiliation rather than isolation, decreased reliance upon denial as a coping mechanism, heightened sensitivity of others' needs, improved communication patterns, adequate controls and limit setting, establishment and maintenance of appropriate boundaries, acceptable need gratification and development of realistic expectations—all are necessary treatment goals for the parental incest family. In addition to holding them accountable for child sexual abuse, therapists must help adults in parental incest families to recognize and avoid high-risk situations. (See also chapter 8, "The Incest Offender.") Although it is important for the adult clients to acknowledge their responsibility for the incestuous child sexual abuse, saying the words and "getting in touch with feelings" is not enough. The child sexual abuse *must* stop, treatment needs for the family and victim *must* be acknowledged and addressed, the associated dysfunctional and pathological behavior *must* also stop.

How to avoid becoming overwhelmed by the complexity and multiplicity of problems exhibited by these families? Therapists will find that a careful diagnostic assessment followed by the development of a problem list are invaluable. Chapter 3, "An Approach to Case Management," presents a step-by-step description of diagnostic assessment, development of a problem list, formulation of a treatment plan, treatment intervention and monitoring. All are essential steps for avoiding confusion, duplication of efforts, "overkill" on some problems and inattention to others. Chapter 13, "Evaluation of Child-Sexual-Abuse Programs," presents a list of nine problem categories developed for Connecticut's Sexual Trauma Treatment Program.[a] The number and type of problem categories can and should be tailored to fit the treatment program. However,it is extremely important to define the family's problems as clearly as possible, to decide which problems will be addressed by the treatment program, and to formulate a treatment plan to address the problems as specifically as possible. Treatment intervention and monitoring should always be in the context of the treatment plan. It will obviously be necessary to negotiate the specifics of the treatment plan with the clients. Once agreed upon, both therapists and clients should make contracts for treatment intervention. Monitoring of treatment intervention should be done in the context of these agreed upon contracts as well.

Treatment Outcomes

Therapists and treatment programs have a responsibility to monitor treatment outcomes over time. It is, of course, necessary to monitor for repeated child sexual abuse. However, working with involuntary clients and applying unconventional treatment methods carry an associated responsibility to link treatment outcomes with the intervention strategies employed to as great a degree as possible. Chapter 13, "Evaluation of Child-Sexual-Abuse Programs," discusses the difficulties inherent in designing evaluation methodologies. Nevertheless, it

[a]Supported by National Center for Child Abuse and Neglect, DHEW, Grant No. 90–C–399.

can be done, as the evaluation data for Connecticut's Sexual Trauma Treatment Program demonstrate. These data are conservative in their claim for "successful" outcomes of treatment intervention. They do compare favorably, however, with Dr. Ann Harris Cohn's data on success of treatment in other child maltreatment programs funded by the National Center on Child Abuse and Neglect. Cohn (1979) reported a 30 percent repeat-abuse rate while families were under treatment, an estimate by therapists that in only 42 percent of cases was the likelihood for further abuse reduced at the termination of treatment and that a substantial number of problems of the victims (that is, the maltreated children) were not being addressed by treatment. Although undeniably grim, these data are probably a realistic appraisal for treatment outcomes for abusive families when strategies for working with involuntary clients are not systematically applied. They should both stimulate and challenge (rather than discourage) us for the task which lies ahead!

References

Anderson, Lorna M., and Shafer, Gretchen. "The Character-Disordered Family: A Community Treatment Model for Family Sexual Abuse." *American Journal of Orthopsychiatry,* 49 (3), July 1979.

Beavers, W. Robert. "A Theoretical Basis for Family Evaluation." In Lewis, J.M. ed., *No Single Thread: Psychological Health in Family Systems.* New York: Brunner-Mazel, 1976.

Burgess, Ann W., and Holmstrom, Lynda L. *Rape: Crisis and Recovery.* Bowie, Maryland: Robert T. Brady Company, 1979, p. 60.

Burgess, Ann W., Holmstrom, Lynda L., McCauseland, Maureen P. "Child Sexual Assault by Family Member." *Victimology: An International Journal* 2(1977):236–50.

Cohn, Anne H. "Effective Treatment of Child Abuse and Neglect." *Social Work* (November 1979):513–19.

Glasser, William. *Reality Therapy: A New Approach to Psychiatry.* New York: Harper and Row, 1965.

Gutheil, Thomas B., and Avery, Nicholas C. "Multiple Overt Incest as Family Defense Against Loss." *Family Process* (1975):105–116.

Kempe, C. Henry. "Sexual Abuse: Another Hidden Pediatric Problem." C. Anderson Aldrich Lecture, 1977.

Laury, G.V. "How Parents May Unwittingly Sexually Abuse Their Children," *Behavioral Medicine* (February 1978):33–35.

Poznanski, Elva, and Blos, Peter. "Incest." *Medical Aspects of Human Sexuality* (October 1975):46–76.

Rosenfeld, Alvin A., and Newberger, Eli H. "Compassion versus Control: Conceptual and Practical Pitfalls in the Broadened Definition of Child

Abuse." *Journal of the American Medical Association,* 237(May 9, 1977):2086–2088.

10 Arts Therapy with Sexually Abused Children

Connie E. Naitove

Normal persons, children, who are involved in either personal or situational stress (such as sexual abuse) are temporarily vulnerable to developing emotional problems. The arts must be made available to these children to facilitate coping skills in the face of life-threatening trauma.

—White House Commission on Mental Health, 1978

This chapter is an outgrowth of the work of Clara Jo Stember, an art therapist whose contribution became a critical element of Connecticut's Sexual Trauma Treatment Program for sexually abused children.[a] Stember had initially founded and developed a Day Care Child Art Program for traumatized children in a pilot project funded by the New York State Council on the Arts from 1972 to 1976. (It is now the comprehensive Extended Family Support Systems for Families in Crisis.) This experience, plus her background in teaching precognitive skill development through the arts, provided Stember with the vital concepts, techniques, and understanding necessary to her pioneering work with sexually abused children in the last year of her life.[b]

Stember was eclectic in her approach to the arts therapies, integrating a broad professional background in the arts and a wide variety of psychological and psychoanalytical theories with the humanistic traditions of the artist and the behavioral sciences. As an artist and educator, she had profound respect for the creative process experienced through artistic expression and for the necessity to accept both the artist and the work unconditionally without concern for the aesthetic, stereotypical, or incomprehensible and occasionally shocking content. Primarily, she employed the principles of play and play therapy, art training and art therapy, creative drama and puppetry, developmental education and

Connie E. Naitove, M.A.L.S., A.T.R., is the president of the National Educational Council of Creative Therapies, Inc. She is a teacher in Hanover, New Hampshire, and is the author of numerous publications on the arts therapies.

[a]Supported by National Center for Child Abuse and Neglect, DHEW, Grant No. 90–C–399.

[b]This chapter is an abstract from a larger volume being developed on the work of Clara Jo Stember, who died in July 1978.

psychology. Like many other therapists with whom she regularly consulted, she occasionally used poetry, dance, movement and music, separately or as facilitators of expression in new or unfamiliar media or modalities.

Why Employ the Arts Therapies?

The arts therapies are the purposeful use of media and techniques derived from the arts themselves and psychotherapy in order to help people to understand themselves, release tensions and anxieties, learn specific coping and communication skills, and facilitate the resolution of conflicts. The premise underlying all of the arts therapies comes from Plato, who stated that all the arts are an expression of the emotions and that all works of art have the power to elicit an emotional response. The rationale for using arts modalities and play with traumatized or disturbed clients lies in the innate qualities of play as a rehearsal for living and of the arts as haptic (meaning primarily sensory responses to stimuli) and nonverbal or symbolic modes of communication and conceptualization. The *Flight of the Bumblebee*, by Rimskii-Korsakov, is an example of melodic, nonverbal, symbolic response to a haptic (auditory) stimulus (the humming of a bee). Each individual responds to sensory stimuli in a unique manner, combining the experience with memories of related prior experiences and developing a symbolic repertoire or constellation around that particular stimulus. Thus the word *rose* might symbolize a flower, a fragrance, a person, a thorn, a color, or a host of other associations. The substance and manner of formulating these symbolic repertoires can provide vital information about how the individual is handling the particular stressful situation.

Unfamiliar modalities and media also circumvent inhibiting aesthetic or skill standards, since few of us have developed such standards for styrofoam packing material or for pantomiming the movements of an elevator. Young children rarely suffer from such inhibitions and will frequently give objects a humanoid existence: a boulder becomes a daddy, a rock becomes the mommy, and a pebble becomes the child or baby. It is not until after the child identifies people with objects that he or she can separate him or herself from them. In figure 10–1, showing some styrofoam structures, an abused child and a neglected child each made separate "family-scapes." The neglected child made a larger, but more tightly interlocked encircling wall. He then placed a small form symbolizing himself trapped within the wall. Outside were two other figures in opposite corners: his sister and his mother. The pieces were carefully selected and the larger mother form reflects more upon the importance of this person to the neglected child than her actual size in proportion to himself. The abused child, attempting to contain and control the enormity of his family situation, carefully selected smaller pieces, grouping them loosely around the perimeter in proximity to one another according to his perception of relationships

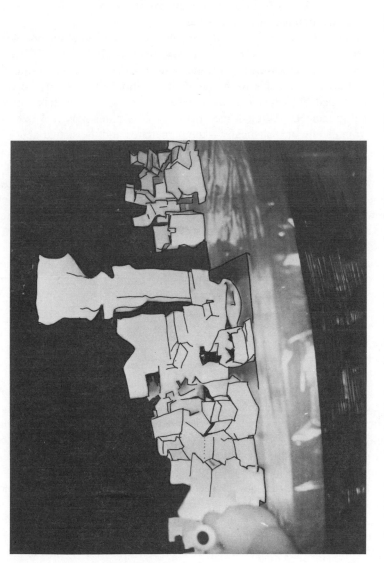

Figure 10–1. Styrofoam Constructions

Note: The small group of forms on the right is by an abused child, the construct on the left is by a neglected child. All of the children had a choice of all sizes and shapes.

between family members. He may not be able to allow these pieces to touch because of his own traumatizing experience.

Sexually abused children commonly perceive the usual verbal methodology for assessment and treatment as threatening and emotionally "loaded." Verbal communication during assessment and treatment may demand a skill level and specificity not always available to the child. In addition, victims may be cautioned or threatened by family members and perpetrators not "to talk" about the traumatizing incident. Through the creative arts, victims may feel freed to express—symbolically or realistically—the perpetrator and the sexual abuse in modalities not perceived to be covered by the cautionary injunction. Figure 10–2 is such an example. This unsolicited family picture was slipped to the therapist when the mother left the room to make coffee. The child put her finger to her lips, indicating secrecy, while glancing in the direction of her mother. After showing the drawing, she slipped it into the middle of the pile of completed drawings and pushed them into the therapist's hands. In this picture the two sexually abused family members are obliterated by being covered with an additional piece of paper. In other portraits of herself and her sibling, this abused child left out mouths (while putting them on other family portraits), indicating an injunction against mentioning the offending incident.

Integration of the Arts Therapies into a Multidisciplinary Program

The arts therapy component of the multidisciplinary team approach in Connecticut's Sexual Trauma Treatment Program operated on several levels. Clara Jo Stember sought to integrate the verbal and nonverbal disciplines with the more familiar approaches used in social work and psychotherapy. She designed an arts therapy component that would permit both autonomy of the arts therapist and his or her integration into the total program. Acceptance by the rest of the treatment team demanded the development of techniques and instruments designed to serve assessment and treatment requirements as well as contribute to the essential body of case-related data. Stember's task demanded cooperation and innovation in order to meet these demands successfully.

The arts therapies are a relatively recent (post-World War II) development in the treatment of situational stress. Most of the professional members of the Sexual Trauma Treatment Program were unfamiliar with the application of arts therapies to assessment and treatment of a client. It therefore became necessary to build staff training sessions into the program. Stember trained interested and capable therapists in basic, simple introductory steps to art media and techniques. After the trainee had used these introductory techniques with a client, Stember reviewed the results and conclusions, and together they determined the next step. Their mutual purpose was to strengthen the alliance between the

Note: The two figures at the bottom of the page (numbered 1 and 2) are covered by pieces of paper and were identified as the artist and her sibling, both of whom had been sexually abused. The other figures had been cut out and taped to this picture by the child.

Figure 10–2. Family Portrait by a Five-Year-Old Abused Female

therapist and the client and facilitate the acquisition of vital information as quickly as possible. Stember acted as consultant, helping the therapist to sequence these activities. For example, when a client, without any direction from the therapist, spontaneously drew a self-image which demonstrated a reasonable degree of body awareness and acceptance, Stember suggested that the next step might be an adaption of the house-tree-person concept. If the resulting drawing implied elements of home and family, the next step might be to suggest a kinetic family drawing showing the family doing something together. Interspersing these assignments with portraits of the therapist by the client was useful in determining the changes in levels of anxiety present in this relationship. In figure 10–3, a child depicted the therapist with a sharply pointed nose and a broad mouth which, although emphasized, is not fully smiling. This indicated to Stember that the child still felt slightly threatened by therapeutic intervention (she was hospitalized at the time). Later drawings of the therapist did not emphasize these characteristics, which may have been thought of initially as symbolizing a "nosey-body." Such colloquilisms often find their way into drawings.

When the therapist encountered a child who could not verbalize well, or found it extremely difficult to establish a trust relationship, or that the victim or other family members might be responsive to the arts therapies, Stember was asked to work directly with the client(s). As the arts therapist she was also available to all team members to conduct arts assessment interviews. These might be requested when there was a question of validation of sexual abuse or when there was a question of underlying organic deficit or temporary functional arrest due to emotional trauma.

The philosophy of Connecticut's Sexual Trauma Treatment Program was to maintain and enhance the integrity of the family unit whenever possible. There was a commitment to provide outreach services in the home to strengthen the family. Stember's earlier experience with the Day Care Child Art Program had led her to an innovative approach to service delivery—the creation of an Artmobile. She extended this concept to her work with victims of sexual abuse. The art therapy mobile unit, Stember's car, was equipped with a variety of materials which enabled her to provide the clients with a broad spectrum of inexpensive and sensory stimulating opportunities for self-expression. It facilitated reaching out to those living in remote areas where isolation might be compounded by poverty. It made it possible to reach parents and families under stress who lived in low-income housing projects. By working through the arts in kitchens, dining rooms, basements, backyards, the frequently unused recreation rooms of housing projects and churches, a relatively familiar and non-threatening environment could be provided where disintegrating families and social systems could be rebuilt.

These settings require the arts therapist to adapt to diverse circumstances and attitudes such as compulsive cleanliness, utter disarray, chaos and filth, or

Figure 10–3. Portrait of the Child Advocate by a Sexually Abused Girl

attempts to manipulate, ignore, or discredit the intervention. Flexibility becomes "the order of the day." Often there is little or no privacy and the therapist's and client's work may be interrupted frequently. These situations have to be evaluated in terms of the norm for that unit's dynamics, resistance to therapeutic intervention, or a variety of "impact reactions" as described by Burgress and Holmstrom (1979). Figure 10–4 shows a typical situation. In this photograph, it can be seen that the kitchen table served as the work surface, while the family cats played amongst the papers and people. The therapist must accept family ties, whether or not they include pets or perpetrator, accommodating to them and finding ways to work with what is available.

Stember soon learned to enlist support by sharing her intent and methods with fellow team members as well as parents, daycare mothers, foster families, and the victims themselves. Interest and support evolved once these people understood that contact with arts media could contribute significantly to the enhancement of learning skills needed by school-aged children (such as concentration and discrimination of size and shape) as well as language and social skills. In addition, families and therapists were encouraged to discover that participation with children in arts activities could stimulate their own creativity and lead to changes in attitude or perception of one another.

Cojoint therapeutic sessions were initiated, involving the victim, the therapist, and the arts therapist. These often took place in the home. Stember would accompany the primary therapist, who either came to observe, talk to another family member, or introduce the arts therapist. The cojoint approach provided additional opportunities to observe family interactions as well as the development of parent-child dyads, sibling dyads, and family arts therapy activities. Afterward Stember and the primary therapist compared notes, delineated problem areas, and developed a treatment plan which they presented at a team meeting and then initiated.

The arts therapist also provided sole or cojoint leadership of arts therapy sessions for various peer groups such as those developed for adolescent victims, mothers, parents, and multiple family groups. These groups offered relief from isolation, feedback on behaviors and views, and an opportunity to test concepts and hypotheses in a socially responsive environment.

Stember initially encountered resistance to the contribution and participation of the arts therapist. Her defined role was ambiguous and some team members were reluctant to involve her in case assessment and in the development and initiation of the treatment plan. However, as the team became familiar with the scope and quality of Stember's work, the role of the arts therapist was more comprehensively applied. Her case assessments and treatment methodology became an integral part of case management, and her records were included in case files and presented at team meetings.

Goals and Objectives of Arts Therapy with Sexually Abused Children

It is axiomatic that, in order to be effective, goals and objectives of treatment must be clearly stated and mutually acceptable to *all* members of the therapeutic team. The goals and objectives of arts therapy with sexually abused children were broadly defined as follows.

1. To introduce the client to creative expressions media and modalities for the purpose of providing gratifying arts experiences. The underlying premise is that success is ego-strengthening and that such experiences provide opportunities to reintegrate impaired egos and to enhance self-esteem.

2. To elicit verbal and nonverbal statements and expressions (ventilation) of overt and internalized areas of conflict, facilitating their definition, delineation, and recognition. This is done by eliciting and identifying individual symbolic repertoires, referred to earlier, and encouraging externalization of the trauma. The premise here is that it is essential for the victim to be able to separate his concept of himself from the traumatic event in order to facilitate desensitization and appropriate integration. In addition, it is subsumed that both verbal and nonverbal behaviors are related and that each of us has developed and acquired a uniquely significant symbolic repertoire.

Symbols are the means by which human beings assimilate information and form concepts. Their expression is a personal metaphor which defines the individual's methods of coping with his perceptions of reality. Understanding the dynamics of this synthesizing process can provide the tools for rehabilitation of dysfunctional behaviors and the resolution of ambivalent feelings toward parents, siblings, other family members, surrogates, and even the perpetrator of sexual abuse. The arts provide an opportunity for the expression of these symbols and for the development of body awareness, the somatic reintegration of the trauma and the acceptance of self. This was classically demonstrated in the drawings of a 5-year-old girl molested by her father. Her first self-image drawing (see figure 10–5) shows an armless, tilted figure "in jail"; a later self-portrait shows a fully age-appropriate female figure leaning only slightly.

3. To provide an opportunity for the development of an alliance (rather than the psychoanalytic process of transference, which would be inappropriate for short-term therapy) with the therapist and to provide for exchange of dependence for independence by reaffirming the client's strengths. This involves acknowledging and totally accepting the individual on a physical, emotional, and ethnic basis while encouraging him or her to recognize that situational disturbances do not necessarily incur permanent physical, emotional or social stigma or impairment. The premise is that understanding and support can help combat long-term negative effects for clients and families who are overwhelmed

Figure 10–4. The Child Advocate with the Clients' Family Looks over Drawings

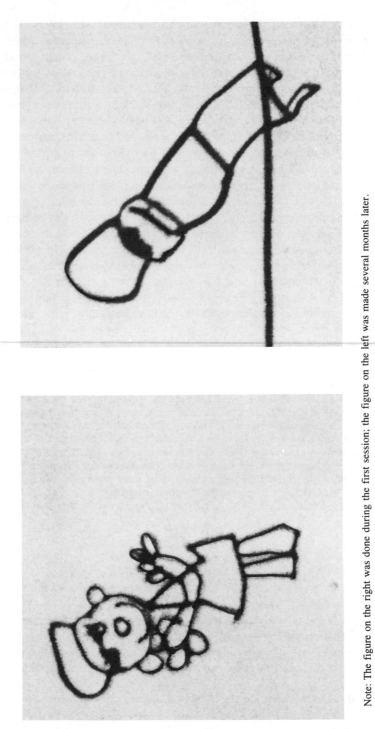

Note: The figure on the right was done during the first session; the figure on the left was made several months later.

Figure 10–5. Self-Portraits by a Five-Year-Old Sexually Abused Girl

by the facts and implications of the child sexual abuse. Desensitizing a child who has undergone abortion to the issues of rape, parenting, maternity, and trust relationships with adults and peers is essential to a healthy readjustment. Thus a hostile, acting-out, recently aborted, 13-year-old was placed in the adolescent treatment group where arts therapy was introduced. Here she developed a supportive relationship with another girl who was sexually active. During her second session with the group, she was noted to be responding to the weight and density of clay; this was the first time she had begun to demonstrate impulse control and sustained concentration. She also responded to poetry and "quiet" music played during mural-painting sessions. The treatment goal: "To build enough self-esteem to accept some kind of impulse control; to offer materials and activities that help fill her sense of emptiness; to offer opportunities for success in self-directed areas." These objectives were clearly being met.

4. To accelerate maturation of delayed cognitive and functional behavior patterns to an age-appropriate level when necessary. Stember (1976), Burgess (1975), and others have repeatedly witnessed behaviors in traumatized children which imply a developmental lag or arrest. Because the arts also provide clues to auditory, visual, and kinesthetic modes of learning and deficit, they add vital information to the data base used for the development of a treatment plan.

> My experience with a child who attended a daycare center for just one day dramatically illustrates both the pent-up need for art therapy services and the ability of some children to make up quickly for delayed expressive growth. At the age of 4, Kia had never seen crayons. In one hour we watched her go through developmental stages that normally take several years: scribbling, the naming of implied forms, and the making of recognizable forms and mandalas. She even began to make whole pictures that included a few humanoid creatures. All of this she accomplished in an uninterruptable frenzy, one drawing on top of another or growing out of the previously drawn form. Kia refused an offer of fresh paper, wanting to paint over her crayon drawings. When she discovered [that crayon resisted the paint while the adjacent paper absorbed it] what she had created, she painted over and around until she was through. She sat until lunch, staring at what she had created. "Me," was all Kia said. [Stember, 1976]

Application of the Arts in Treatment of Child Sexual Abuse

Ignorance and misconception surround the application of the creative arts therapies. This can be compounded by the misuse of media and abuse of techniques by the unskilled who have sought neither training nor accreditation from existing national organizations established to protect the standards and ethics of practice.

All art(s) therapists must be able to design activities that will foster growth, [elicit] information, or reveal the emotional state and personal conflicts of the child in question. An art(s) background is essential. The therapist must be in full control of the medium being used. For example, John, sodomized by his father at the age of seven, was on the verge of exploding [with emotion]. His father had been arrested; his family was shattered. He also was grieving over the loss of his father. He needed a way to channel these . . . feelings. The art therapist knows that clay is a great material for ventilation. Pounding and wedging to get the air bubbles out is a concrete activity; kneading and pulling and smashing the clay help provide a focus for pent-up emotions. But when the wild catharsis turns to the creation of form, the artist must know how to keep the evolving object intact. If, for instance, lack of knowledge about the proper consistency of clay causes the work to fall apart as it dries, the mastery, gratification and good feelings about having created something can [also] be destroyed. This type of negative experience may only reinforce what the child already thinks about himself. If our goal is to help children gain control over their own actions, and the products of their artistic efforts are proof of this growing skill, then their works must be sound. [Stember, 1978]

Selection of media, modality, and techniques are usually made on the basis of judgments concerning the child or group's need for greater freedom or control. Chalk on dry paper presents an opportunity for reasonable control. Chalk on wet paper provides increased opportunity to take risks but, with the use of paper towels, still permits a reasonable degree of control. Wet paint on wet paper provides for considerable risk taking, discovery of the natural properties of gravity, pigments and freedom from responsibility. When to offer which technique, where to offer it (for the child may feel either freer or more constrained in the home or agency setting) and what responses might cause concern are judgments which might best be made in concert with the client.

Fear that the arts might provide too much freedom and might even increase anxieties if the client is offered too much choice arise from ignorance of the limits and structure of the arts therapies. Dr. Judith Rubin (1978) has written:

In my own work with seriously ill schizophrenic children, where they had freedom of media choice, it was striking that those with poor ego boundaries consistently avoided such fluid materials as fingerpaints. They often provided their own kind of structure, such as one regressed twelve-year old who always pulled a chair up to sit at the easel, in order to 'contain' his usual aggressive hyperactivity. . . . Another child, blind and retarded, 'contained' his experimentation with fingerpaint, previously threatening to him, through the use of a tray. He was surprisingly calm and relaxed throughout, the physical boundaries of the tray apparently allaying his anxieties about edges. . . .

Peter Slade believes that " 'dramatic play provides the child with a great safety valve—an emotional catharsis . . .' [and] in providing emotional release, it also offers opportunity for emotional control, and thus it provides an inner self-discipline." (Courtney, 1974)

Arguments opposing the use of arts therapy modalities in social services maintain that they are imprecise tools: difficult to evaluate, record, substantiate and replicate. Carter and Miller conducted a six-week program using art activities with brain damaged children which "showed significant gains made by each child on the Frostig Developmental Test of Visual Perception." (1975) Demonstrating one method for evaluation, it also demonstrates the value of art in education.

Connecticut's Sexual Trauma Treatment Program records were kept on a variety of forms. A Problem Oriented Record was maintained on every case; a Treatment Plan sheet was maintained for every problem appearing on the Problem list and described the treatment method that was planned. Both of these forms concerned team functions, referrals, delineation of responsibilities, and actions taken—not the actual content of therapeutic sessions. Stember maintained two additional forms for each case record: a Consultant's Activity Log (which defined the activity, with whom, its purpose, and outcome) and an Art Therapy Consultations Form (which listed the cojoint therapist, date, client, a review of each session, and recommendations). Because these forms were filled out by hand and well after the fact, Stember made tape recordings shortly after each session which comprehensively described every aspect of each session.

One of the major difficulties in recording arts therapy sessions is selection of an appropriate vocabulary which maintains objectivity and provides sufficient data which is both informative and quantifiable. One such form, the CENDEX, recently developed by this author but as yet unverified (Naitove, 1979), lists and measures attention span, attitudes toward staff, peers, group, and activity, symbolic content in gross and fine motor movement, graphic, verbal, nonverbal, oral, and plastic expressions, and includes as many as thirty specific observations to be checked off in each arts modality. Such a comprehensive form might be considered cumbersome, but without it Stember found that she was putting in at least two hours of record keeping for every hour of treatment.

Play Therapy

Investigations into the developmental, cultural, and social importance of play conclude that the young of many species learn through play. They learn to interact with their environment, control aggression, clarify social relationships, enhance concentration, and comprehend the boundaries of personal achievement, time, and space. Play may provide the therapist with an initial opportunity contact and rapport with the frightened or severely deprived child. It can provide a catalyst for the discharge of emotion and thereby reduce the anxiety level. A pillow, wax, or plasticene figures and puppets offer the child an opportunity to reenact situations and release aggressions. Accepting these behaviors in this milieu and with these materials, while simultaneously offering or reinforcing insights the child may gain during these activities, helps the client to develop confidence in the therapist and the treatment process.

Some therapists view arts expression as a concentrated form of play while others regard the arts therapies as a development of the play impulse. It is true that play and arts activities can be recreative and therefore beneficial; however, in their therapeutic application, a durable—rather than momentary—contribution to cognitive growth and behavioral change is the primary objective. Keeping in mind the goals of treatment, the therapist encourages the transition from nondirective play into intentional communicative and therapeutic activity. Free play or undirected arts activities, in and of themselves, will not bring about insight, growth, or rehabilitation for the victim of sexual abuse. It is vital that the therapist make this clear to staff, the child, and the family.

Symbolic Expression and Identification of Learning Modes

It is the aim of the creative arts therapies to elicit symbolic expressions which contain and communicate ideas. The creation of such statements is a combination of complex cognitive and functional behaviors. While it is certainly necessary to allow sufficient time for the exercise of defences and the exploration of media when introducing the arts therapies, it is equally important to stress to clients that therapeutic sessions cannot be allowed to dissipate into uncontrolled or purposeless activity or destruction. As has been pointed out, this is rarely an issue with young children, but with adolescents and adults it may be necessary to point out correlations between disruptive or inappropriate behaviors during the therapeutic session and their other social behaviors, including the willingness to face and resolve conflicts.

Creative arts expression not only may bring out fantasy or imaginative or symbolic content but also the artist's relationship to that content. Often, fantasy may be the child's solution to problems involving acceptance by significant adults in his or her life. A 5-year-old girl, molested by her father, made a multimedia figure of a bird with wings, legs, and a phallus in its middle. She named the bird "Bozo" and told a lengthy and elaborate story of how the bird needed his wings for flight to a television station where it was going to sing and dance. No purpose was described for the object in the bird's mid-section. "Bozo" was very talented; everyone loved him. Although the child may not have been ready to discuss the traumatic event directly, the desire for acceptance and possibly flight (signifying a possible desire for independence or escape) was clearly related to it.

Opportunities to explore the "Bozo" fantasy further through music and dance were clearly present. Through such exploration, the child's preferential modes for learning and communicating might be ascertained. Such information gives the therapist the means to enhance the child's ego structure, behavioral change, and developmental growth. The rationale for selecting specific arts therapies lies in the specific attributes of the art and the learning modes through which individuals process information and learn. Some people are kinesthetic attenders: they need space because they need to move; they process information through action (Einstein was one of the more famous kinesthetic learners not involved in the arts). Dance, movement, and drama are useful modalities with these people. Some are auditory attenders: their moods may be affected by the volume, pitch and tempo of sounds in the environment. These people are often highly distractable, unable to concentrate when disturbed. Appropriate musical and poetic activities may be helpful for them. Visual attenders respond to impressions, color and movement, and are also easily distracted when disturbed. Graphic and plastic arts may prove most absorbing for these individuals. Persons with mixed dominance or right hemispheric brain dominance often have difficulties with such symbolic disciplines as reading or arithmetic. Many compensate through tactile experience, available in modeling or collage, or through one of the other learning modes mentioned.

By understanding the learning modes of clients, the arts therapist can select appropriate perceptual techniques to enhance their skill development and self-image. Using the individual's preferred mode of learning helps to engage his or her attention, extend that attention span, and enhance concentration. Selecting the appropriate perceptual technique for a client also enhances possibilities for constructive motivation while providing an opportunity for him or her to respond to situations appropriately. In addition, creative arts expression offers the client an opportunity to increase control over voluntary muscles and enhance coordination. These activities engage perceptual motor, sensory motor, and cognitive skills; object relatedness; interpersonal and group skills; reality testing; personal awareness and identity. Creative arts expression may reduce or relieve tension and anxiety by allowing the client to recognize potentials for control, failure, mastery, rejection, hostility and acceptance while developing the abilities to cope with these risks in safe, socially acceptable arts experiences.

Music and Sound

Music and nonverbal sound making (for example, "giving the razzberry") can be used as facilitators of other activities. For example, music may facilitate movement or dance with someone who presents himself or herself as being "uptight," the combination can then be used to facilitate freedom of movement in graphic mural work. They can also be used as core activities to enhance auditory perception and expression as well as putting the individual in touch with his or her own natural body rhythms (for example, the heartbeat). Emitting sound provides the infant's first sense of power, and the child quickly learns to attend to the rhythm, pitch, and volume of verbal communications before he can attend to its content. Activities in this modality might include a nonverbal sound dialogue which includes greeting, debate, and departure, or the employment of the group to echo back, as precisely as possible, the speaker's statement of his or her name in a natural, angry, and finally, loving manner.

Movement and Dance

Movement is inherent; we cannot escape our bodies. Movement makes our presence known. Children are sexually abused while they are still developing a sense of autonomy and control over their bodies. Some have been sexually abused at the moment of intensive physical, emotional, social, and cognitive changes. Perception of identity, control, authority, and sexuality are paramount sources of concern to the victim of sexual abuse. Kinesics, or body language, frequently corresponds to idiomatic language (being "uptight" or a "pushover") and is more closely allied to individual and cultural rhythms, patterns, and defences than the individual's verbal language. Therapeutic exercises may include body writing (the use of body parts to write a word or name in the air as large or as small as possible, as rapidly and as slowly as one is able), or exercises which demonstrate consistencies and inconsistencies with verbal language (such as acting out the phrase "going around in circles" in order to define options which might be available to altering this perception and behavior).

Color, Form, and Line

Color, form, and line are inherent in our environment as well as being common to idiomatic speech (feeling "blue, down, high, or square"). Line, shape, and placement can be correlated to conceptualizations and uses of space, object and human relationships, as well as self-image. Illustrations for this chapter, descriptions of Stember's assessment procedures as well as other techniques mentioned, should suffice as examples.

Mime

Mime is a nonverbal drama approach to problem areas. It stimulates body language and gesture which may be in conflict with the client's verbal statements. Such gestures, consistencies, and inconsistencies can be explored, focusing on cognitive processes and their physical expression. It joins mind and body, so easily separated in the "brain versus brawn" conflicts of adolescence, and provides a modality for the integration of the trauma and psychological effects.

Drama and Poetry

The verbal therapies of drama and poetry are also process-oriented. They offer an opportunity to explore metaphor and real-life situations in a safe, protected, constructive environment. Potentially threatening situations can be dealt with either by direct confrontation, as in psychodrama, or indirectly through creative drama techniques. Drama conveys the essence of human relationships, and through it the child assimilates experience. Dramatic activities permit somatic and verbal modes of communication to be separated, as in mime, and then combined in creative drama. This permits an opportunity to explore and focus on the individual elements of gesture, phrase, and context.

Poetry restores the joy inherent in the sound and meaning of language and teaches us that sound is meant to be listened to. It liberates verbal expression and clarifies it; it restores the "me" in meaning. By means of the symbol, man forms concepts; by means of poetry, man can express this metaphoric process. Exercises in poetry therapy might begin by having the client maintain a journal of thoughts and feelings. A group of clients might create a group poem with each member contributing a line (an opening metaphoric line contributed by the facilitator will often help to get the group started). A dramatic warm-up activity might involve the miming of a sport activity or juggling or perhaps a tightrope walking act. Selecting a personal idiosyncracy for focus in learning the art of clowning can bring the whole aspect of façade, self-image, and reality into focus. The child who depicts clowns in graphics or disrupts group activities with clownish behavior might benefit from such an exercise.

Basic Considerations

The arts therapist must be convinced that these modalities have the potential for enabling the individual to draw upon the strengths of the "remembered" self. The therapist must respect the individuality of the people with whom he or she works, regardless of age, and provide opportunities for the reintegration, reassurance, and reassertion of the identity of that individual. Believing in the educational and rehabilitative merits of the activities proffered, the therapist must be able to accept and, to some degree, comprehend the results of creative expression.

As has been stated, the arts therapies are the purposeful use of media and techniques derived from the arts themselves and psychotherapy in order to help people to understand themselves, release tensions and anxieties, learn specific coping and communication skills, and facilitate the resolution of conflicts. Therefore all such activities must be rewarding and must not increase anxiety or confusion. It is important to keep instructions clear, concise, and simple. The activities should offer variety in order to sustain interest and motivation. They should be within the abilities of the individual, in terms of physical, perceptual, and cognitive skill levels; and compatible with the dignity, individuality, and independence of the client. They should provide neither too much nor too little freedom. Too little freedom impinges upon the creativity of the individual; too much freedom can often lead to frustration. Although the therapist should be supportive (for example, demonstrating "tricks of the trade" where specifically requested or indicated), he or she must be ever-vigilant against usurping the clients' prerogatives to devise their own solutions and function independently.

Structure of Arts Therapy Sessions

The adequacy and appropriateness of space allotted for creative arts expression in any program is rarely ideal. Therefore the thrust should be the creation of a climate for creativity (that is, an opportunity for the flowering of the individual and the potential for satisfaction). This is accomplished by establishing and emphasizing realistic goals resulting from the activities in order to reinforce the abilities of the individual. Structuring the sequencing of activities within a session must always remain flexible. The personalities of, and circumstances surrounding, the clients will determine the media and activity, program and sequencing. It is vital to remember that the clients' defences may be well entrenched and that avoidance maneuvers or acting out may be indications of survival tactics that have been developed.

One victim, Caren, subjected to a progression of sexual abuse over a long period of time, was impregnated by her father who was arrested. The pregnancy was terminated and Caren was incorporated into the adolescent treatment group. Although there were others in the group who had been subjected to incest and abortion, this 13-year-old remained quiet and withdrawn. Although she was capable of working in dyads on mural paper, her work was stereotypical, and she kept herself to one corner of the paper, continuously withdrawing and making smaller and smaller drawings if others encroached upon her work space. Work in the home was more relaxed and she was able to do dyadic work with her sister, who was also in the adolescent group. In this environment, she was able to break away, momentarily, from her stereotypical depictions of flowers and execute a free-flowing painting which covered the entire page. The pattern demonstrated her own diffusion and inability to deal with content. She could project nothing into it other than to call it "Ribbons and Worms." The painting has no core, no vortex, the colors and patterns meander about in no particular pattern of verticality or horizontality, only a vague relationship exists between colors, lines, forms and composition (see figure 10–6). It was decided, with the victim's consent, to break off the increasingly dependent relationships built into the dyadic activities, and she began cojoint psychotherapy with the team psychologist and the arts therapist. Despite her mother's active cooperation with the program, the girl expressed feelings that her mother should have protected her and now the family was blaming her and trying to keep the whole thing a secret. That this was true only increased her anxiety and acting-out behaviors— failures in school and withdrawal from friends. Her drawings clearly demonstrated a need to maintain tight control over her feelings as she began the progressive withdrawal behavior. The parents' divorce was finalized, the father released from jail, plans were made to move the family out of state. Her fears were certainly reality-based; she could not know what was ahead for her.

Did the arts therapist fail with this child? Who can be sure? Certainly others who worked on dyadic murals with her demonstrated real progress and growth; perhaps she learned vicariously from their experiences. One of these was a 12-year-old girl, Lynn, whose impregnation by her stepfather had been terminated early in the first trimester. In her dyadic experience with Caren, Lynn was able to paint a large, emotionally charged symbolic representation of the sexual abuse and abortion. (Illustration 10–7.) The arching form resembles a vagina, colorful and complete with ovum. Flowing from it is a hastily executed blood-red color. Lynn was unable to discuss it at the time and inference concerning its significance to the child was drawn both from the content of the symbol and her intense emotional reaction to it. Two weeks later, in a similar dyadic exercise, Lynn was able to reduce and therefore control a recreation of this form in clay. "As she finished the clay model, she placed herself with her back to the painting [which hung on the wall]. After this, she was able to verbalize her experiences in the Adolescent group meetings."(Stember, 1978)

Certainly Caren could not ignore Lynn's revelations and behavioral changes. Perhaps she internalized them along with her own traumatic experience. Since she would soon be leaving, perhaps she was protecting herself against any further despair and loss by withdrawing. Hope and supposition is sometimes all that remains in such cases.

In addition to a climate for creativity, it is important to provide a variety of situations in which to experience the arts therapies. The therapist must have an opportunity to work alone with a frightened, dominated, or deeply disturbed individual, without interruption or distraction. Similarly, where possible and indicated, opportunities should be made for creative arts expression in parent-child dyads and sibling dyads. This enables significant family members to experience, communicate, and get to know one another through these less familiar—and therefore less well defended against—forms of activity.

> Unquestionably, the most important and influential dyad in a child's life is himself and his mother, and it is useful to have occasional mother-child sessions both early and late in treatment. (Rubin, 1978, pp.141–44.)

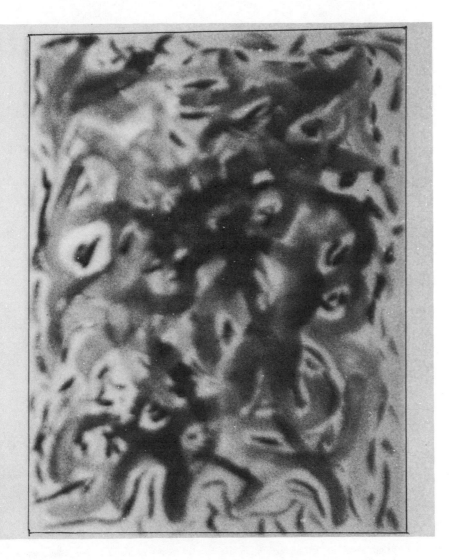

Note: This painting by a fifteen-year-old sexually abused female was done at home.

Figure 10–6. ''Ribbons and Worms''

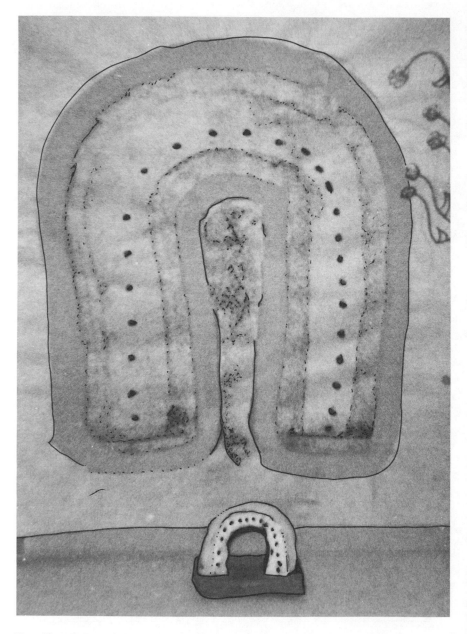

Note: The painting was the first representation and the clay form was done two weeks later when she was able to talk about it.

Figure 10–7. Symbolic Representation of Rape and Abortion by a Twelve-
                  Year-Old Victim

Stember and Rubin both point out the advantages in observing intrafamilial interactions and competitive behaviors and the potential for clarification of perceptions (that is, abilities, potentials, affections, resentments, respect, and relationships of other family members and household personages) during such dyadic activities.

Other appropriate situations for introducing the arts therapies are peer groups for adolescents, parents, mothers, and multiple family groups. These situations offer an opportunity to share the burden of the therapeutic process by working together on projects, sharing problems, perspectives, and potential solutions, humor and laughter. Such groups may offer some members a chance to excel or "shine" where no such opportunity had previously been available. Others, uncomfortable in verbal group therapy, find the opportunity to communicate through the arts more agreeable. Often these activities will provide the group with the only form of recreation and social intercourse that the individual or family unit may experience. Peer groups tend to break down barriers of isolation, provide opportunities to test perceptions, receive feedback, find role models, and reduce dependence upon the therapist and team. Socialization and communication skills are enhanced while inappropriate or disruptive behaviors seem to be more amenable to remediation by peer pressure than from "authoritative" sources.

Rubin describes two kinds of families which seem to benefit most from experiencing the arts therapies, "those who either talk little and distrust words, or those for whom talk has become a way to escape and hide." (1978, p. 146.) Often these people are neither confident artists nor are they comfortable conversationalists. It is often easier for them to talk about an object or product of an activity than to discuss the constellation of emotions and events which gave rise to it. In eliciting information concerning the work created, perceptions and psychodynamics of the individuals and groups are also forthcoming. When the product is graphic, plastic, or has been recorded on film or tape, the work itself remains as a witness, available for immediate review or later to evaluate changes over time. The original work can be altered or revised to suit the needs and desires of the clients.

A sexually abused child playing with a lump of clay created first a mountain and then a strange "house without windows." (figure 10–8.) In previous drawings, she had indicated other dwellings in her neighborhood with windows open, but her own house with closed shades and windows. She had neither a room nor place of her own to sleep. Doors within the home were frequently closed to her. Referring to her clay "house," she said, "I want the house open, so I can see inside." Finding the therapist receptive to this concept, the child changed the form to a sort of open, curving wall on a slab foundation, into which she was able to move several figures, creating dialogues and whole stories about

Note: The water and sun are filled in with color (the sun is a yellow-green) but the boat is only outlined in red with solid red portholes.

Figure 10–8. The First ''Free'' Painting by a Seven-Year-Old Sexually Abused Boy

what had taken place in the house in the past, present and future. It became possible to establish correlations to real people, relationships, and situations in the child's life and to reconcile the child's desires for change with the potentials for intervention by the Sexual Trauma Treatment Program.

A brief discussion, introducing the therapist, media, and techniques may be useful when working with older children, adolescents, and adults. Very young traumatized children may wish to explore or to play with the materials on their own, disregarding the therapist and frequently turning their backs to him or her by way of emphasis. Others may prefer to watch the therapist as he or she paints, draws models or mimes an activity. If rapport can be established quickly, a brief ten-minute introduction to the media and warm-up activity may be all that is necessary. However, it may take as long as two hours or two sessions to establish the beginnings of a trust relationship.

> It is not until later in the treatment strategy that you can begin to help the client understand the reality of time (their time, your time, and the time you share together). How much time you have together is a very real part of their re-entrance into a pattern or system which will facilitate their functioning in the real world. [Stember, 1978]

The structure of the therapeutic arts therapy session usually consists of a warm-up activity (familiarizing clients with the therapist, modality, and media), a core activity (designed to further therapeutic objectives), and a closure or declimaxing activity (designed to restore clients to a functioning level no less than when they arrived or began the session). The warm-up activity is usually a playful introduction to the media or modality which facilitates involvement and concentration upon the core activity. It provides a transitional experience from the client's physical and emotional "set and setting" prior to the session and the "here and now" of the therapeutic agenda. In some instances it may be necessary to discourage innovation or sterotypical practices tried out in the warm-up activity, in favor of an awareness of the potentials of both the media and the client. This is rarely a problem with young children; however, adolescents and adults may feel more secure drawing cartoon-like figures and animals or flowers. They should be encouraged to portray these objects and creatures in action, doing something, or in a manner which expresses a variety of emotions of their own choice.

Once the arts therapies have been introduced, they may be audio or visually tape-recorded or photographed. This provides vital records of the therapeutic process long after the activities have been abandoned and the therapeutic sessions are over. Carefully introduced, clients are rarely disturbed or distracted by these recording methods. Often they wish to try their own hands at it and are eager to see the results. This provides an opportunity to, quite literally, see from the clients' perspective and to review with them what they were feeling at the time and can often enhance behavioral change. Sharing the record-keeping with the client helps to dispell the mystique of administrative procedures and the therapeutic agenda, reaffirms the identity of the client, and offers proof of his or her own contribution to the therapeutic process. The client's independence and prerogatives are reaffirmed and sharing the record-keeping is usually interpreted as evidence of the therapist's commitment, interest, and investment of time and concern beyond the limits of the therapeutic session.

The arts are truly evocative, providing the client with a highly subjective experience and bringing forth emotionally charged material remarkably quickly. Therefore time and opportunity must be allotted in each session for declimaxing or closure. This may be accomplished by discussing the work accomplished and the client's or group's reactions during and after completing the activity. It may simply be a quiet time—listening to music and relaxing—or an unhurried cleaning up activity restoring the home or work room to its original state.

Arts therapy sessions are usually scheduled to last from one to two hours, dependent upon factors such as the client's ability to concentrate and variables in the environment and group. Five to twenty minutes of discussion time is usually allotted at the end of each work session. One or two modalities may be incorporated into the activities of a given session or a single modality may be carried over into several sessions (such as the creation of a sculpture or mask, firing, sealing, glazing, or painting).

Sessions scheduled for the home or current residence of the client may, due to lack of privacy, turn into dyadic parallel, or family activities, making it difficult to provide the desired focus on the victim. Such sessions may apparently be willingly scheduled by the parent or victim and then avoided, disrupted, or terminated by either the client, his or her friends, or by other family members. However, Stember found that by leaving attractive or requested arts materials with someone in the household or a neighbor, the chances for future contact and productivity were greatly enhanced. Persistence and demonstration of continued interest, concern, acceptance, and understanding are among the many ways to counter client resistance.

Arts Therapies and Developmental Stages

Stember, Burgess, and others report that abuse, neglect, and sexual trauma may result in behavioral and developmental "lags" or arrest. In order to counteract this effect in very young children, a haptic or sensory approach to media exploration may be essential. It is beginning with what is innate, available, and least threatening: sensory awareness. Providing age-appropriate media and techniques while circumventing inhibitions (such as getting messy or dirty) are among the challenges facing the arts therapist. During the first fifteen months of life, the average "normal" child experiences his world through sensory perception. He should be responding to his environment with pleasure, on the whole, and developing trust relationships. He enjoys the quality of sound and mimicry and begins to use words to gain needs and for clarification and discrimination. He is beginning to trust his body and develop coordination. His art is dominated by random marks and uncontrolled scribbling. Neglect and sexual abuse can arrest or cause regression to this stage, and it is important to be cognizant of developmental levels and to treat the whole child—physically, emotionally, and developmentally.

The toddler or preschooler, aged two-to-five years, is learning about himself in relation to his parents and peers. He is beginning to develop autonomy and initiative as well as a certain degree of mastery over impulses and fears. He is developing increased coordination leading to a sense of accomplishment and skill. Although he still has needs for immediate gratification—which the arts provide—and sees adults as needs-providers, he is beginning to attempt cooperative activities and simple group activities are possible with this age level. He has begun to discriminate similarities and differences, use labels and words to define his own behavior and to affect others. He is capable of ordering and classifying objects, recognizing color and using it, and of separating reality from fantasy. According to some authorities, he is also developing a sense of guilt. His drawing may be defined as "preschematic" although form is beginning to come into focus (circles, vertical and horizontal movements, and placement). He may not be ready to read but enjoys telling and hearing lengthy and complex stories, as shown in the earlier example of the little girl's bird, "Bozo," who sang and danced on TV.

The six-to-twelve-year-old group is beginning to develop skills for successful group participation and the application of individual skills to group procedures, including cooperating and sharing. He is developing self-esteem, verbal self-expression, expectations for himself and others, and is capable of approximating real-life situations in his activities. His developing symbolic forms of expression are said to function as "semi-concrete concepts of conservation," a sort of shorthand for his synthesizing processes. He is capable of schematic drawing (the representation of base and skylines, space relationships which are individualized and ordered and may reveal social behaviors, attitudes and interactions).

A seven-year-old boy, sodomized by his father who was then incarcerated, presented himself as quiet and compliant but was said to have begun hitting and rejecting his younger siblings. The arts therapist was asked to see the boy, and he selected paints for his first "free," or self-directed, picture. He outlined a ship in red and later added a blue sea and a strange yellow-green sun. Asked who might be on the ship, the boy replied that it was empty; no one was on it.

Stember felt this first picture to be vitally important. The experience of many arts therapists agree with Stember's conclusion concerning the initial representation made by a client.

> These first drawings relate intimately to the impulses, anxieties, conflicts and compensations that are characteristic of that individual. In some sense, these drawings are that person at that moment. [Therefore] we can analyze some of the work, process behavior and product in terms of where symbols, forms were placed on the sheet [of paper], and the [rapidity and repetitiousness] of graphic movement (whether they start small and tight and move outward or start large, scrawling, chaotic and diffused) and—in the recognition of diffusion and chaos—attempt to integrate the forms into a unified whole. [Stember, 1977]

The large, centrally placed ship implied a sense of self-control, of being "centered" and the boy's behavior supported this conclusion. The choice of red to outline it and the yellow-green sun alerted the therapist to conflict. (This strange yellow-green has been reported in the work of other sexually traumatized individuals.) The fact that the child said that there was no one aboard emphasized the quality of emptiness of the ship. Opaque red portholes would be hard to see through (as is anger). Here again, the behavior and verbalizations of the child add to the significance of the symbol; placid and empty are uncommon qualities both in a boy of seven and in so large a vessel on the high seas.

In consultation with the team, it was decided that this child needed an opportunity to ventilate his feelings fully and to reestablish his relationship with his siblings through work with the arts therapist. At the next session he was offered clay which he pounded, cut, wedged, pinched, and squeezed for a full hour. He appeared happy but still not satiated by the end of the session, so the clay was left with him for further exploration. Offered the opportunity, in a later session, to create box puppets, he created himself ("I'm Jehovah!") and his younger sister, also victimized by the father, and proceeded to create a drama by hiding and projecting his voice from behind these forms. Gradually, dyads and parallel play with the sister were introduced. His behavior toward his siblings improved, and he became protective and concerned about them. Six weeks after the initial arts therapy session, he made a depiction of his father in jail and added a woman in another cell (possibly his dominating mother—he didn't say, but smiled when asked who it was). The puppet head, made from a carton using colored tapes to illustrate features, done during the session mentioned, shows the father with one dark eye and one light-colored eye. This was more symbolic of a conflict of feelings concerning his affection for and awareness of betrayal by his father than a statement of fact about his father's eyes. (See figure 10–9.) The boy had progressed from being depressed and grieving for his absent father through a haptic regression and ventilation of his emotions (the clay experience) to a reality-based acknowledgment of the current situation.

Note: After six weeks of therapeutic intervention, this seven-year-old male victim of incest depicts his father in two different media. The drawing shows the father and "a woman" in different cells in jail. The box puppet shows the father with one dark and one light-colored eye, demonstrating ambivalence.

Figure 10–9. Drawn by a Seven-Year-Old Male Victim of Incest

Because children do not mature at uniform rates or achieve certain cognitive, functional, biological, and emotional levels at precisely the same chronological point in their lives, there is considerable overlap in the definitions for developmental stages, particularly those of the middle years of childhood. This is evident in such labeling attempts as: latency (6–10 yrs.), preadolescence or middle years (9–14 yrs.), adolescence (11–26 yrs.), young adult (18–25 yrs.), adulthood (21–60 yrs.), old age (60 yrs. and above). Therefore it is vital to maintain a certain degree of flexibility in making assumptions concerning the capabilities of any child. Similarly, it is equally important to remain flexible in the interpretation of symbols appearing in the work of clients.

Interpretation of Symbols

A case in point is one concerning a nine-year-old girl treated for pediatric venereal disease. It was unclear if the child had been victimized by an adult or older person or if she had been engaged in peer sexual activity. The initial art assessment and follow-up was done in the home and Stember had an opportunity to observe a continuous flow of males visiting the mother, a prostitute, older siblings known to be sexually active, and the client.

The first picture was done cheerfully and eagerly; it portrayed a city scape. Smoke was emerging from all of the chimneys on all of the buildings depicted. Chimneys are said to be a phallic symbol and smoke coming from them has been said to depict warmth and nurturing. All of the buildings had windows and doors, implying freedom of access and egress. There was evidence of the strange yellow-green mentioned earlier. The sky was a red (said to signify anger or fear) and the street was a compatible shade of blue (an inversion of color placement which might indicate confusion or turmoil).

Stember described the child as "smiling, outgoing, carefully dressed, self-possessed, responsive with a lively affect and quick, playful communication, [and evidencing] unusual organization of self and attention to detail in the midst of chaos." Although there seemed to be elements of jealousy between the siblings and the mother and daughters, the client seemed to be secure and to be coping well. Posing for a photograph taken by Stember, the child clearly exhibited seductive behavior. Her three-dimensional work demonstrated consistent, age-appropriate, imaginative, and physical skills. Frequent substitutions of male and female figures, first identified as one and then another person—identities being changed as various scenes were enacted in a diorama—acknowledged frank sexual activity on the part of all family members. Stember concluded that this child was frankly and cheerfully emulating the behaviors of her mother and older sibling, both known prostitutes.

In this instance, the red sky could have been simply a depiction of a cityscape at night, blue being appropriately selected for the glistening pavement.

The choice of green might have been selected on the basis of chromatic consistency with the other hues and shades in the picture. Green, in our culture (and color selection is often culture dominated), is usually interpreted as a positive statement (the green light for "go" in traffic or the color of growing grass). On the other hand, children often depict green monsters (note the color of the "Incredible Hulk," a television characterization of the darker side of human nature) and "feeling green" (being ill or envious). In this case, the arts therapist balanced clinical observation with interpretation of the child's product and was not misled and was able to assist the team in their assessment and treatment plan in an extremely meaningful fashion.

Similarly, psychologic tests showing below-average functioning may not be an indication of permanent developmental arrest but rather a symptom of temporary regression brought on by the sexual and emotional trauma. In one such case, the arts therapist was able to help the team untangle the web of functional and learning disabilities (which had led to disruptive school behaviors) and establish the functional strengths and capabilities of one six-year-old. Stember's report is as follows:

> While her motor coordination appears appropriate (Ulman Diagnostic Series, etc.), she appears to process information slowly. Though comprehending instructions involving body movement, had difficulty in using the same movement to create a line using that movement. Characteristics of her drawings, in terms of personality or trauma, indicate average intelligence (she spoke matter-of-factly, if a bit distractedly, about her father's doing "you-know-what") and immaturity. There is a developmental lag, no evidence of neurosis or arrest, and obvious age-appropriate forms were readily produced. There are signs of clinical neurological deficit: her concept of body image is considerably below the expected maturational level and she exhibits signs of perceptual difficulties in her bizarre and diffuse drawings of "dogs." . . . [Stember, 1977; see figures 10–10 and 10–11]

In cases of incestuous child sexual abuse, the victim may feel "forced into passive aggression, that is they are too afraid of losing the parent's love to oppose the parent openly. . . . conflict and guilt result when a child has anxiety about adequacy, punishment or loss of love." (Williams and Wood, 1977, p. 77.) Pressure from the family on one young victim to recant her accusation concerning her stepfather led to her compliance and the case against him was dropped. Shortly thereafter she did several black drawings and scribbles, including an angry, tempestuous piece she titled "House Torn by the Worst Tornado." This was followed in a subsequent session, by a self-portrait (figure 10—12) in which she was "all dolled up" in make-up and jewels and left with her stepfather. Finding security both in the adolescent group and the activities, she was able to share the fact that her mother had bought her the make-up and jewelry for a visit to her stepfather and to express the fact that the sexual abuse had been resumed. This information led to her placement with a foster family

Note: The lack of arms (possibly implying helplessness) and bird-like feet are significant of functional and possibly organic deficit.

Figure 10–10. Self-Portrait Requested during a Diagnostic Interview with a Six-Year-Old Girl Suspected of Having Been Sexually Molested

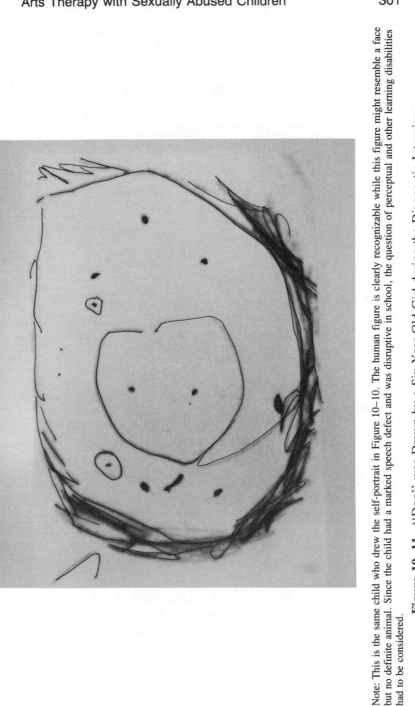

Note: This is the same child who drew the self-portrait in Figure 10–10. The human figure is clearly recognizable while this figure might resemble a face but no definite animal. Since the child had a marked speech defect and was disruptive in school, the question of perceptual and other learning disabilities had to be considered.

Figure 10–11. "Dog" was Drawn by a Six-Year-Old Girl during the Diagnostic Interview

Note: The appearance is that of an older woman and the lack of arms could imply a sense of helplessness in coping with an adult situation.

Figure 10–12. Self-Portrait by a Twelve-Year-Old Sexually Abused Girl Painted During an Adolescent Group Art Therapy Session

and an expression of her mixed feelings about separation from her family through the arts. She was, in time, able to accept this new placement and to begin to think about her future. With Stember's guidance, she began to work on skill development in art expression, was cheerful, and could often be heard singing softly to herself as she worked.

This is not to imply that all cases of arts therapy intervention have successful outcomes. These modalities are not a panacea for all situations. As was shown earlier, the response of some clients is minimal, and one child who had been smothered with a pillow while being sexually abused was too traumatized to respond at all. Three girls in the adolescent treatment group refused in any way to deal with portraiture, body image, or human figure drawing. Many evidenced a sort of approach-avoidance attitude toward new experiences, new media or modalities, and even new people. Those who have suffered severe, long-term physical abuse are apparently terrified to the point of rigidity and withdraw from anything new or different.

Arts Therapy Assessment and Treatment of Sexually Abused Children

Designing an arts therapy assessment and treatment procedure for sexually abused and traumatized children must include the following considerations:

1. The effect of the task, media, and therapists upon the victim (that is, responses to the people, the materials available and the decision-making process associated with the situation).
2. The victim's willingness to engage in the arts therapy activities as well as any verbalizations associated with them—whether spontaneous or in response to questions about the product (that is, degree of detached, passive, or confronting behaviors observed).
3. The victim's nonverbal behavior, how the victim reacts to structured and unstructured tasks as well as to the creative process (that is, qualities of communication during and after the assignment, disclosure attitude; willingness or ability to handle reality testing and feedback; expressive, defensive or stereotypical forms and the use of imagery).
4. How the victim identifies him or herself (that is, the degree of data about self and self-awareness imparted).
5. The victim's capacity to project a potential or future identity or situation involving him or her; the nature of this projection must be explored.

Stember's assessment procedure was an outgrowth of the Ulman Diagnostic Interview (Ulman, 1965, p. 63). As may have become apparent, Stember carried with her a variety of stimuli, objects and media with which to introduce herself and the tasks at hand. The choice of activities and media often depended upon the age, degree of defensiveness exhibited, and opportunities or the lack of them which the home environment might present. It sometimes took Stember several visits to accomplish her assessment procedure.

Usually, regardless of age, the first task was the production of a spontaneous or "free" drawing. This exercise might produce a liberating effect of relaxing and freeing the client to explore either the potentials of the media or to express "habitual modes of response" to adult authority. The importance attributed to this first drawing has already been discussed; however, this particular technique was regarded as so informative that the team psychologist began to incorporate it into his intake assessment procedures as well.

If the child was particularly inhibited or defended, the process was sometimes begun with the Winnicott Squiggle Game. (Winnicott, 1971, pp. 14–27.) In this exercise, the therapist and client each select one contrasting color to use so that their contributions to the mutual drawing may be distinguished. The therapist closes his or her eyes and makes a mark on the paper and offers the child an opportunity to make it into a picture. The therapist then encourages the child to tell about the picture (what happened, what might happen, and so on). The procedure is reversed. The child draws the squiggle and the therapist completes the picture. By taking turns, the therapist is able to be somewhat directive in bringing up forms and subjects or allegories which might elicit an emotional response.

> The structure of this exchange reflects a basic issue which relates to all psy-chotherapeutic interactions: establishing contact and initiating rapport. Like many art therapy activities, this process is without rules, except, of course, for the primary ones of therapeutic exchange. First the child is given permission for spontaneous and active participation. Second, based on the child's picture (or a refusal to draw one), the therapist actively joins in an exchange through the picture he or she creates in turn. Consolidation of the relationship occurs through this flow, and reciprocity grows. [Stember, 1978]

Levels of trust and eye contact evident during this first task, the quality and quantity of symbolic material expressed, any discussion which might have occurred during or after the task, all help to determine the second step of the procedure. In both the Ulman and Stember procedures, this activity usually involved an element of exercise, body awareness, and free movement. This might include the miming of the creation of a large mural, led by the client and "mirrored" by the therapist (leadership in such mirror exercises may alternate or evolve simultaneously in this and other sessions). It might be the miming of large muscle sport activities or the movements of large and small animals. Doing these movements normally, then rapidly, then in slow motion, and finally normally once more tends to release physical tensions and provide the therapist with insights into inhibitions, limitations in range and control of motions, natural rhythms and, as had already been noted, the ability to translate verbal instruction into action.

This activity was followed with the request that the client do a sort of rhythmical scribble based upon the motions just experienced. According to Ulman, this may result in a "lowering of defences and the emergence of stronger feelings and more unconscious material." (Ulman, p. 64.) This may then be followed by a request that the client do another scribble (this time with eyes closed, if possible) which is then developed through the addition (if desired) of lines, forms, and colors to create a picture. Discussion, or at least increased verbalization, often occurs after this exercise, allowing the opportunity to de-velop a degree of focus in subsequent tasks.

The Ulman model, which consists of four drawings and one movement exercise, concludes with a final free drawing. The purpose of this is to give the client an opportunity to continue to explore the potentials of the media and his or her own creativity or to return to the defensive posture assumed in his first picture. The work may express strengths and the confidence to take modest risks or the desire to express limits on risk taking. These five tasks were completed in a one-hour assessment interview conducted in a therapeutic setting. Because Stember's assessments were rarely conducted at the agency, she adjusted her assessment format to the age of the client and the environmental site and situation. She also adjusted the number of tasks, and the time necessary to accomplish them, to include some in the expressive mode preference of the client. Thus her assessment might include as many as seven tasks in art drama and play therapy.

While initially offering chalks, paint, clay and plastic media, mask-making and construction materials, as well as toys and objects for play, specific themes might be suggested for later sessions. These themes might include a kinetic family expression ("Can you make something showing your family doing something?"), a portrait or a mask ("Of someone important or someone you would like to talk to.") a self-portrait ("Draw yourself as you would like to be.") and a portrait of the therapist ("Draw a picture of me.") The child might also be asked to draw a favored place where he or she has been or would like to be (" . . . in a week, a month and a year.").

In cases of child sexual abuse, it is important to assess the strengths of family ties. The child's emotional relationship to parents, other family members, and the perpetrator plays an important role in symptomatic behaviors. Assessing these relationships and bonds helps to determine the best course of action for the victim. Identification by the victim of his parents as positive, caring, and nurturing figures is regarded as indication for an optimistic attitude for reintegration of the trauma and the family unit. Rapid recovery on the part of the victim, as indicated by behavioral improvements and a quality of increased "intactness" of his work, seems to indicate "a fairly stable ego structure and could define developmental lags as being situational in nature." (Stember, 1977.)

The next vital step is to help the victim separate the percept of the ego (the merger of self and the traumatic incident) from the reality of the abuse. This, in itself, may be extremely painful and difficult. The impact of the sexual abuse itself, the consequences following disclosure, the implied or imposed sense of guilt, betrayal, and rejection may incur such self-protective devices as deep repression, total loss of recall or denial of the event. There would seem to be no question that the sexually traumatized child suffers intense conflict of emotions and an affect of confusion. Most vital and frequent are expressions of low self-esteem, guilt, and bewilderment.

> They often become lost in swirls of anguish as they try to find a sense of themselves separate from the violated forms of their bodies. To rebuild the self . . . separate from the incident takes different lengths of time. The length of recovery time appears to be correlated with the point of development the abuse interrupted, the length and severity of the abuse, and the character of the victim. Individuality in victims of sexual abuse appears to override commonalities of symbolism. [Stember, 1978]

As the victim begins to integrate the trauma, it becomes evident in her or his creative arts expressions. The example given earlier demonstrating the ability to contain and reduce the symbolic expression to a controllable size, the use of the stronger colors or the containment and reduction of self-perceived negative colors, the exchange of stereotypical forms and gestures for, or the introduction of, more naturalistic, age-appropriate expressions are all indicative of change and progress. Stember also found a commonly expressed fantasy of moving people from large global areas into smaller spaces close to the victim. This wish fulfillment, facilitated by the use of clay and wax figures, maps, murals, and segmented cartons for doll houses, provided the child with an opportunity not usually available to him: to control and reestablish a satisfying family situation. Having thus realized his fantasy, the child often became more available to the acceptance and reintegration of the full situation.

Summary

In crisis intervention and short-term therapy, the arts therapies provide a quick, inexpensive, and dynamic access to vital information and rehabilitation. The skilled arts therapist brings the team vital techniques and training which have not been traditionally available, but which facilitate assessment and treatment as well as enabling team members to accomplish their goals more effectively. Clara Jo Stember was a pioneer committed to the use of a multiarts, multimedia approach to the problems of abused, neglected, and sexually traumatized children and youth. Only a brief sample of her work and views have been presented here; more will have to follow. The chapter attempts to demonstrate how verbal and nonverbal behaviors relate to each other and how they are expressive of the structuring of sensory input resulting in behavior. By avoiding dwelling on commonalities in symbols expressed by sexually abused and traumatized children (which, at best, should only serve to alert the therapist to the possibilities of distress), I have attempted to show that each of us has a unique symbolic repertoire of expressions, and the multiple or singular significance applied to that symbol is unique to that individual.

The multimedia and multiarts approach to individual expressive and learning modes facilitates the communication and conscious awareness and integration of this symbolic repertoire. They are the purposeful use of media and modalities for the creation of an expression which is neither haphazard, unintentional, or accidental but rather the immediate result of a synthesizing process. These expressions stand as metaphor for that process and are therefore, in and of themselves, structures. Ventilation in a socially acceptable milieu reduces anxiety and the need to act out negative feelings. Because they allow for the expression and objectifying of conflicts and emotions, the arts therapies can enhance control of such behaviors. Exploration and the successful resolution of conflicts in one area can lead to the willingness to take risks in other areas. By enhancing learning skills such as concentration and communication, the arts therapies also enhance self-esteem.

When the arts are introduced in a congenial and nonjudgmental manner, they provide a pleasurable and valued experience for individuals (children and adults), families, and other groups. It is important that the therapist maintain a supportive attitude which does not usurp the client's prerogatives to contribute to his or her own recovery from the trauma. A tendency, inherent in nursing for example, to anticipate the client's needs may actually increase insecurity and dependence upon the therapeutic team. In applying the arts therapies, it is important to act as an interested observer or facilitator of creative expression than to be helpful and directive in the creative process.

It is equally important to keep in mind that the arts are very evocative tools and, when used in a therapeutic context, imply a knowledge of psychodynamics as well as the emotional and physical effects of the media and techniques. Misuse of the media and techniques by individuals familiar with arts practices but not their emotional effects, or any other incomplete combination of these variables, could easily compound the client's difficulties. Both training and trained arts therapists are readily available in many parts of the United States, and the national organizations of the various disciplines are available to respond to inquiries.

In the therapeutic session, as in treatment or the writing of a chapter or story, it is important to remember the dictim to have a beginning, middle, and end. In the therapeutic applicaiton of the arts, these are referred to as the warm-up, the core activity, and the closure. Experience in the various techniques and exercises leads to an approximation of how much time to allow for each aspect of the session. It is important to allow enough time for the completion of each activity in order not to frustrate or discourage participants.

The importance of closure cannot be underestimated. Time, in every session, must be alloted to this element. To leave it out would be like sending children into the library after recess; the emotional energy invested in the therapeutic activities is too valuable to be allowed to dissipate carelessly. It is within the potential of the arts therapies to reveal the psychodynamics and events of the past and present, as well as the capabilities of the victim to anticipate and cope with the future. By enhancing developmental and psychological growth, communication and learning skills, ventilation, gratification and success, the arts also provide an opportunity for lifelong enjoyment. It is extremely rare, in short-term crisis intervention, that we have an opportunity to provide such an attractive and enduring method for coping with life's vicissitudes.

References

Rape

Burgess, A.W., and Holmstrom, L.L. *Rape: Victims of Crisis.* Bowie, Maryland: Robert J. Brady Co., 1975; p. 65.

Art

CENDEX. Naitove, C.E. 1979; unpublished.

Carter, J.L., and Miller, P.K. *"Creative Art for Minimally Brain-Injured Children" Academic Therapy:* 6:245–52.

Ulman, E. *"A New Use of Art in Psychiatric Diagnosis." Bulletin of Art Therapy* 4(April 1965).

Rubin, J.A. *Child Art Therapy.* New York: Van Nostrand Reinhold Co., 1978.

Williams, G.H., and Wood, M.M. *Developmental Art Therapy.* Baltimore: University Park Press, 1977.

Stember, C.J. *"Art Therapy: A New Use in the Diagnosis and Treatment of Sexually Abused Children" In Sexual Abuse of Children: Selected Readings,* MacFarlane, K., ed. National Center on Child Abuse and Neglect, U.S. Government Publications: 1980.

———. *"Graphic Clues Predictive of Child Abuse/Neglect."* Topeka: Archives of the American Art Therapy Association, 1976.

———. Case Reports, Articles and Art Therapy Session Records, 1976–78.

Play

Axline, V.M. *Play Therapy.* New York: Houghton-Mifflin, 1947.

Erickson, Erik. *Childhood and Society.* New York: Penguin Press, 1965.

Woltman, A.G. *"Concepts of Play Therapy Techniques." American Journal of Orthopsychiatry* 25(1955):771–83.

Courtney, R. *Play, Drama and Thought.* New York: Cassell & Collier Macmillian, Publishers, Ltd., 1974, pp. 80–95 and p. 39.

Kiefer, C. American Anthropological Association Annual Meeting Presentation. Boston Globe, 1976.

Melville, Keith; *"Play's the Thing." The Sciences* 14, 1(Jan.–Feb. 1974), pp. 12–14.

Miller, S. *The Psychology of Play.* Baltimore: Penguin Books, 1968.

11 Law Enforcement and Child Sexual Abuse

Patricia A. Graves, and
Suzanne M. Sgroi

Helping sexually abused children depends on the combined efforts of law enforcement, medical, social service, and prosecution personnel. It is essential for those in each field to recognize and understand the others' responsibilities in dealing with child sexual abuse. Only then can we learn how best to help each other to help the victims and their families. As experience, research, and learning advance, it becomes increasingly clear that the police officer—and indeed the entire criminal justice system—are an integral part of identifying the problem, protecting the victim, and remedying the situation.

Law enforcement and the criminal justice system have significant impact on all child-sexual-abuse cases after disclosure, even when the police are *not* notified and criminal prosecution of the offender does *not* occur. Sexual abuse of children is a crime in every state in the United States, although definitions of criminal conduct vary from one jurisdiction to another. Because they abhor the punitive aspects of the criminal justice system, professionals from the fields of health, mental health, and social work often shy away from reporting cases of child sexual abuse to law enforcement authorities. By refusing to work cooperatively with police and prosecutors, helping professionals often deny child-sexual-abuse victims the potential assistance of law enforcement and the courts.

Nevertheless, the offender's desire to avoid accountability for his or her criminal behavior is a powerful "behind-the-scenes" factor in every unreported child-sexual-abuse case. Such offenders sometimes appear initially to cooperate with treatment plans. Their "cooperation," however, usually fades away when they perceive that a report to the police or prosecution is not likely to occur or when they believe they have "neutralized" the threat to themselves by under-

Patricia A. Graves has been a member of the Manchester, Connecticut, police department for fifteen years and is a lieutenant in the detective bureau in charge of youth services. Lieutenant Graves has a degree in police science from the Graduate F.B.I. Academy in Quantico, Virginia. She has been an instructor for the Manchester Regional Training Academy and for the Connecticut Department of Children and Youth Services. Lieutenant Graves is currently the chairperson for the Manchester Child Advocacy Team and a member of the Hartford Bar Association's Child Law Committee. From 1977–1979 she served as a consultant and multidisciplinary case-review team member for the Sexual Trauma Treatment Program of the Connecticut Department of Children and Youth Services.

mining the credibility of the allegations against them (usually by pressuring the child victim to recant his or her allegations or to remain silent).

Cooperative Intervention

One possible solution is for police and prosecutors to work cooperatively with professionals from health, mental health, and social work to assist child victims of sexual abuse to make complaints against offenders that will be upheld in court. This can be accomplished by joint investigation of cases and by supporting the child victim and his or her family through the process of case prosecution. In locations such as Seattle, Washington, where such cooperation does exist, skilled investigation of cases results in a high proportion of guilty pleas by offenders (Berliner, personal communication, 1980), thereby eliminating the need for a lengthy prosecution. The key to success of such cooperation between police, prosecutors, and "helping professionals" is to create a community-based offender treatment program that represents a humane alternative to incarceration without rehabilitation. (Giarretto et al, 1978). When criminal court judges have the option of sentencing offenders who are convicted of some type of nonviolent child sexual abuse (or who plead guilty to charges) to participate in a treatment program as a condition of a suspended sentence or as part of a work release program, the authority of the criminal justice system can be used humanely rather than punitively. Child victims of sexual abuse and their families can thus be helped by authoritative intervention. The community has a realistic hope of helping a greater number of nonviolent offenders and preventing further child sexual abuse rather than incarcerating and punishing a few offenders and allowing most to evade accountability and to continue their sexually abusive behavior toward children.

How can we achieve these goals? It is not enough for us to want the circumstances to improve. Police, prosecutors, and helping professionals need to trust each other much more than they do now in order to be able to work together more effectively on behalf of child victims. A significant part of trusting another professional person is a better understanding of what he or she does. Few helping professionals understand the police officer's responsibilities in child-sexual-abuse cases. There is little understanding of proper police procedures to investigate these cases and to collect evidence for use of prosecutors.

What do the police have to do (in investigating a child-sexual-abuse case) and why do they have to do it? How much discretion do the police have and how is it exercised? How can other professionals help the investigating officer, and how can he or she help them to help the child?

The purposes of this chapter are fourfold:

1. To explain how sexually abusive behavior toward children is translated into "elements" of crimes.

2. To explain the "how" and "why" of police investigation of child sexual abuse.
3. To show how evidence collected by police investigation leads to decisions for arrest and prosecution.
4. To point out methods to achieve improved cooperation between police, prosecutors, and helping professionals.

One of the authors (P.A.G.) is a lieutenant in a community police department in Manchester, Connecticut who presently heads a youth services bureau and has fourteen years of experience with police investigation of child-sexual-abuse cases. The other author (S.M.S.) is a physician who has served as a trainer on physical and sexual abuse of children for Connecticut's Municipal Police Training Council since 1972 and has extensive experience with investigation and management of child-sexual-abuse cases. Both authors served as part of the multidisciplinary team that reveiwed cases for Connecticut's Sexual Trauma Treatment Program.[a] This chapter represents a distillation of our combined experience in investigation and management of child-sexual-abuse cases by police and helping professionals.

The Laws and Their Use

What are the criminal aspects of sexually abusive behavior toward children? How do the police decide if a crime has been committed? What determines the type and number of charges that are made?

In order to understand police procedures, a basic knowledge of the state's laws pertaining to all elements of sexual abuse of children is essential. In many states, one or more organizations have compiled, printed, and distributed compendiums and summaries of the statutes. Such compendiums are invaluable for teaching and quick reference. All agencies who deal with troubled children and families should acquire a compendium of the statutes if one is not already available; it must be complete and continually updated. Any helping professional in the field of child sexual abuse must be familiar with these laws and be able to refer to the statutes quickly and easily.

Elements of Crimes

Law enforcement officers are trained to assess a complaint of child sexual abuse and analyze the specific elements of the behavior in order to determine what

[a]Supported by the National Center for Child Abuse and Neglect, DHEW, Grant No. 90-C-399.

crimes have or have not been committed. In other words, the behavior will be evaluated to see if different aspects can be categorized as criminal behavior. The elements of crimes will differ from state to state, depending on the definitions found in the statutes. However, we can suggest a list of important categories to be considered in determining elements of sexual behavior with children that may be crimes. We encourage readers to examine their own state laws and to check them against these categories.

Age of the Participants.
Offender's Age. This is usually pertinent only if the "offender" or "actor" (the person who initiated the behavior) is a minor (younger than the statutory age of majority). In some states, the law does not speak to this issue. In other states, the statutes require that a minimum age difference be present when both participants are minors. For example, the offender who is also a minor, may have to be at least four or five years older than the younger child in order to be charged with sexual assault in some jurisdictions.

Victim's Age. As stated above, the victim may have to be younger than the offender by a designated number of years if the offender is a minor. If the offender is an adult, there are two important cutoff points for the victim's age. First, most statutes will identify an "age of consent" for all minors. Below this age of consent, it is assumed that a child cannot voluntarily and knowingly engage in consenting sexual behavior. Accordingly, a child who is younger than the age of consent may be considered a victim of "statutory rape" if he or she engaged in sexual behavior with an adult, regardless of other circumstances.

The age of consent varies widely from state to state; in most locations, it will vary from age 12 years to age 15 years. Many states make a further age distinction for victims if the offender is the victim's parent or guardian or an adult with whom the child resides. In these cases, the age of consent may be as old as sixteen or eighteen years. The implication is that the added factors of parenthood, guardianship, or residence with the offender influence the victim's capacity to give consent so strongly that even older children cannot freely consent to sexual behavior under these circumstances. Likewise, some states make further provision for raising the age of consent when the victim is in the custody of the offender (as in a hospital, group home, or the like). Again, the implication is that the offender has a special position of power over the victim that influences the child's capacity to give consent, even if he or she is older than the minimum age below which statutory rape can be charged. For example, Connecticut identifies sexual assault in the second degree if the victim of sexual intercourse is under age 15, or under age 18 and the actor is the victim's guardian or responsible for the general supervision of the victim's welfare. Sexual assault in the fourth degree (a lesser charge) is used with the same age parameters if the behavior was limited to sexual contact.

Relationship between the Participants. Is the offender a parent or guardian or someone who serves as custodian for the victim in an institution? If so, the age of consent may be greater than the age for statutory rape as explained above. Further, are the participants related to each other in a way that the state identifies as a barrier to marriage? If so, an essential element for the crime of incest is fulfilled. In most states, the incest statute specifically mentions that the participants must be related to each other in the "degrees of kindred who are prohibited to marry." These specified relationships vary from state to state but, in general, include parents, stepparents, grandparents, aunts, uncles, brothers, sisters and stepsiblings.

Type of Sexual Behavior. It is extremely important to identify every type of sexual behavior that occurred. States differ in their definitions but, in general, the following can be expected to appear in sexual assault statutes.

Exposure. Exposing one's genitals to a child, depending on the circumstances, will be an offense in most states. Forcing or encouraging the child to disrobe and expose his or her genitals may also be an offense.

Fondling or Sexual Contact. Touching certain areas of the child's body as specified by the statutes may be termed fondling. Usually the specified areas include the genitals, rectal opening, buttocks, inner aspect of the thighs and breasts. Sometimes this behavior is termed "sexual contact." In general, "touching" behavior is considered a more serious offense than exposure.

Sexual Intercourse. This behavior may include oral intercourse, vaginal intercourse, or rectal intercourse. The essential element is penetration of one of these openings of the victim's body. Sexual intercourse is always considered to be a more serious offense than sexual contact or exposure.

1. Vaginal intercourse. The legal definition of vaginal intercourse in all states includes penetration of the vagina by the penis. In some states, penetration may also include an object or finger inserted into the vaginal opening. In Connecticut, penetration "however slight" is nonetheless penetration and emission of semen is not necessary to complete vaginal intercourse. In many states, penetration of the vaginal opening by the offender's lips and tongue (cunnilingus) is also considered to be a type of vaginal intercourse.

2. Oral intercourse. This behavior always involves some type of oral-genital contact. Usually, oral intercourse is defined as fellatio: the male offender inserts his penis into the victim's mouth or the penis of a male victim is taken into the mouth of an offender of either sex. Sometimes this behavior is termed oral sodomy. Emission of semen is usually not an essential element of oral inter-

course. The definition may also include cunnilingus as described above. Oral intercourse in child sexual abuse may also involve contact between the child's lips and tongue and the vulvo-vaginal opening of a female offender.

3. Rectal intercourse. In some states, rectal intercourse is narrowly defined as penetration of the victim's anal or rectal opening by the penis of a male perpetrator. Broader definitions include penetration by a finger or by an object. Statutes vary as to the degree of penetration required; some states may require that emission of semen accompany the penetration. Sodomy is a term sometimes used interchangeably with rectal intercourse.

Incest. The legal definition of incest varies widely from state to state. The relationship of the participants is a key factor: they must be related in a way for marriage between them to be prohibited. Usually, some form of sexual intercourse is an essential element for a charge of incest. The severity of the penalty for incestuous sexual behavior is highly variable. In Connecticut, incest has carried a lesser penalty than second degree sexual assault, although both charges include the element of sexual intercourse and neither charge requires that the elements of force or threat of force be present.

Degree of Force Employed. The degree of force employed in engaging the child in sexual behavior is an important element to be considered in filing charges. Any of the following circumstances may apply.

No Force or Threat of Force. In this situation, the offender does not use force or threat of force to compel the victim to engage in sexual behavior with him or her. This may often be the case in child sexual abuse because offenders are more likely to try to persuade the child to take part in sexual activity than to frighten or compel him or her to do so. If the elements of force or threat of force are absent, the offense is usually viewed as less serious.

Threat of Force against the Victim or a Third Party. Some offenders will tell a child that they will force him or her to engage in sexual activity. The threat of force may be directed at the child himself or herself or it may be directed against a third party. For example, the offender may say to a child, "If you cry or scream, "I'll beat you up." Or, the child may be told: "If you don't let me do this, I'll beat up your sister." The element of a threat of force if the child fails to comply with the sexual behavior usually makes the offense more serious. Some statutes add the provison that the threat must make the victim fear bodily harm to himself or herself or to a third party.

Use of Force against the Victim or a Third Party. In other instances, the offender may actually use physical force to compel the victim's cooperation. The element of use of force, when present, virtually always increases the severity of the offense. Some statutes only designate force used against the victim; others include the element of force used against a third party to compel the victim's compliance as well.

Use of a Firearm or Dangerous Weapon. Some states have a separate statute that covers sexual assault with a firearm or dangerous weapon. If these elements are present, such statutes are likely to carry very severe penalties.

Corroboration. Since child sexual abuse is frequently nonviolent, with no physical force employed against the victim, there is usually little or no evidence of physical trauma to be found. There may not be emission of semen when children are sexually abused by male offenders; absence of semen is to be expected when the offender is a female. Child sexual abuse usually involves a secretive one-on-one relationship between the victim and the offender. Witnesses to the sexually abusive behavior are rare; when present, they are likely to be other young children. Nevertheless, some states require one or more of the above types of corroboration for a charge of sexual assault against a child. Thus the presence or absence of corroborating evidence is important in determining the type of charge that is filed when a complaint of child sexual abuse is made.

Child Pornography. Some sexually abusive behavior directed toward children is associated with child pornography: the elements of direct or indirect (via photograph or film) exhibition of the child in some type of obscene performance. This common practice is now more widely recognized and many states have statutes that deal specifically with child pornography or "kiddie-porn." Penalties for child pornography are highly variable.

Risk of Injury to a Minor or Impairing the Morals of a Minor. In many states, sexual behavior with a child also falls within the definition of broader statutes dealing with issues such as risk of injury to a minor or impairing the morals of a minor. Sexual offenders against children may also be charged under such broader statutes. Although the language of the statutes is highly variable, law-enforcement officers in most jurisdictions can file charges of this type when they receive a complaint of child sexual abuse.

Charges against Offenders

The foregoing list of factors should be assessed in determining the elements of crimes that may be present in cases of child sexual abuse. The presence or absence of specific elements of crimes, in turn, determines the type and number of charges that may be filed. Frequently nonpolice professionals oversimplify the sorting out and selection of the charges that are appropriate and necessary for successful prosecution. The fact that police file a variety of charges and multiple charges is sometimes misinterpreted as "being out to get the guy."

It is not unusual for police, after making the decision to arrest someone in a child-sexual-abuse case, to file more than one charge against the accused. In most cases, more than one type of crime has been committed. For example: If a father has sexually molested his seven-year-old daughter by having forced sexual intercourse with her, the offenses in Connecticut that could be charged are sexual assault in the first degree, sexual assault in the third degree, and risk of injury to a minor. The charge of sexual assault, first degree would be appropriate because the offender has compelled (by use of force) another person to engage in sexual intercourse. Sexual assault, third degree, would be an appropriate charge because the child is related to the offender in the degrees defined in the statute and sexual intercourse was an element of the behavior. Risk of injury to a minor would be an appropriate charge because the father placed his daughter in a situation likely to impair her health or morals.

Knowledge of the laws and the process used by police to assess criminal behavior and to determine which, if any, charges will be filed is a powerful tool for any helping professional who deals with the child sexual abuse. Armed with this knowledge, he or she is far better equipped to assess the seriousness of the sexually abusive behavior and to support and assist the victim and the family. Lastly, knowledge of the laws and their use is key for those who are willing to utilize authoritative incentives for treatment of child sexual abuse.

Police Investigation

Cases of child sexual assault demonstrate the accuracy of the statement that police work is both an art and a science. It is true that the officer's primary goal in investigation is to gather evidence to be used to prove that a crime has been committed and to determine, and later prove in court, who committed that crime. When the complaint under investigation is that of child sexual assault, the victim's physical and emotional well-being must always be the police officer's first responsibility and concern. Meanwhile, the officer must carry out the tasks of gathering, evaluating, and preserving evidence for possible prosecution. Sometimes the investigation fails to produce evidence that a crime has taken place.

Every case of child sexual assault must be individually assessed to determine how the investigation will proceed and what will be required in that investigation. We cannot offer a fixed and predetermined protocol to be used without variation in all cases. Only guideposts can be established. For example, the requirements and findings for an investigation of an immediately reported sexual assault of a six-year-old child by a stranger in a park will differ markedly from the particulars of a father-daughter incest case in which sexual activity occurred regularly over a three-year period prior to the report. Also, police investigation of child sexual assault is often accomplished in concert with other disciplines. Frequently, the child and other family members are interviewed by child-protective-service workers, health or mental health professionals, counselors or social workers, before a report to the police is made. Nevertheless, a police investigator must collect detailed and complete information about the situation in order to determine which, if any, elements of crimes are present.

Members of other professions, family members, and even victims themselves are likely to be impatient with the process used by police investigators to determine if a crime has taken place and to gather and preserve evidence. Although the process can and should be altered, whenever possible, to protect and support the child victim, the police officer cannot neglect his or her responsibility to gather facts. What happened, how it happened, the exact sequence of events that occurred, background information about the victim, the victim's family, the suspect, and any potential witnesses—all this information must be gathered and recorded in detail. One way to assure that all the pertinent information is collected is to use the following format:

Basic Information about the Complaint

1. *Victim*. Name, date of birth, home address, telephone number, school and grade, guardian of the child, birth certificate (if it is an incest case), date of last intercourse or sexual contact and identity of partner, dates of any prior sexual assault or sexual activity, details about relationship with the suspect and its duration.
2. *Family*. Parents' names, dates of birth, home addresses, places of employment and occupations, marital status; siblings' vital statistics; physical environment; relationships of family members to each other; reactions of family members to the complaint and to subsequent police involvement and posture toward the victim and the suspect.
3. *Offense*. Exactly what occurred, when and where it occurred, just how it occurred, what happened prior to the incident, what happened after the incident, and any reason for its occurrence, if one can be ascertained.
4. *Suspect*. Name, address, vital statistics if known or full and complete description from the victim and witnesses.
5. *Witnesses*. Names, addresses, and telephone numbers of all parties who saw the victim before the incident or incidents; who saw or heard any part of the incident or incidents; or who talked to the victim prior to police involvement. Neighbors may be interviewed.

Several factors are likely to determine how the police will begin the investigation after a complaint has been received.

Elapsed Time. Did the sexual assault of a child just happen or did it occur several days, weeks, months or even years prior to the complaint? If the sexual maltreatment is reported long after the last incident occurred, there is probably little physical evidence to be gathered. These children should nevertheless have a complete physical examination but it is less crucial to do an immediate physical examination.

However, if the sexual maltreatment is reported immediately after an incident has occurred, the police will try to obtain as much physical evidence as possible. This may include the folowing:

Victim's Clothing. The police will wish to obtain and preserve the clothing worn by the child at the time of the incident before it has been cleaned or altered in any way. Tears, dirt, bloodstains, and semen may all be present and can be used to corroborate the victim's story of the sexual maltreatment.

Photographs of the Victim. Color photographs of injuries to the victim's body may be very important and should be obtained whenever possible. The cooperation of the child and the examining physician are essential. In addition, the police may wish to obtain photographs of the child's facial expression and general attitude. If the child appears in a photograph to be frightened, dejected, or otherwise traumatized, this may also convince others that an injury has taken place.

Physical Examination of the Victim. An immediate physical examination of the victim is essential if the sexual maltreatment has taken place within the past 24 hours. This examination should be conducted by an experienced physician whose findings can be introduced as evidence before the court. The physical examination should identify and record evidence of any trauma, any condition of the vaginal or rectal openings that may be abnormal considering the age of the child, presence of sperm in the vagina of a female child, and the presence of sexually transmitted diseases (especially gonorrhea infections of the throat, urethra, vulvo-vaginal area, and rectal opening). Establishing that a female victim (ages 9 years and older) is pregnant may also be an important contribution of the physical examination. Any or all of the evidence obtained from a physical examination may be used to corroborate the complaint of child sexual assault. Obviously, the physical examination is far more likely to reveal physical findings that support the child's story if the sexual activity was carried out by force. If no force was used, there is less chance that findings from the physical examination will be helpful.

Location of the Sexual Assault. Where did the sexual activity occur? The police officer may wish to visit the scene of the sexual assault for two reasons.

Collection of Evidence from the Scene. Depending on the elapsed time between the incident and the report, the scene of the crime may still contain physical evidence of the assault. The police officer may wish to visit the scene to identify and collect physical evidence (signs of a scuffle, blood stains, semen, fragments of clothing or any other pertinent physical signs). The degree of force or violence reported by the victim will also be important in deciding if the scene of the crime should be visited and how soon the visit should take place.

Diagramming or Photographing the Scene. Even when physical evidence of the assault is not present at the scene, it may be helpful to diagram or photograph the location where the sexual assault took place. Reviewing the activity in relation to a photograph or a diagram is likely to increase the investigator's understanding of exactly what took place as well as to enhance the victim's recall of what occurred. Photographs and diagrams may also be very helpful to the prosecutor in explaining the crime to a judge or to a jury.

Relationship of the Accused to the Victim. Was the accused person known to the victim? Was he or she a family member? Did the sexual maltreatment take place in the victim's home? If the accused person is known to the victim or is a family member, the police officer must consider the potential family pressure upon the victim during the investigation. Victims may be placed under extreme pressure by the accused person or by other family members to withdraw the complaint or to withhold details of the story. Also, if the sexual maltreatment took place in the victim's home, the officer may need to obtain a search warrant or a consent to search in order to examine the scene for physical evidence or to obtain photographs.

Nature of the Sexual Assault. What exactly took place between the victim and the accused person? Was physical force or violence used? Was a firearm or other dangerous weapon employed to threaten the victim? Did the sexual assault include a beating or other forms of physical abuse? Was the child photographed or filmed as part of the sexual activity? All of these possible factors will influence the police officer's decision on how to proceed with investigating the complaint—the timing of physical examinations, visiting the scene, obtaining of search and arrest warrants, and so forth. If a weapon was used or if photographs or films were taken, the obtaining of a search warrant or a consent to search may be crucial, especially if the scene of the sexual activity was the victim's home or someone's private residence.

Although the above-described factors will influence the direction of the investigation, the police officer will probably wish to conduct a detailed interview of the victim first, if the condition of the child permits. Many considerations must be kept in mind during this interview.

Interviewing the Victim

Interviewing a child-sexual-assault victim is a very difficult and delicate assignment. The investigating officer must remember to consider the psychological condition of the victim and his or her family at all times. Questioning the victim should not cause additional emotional problems to occur. The following circumstances of the interview are all important.

Location. The interview should take place in a quiet pleasant room with no distractions. Comfortable chairs and the absence of ringing telephones go a long way toward helping a child to relax. It is always preferable for the interview to take place in a neutral setting. Interviews should never be conducted in the child's home if incest is suspected or if a parent or family member has any reason to wish to suppress information or if the assault took place in the home. However, in selected cases (for example, an assault of a young child in a park by a stranger), conducting the interview in the child's home may make the process easier for the child. In all cases, the officer will have to judge what arrangements are best, keeping the welfare of the child in mind.

Persons Present. Sometimes it may be very helpful to interview the child with someone else present. This second person should be someone whom the child knows and trusts. If someone else is present during the interview, it is preferable that he or she be a social worker or counselor (rather than a relative). Sometimes another professional person will have already interviewed the victim and will have already established a trust relationship. In general, the younger the victim, the more important it will be to have another known and trusted person present during the interview.

Why not a relative? The reason for excluding relatives is obvious in an incest case. Any relative is likely to be upset by information elicited from the victim about the incestuous sexual behavior. The officer must remember that some relatives may wish to suppress incriminating information that the child might reveal. Although some police agencies require that a parent or guardian must always be present when officers interview children, this should not be required for child *victims* (as opposed to juvenile *offenders*).

When police officers conduct interviews with child victims of sexual assault, they will usually ask anyone present during the interview to remain silent and not to interrupt. This enables the officer to elicit information from the child and to assess its credibility without distractions. On the other hand, the second person may be able to assist the officer by being supportive of the child and perhaps by clarifying the child's terminology or the sequence of events described. We recommend that the police officer discuss the interview procedure with the second person first, in the child's absence. The police officer can thus hear any information that the second person can supply about the facts of the incident or about the child. Also, they can establish some ground rules about input from the second person. Although the investigating officer should clearly be in charge of the interview, he or she would be wise to turn to the second person at intervals and invite input or clarification. They may wish to set a prearranged signal to be used by the second person to alert the officer to the second person's concerns about the victim. All these prearrangements show a concern for the child's well-being and will, in the long run, be helpful in the investigation.

Timing. When should the interview take place? Most investigators would prefer to talk to the child as soon as possible after the incident is reported. The timing of the police investigator's interview with a child victim of sexual assault will nevertheless depend upon many other considerations. Was the child physically injured? If so, a medical examination should be performed and medical treatment initiated before the officer attempts to conduct a detailed interview with the child. Is the victim emotionally upset or perhaps hysterical? If so, again, the officer should not attempt to interview the child immediately but rather should defer talking to the child until after he or she has had an opportunity to calm down. With a young child or perhaps a child who appears to be very fearful, the interview should take place at a time when a known and trusted person can be present.

The timing of an interview can also be crucial in an incest case or in a child-sexual-assault situation involving an offender who has continuous access to the child. When the offender is likely to be in a power position over the child after the disclosure of sexual activity between them, the investigating officer must appreciate the importance of interviewing the victim before the disclosure. Otherwise, the child may be too frightened to tell a police officer what has really occurred for fear of retribution by the offender. In all cases, the investigating officer must try to interview the child at a time that will be least upsetting for the child but will also be likely to elicit responses from the child which are accurate and "uncontaminated" by pressure from others. If the timing of the interview cannot be controlled by the investigating officer, at least he or she should be aware of the implications of the timing as just described.

After the circumstances of the interview have been determined, the police officer has three major tasks: establishing a rapport with the child, interviewing for facts, and victim evaluation. Chapter 2, "Validation of Child Sexual Abuse," contains a detailed discussion of the process by which these tasks can be accomplished. The issues are the same, regardless of the identity of the interviewer (police officer, child-protective-services worker, health professional, social worker, or the like).

Probably the most important part of the interview is the officer's ability to establish a rapport with the victim. The officer should never begin an interview by asking questions about the incident. Learning to establish an informal and friendly relationship with the child not only will assist in the relationship between the officer and the child, but will help the child become accustomed to answering the officer's questions. The officer should let the child describe the incident in his or her own words and refrain from asking detailed questions until the child has related the complete story. When asking questions, the language of the officer must suit the age and level of development of the child. Questions should be phrased in words that the child can understand. Again one cannot stress strongly enough the importance of asking personal questions. This gives the officer the opportunity to assess the information in relation to the child's capacity to recall and relate the facts. It also assists in determining that the child understands the importance of telling the truth and can distinguish between fantasy and fact.

Police officers usually understand that a child may be reluctant or embarrassed to relate information about sexual activity. It helps to maintain a calm, matter-of-fact attitude and to avoid conveying to the victim that the child's story is disturbing to the interviewer. Oftentimes it may be necessary for the officer to clarify terms that are used by the child. It may help to use a picture or a diagram of the human body to describe sexual activity. With young children, pointing to body parts on an anatomically correct doll can be useful. Sometimes having the child point to parts of his or her own body or to the interviewer's body will be a good way to begin to describe the sexual activity.

It is important to keep in mind the crime against the victim while investigating the case and interviewing the child. In a case of sexual assault, the child has not only suffered a violation of his or her rights but has also been the victim of a violation of the body. Not only do we know that many victims are confused, angry, and bewildered by their own feelings but they must also cope with the confusion, anger, and frustration displayed by the family, even though this may not be verbalized. The nonverbal communication at times says it all. In particular the victim of incest frequently is made to feel as if he or she is the guilty one.

These feelings of guilt are not unusual and indeed are to be expected. They may stem from a variety of sources such as:

1. Growing awareness of society's sex mores frequently results in guilt feelings after the act has taken place.
2. Reaction of the victim's peer group of scorn or pity leads to feelings of alienation and feeling "different."
3. Family reaction that conveys blame on the victim not only for the sexual activity but for the family disruption which results after it is disclosed.
4. Realization that pleasure was experienced although the act was a "forbidden one."

Trying to overcome these feelings of guilt, many times reinforced by their families, requires skilled clinical assistance. However, the investigating officer can help the child at the outset by anticipating guilty feelings and by conveying respect for the child's feelings and supporting him or her at all times. A nonjudgmental yet supportive attitude is crucial.

At the time the interview is conducted, the officer has a resonsibility to evaluate the child's capacity accurately to relate the event to determine that the child can distinguish between fantasy and fact. In obtaining the verbal or written description, the officer must also evaluate the victim's potential as a credible witness as well as attempt to determine the truthfulness of the child's account of the situation. The age of the victim is a major consideration. A verbal description may be the only type of statement the officer can obtain if the child is too young to read or understand a written description.

Very few child sexual assault cases are proven to be unfounded. In general, when a young child can relate explicit details of sexual activity, the interviewer must be aware that the child has either participated in sexual behavior or else has been an observer of sexual behavior. However, in the authors' experience, it is unusual even for older children to make false allegations of sexual assault.

A crucial factor to be assessed during the interview is whether the child can tell time or has any sense of passage of time. Adults are accustomed to describing the passage of time in minutes, hours, days, and so forth and to supplying specific dates and times to describe when an event occurred. Older children use the same methods to describe time factors.

However, a child can still be credible (that is, show a comprehension of time), without having to understand what a day or hour is, through the use of "event time." For example, if an officer is trying to establish when the assault occurred, some knowledge of recent family events might be useful as a part of reference. The interviewer can relate important events (from the child's perspective) such as birthday parties, visits of relatives, school events or when school was in session to the timing of the sexual activity to establish the child's comprehension of when the assault took place. Care in establishing "event time" may be the key to possible future testimony in court. There are times when a defense attorney can discredit the victim's testimony or discover lapses of memory. This may weigh heavily with the judge and jury in making a decision in the case. Use of "event time" helps the child to avoid confusion and improves the credibility of his or her testimony.

An interview should never be ended abruptly. Asking if the child has anything to add to the statement, or if he or she has any questions of the officer are important and useful methods of concluding. The interview should be ended as it began—with warmth, compassion, and talking to the child about other subjects that are not related to the case. Pertinent information should be given to the parent or guardian regarding the next step in the investigation and agencies available to work with the child and family. The victim, parent, or guardian should be told to feel free to contact the officer afterward with any concerns or questions.

Interviewing Witnesses

If the sexual assault occurred recently, statements should be taken from all parties who saw the victim before or after the incident, or who may have seen or heard anything that might be pertinent to the case. Statements made by the victim to other persons about the crime or suspect within a reasonable time after the offense are admissible in their entirety in court by those persons. This is an exception to the hearsay rule known as "constancy of accusation." According to this premise, "in rape cases the police officer must be aware that under a theory of law called constancy of accusation, statements made by the victim concerning what happened to her, made within a reasonable amount of time after the crime to other persons, can be testified to by these persons" (Markle, 1968).

The statements that are made to third parties immediately after the assault are also admissible as evidence because they substantiate the victim's testimony and historically have been viewed by the court as "probative evidence." Here the premise is that the victim of such a crime would not readily relate those facts to others unless they were true. Accordingly, police officers are likely to interview many of the victim's family members, acquaintances and neighbors. This process is frequently viewed by the victim and family as disruptive and as violating their confidentiality, since they may wish to keep the sexual assault a secret or to de-emphasize its importance. Therefore, it is best for the investigating officer to interview the victim first and to obtain statements from others depending on the victim's recall of the events. Indiscriminant questioning of large numbers of people is liable to antagonize the victim and his or her family and unlikely to elicit valuable information.

Writing the Report

Report writing is a responsibility of the police officer that often receives little consideration, despite its extreme importance. All agree that a thorough and complete investigation is essential. However thorough, the investigation is of little value if the written report cannot communicate all the aspects of the case to those who read it. The report should include photographs, diagrams, the results of interviews, medical information, and any other evidence that may be pertinent to the case.

Investigative reports should reflect only facts, not opinions. Care should be taken to distinguish observation from inference. *Inference* is that which is interpreted and *observation* is that which is seen. For example, the phrase "the victim appeared agitated," raises several questions. What did the officer observe? What nonverbal communication was present? The five categories of nonverbal communication must be taken into consideration: the eyes, general facial expressions, general body movements or positions, physical distance changes between the child and the interviewer, and the tone of voice. The officer's report may make the difference between a conviction or an acquittal. Justice depends upon good police work, including careful report writing.

Decisions for Arrest and Prosecution

Probable Cause

The major reason for conducting a police investigation is to determine if a crime occurred and if probable cause exists to make an arrest. The definition of probable cause is found in the Fourth Amendment to the Constitution of the United States, which requires that "no warrant shall issue, but upon probable cause, supported by oath or affirmation, and particularly describing the place to be searched and the person or things to be seized." The Supreme Court of the United States has defined probable cause as follows: "Probable cause exists where the facts and circumstances within [the arresting officer's] knowledge and of which they had reasonably trustworthy information are sufficient in themselves to warrant a man of reasonable caution in the belief that an offense has been or is being committed" (Klotter and Kanovitz, 1968).

The definition of probable cause is of necessity vague. Any kind of fact may be an element in showing someone's apparent guilt. It is a combination of those facts and circumstances developed in an investigation, when taken as a whole and presented in a logical and reasonable manner, which leads one to believe another's guilt. Probable cause is much more than mere suspicion or belief because it must be based on provable facts. However, facts and circumstances which add up to probable cause do not need to have the weight required to prove "beyond a reasonable doubt" (the standard of proof required for conviction in criminal courts) that a crime has been committed.

Decision to Arrest

When the investigation of a child-sexual-assault case is complete and all facts and circumstances are recorded, a decision must be made to arrest the suspect if probable cause to make an arrest is present.

The decision that probable cause exists to make an arrest is not made independently or in isolation. The police officer's supervisors are kept informed at each step of the investigation. At times the prosecutor is consulted during the investigation. This consultation is of primary importance since it is the prosecutor who must present the case in court if an arrest is made. The prosecutor advises the investigator what evidence or additional evidence is needed to prove a case and to obtain a conviction. After consulting with his or her supervisors and the prosecutor, if it appears that probable cause exists, the investigator must then complete an application for an arrest warrant to present to the court. This affidavit includes:

1.   A brief description of the initial complaint to the police.
2.   A summary of the investigating officer's experience in police work (for reasons of credibility).
3.   Any medical findings.
4.   A summary of statements obtained from the victim and witnesses.
5.   Any evidence found by the investigator.
6.   The charges against the accused.

This application for an arrest warrant must be notarized and reveiwed for accuracy prior to its presentation to the prosecutor and judge. Once the warrant application has been completed, it is presented to the prosecutor, and if he or she believes that probable cause exists, the application is signed. It is then reviewed by a judge of the criminal court of jurisdiction, and if the judge believes that probable cause exists, the application is signed. When the prosecutor and the judge have signed the application, an arrest warrant has been completed. This warrant then becomes an order from the court to place the accused person under arrest and to summon him or her to court to answer the charges.

Arrest without Warrant

It has been recognized in common law that under certain circumstances, an arrest can be made without a warrant. For example, the person making the arrest can do so without a warrant if he or she witnessed the commission of a misdemeanor or a felony. Greater latitude is given in making warrantless arrests in felony cases because of a more serious threat to public safety. An arrest may be made without a warrant in a felony case under common law if reasonable grounds exist to believe a felony was committed and the person to be arrested has committed it. It should be noted that the Uniform Arrest Act defines a felony as any crime which is or may be punished by death or imprisonment in a state prison. Since the laws of most states do not provide for imprisonment in a state correction institution unless the sentence is at least one year, it is generally agreed that an offense is not a felony unless the penalty is at least one year of incarceration. All other offenses would then be misdemeanors.

Although much sexual behavior with children contains elements of crimes that are classifiable as felonies, police officers usually prefer to wait until an application for an arrest warrant has been granted by the criminal court before arresting the accused person. This is because the grounds for a warrantless arrest are subject to the most severe scrutiny. It will be rare, indeed, that the arresting officer has actually witnessed the commission of the crime of child sexual assault. Since physical evidence of a crime is frequently lacking, the investigating officer may only have the unsupported accusation of a child against an adult in preparing the affidavit. Under these circumstances, the police officer and his or her superiors may prefer to share the responsibility of ascertaining that probable cause exists to make an arrest with a prosecutor and a judge.

Helping professionals are likely to view the methodical process of establishing probable cause and applying for an arrest warrant with impatience, especially if they fear that the accused will escape or injure the victim or others in the meantime. While the process may be lengthy, the police agency must determine if a crime has been committed and who is responsible as well as protect the constitutional rights of the accused person. Sometimes the procedure is rapid and efficient. Too often, it may seem to drag on interminably to those who are fearful for the child's safety. Nevertheless, complete and thorough investigation are necessary for successful prosecution following the arrest.

Setting Bond

Once the accused person has been arrested, a decision must be made regarding the type and amount of bond to be set. In some states this decision is made only by the court; elsewhere, the police decide about setting bond. The major consideration in setting bond is whether the person who has been arrested is likely to appear in court when his or her case is presented. The seriousness of the offense that has been charged and the person's prior criminal record are also considerations. The judge of the criminal court always has the final authority in setting bond and can raise or lower the amount that has been set. A person who is accused of a nonviolent crime and who has no prior criminal record may not have any bond set upon him or her. Instead, that person may be released after the arrest simply by signing a written promise to appear in court when the case is called. Likewise, a person with a prior criminal record who has nevertheless always appeared in court when previously summoned, may also receive a low bond or not have a bond set upon him or her.

Again, nonpolice professionals who are working with a child-sexual-assault victim may be concerned or even outraged by these procedures. They are more likely to be concerned about retribution or pressure brought by the accused person upon the victim (a reasonable fear) than about the likelihood that the accused person will appear in court. Since those who are responsible for setting bond must always be mindful that an accused person must be regarded innocent until proven guilty by a court, it is often difficult both to protect the rights of the accused and to insure the safety of the victim.

Restraining Orders

One alternative to continued incarceration of a person accused of child sexual assault prior to the trial is to obtain a restraining order from the court at the time the case is presented. Such a restraining order may limit the accused person's contact with the victim as a condition of his or her release pending the trial. The difficulty with restraining orders is that they are hard to enforce and, in the case of child sexual assault, depend upon the presence of an adult ally for the child to monitor the situation and to report any violation of the restraining order. Professionals who are concerned for the child's physical safety may fear that the child will be injured by the accused person before a violation of the restraining order is detected or reported. Even more likely, the accused person may violate the restraining order by pressuring or threatening the child without actually using physical force against him or her. Once again, it may be the child's word against the word of an adult that this violation is taking place.

Child Custody Orders

In Connecticut, the criminal court also has the alternátive of limiting the accused person's access to the victim in certain circumstances. Whenever a person is arrested and charged with risk of injury to a minor or with sexual assault upon a minor child who resides with the defendant, the judge who signs the arrest warrant has the statutory authority to give immediate custody of the victim and any other children residing with the defendant to the Connecticut Department of Children and Youth Services for a period of seven days. (Connecticut General Statutes, Chapter 3d, Section 17–38e). This provision provides protection for the child victim and other children who live with the defendant if the adult who has been charged with the offense is released and able to return to the home.

Police Discretion

It is necessary to understand the legal constraints of the police agency and proper criminal justice system procedures in order to understand how much (or little) discretion can be used within the system while still fulfilling the requirements of the law. Today many police personnel are trained in basic psychology, crisis intervention, and domestic violence for the purpose of utilizing discretion in the performance of their duties.

The police agency can and should exercise discretion in making decisions to arrest and setting bond in child-sexual-assault cases. This limited discretion should be exercised in the best interests of the child involved, whenever possible. We believe that in most cases of child sexual assault, the accused person should be arrested and the authority of the criminal justice system should be used to protect the child from being pressured or threatened.

As experience, research, and learning advance it becomes increasingly clear that the police agency and indeed the entire criminal justice system are an integral part of the process of identifying the problem, protecting the victim, and remedying the situation. Unfortunately perceptions of the police role are, even today, frequently based on experience of other disciplines with police personnel of yesteryear. At one time the pervading and pervasive attitude of the police was the narrow one of investigation, apprehension, and arrest.

While all of those elements remain in the modern police philosophy, there is increasing emphasis on the role of keeping the peace, protecting the weak, and aiding the distressed. As early as 1963, O.W. Wilson stated "the primary purpose of police departments is to serve the citizens of a community and their guests. Police service today extends beyond mere routine investigation and disposition of complaints; it also has as its objective the welfare of the individual and of society."

Some cases of child sexual assault are not prosecuted even when prosecution of the accused person would be most helpful for the victim. What types of cases are likely to be dropped by the criminal justice system?

1. Inefficient police investigations.
2. Violation of rights of the accused.
3. Poor police documentation of the facts of the case.
4. Lack of support for victim or witnesses when testifying in court.
5. Poor testimony on part of the police officer.

All of the above are more likely to occur in child-sexual-assault cases if the police and helping professionals within the community are unfamiliar with the problem and fail to work together. Biases against the problem of child sexual assault and against each other abound.

How can the limited discretion of police and prosecutors be used to enable the criminal justice system to be most responsive to the problem of child sexual assault? An improved working relationship between police, prosecutors, and the helping professionals within the community is essential.

Interface between Police and Helping Professionals

No agency can stand alone and properly care for the needs of child-sexual-assault victims and their families. History and experience in working with these types of cases have proven this to be true. Many helping professionals at times are reluctant to communicate with each other and, in particular, refuse to work with the police. Usually they believe that volunary participation in treatment can be achieved and will be less disruptive to the family than prosecution of the offender. On the other hand, many police agencies are reluctant or refuse to discuss the case with helping professionals in the community because of fear that these professionals may interfere with police investigation. There is no doubt that lack of trust and, in some cases, lack of mutual respect are involved.

It is not enough to wish that "things would be better." These problems will continue to exist unless some professional person takes the initiative in each community and begins an outreach process. Little benefit will be derived unless individuals from each group begin to understand that increased cooperation can make everyone's job less trying and more rewarding in cases of child sexual assault.

We have both had the experience of working together with a multidisciplinary team of professionals whose goal was to improve child-sexual-abuse intervention. Although sometimes frustrating, the participation was both meaningful and helpful. As a result, we believe that sexually abused children can best be helped in communities in which police, prosecutors, and helping professionals are willing to sit around a table together, discard old fears and prejudices, and painfully learn to work together to improve intervention. Based on that experience, we learned the following lessons about cooperative intervention in child sexual assault.

Confidentiality

Although undoubtedly a problem, confidentiality issues can be resolved. Cases can be presented anonymously with police and prosecutors giving their "expert" opinion regarding police intervention and prosecution. We found that, most often, helping professionals were convinced that a police report should be made when the known facts of a case had been reviewed and discussed and child-protection issues were properly explored. Likewise, police reluctance to trust nonpolice personnel could be overcome when it was demonstrated that support by helping professionals was a key factor in assisting children and family members to appear in court.

Accountability and Treatment

Being held accountable by the criminal justice system was essential for offender and family treatment in incest cases. Those offenders who focused their efforts entirely on evading prosecution were also the same individuals who continued to try to maintain their power positions over the child and refused to acknowledge their own responsibility for the sexually abusive behavior. In other words, "therapy" was not possible for these offenders unless or until the cases were reported to the police. In a limited number of cases, we saw police discretion (deciding not to arrest) used creatively to persuade the offender to get therapeutic help. In other cases, we were able to persuade judges and prosecutors to be less punitive and more supportive of offenders who were willing to be held accountable by the criminal justice system and who wanted to be helped. One technique does not work—that of the old-time "tough cop" who decides to "scare the guy" instead of making an arrest. Talking to an offender will not stop the sexual abuse and protect the child; instead the offender simply increases the pressure on the child and family to keep the secret.

Investigation

Increased knowledge of sexually abusive behavior toward children, motivations of offenders, impact of sexual abuse upon the child, and family dynamics of incest coupled with increased understanding of police and therapeutic procedures—all combine to improve case investigation. Joint interviews and preparation of child and family members resulted in less trauma for the victim and fewer withdrawn complaints.

Court Appearances

We found that careful advance preparation, jointly conducted by police officers and therapists, made the experience of testifying in court far less traumatic for the child. Knowing what to expect of criminal justice procedures was very helpful for therapists, victims, and family members. At the same time, through role playing, these individuals were able to make a more convincing appearance in court. Lastly, the criminal justice process could be put in a more acceptable and less alien context for all concerned.

Coordinated Follow-Up

Both police and helping services professionals must be committed to follow-up of cases of child sexual assault. A police investigator who stops following the case after he or she has filed a report or arrested the offender will, more often than not, discover later that the charges against the offender have been dropped and that the victim is once again unprotected and without treatment. A protective services worker who stops following a case after an arrest has been made or after a victim has been temporarily separated from the offender or after the family has been referred to a mental health agency will, more often than not, discover that the "case falls apart" over time: the charges are dropped, the separation of the victim becomes permanent by default, there is no accountability component to the treatment plan for the victim, offender and family, and the treatment plan fails or never "gets off the ground." Coordinated follow-up by the two agencies with statutory authority for child sexual assault is essential to prevent these problems.

Conclusion

Neither police nor helping services professionals can manage cases of child sexual assault effectively if they work alone instead of working cooperatively. Helping services professionals must understand that the police *do* care about the well-being of victims and families in addition to fulfilling their responsibility to enforce the law and to arrest offenders. Police officers must understand that there are no magical treatment solutions to child sexual assault and that some law enforcement procedures are unnecessarily traumatic to victims and families. Both groups must understand that their efforts will be far more effective and less frustrating if they work together.

Unfortunately, the sexual assault of children is a subject that most people wish to ignore. It will be necessary for concerned professionals from police and helping services agencies to recognize that *they* must begin to take responsibility for making constructive changes and minimizing the frustrations inherent in these cases. And there *are* frustrations: the limitations of the criminal justice system, inadequate facilities and resources for treatment, laws which are unnecessarily punitive for offenders and restrictive with respect to admission of evidence, professionals who withhold information, refuse to testify, or decline to learn more effective investigative and treatment skills. The changes must begin now; the future management of child sexual assault will be as good or as bad as we allow it to be.

References

Berliner, Lucy. Harborview Sexual Assault Center, Seattle, Washington. Personal communication, 1980.

Giarretto, Henry, Giarretto, A., and Sgroi, Suzanne M. "Coordinated Community Treatment of Incest." In *Sexual Assault of Children and Adolescents* by Burgess, A.W., Groth, A.N., Holmstrom, L.L., and Sgroi, S.M. Lexington, Massachusetts: Lexington Books, 1978, p. 231.

Markle, Arnold. *Criminal Investigation and Presentation of Evidence.* Saint Paul, Minnesota: West Publishing Company, 1976, p. 27.

Klotter, John C. and Kanovitz, Jacqueline R. *Constitutional Law for Police.* Cincinnati, Ohio: W.H. Anderson Company, 1968, p. 68.

Wilson, O.W. *Police Administration.* New York: McGraw Hill Book Company, 1963, p. 4.

12 Multidisciplinary Team Review of Child-Sexual-Abuse Cases

Suzanne M. Sgroi

Nowadays it is practically "un-American" for a community to lack a multidisciplinary team of professionals to review cases of child maltreatment. Barton Schmitt's *Child Protection Team Handbook* is a comprehensive, practical, and highly readable book that is virtually indispensable for anyone who wishes to start a team or to serve as a member. Nevertheless, I believe that there are some additional useful comments to be made about multidisciplinary team review of child sexual abuse.

First, *multidisciplinary team review of child-sexual-abuse cases works*. Although far from being a panacea, it can be a useful tool in case management. Bringing an individual case of child sexual abuse before a group of professionals from a variety of disciplines has the obvious potential of assisting the clients and staff who are involved. There is, however, a broader potential for improving the community's response to the problem as well.

Second, most *child-protection teams are ill-equipped to deal with child sexual abuse*. At the risk of sounding elitist, I submit that in most communities, it is unrealistic to expect that the local child-protection team will be able to address this problem. Instead, it may be preferable for a second group of professionals to work with child-sexual-abuse cases. Since there are likely to be few, if any, local "experts," team members should be recruited on the basis of a willingness to learn and a solid professional background in one of the disciplines which touches the problem. This should not cause duplication of service. Most child-protection teams are able to address only a small proportion of the total number of cases of child maltreatment. Splitting out the sexual abuse cases should alleviate this problem to some degree. In addition, the team which reviews the sexual abuse cases should be able to address most of these cases occurring in the community since the proportion of reported cases of sexual victimization of children is smaller.

Third, despite current mythology about child-protection teams, *the application of this tool for child-sexual-abuse cases will not be easy or cheap; nor will it constitute a simple one-step solution to the problem*. Unfortunately, many administrators of helping service agencies have such unrealistic expectations. Teams take time, and hard work is required before they slowly develop into highly effective community forces to combat child maltreatment. Although the out-of-pocket startup cost is negligible, the average two-hour multidisciplinary team meeting represents an expensive contribution of professional time by those who are seated around the table. Multidisciplinary team review rarely results in a dramatic and simple solution to the multiproblem and complex cases which are presented. Many of the benefits are intangible and do not lend themselves to embellishing score cards or track records. The same experience can be anticipated for a child-sexual-abuse review team.

I have served continuously on multidisciplinary child abuse teams since 1975 including a child-sexual-abuse review team since 1977. The experience has been time-consuming and often frustrating as well as educational and rewarding. At the present time, I am serving both on a community child-protection team and a regional child-sexual-abuse team. Although there are some similarities, the demands, challenges, functions, expectations, and contributions of these two types of teams are, for the most part, radically different. A multidisciplinary review team which focuses on child sexual abuse is not just another child-protection team. Here is what it can and should be doing.

Functions

A multidisciplinary child-sexual-abuse case review team may be able to serve as a vehicle for the following:

Development of Experience and Expertise in Case Management. In the beginning, most of the team members and, indeed, most of the professional people within the community will lack both experience and expertise with child-sexual-abuse cases. Reviewing multiple cases at team meetings is an efficient way of augmenting one's experience and in developing expertise in case management. It really is possible to learn from someone else's mistakes and successes.

Consultant Training. To be effective, team members must also be willing to serve as consultants and to work directly with the clients in some of the cases which are reviewed. Since few communities have child-sexual-abuse "experts," consultants must be trained to address this problem. Service on a multidisciplinary team in conjunction with acting as a consultant on some of the cases that are reviewed by that team can be an effective training tool for psychologists, social workers, physicians, and the like.

Liaison and Linkage Building. If team members are sincerely interested in learning more about working with child sexual abuse, they will inevitably become involved with cases at earlier stages. If the team membership represents the key disciplines which are touched by child-sexual-abuse cases, it will be hard to avoid improved communication among the agencies and institutions where they work. Liaisons and linkages based on working relationships between individuals are generally far more effective than those which are based on policy and administrative edicts alone.

Community Program Development. A functioning multidisciplinary review team is an essential first step in developing a community child-sexual-abuse intervention program. Professionals who review cases together are far more likely to work cooperatively to fill gaps in service. They are also likely to be the most effective emissaries for their coworkers in their respective agencies.

Start-Up

A core of three or four professionals who have direct experience with cases is adequate for start-up purposes. The essential ingredients are as follows:

Interest in Learning. Team members must be intrigued and excited about the problem and want to learn more about child sexual abuse. It helps if their interest is both practical and theoretical. The incentive for most professionals to form a review team is likely to be based on a desire to be able to address case management problems more effectively. A theoretical "study group" with no ongoing case experience would be unlikely to progress very far. A capacity to apply a theoretical context without losing sight of the practical issues addressed by case review is ideal.

Willingness to Participate. It is necessary for team members to be willing, if not eager, to participate. If individuals are pressured or coerced to join the team, their participation can only have a negative effect. It is preferable to leave a discipline or organization unrepresented until a professional who really wants to belong can be found to fill the gap. Sometimes it is possible to convince a key person that the effort is worthwhile. This can usually be accomplished by demonstrating that multidisciplinary team review has been of practical assistance in an individual case. Probably the most common mistake which is made is to force participation by staff of the local child-protection agency. In my experience, this is almost always destructive and fruitless. Other methods have to be found to convince individuals that their participation can be helpful to them.

"Hands-On" Experience. The credibility of a multidisciplinary child-sexual-abuse review team will depend on the degree to which its members are directly involved with cases. Since no discipline has yet incorporated a body of knowledge about child-sexual-abuse intervention into its professional training curriculum, it is essential for team members to have ongoing hands-on experience with perpetrators, victims, and their families. Although it would be unwieldy

and unrealistic to expect every team member to be involved directly with every case which is reviewed, the team members should nonetheless be willing to see some clients in consultation.

Willingness to Share Case Experience. Every team member must be willing to present his or her own cases. Willingness to share case experience is the sine qua non for effective multidisciplinary team review. One of the most effective ways to break down defensive barriers and facilitate communication and trust among team members is for each to present one of his or her own cases to the others in rotation during the initial sessions. Names can be changed or withheld to protect confidentiality whenever necessary.

Membership

To be effective, a multidisciplinary child-sexual-abuse review team must eventually be comprised of professionals from those disciplines with knowledge and skills which are applicable to this problem. Some of the choices are obvious; others less so. I believe it is preferable for the permanent members to represent themselves and their own body of professional knowledge rather than the agencies which employ them. Professionals who are involved with specific cases in an official capacity can be invited to participate at meetings when these cases are being reviewed. Permanent membership and regular input from members representing these disciplines is desirable.

Child Protective Services. This discipline should be represented by someone with professional training in social work and direct case experience with sexual abuse who now occupies at least a supervisory level. Child protective services is the only "helping service" which has statutory authority to remain consistently involved with validated cases.

Law Enforcement. The team member who is engaged in law enforcement should also be someone with professional training and direct experience in investigation of child sexual abuse. He or she should have detective rank, at minimum.

Law. The attorney should be someone with criminal court experience preferably with child-sexual-abuse cases. He or she should at least have a working knowledge of laws and court procedures dealing with sexual assault, child maltreatment, commitment, and guardianship.

Health Services. This person could either be a physician, a nurse, or perhaps a nurse-practitioner who has worked with cases of child sexual abuse. The essential ingredient is knowledge of the medical aspects of collection of physical evidence as well as proper medical treatment procedures for sexual assault.

Mental Health Services. This could encompass several disciplines—psychiatry, psychology and social work, for example. It may be helpful to invite someone from each of these disciplines to serve on the team. Knowledge of behavioral pathology, diagnostic procedures, and capacity to assess amenability to treatment are essential. In addition, representatives from several of the specialized areas of mental health services have special expertise to contribute.

   1. Victimology. This often neglected discipline has much to offer to a multidisciplinary child-sexual-abuse review team. Much of the therapy for child sexual abuse is aimed at reducing the traumatic effects of victimization.

   2. Sex therapy. Although sex therapists do not, as a rule, receive specific training to deal with child sexual abuse, professionals with sex therapy training are remarkably desensitized to most issues dealing with human sexuality. Although I do not advocate treating child sexual abuse primarily as a sexual aberration (rather than a power disorder), the sex therapist's perspective can be an invaluable asset in multidisciplinary team review.

   3. Arts therapy. An arts therapist also can offer a frequently neglected perspective on both diagnosis and treatment. Since treatment approaches to child sexual abuse are still in very early developmental stages, the application of the arts therapies, especially for the severely traumatized, withdrawn, and isolated clients who are so frequently seen, should be described by a registered arts therapist.

   4. Involuntary client therapy. There are relatively few therapists who choose to work with involuntary clients and who have expertise in this area. Nevertheless, a professional with such a background should be sought as a team member. A therapist who has worked within a court-related or correction system or for a psychiatric institution which deals with committed patients may have such expertise to offer. Since the great majority of cases which come to team review will involve involuntary clients, a professional with this experience can contribute much to the discussion.

Organization

The organization of a multidisciplinary child-sexual-abuse team should be as simple as possible. I view with alarm the recent trend toward hiring full-time coordinators for child-protection teams. Creating such positions inevitably tends to increase the amount of paperwork and bureaucratic proliferation involved. In addition, the child-protection team can easily become institutionalized to the point of becoming just one more community agency competing for funds, prestige, power, and turf. Ideally, a multidisciplinary child-sexual-abuse case review team should be a relaxed group of sleeves-rolled-up professionals who trust their colleagues' integrity and expertise and are willing to volunteer their time on a regular basis to discuss cases involving a little-understood societal and clinical issue with an aim toward increasing their knowledge and assisting in problem solving. Most will be extremely busy persons with multiple professional responsibilities. It is unlikely that any of them will be willing or able to devote much time to organizational matters. On the other hand, it is likely that there will be several members who will be in a position to offer a modest amount of secretarial support to the team. It is also likely that an acceptable meeting place that will be available on a regular basis will not be difficult to find within the community.

"Housekeeping" Details. In the first meeting, the group should select a meeting place, decide how often it will meet and set up a calendar of future meetings. If possible, a reminder system regarding subsequent meetings (by telephone or written notice) should be compiled. Several other responsibilities should be addressed.

1. Selection of cases for review. I recommend that team members each present a case in rotation for the initial series of meetings. This will afford the most efficient opportunity for each member to grasp the essential elements of case presentation to the group. The initial series of meetings should be regarded as a group learning experience. It will be helpful if members can agree to assist each other by offering helpful criticisms of the presentation and discussion format. Each presentor should take the responsibility of inviting other professionals to the meeting who know about the case to be presented and can contribute to the discussion. The group should decide how many cases are to be presented each meeting; in the beginning, one case will probably occupy an entire session.

2. Chairing the meeting and leading discussion. Some groups will have an organizer who is the logical chairperson and will be accorded that position either by election or by tacit agreement. The chairperson's primary responsibility is to serve as discussion leader. Again, in some groups it will be better to rotate this responsibility. Eventually the chairperson may also take on the responsibility of deciding which cases to present. He or she should be accorded the authority to redirect or conclude group discussions when time and circumstances require as well as to summarize the group's consensus for case management recommendations.

3. Record-keeping. This responsibility should be equally distributed and kept to a minimum. A log of the case reviews should be kept along with a group attendance record for each meeting. Using a preformed outline, the recorder should note the group's major findings and recommendations. These should be summarized by the chairperson at the close of each review and recorded. If members take exception to the summary, the group should attempt to reach a consensus. If this cannot be done, the recorder should note any minority opinion

that a team member requests to have entered in the log. A clear distinction should be made between the team's recommendations on the one hand and any participant's acceptance of an assigned task with respect to a case. The participant who agrees to perform a task should be asked by the chairperson if he or she accepts this responsibility before it is recorded. A copy of the log for a given case review should be made available upon request to any of the professionals who were invited to attend the meeting.

Confidentiality. The team should decide at the outset if cases are to be presented with names disguised or not. In general, it is preferable to disguise cases so that the identity of the clients is protected. The chairperson should begin each meeting with introductions if guests or new team members are present. He or she should briefly state the group's professional commitment toward maintaining confidentiality for clients. Guests at any team meetings should always be limited to persons with a professional ethic related to confidentiality if cases are to be discussed.

Roles of Team Members. One of the greatest pitfalls in organizing a multidisciplinary team is to become bogged down in defining what each participant's role should be or indeed the role of the team itself. In my experience, these discussions are frustrating, fruitless, and a waste of time for all concerned. A major benefit of multidisciplinary team review of cases is to identify problems and suggest ways of approaching them effectively. The roles of the participants are truly irrelevant. Instead the discussion should focus on the problems and needs of clients and the responsibilities and potential contributions of those who are involved with the case.

Efforts to mold the input of participants into stereotyped definitions of a police officer's role, a social worker's role, a therapist's role, and so forth will invariably be counterproductive. Neither the clients nor the intervenors are likely to be helped by the application of role therapy to the problems of case management. Frequently the team can help the intervenors to decide who can be most helpful to whom and in what capacity. In a given case situation, it may be highly effective for a police officer to be supportive, for a health professional to offer guidance about money management, or for a therapist to be authoritative and confronting despite traditional perceptions of the "roles" of these professionals. Not everyone is temperamentally suited to belong on a multidisciplinary child-sexual-abuse case review team. It demands flexibility and a pragmatic approach to problem solving, coupled with a respect for the perspectives of others even if one does not always agree with them. Professionals who require rigid role assignments in order to feel comfortable will probably be too discomfited to remain long on the team.

Content of Meetings. The primary focus of team meetings should be review of cases. Housekeeping matters should occupy a minimum amount of time. Although the case review process is indirectly supportive of the intervenors, the meetings should remain case review sessions, not commiseration or "hand-holding" sessions.

I believe that the focus of the review should be case management. The group should decide ahead of time on a framework for case assessment. It may be convenient to assess the case according to the principal phases discussed in chapter 3: reporting, investigation, validation, child-protection assessment, initial management planning, diagnostic assessment, developing a problem list, formulating a treatment plan, treatment intervention, and monitoring. All of the team members should clearly understand which phase is under discussion; otherwise it will be extremely difficult to keep the discussion focused.

At the close of each case discussion, three questions should be addressed:

1. How can community response to this case be improved?
2. How can we be helpful to these clients and the intervenors?
3. What can we learn from this case?

Identifying the ways that community response can be improved is, of course, the essential first step toward implementing the improvements. It may not be possible or appropriate for team members to help directly in all the cases. However, the willingness to help is bound to be appreciated by those responsible for case management. If unable to be of direct assistance, a team member may be able to put the intervenor in touch with someone who can help with a specific task or problem.

Asking what can be learned from each case is extremely important. Although the approach to each case should be practical, expansion of the overall knowledge base of individual members as well as the professional community is the ultimate *raison d'être* for the team. Time for critical attention to this question should be allotted in every case review.

Summary

Formation of a special multidisciplinary team to review cases of child sexual abuse only is a viable approach to improve case management, increase the reservoir of professional knowledge within the community, train consultants, and improve liasons among intervenors. Team members should be willing participants who have hands-on experience with cases. A simple organizational structure for the team is preferable, and a focus on case management is encouraged. In addition to addressing the practical problem-solving issues, the team has a responsibility continuously to assess how community response can be improved and what can be learned from each case that is reviewed.

Reference

Schmitt, Barton, ed. *The Child Protection Team Handbook*. New York: Garland
S.T.P.M. Press, 1978.

13 Evaluation of Child-Sexual-Abuse Programs

Karen W. Bander,
Edith Fein,
and *Gerrie Bishop*

The growth of human services in the past decades, and especially the rapid growth of government-funded programs in the 1960s and 1970s, have created pressures to make judgments about the worth of programs as they compete for inevitably limited resources. (Quie, 1974). That judgment process led to the development of program evaluation as a research technique. The technique had its detractors since any methodology that can be used to choose one program over another may be viewed as critical, unfair, or subjective. Historically, evaluators have also been charged with being insensitive to the ambiguities, complexities, and idiosyncratic work demands of human service programs. To change this image, efforts in the 1970s have been focused on making program evaluation more constructive and useful (Attkisson and Broskowski, 1978). In the process, program evaluation has evolved as a special type of research effort, adapted to the challenge and demands of working in a real-life setting alongside the service providers.

This chapter will address evaluation of clinical intervention in child sexual abuse. In order to provide a background in evaluation, we will first focus on

Karen W. Bander, Ph.D., is a practicing clinical psychologist trained in program evaluation. She is presently the coordinator of Research and Clinical Evaluation for Alcoholism Services in the Department of Psychiatry, Saint Vincent's Medical Center, New York City. From 1977–1979, while employed in the Research Division of Child and Family Services of Connecticut, Dr. Bander served as program evaluator for the Sexual Trauma Treatment Program of the Connecticut Department of Children and Youth Services. She continues to conduct workshops and training on program evaluation and child sexual abuse.

Gerrie Bishop received the bachelor's degree from Central Connecticut State College and has worked as a research assistant at Child and Family Services of Connecticut since 1975. Her experience includes evaluation of a residential acoholism treatment program, an outpatient alcoholism program, a family day-care program, and a child sexual-abuse treatment program.

Edith Fein, M.A., is currently the Director of Research for Child and Family Services of Connecticut. She has been involved with mental-health and child-welfare service delivery and research since 1949. Mrs. Fein's graduate study was with the Committee on Human Development at the University of Chicago. Recent research interests include services to unwed teenagers, alcoholics, the foster-care system, sexual-abuse victims, and management information systems for social-service agencies. Her concern with fostering a critiquing attitude among service providers has contributed to the development of a large and active research department in a voluntary social-service agency.

some differences between research and evaluation in order to appreciate the limits of each. Then we will consider evaluation as a way of using information by discussing the types of questions that might be asked, the different points in time that may be relevant, and the variety of issues that arise as questions are asked and information is generated. We will report our experiences in designing and implementing an evaluation plan for Connecticut's Sexual Trauma Treatment Program for child sexual abuse.[a] Last, and most important, we will make suggestions for evaluation of new child-sexual-abuse programs, based on our recent experience.

What Is the Difference between Research and Evaluation?

To understand program evaluation as a special type of research undertaking, it may be instructive to begin with a definition. Research is generally accepted to be "systematic, controlled, empirical, and critical investigation of hypothetical propositions about the presumed relations among natural phenomena." (Kerlinger, 1973.)

That is, to study the questions one wishes to answer, a research scientist will typically state the problems in a conjectural way and thus *hypothesize* the relationship between phenomena. Ideally a cause-and-effect relationship will be sought. In considering child sexual abuse, for example, one hypothesis worth investigating might be, "Those sexually abused youngsters who participate in a multiservice program designed to protect and support them will do better than those who do not participate in such a program." Another hypothesis might be, "Those families of sexually abused youngsters who take part in a multiservice program will have a more integrated family life than those who do not participate."

A further step in the application of the scientific method is to design a test, observation, or *experiment* that will give data leading one to accept or reject the relationship stated in the hypothesis. This research design is subject to a number of requirements. Chief among them are:

1. The experiment (or treatment or program) must be the same for all the subjects so that conclusions may be drawn about the presence or absence of the experimental condition. This requirement of *constancy*, in the sexual abuse examples used above, would mean that all children and families who participated in a multiservice treatment program would have to receive the same amount and kinds of treatment in order to determine if the treatment led to better outcomes. If children and families do better with, without, or with varying amounts of treatment, there is no way to conclude if the treatment had any effect and whether the relationship stated in the hypothesis is true.

---

[a]Supported by National Center for Child Abuse and Neglect, DHEW, Grant No. 90-C-399.

2. There must be *control* or *comparison* groups that do not receive the experimental condition, in order to determine if its absence had any effect. The program subjects, further, must be assigned randomly to the experimental or nonexperimental condition so that, by the luck-of-the-draw, the two conditions will end up with similar subjects. If random assignment is not possible, then subjects may be matched on a number of variables or assigned to the experimental or nonexperimental condition in such a way as to end up with similar groups. It must be feasible, that is, to give or withhold treatment so comparisons can be made.

3. Measurements of the effect of the experimental condition must be done in such a way that the resultant data are both *valid* and *reliable*. Validity implies that evaluation instruments are measuring what they purport to be measuring, and reliability assumes that measures repeated over time will have stability or dependability. To measure outcomes in a child-sexual-abuse program, for example, it may be appropriate to measure changes in a sexually abused youngster's self-esteem; the instrument, however, must be a reliable measure of self-esteem, and it must be clear that it is not being assumed to measure another outcome such as decreased sexual contact.

This brief discussion of requirements for an adequate research project makes apparent the difficulties of doing research in the human services delivery system. In the formulation of hypotheses, for example, problems arise with defining the variables operationally so that an experimental condition can be designed and the measurement phase can proceed. What is "doing better"? No further sexual abuse? Adequate social and emotional relations with peers? Ability to continue with schooling? What is a "more integrated family life"? The unity of the nuclear family? Closeness of mother and daughter though the father may be out of the house? Psychological and emotional rapport between siblings and parents?

Human services programs also impose research design difficulties in that they are rarely constant and unchanging enough so that the same intervention may be said to occur for all participants over time. Availability of funding, service delivery policy changes, administrative edicts, community pressures, or political influence may have an impact on the way services are delivered, and to whom, so that a program may look very different as time passes. Without a constant experimental condition no conclusions can be drawn about the experiment.

Real-life programs present further difficulties with the measurement of change, difficulties in addition to those inherent in the ordinary measurement problem. The question of *how* to measure outcome, and what instruments will give the greatest validity and reliability, are no small technical challenges, but they pale in comparison with the question of *when* to measure outcomes. Is "success" of intervention determined after a specified time period such as six months or a year? Is discharge from the program the criterion? In that case, is there a difference between planned discharge (treatment completed) and premature discharge (client refuses treatment)? And how does the experimenter obtain data from clients who want nothing more to do with the program? Should the program's success be measured a year or two after treatment to determine if there are any long-term benefits? Related issues deal with informed consent, the difficulty of obtaining subjects' participation, maintaining their motivation, and locating them after a period of time.

The realities of delivering human services also hamper the use of control or comparison groups. A program is usually funded because of the belief that it will have some effectiveness; to withhold treatment from some clients and assign them to a control group is ethically indefensible. Even if an elaborate permission and choice process could be devised to overcome the ethical objections, as has been suggested in medical research where some of these same problems exist (Zelen, 1979), community pressures would probably never permit the experimental design to be implemented. It would be unthinkable, for example, to withhold treatment from a sexually abused youngster in the name of research design when the child-protection agency is charged with delivering services.

However, the difficulties encountered in conducting human services research in as elegant and scientific a manner as one would wish are no reason to forego information gathering that can help the providers of service to make more informed and rational decisions, especially in program planning. Such information gathering, or program evaluation, is research undertaken in a real-life setting and therefore without the luxury of experimental design and controls. It deals with the constraints that the realities of an operating human service program put on a research effort; it investigates a service delivery system as it functions; it is a technique of using information to make decisions and plan programs without the comfort of scientific rigor as clear justification.

Types of Evaluation Questions

If program evaluation is a form of research, how will the scientific method need to be modified to make it an appropriate mode of inquiry in its evaluation application? Can an analog be found for hypotheses, experiments, and other conditions of research? Suchman (1967) creates such an analog by describing evaluation as the "process of stating objectives, in terms of ultimate, intermediate, or immediate goals, of examining the underlying assumptions, and of setting up criteria of effort, performance, adequacy, efficiency, and process. . . ." In essence, information is gathered on:

1. What *effort* is going into the program? How many people are delivering services, in what mix, at what cost?
2. What is the *efficiency* of the program planning? What is the relationship

between what is actually occurring and what the plans or objectives were? (If 50 percent of program time is spent in interviewing clients, was the planning for 30 percent, 50 percent, or 70 percent?)

3. How *adequate* is a program in relation to the community's needs? Typically such data are difficult to obtain (the methodology for needs assessment is cumbersome and validity is hard to gauge), but it obviously makes a difference if a program is serving 60 sexually abused youngsters a year in a community where 100, or 1,000, cases were identified.

4. What is the *effectiveness* of a program? Is it doing any good, is it achieving its ultimate goal? It is extremely difficult to obtain any valid answer in this area without resorting to the kind of rigorous research design described above, but some complex program evaluations may attempt such a design.

To such questions about a program's effort, its efficiency of planning, its adequacy, and its effectiveness, may be added the dichotomy of formative evaluation/summative evaluation. *Formative evaluation* is concerned with how an ongoing program is implementing its goals and objectives, while *summative evaluation* is based on completed programs and their effects. The difference is related to completeness of measurement at different times; and whether results are entered into a feedback loop, as it were, for ongoing program modification or whether they are used at the end of a program for determining effects, for refunding or for other such program planning decisions. The formative/summative dichotomy is only an approximation, but used in conjunction with the effort-efficiency-adequacy-effectiveness classification of evaluation questions, it can be useful to delineate the parameters of evaluative studies.

Evaluation of Connecticut's Sexual Trauma Treatment Program

Program evaluation was planned to be an important component of the project by a project director who wanted evaluation data and made use of it. The sponsoring agency, the Connecticut Department of Children and Youth Services, arranged, via contract, for the evaluation to be done by the Research Department of Child and Family Services of Connecticut, a private social service agency with experience in evaluating human service programs as well as in delivering social and mental health services to children and their families. The relationship of the evaluators to the staff of the Sexual Trauma Treatment Program was carefully nurtured by both groups; positive attitudes toward evaluators were modeled by the project director, while, for their part, the evaluators were careful to be nonjudgmental team members who understood their roles as objective "outsiders" let "inside" the program's operation.

The program staff and the evaluators met together at the beginning of the project to design an evaluation plan that would be relevant to the program's operation. Those areas that would be studied, as well as the methodology for studying them, were the subject of evaluator-staff negotiation. The evaluation was designed to be a formative evaluation, that is, interactive with the program, giving project staff periodic information and reports that could be incorporated into program planning and program change. It was hoped that by this means program change would occur in a timely fashion rather than at the end of an arbitrary evaluation period; that program planning would be rational, based on data rather than reaction to events; and that evaluation results would be used rather than only published in reports.

The evaluation plan, moreover, was designed to gather information in a way as nonburdensome to the program staff as possible. Wherever feasible, existing data sources were used. When special information was needed, the record-keeping was designed to be integral to the program's operation as well as to the evaluation plan. For that reason special reporting forms included only a Problem Oriented Record (to be discussed later), and a time-keeping sheet. Structured interviews with staff were conducted two times during the evaluation. Other alternatives, such as school reports, client self-reports, client satisfaction forms, behavioral rating forms, and narrative recording were considered too specialized a research form, too time-consuming to obtain, or too peripheral to the program's functioning to be justified.

The Evaluation Plan, in table 13–1, can be seen to address a number of questions, all of them related to effort and efficiency of planning as outlined above.

1. Who is the client?
   What happens to the client?
   What problems exist, what plans are made, what occurs in treatment?
2. What is the model for treatment?
   Did the team treatment actually occur?
   Were multiple modalities of individual, group, family, and art therapy actually used?
3. How is the treatment model implemented?
   What was the function of the multidisciplinary team?
4. How are outside systems used and affected?
   Are there formal or informal agreements?
   Do they work?
5. What are the training needs of staff?
   Do they need more help with defining client problems, formulating treatment plans, using consultants efficiently, managing groups, and so forth?

The remainder of this chapter reports the results of the STTP evaluation,

Table 13–1

Connecticut Department of Children and Youth Services Sexual Trauma Treatment Program—Evaluation Plan

Project Questions	Possible Issues or Concerns	Data Sources
What happens to the client?	Who is the client?	DCYS Form #535
	What problems and defenses exist?	Problem Oriented Record Contract
	What plans are formulated to deal with the problems and defenses?	Intake Summary Closing Summary
	What occurs in treatment?	
What is the model for treatment?	What are the roles of the consultants, multiple modalities, and team treatment?	DCYS Form #535 Case Review Form Attendance Decision-making
	What are the decision points?	Problem Oriented Record
	Is there a written contract?	Interviews with staff treatment team
How is the treatment model implemented? on therapist level? on system level?	How is the multidisciplinary team used?	DCYS Form #535 Case Review Form
	How are community resources used by staff in treatment?	Problem Oriented Record Interviews with staff, treatment team, others
	What is the systemic interplay with other agencies? mental health? law enforcement?	
How are outside systems used and affected?	What is the role of the treatment team?	DCYS Form #535 Case Review Form
	How are formal and informal working agreements arrived at? Do they work?	Interviews with staff, treatment team
What are the training needs? present staff? regional staff?	Contract writing	Interviews with staff, treatment team
	Formulating treatment plans on appropriate behavioral level	Problem Oriented Record
	Use of consultants, treatment team	
	Use of groups	
	Record-keeping (joint record-keeping by all?)	
	Supervisor to work with records to train in contracting and formulating treatment plans and to do careful monitoring	

provides insight into the functioning of a child-sexual-abuse program, and illustrates the uses of evaluation in the development of clinical interventions.

Program Description

A brief review of the major aspects of Connecticut's Sexual Trauma Treatment Program (STTP) will show the relevance of the evaluation to the program as planned. STTP was funded by the National Center for Child Abuse and Neglect (Grant No. 90-C-399) to demonstrate new and effective ways of assisting child victims of sexual abuse. Established within the Connecticut Department of Children and Youth Services (DCYS), the state agency with statutory responsibility for all child welfare, child mental health, and juvenile delinquency services, STTP operated within a child protection framework. The program proposed to (1) set up a treatment center for incestuous families; (2) develop a model treatment program that used approaches different from those used in other types of child abuse cases; (3) improve the handling of the sexually abused child at entry point into the helping services system by coordinating the services of the police, hospital, school, and social agencies; (4) increase cooperation between child protective services and the legal justice systems; and (5) formulate training guidelines for medical, legal justice, and treatment personnel.

Aimed specifically at therapeutic intervention in cases of child sexual abuse, STTP developed a multiple impact model of therapy for the incestuous family. The model included multiple modalities of therapy, team treatment, consultation, and multidisciplinary team review. Multiple modalities of therapy were expected to allow the team to enter the family system in a variety of ways, thereby making it difficult to maintain old and dysfunctional patterns of interaction. Given the hypothesized family power structure of a dominant father, psychologically absent mother, and victimized child, multiple therapists were to be utilized to provide each member of the family with an ally and confidante, thereby changing the balance of power. A team of therapists could also potentially increase the information data base and permit more effective crisis management. Team treatment was to be augmented by the direct services of an internist, a psychologist, an arts therapist, and a psychiatrist. In addition to the treatment team, a multidisciplinary team of these consultants and a police officer, assistant attorney general, prosecutor, and the program evaluators was to meet regularly with the project staff in biweekly reviews of selected cases. Team reviews of cases were to provide information from specialized consultants in areas beyond social work expertise to facilitate coordination of treatment with the legal justice, health care, and law enforcement systems, and to maximize utilization of available resources within the community.

The model was to operate in the following manner: following the disclosure of the sexual abuse and referral to STTP, a core treatment team consisting of a therapist for the mother and a therapist for the child victim was to be assigned to each family. the first two weeks of intervention were to be devoted to assessment, investigation, and validation of the sexual assault. Since corroborating physical evidence was known to be found in only a small portion of the cases, STTP's validation of the referrals was to be dependent upon investigative interviewing by workers experienced in assessment and knowledgeable about sexual abuse and child development. The team was therefore to gather information about the family as a unit, what family conditions led to the sexual abuse, whether it was a secret, and why it came to light at the particular point of referral. Medical, psychological, and arts therapy assessments were to be arranged during this time, if appropriate. At the end of the assessment period a team meeting was to be held to determine the validity of the complaint and to plan the treatment strategy.

Treatment planning was to be based upon STTP's assessment as well as the legal justice status of the case. Since this was a program of the state agency whose primary responsibility is child protection, the first team decision was to be concerned with the safety of the child and the necessity of temporary child placement or separation of the family from the perpetrator. Plans were then to be made regarding the use of the multiple modalities of individual, group, family, marital, and art therapy. Each modality was assumed to be appropriate at particular times with particular families. Individual treatment, for example, was to be used initially to build up a trusting relationship; group treatment to break down massive denial and isolation; family or couples therapy to effect systems change; and arts therapy to overcome resistance and build trust with young or nonverbal children. The team was therefore to decide which modalities to use and when to use them. Treatment decisions were also to be made about the timing of interventions with the perpetrator fathers and were dependent upon his presence in the home, his pressure on the child to recant, his acceptance of responsibility for the incestuous act, and the stage of the case in the criminal court or juvenile court. Finally, the team was expected to map out STTP's interface with outside agencies. Whenever possible, the orientation of STTP's treatment was to maintain family integrity.

STTP intended to serve children and families within a thirty-six town catchment area of DCYS, a region with a population of 700 thousand containing urban, suburban, and rural communities. Intake was to be mediated via the existing child-protection intake system. All cases of child sexual abuse were to be accepted, although a preponderance of incest cases was expected.

Program staff was to include a program chairman, program vice chairman, case supervisor, three full-time and two part-time social workers, and consultants as listed above. None of the program staff devoted full time to child sexual abuse in the first year of the program. In-service training was to be accomplished through a series of teaching sessions on child sexual abuse, workshops with nationally recognized experts, and weekly case supervision.

Given this program outline, it can be seen that the scope of the evaluation was compatible with the program's emphases. The evaluation was to collect and examine data concerning client characteristics, the model for treatment, the use of the multidisciplinary team, the interaction with outside agencies, and the training of staff. At the same time, the plan called for the evaluators to supply information pertinent to the functioning, decisionmaking, and growth of a developing treatment program on an ongoing basis.

Evaluation Findings: Client Characteristics

Intake. During its two years of operation, STTP accepted 82 families for treatment of child sexual abuse. At intake, these cases were categorized as to the nature of the sexual abuse and the relationship of the perpetrator to the child victim. The abuse was defined as "sexual contact" if the acitivity involved genital exposure, masturbation, or fondling without penetration. "Sexual intercourse" described penetration of any part of the child's body including the mouth, rectum, or vagina by the perpetrator's penis, tongue, fingers or any object manipulated by the perpetrator into the victim's body. Cases were classified as intrafamilial, as compared to extrafamilial, if the perpetrator was part of the child's psychosocial family, that is, a parent, stepparent, parent figure, or relative. Table 13–2 displays the categories of sexual abuse for STTP's 82 cases. As expected, intrafamilial cases comprised the largest portion of the caseload (66 percent) with extrafamilial cases making up an additional 22 percent. Another 10 percent were considered sexually "at risk,"[b] and 3 percent venereal disease, perpetrator unknown. Since the program's stated emphasis was the treatment of incestuous families, the focus of the evaluation presented here will be the 54 cases of intrafamilial sexual abuse.

Referral Source. Table 13–3 shows the referral sources for the 54 intrafamilial cases. The largest number of cases (26 percent) was referred to STTP by the police. The remainder of the intrafamilial referrals were made by a variety of

Table 13–2
Classification by Type of Child Sexual Abuse

Type of Sexual Abuse	Cases (#)	%
Intrafamilial intercourse	(26)	32
Intrafamilial sexual contact	(28)	34
Extrafamilial intercourse	(7)	9
Extrafamilial sexual contact	(11)	13
Sexually at risk[a]	(8)	10
VD, perpetrator unknown	(2)	3
Total	(82)	101

[a]The "at risk" category was never fully defined by the program, but it typically referred to cases of young children who had not been assaulted but were living in risky sexual situations.

Table 13–3
Referral Sources of Intrafamilial Cases

Referral Source	Cases (#)	%
Police	(12)	22
School	(8)	15
Careline	(6)	11
Family member	(6)	11
Hospital	(5)	9
Mental health professional	(4)	7
Youth services bureau	(4)	7
DCYS	(3)	6
Neighbor	(2)	4
Attorney	(1)	2
Priest	(1)	2
Physician	(1)	2
Anonymous	(1)	2
Total	(54)	100

different sources including school social workers, the child abuse hotline, hospital emergency rooms, mental health professionals, and youth service officers.

The data showed that no one referral source was significantly more likely than any other to recognize and refer intrafamilial child-sexual-abuse cases to the statutory child-protection agency, and that some mandated sources such as schools, private physicians, and mental health professionals were making very few sexual abuse referrals. It was apparent that further attempts at educating the community and professionals would be required to overcome the taboo of recognizing and reporting incest.

Demographic Characteristics.   Selected demographics of the 54 incest cases are highlighted in table 13–4. Of the 63 victims of intrafamilial sexual abuse (2 or more children were referred in 7 families), adolescent and preadolescent girls were the most frequently reported victims of perpetrator fathers or stepfathers. The relationship of the perpetrator to child victim is shown in table 13–5. Most typically, the families were white (57 percent), intact (63 percent), self-supporting (67 percent) families of Catholic (47 percent) or Protestant (47 percent) religious affiliation, living in the suburbs adjoining Hartford. Examination of the figures revealed, however, that incest was not specific to any one demographic, socioeconomic, geographic, or religious group. This finding was particularly interesting considering the typical over representation of the poor and minorities in protective-services caseloads (Gelles, 1977). These data provided STTP with information about its own client population as well as with statistics to compare its program with other sexual-abuse treatment programs.

Validity of the Referral. As previously stated, STTP's validation of sexual

Table 13–4
Selected Demographic Characteristics of Intrafamilial Cases

	Clients	
Characteristic	(#)[a]	%
Age of Victim		
1–9	(16)	26
10–12	(14)	22
13–18	(33)	52
Sex of Victim		
Female	(56)	89
Male	(7)	11
Ethnic Background		
White	(30)	57
Black	(17)	32
Hispanic	(3)	6
Other	(3)	6
Parental Marital Status		
Married	(34)	63
Separated/divorced	(15)	18
Widowed	(2)	4
Living together	(3)	6
Religion		
Catholic	(15)	47
Protestant	(15)	47
Other	(2)	6
Income		
AFDC	(15)	33
Self-supporting		
Below $10,000/yr	(13)	28
$10,000–$15,000/yr	(8)	17
Above $15,000/yr	(10)	22
Geographic Residence		
Inner City	(21)	40
Suburban	(32)	60

[a]Since demographic information was not always consistently recorded, the number of clients listed for each characteristic varies.

abuse depended primarily on the assessment of the family and victim by an experienced investigating team. According to STTP's assessments, 42 (78 percent) of the 54 reported cases of intrafamilial sexual assault were valid. Validation was considered ''unknown'' in an additional 10 cases due to limited or no access to the family (6 cases) and changing stories as to perpetrator (4 cases). In only 4 cases was the complaint assessed as being false or invalid—in 2 cases the child was assumed to have lied and in 2 cases, the mother had made a false allegation. This finding supported the belief that most reports of child sexual abuse are legitimate and well founded.

History of the Abuse. Detailed information concerning the history of the sexual abuse was gathered to gain further understanding of the situation. As seen in

Table 13–5
Relationship of Perpetrator to Child Victim

Relationship	Cases (#)	%
Father	(27)	50
Stepfather	(9)	17
Father & mother	(1)	2
Mother's boyfriend	(4)	7
Uncle	(4)	7
Grandfather	(3)	6
Brother	(6)	11
Total	(54)	100

Table 13–6
History of the Sexual Abuse

History	Cases (#)	%
Length of Abuse		
one incident	(2)	5
less than one month	(5)	13
2–12 months	(14)	35
1–2 years	(4)	10
over 2 years	(15)	38
Female Adolescent Pregnancy	(9)	27
Secret between Victim & Perpetrator	(30)	75
Perpetrator used threats to maintain secret	(19)	46
Perpetrator used bribes to maintain secret	(10)	24
Other Family Members Aware	(27)	66
Other Family Members Involved	(16)	39
Sexual Abuse in Mother's Background	(9)	22
Sexual Abuse in Father's Background	(4)	10

table 13–6, which reports this historical information for the 41 validated cases, in 48 percent of the cases the child victim was sexually assaulted for more than a year's duration. (One valid case was accepted into the program after these data were collected.) Only in 18 percent of the cases was the abuse a single incident or a problem for less than one month. The assault resulted in pregnancy in nine (27 percent) of the 33 postpubertal female adolescents.

As expected, the relationship had been a secret between the child and the perpetrator in a majority of the cases (75 percent) with either physical or verbal threats frequently utilized (46 percent) by the perpetrator in order to maintain the secret. Secrecy was also encouraged with financial rewards, bribes, more attention, and special favors in 10 cases. Despite the assumed secrecy of the abusive relationship, however, other family members often admitted some awareness of what was happening (66 percent). In 16 cases mothers were aware;

other siblings knew of the relationship in 17 cases, and grandmothers were cognizant in 5 instances. Other family members had been involved in the abuse in 39 percent of the validated cases. In 7 families other siblings had been victimized by the same perpetrator; siblings participated in the abuse of the referred victim in 3 cases; and one uncle and one mother had been additional perpetrators in 1 case each.

Inquiry into the parents' backgrounds provides some evidence for a multiple generational aspect of sexual abuse. Nine (22 percent) of the mothers and four (10 percent) of the fathers revealed a history of sexual abuse as children. While the percentages are small, they probably underestimate the multiple generational history since background information was "unknown" for 34 percent of the mothers and 80 percent of the fathers. If the figures are recalculated eliminating the "unknowns," 33 percent of the mothers and 50 percent of the fathers had been abused as children.

In sum, the historical information disclosed a somewhat chronic picture of sexual abuse. The identified relationship was generally ongoing and progressive over many months or years; other family members were often aware; multiple victims were found in the same home; and some parents had themselves been victims as children. It seems, then, as in other types of child abuse, there may be a familial pattern in sexually abusive families, a pattern that must then be taken into account in the families' treatment.

Family Pathology. In addition to the sexual abuse history obtained from the families, the workers diagnostically assessed each family in a standard manner through the use of a Problem Oriented Record (POR). The POR provided an ongoing record of the family's problems in nine defined categories and the plans for treating these problems. At intake, a problem list was constructed for each family. (Problem Oriented Records were available on the thirty intrafamilial cases admitted to the program after December 1977. Prior to this date workers were being trained in the use of the instrument.) Within each of the nine defined problem categories the worker could describe a problem, state there was no problem, or defer the assessment by writing "unknown." Table 13–7 presents the nine problem areas, subproblems, and the percentages of families for whom each problem was cited. Sexual assault clearly was not an isolated problem in an otherwise optimally functioning family. All of the families had internal difficulties in communication, parenting, or marital relationships. Parent-child or parent-parent relationships were characterized by fear, anger, alienation, and failure to support or protect one another. Physical abuse of children was described in eight families and abuse of the wife in three families. Sexual abuse, therefore, seems to occur within the context of other dysfunctional family interactions.

For a majority (80 percent) of family members, intrapersonal problems were also identified. Eight of the victims were severely depressed—three attempted

Table 13–7
Family Problems for Intrafamilial Cases

	Cases	
Problem Category	(#)	%
Child Sexual Relationship (Referral Problem)	(30)	100
Intrafamilial Interpersonal Problems		
Communication difficulties	(21)	70
Parenting problems	(17)	57
Marital problems	(16)	53
Other	(23)	77
Overall	(30)[a]	100
Intrapersonal problems		
Child symptoms—guilt, depression	(15)	50
Mother symptoms—helplessness, low self-esteem	(12)	40
Other	(14)	47
Overall	(24)[a]	80
Environmental Problems		
Educational	(14)	46
Financial	(8)	27
Employment	(6)	20
Other	(12)	40
Overall	(23)[a]	77
Criminal Justice Involvement		
Previous criminal history	(4)	13
Present police involvement	(21)	70
Overall	(22)[a]	73
Interpersonal/Social Problems	(18)	60
Adult Sexual Problems	(17)	57
Substance Abuse		
Alcohol	(10)	30
Drug	(7)	23
Overall	(17)[a]	57
Health Problems	(16)	53

[a]Numbers and percentages refer to the total families for whom the problem was identified. Since families could have more than one subproblem cited within each category, the numbers and percentages listed for the subproblems do not necessarily tally to the figures cited for the overall category.

suicide and three admitted to suicidal ideation. Guilt and poor self-image were characteristic child problems as well. Low self-esteem, inadequacy, and dependency were problematic for many mothers. A majority of the families also had environmental difficulties with school, employment, or finances (77 percent), problems with criminal justice involvement (70 percent), adult sexual problems (57 percent), alcohol or drug abuse (57 percent), and health problems (53 percent).

In sum, an average of seven problem categories was identified per family—six in addition to the referral problem of the sexual abuse. STTP was clearly serving a multiproblem population. It is interesting to note that as the STTP workers become more experienced and more proficient at interviewing, the number and types of problems diagnosed by the workers increased. Since it is unlikely that the population changed over these two years, it is probable that these families were even more dysfunctional than had been assumed at the start of the program.

The STTP evaluation therefore began by providing information to the program staff concerning the clients they were serving. General trends, overall patterns, similarities and differences between cases could be gleaned from these data. The information was important for developing appropriate treatment techniques but was also especially interesting to individual staff members who needed the picture of the whole population over and above their individual caseloads.

Evaluation Findings: Service Delivery

Direct Services. Based on the hypothesized, and later demonstrated, pathology of the intrafamilial cases, STTP proposed a multifaceted treatment model including both therapy and concrete assistance with environmental problems. Since the evaluation was to determine whether this planned treatment model was actually in operation, an examination of the provision of primary and supportive services was undertaken.

Primary Services. As stated previously, the multiple modalities of individual, group, family, marital, and art therapy were assumed to offer different strengths which, combined, would create a maximal therapeutic impact. Team treatment, or the involvement of two or more therapists in each case, was assumed also to enhance treatment effects. Thus a multiple therapist-multiple modality approach was to be the recommended treatment strategy. An analysis of data from STTP's first year revealed that multiple therapists had been *assigned* and multiple modalities had been *planned* for the large majority of intrafamilial cases. The second year's evaluation confirmed that, in fact, STTP was employing the proposed treatment model. That is, 86 percent of the cases involved two or more team members, and an average of four different therapy modalities were utilized per family.

Each treatment modality was examined for the frequency of its use with the 28 cases involved in treatment during STTP's second year. As displayed in table 13–8, mothers and child victims were the most frequent focus of therapy through individual sessions, adolescent group, and mother-child dyad treatment. In comparison, interventions involving fathers in individual, family or marital sessions were employed in fewer than half the cases. Similarly, art therapy and group therapy for mothers were infrequently utilized. These data indicated that, as expected, STTP's treatment emphases were: (1) to help the child deal with

Table 13–8
Utilization Frequency of Treatment Modalities

Treatment Modalities	Cases (#)[a]	%
Individual child sessions	(25/28)	89
Individual mother sessions	(24/27)	89
Adolescent group	(11/21)	52
Mother/child dyads	(14/27)	51
Individual father sessions	(11/23)	48
Family sessions	(11/28)	39
Individual sessions with sibs, aunts, grandparents	(10/28)	36
Marital sessions	(6/22)	27
Art therapy	(7/28)	25
Mothers' group	(6/27)	22

[a]The numbers and percentages associated with each treatment modality is the ratio of the number of families for whom the modality is recommended to the number for whom the modality is possible, that is, if a child is not an adolescent, adolescent group is not possible.

his or her emotions, assimilate the sexual trauma, and continue growth and development using individual or adolescent group therapy; and (2) to support and build up the mother's ability to protect the child through individual sessions. The infrequent use of group therapy for mothers and the limited program contact with perpetrator fathers were emphasized by these data and therefore brought to the staff's attention.

An examination was made to determine whether a typical sequence of interventions existed—that is, whether there were typical decision points when modalities were added or changed. It was found that the treatment plan most often involved early individual sessions with the mother or the child victim or both; with this exception, no predetermined sequence of interventions was evident.

Finally, in examining the provision of primary services, the amount of time typically devoted to a case treated through this model was analyzed. Workers were asked to keep detailed records of time spent in various case activities. Time sheets were developed which categorized all case activities and only required the workers to record the daily time spent in each activity per case. These sheets were tallied by the evaluators each month. It was found that intrafamilial cases were seen in treatment an average of seven hours a month, that is, families were seen approximately twice a week. Average time per case per month ranged from 1 to 24 hours depending upon the stage of treatment and crisis status of the case. Average telephone contact with families was an additional one-half hour monthly. Although these figures reflected only direct contact with families, it appeared that a considerable amount of time was invested in treating incest cases.

Supportive Services. In addition to direct treatment, STTP's model called for supportive services or cooperative work with other agencies involved with the family. The model assumed that optimal treatment of sexual abuse entailed close cooperation with the law enforcement system for coordinating the investigation of the abuse and the arrest of the perpetrator; with the legal justice system for the prosecution of cases or the obtaining of custody of the child victim; with the health care system for gathering physical evidence of the abuse or treatment of the physical effects of the abuse; and with the school systems for access to and ongoing monitoring of the child.

A time analysis revealed that collateral contact and case management required between 36 percent and 48 percent of total case time. Workers typically spent three hours a month per case in face-to-face collateral contacts, and two-and-one-half hours in case-related conferences. Virtually every open case necessitated STTP's interaction with one or more outside systems. In order to determine which systems required the most STTP energy, percentages of collateral time were calculated for each and are summarized in table 13–9. Court appearances, court studies, and legal consultations regarding both criminal and juvenile court involvements demanded the greatest amount of collateral time. Working with the health care system, school systems, and law enforcement system comprised another large segment of time. To obtain such services, additional time was used to transport the clients and for worker travel to inter-agency conferences. When all services, including both primary and supportive activities, are tallied, the STTP treatment model typically required about 14 hours of service per case per month.

Treatment Model. The evaluation of service delivery also called for an investigation of the functioning of the treatment model, the use of consultation and multidisciplinary team review, and the relationship of STTP with outside systems. Information regarding these issues was drawn from program records and

Table 13–9
Percentage of Time Devoted to Various Supportive Services and Collateral Involvement[a]

System or Service	Hours (#)	%
Legal justice system (court appearance, court studies, legal consultation)	(111)	46
Health care system (arranging hospital examinations, abortions, visits, medical, and mental health consultations)	(42)	18
School systems (school visits, educational planning conferences)	(36)	15
Law enforcement system (contact with police departments)	(9)	4
Transportation and travel time (transport clients to and from above systems)	(30)	12
Other (financial assistance, placement visits)	(13)	5
	(246)[a]	100

[a]Number of hours devoted to supportive services over a 9-month sampling period.

structured interviews with the staff. While records might be considered more objective data, staff interviews provided an insider's assessment of the program—its workings, its strengths, and its weaknesses. Given the strong relationship of mutual respect between evaluators and staff, it was felt that staff responses would be honest and directed toward constructive program modification rather than personal bias and self-interest.

Multiple Therapist-Multiple Modality Therapy. The unique aspect of STTP, the use of the multiple therapist-multiple modality approach, was developed to increase the potential for change in highly resistant sexually abusive families. Multiple intervenors, one for each of the major actors, and multiple interventions, each with its own strengths, were intended to change the balance of power in the family and quickly disrupt old patterns of interaction.

Staff were queried about the model as practiced. From their perspectives, the major advantage of team treatment was the shared responsibility for case management and decisionmaking. For them, the interchangeability of their roles was as important as the identification of each therapist with one family member. Since one team member could take over the other's role when necessary, they felt that better services could be provided to the family. They also indicated that team treatment allowed more effective crisis management as different aspects of the crisis were handled simultaneously and therefore in a more timely manner by the team workers. For staff, then, team treatment and multiple modalities seemed to permit work to be done more efficiently and to dissipate some of the anxiety of working with the incestuous family.

Effective team treatment demanded a high level of coordination—a quick sharing of important information, a meshing of different therapeutic styles, an efficient division of responsibilities, and effective joint decisionmaking. The use of multiple modalities also required the coordination of therapists and decisions regarding when to offer what modality to which family member and in what sequence. When coordination went awry or when teams had trouble meeting together (an unfortunately common occurrence given the crisis nature of the cases), it seemed to reinforce the fragmentation and dysfunctional communication patterns of the families. This treatment approach where one family member may be relating to five different therapists and four different modalities at once, seemed to have the potential of creating either maximal positive impact or maximal confusion, depending upon the coordination skills of the team.

Another issue of importance in using this treatment model was the number of families that could be served using this multifaceted approach with a finite number of staff members. Data indicated that over the two-year period an average of nine cases per month were seen in this multiple modality-multiple therapist treatment. Since this represented aproximately 40 percent of the active monthly caseload, about two-thirds of the open cases were not receiving the proposed treatment model during any one month. Whether this statistic reflected a limitation of the maximal impact treatment used by STTP, or an indication of the costliness and difficulty of working with the families using any therapeutic model, was not clear at the time of this evaluation. It was concluded, however, that cost-effectiveness comparisons with other intervention models would be important areas for future investigation.

To summarize, the findings concerning the treatment model showed that, despite some limitations of involving multiple therapists and multiple modalities, STTP's treatment model seemed to provide certain advantages to the staff and families. That is, STTP seemed to be treating families who might otherwise elude more traditional services and may have done so with less staff anxiety and more staff support. More extensive analysis of cost-effectiveness of alternative treatment strategies, however, is indicated.

Consultation and Multidisciplinary Team Review. Consultation and multidisciplinary team review, almost institutions in the treatment of child abuse, were included as an important component of the sexual abuse program. STTP's consulting team included a psychologist, and art therapist, a police officer, a prosecutor, a DCYS lawyer, an internist, occasionally a psychiatrist, and the program evaluators. As part of the Evaluation Plan, the use of consultation and team review was examined.

When interviewed, staff and administration confirmed that the multidisciplinary team meetings were functioning to share information and advice from specialized consultants on areas beyond staff expertise, to facilitate the connections with the legal justice, health care, and law enforcement systems, and to identify the existing community resources available for treatment. Over the two years, 32 of the 54 intrafamilial cases were presented and reviewed in these biweekly meetings. Time was devoted primarily to case problem solving, that is, clarifying the model for treatment, particularly regarding the timing of intervention with the fathers; discussing issues related to court and police proceedings; or treatment planning for complicated cases.

While acknowledging the importance of these team reviews, the participants admitted to the difficulties in their functioning. It took time to overcome the initial air of feeling evaluated, being defensive, and feeling anxious, before a supportive atmosphere developed. Early "turf" defending and blame-projection both caused and created tension. The climate was particularly vulnerable to any conflicts in administration or consultation and was highly dependent upon the moderating skills of the leader. The staff, as compared to the administration, felt the meetings were at times used for supervision or case management rather than used to provide expert advice. Finally, there were difficulties in the length and organization of the early presentations. Often they were "process presentations" taking as long as two-and-one half hours for the presentation and discussion. Generally, however, staff attitudes about the meetings became more positive. Feelings of greater staff support, fewer conflicts, more constructive consultation, and shorter, more precise presentations developed over time.

In addition to attending the biweekly team reviews, the psychologist, art therapist, and project internist also were expected to provide consultation through direct case contact. Records indicated that 15 incest cases (28 percent) received art therapy, 13 (24 percent) received psychologial evaluations, and 20 (37 percent) received medical examinations, on-going health care, or both. Analysis of these cases showed that almost every case receiving this expert consultation was an intrafamilial case already being seen in multimodality, multitherapist treatment. This consultation therefore was another facet of the maximal impact treatment.

It was found that staff required contact with *all* consultants outside of the case review sessions. This necessitated the consultants' availability at times of crises and for follow-up, and their commitment to the program and its goals. All of these were vulnerable to the crises and requirements of their other professional obligations. This was particularly true for the attorneys who served on a noncontract basis. In short, while the worth and importance of consultation and multidisciplinary team review to the servicing of intrafamilial cases was apparent, so too were the trials and tribulations in implementation.

STTP's Relationship to Outside Systems. A significant aspect of service delivery is the linkage between the service agency and other agencies involved with the family. Thus the relationship of STTP to outside systems was addressed in the Evaluation Plan. As previously indicated, a substantial portion of staff time involved interaction and contact with collateral agencies. Additionally, in all of STTP's multidisciplinary team meetings there was representation of one or more of these outside systems.

Though the scope and focus of the present evaluation precluded a direct study of the outside agencies and their reactions to STTP, data concerning them were derived from STTP case records and staff interviews. According to the project director, in the two years of the program STTP developed liaisons with key people in the community including municipal police departments, hospitals, social service agencies, the Attorney General's Office, the State's Attorney's Office, the Connecticut Justice Commission, and the Department of Correction. While the awareness of sexual abuse seemed to increase in all these systems, the staff felt that there was continued resistance in recognizing the problem, and inexperience and prejudice in handling the families. Lawyers, doctors, and police officers alike had trouble in interviewing or examining the victims. Law enforcement and criminal justice personnel had trouble arresting and prosecuting the offenders. The adversary nature of the legal justice system often worked for the protection of the perpetrator's rights, sometimes to the detriment of the victim's rights. Also, school personnel saw conflict between their responsibilities as mandated reporters and their obligation to keep information on the child confidential. Thus interagency cooperation obviously required extensive education, reorientation, change, and reform.

STTP, as the first and only Connecticut treatment unit specializing in child sexual abuse, was not only working in a difficult area but was working without a track record of success and experience behind it. In many cases the staff had to rely as much upon their previous agency relationships established prior to STTP as on contacts developed on a case-by-case basis. Formalized, prospective working relationships, though crucial, were difficult to build. STTP seemed to have developed some cooperative relationships with outside systems, though the extent of real impact and change in the 36 towns within the catchment area was difficult to assess.

As an example, STTP's relationship to the criminal justice system was examined in more detail for the 41 validated cases of sexual abuse. Ideally, most if not all the validated cases should have been prosecuted since STTP attempted to use the authoritative sanction of the police or court initially to "motivate families for therapy and maintain access to the target child" (Sgroi, 1979). It was found that 26 of the 41 cases (63 percent) entered the law enforcement system via reports to local police departments. Twenty-three cases (56 percent) were investigated by the police. Thus the first step into the criminal justice system—police investigation—was taken in slightly over half the intrafamilial cases. Of the 20 cases (49 percent) where an arrest was made, six perpetrators pleaded guilty (30 percent), one was convicted (5 percent), six had their cases dropped (30 percent), and seven had litigation pending at the time of data collection. The overall rate of conviction or guilty pleas was 17 percent of the total sample. While these statistics might appear discouraging, they may be compared with a study of men charged with rape showing only a 2 percent rate of conviction (Rape Crisis Newsletter, October 1978). Comparable data for other child-sexual-abuse programs that are not a part of the criminal justice system are not available.

It is clear that barriers to cooperative working relationships between STTP and the legal justice system continued to exist during the life of the program. First, given STTP's assessment of the validity of the sexual assault, the dropping of charges was considered a negative outcome. The child was disbelieved; the family was under pressure; and therapy was often made impossible. It was found that family members in 3 of the 6 cases where charges were dropped immediately withdrew from therapy. Second, even with conviction or guilty pleas the staff often felt that the child had been subjected to traumatic and difficult legal procedures. Third, the fact that all the convicted perpetrators were sentenced to prison usually implied punishment but not necessarily treatment for the perpetrator. Finally, the statistics revealed the lack of disposition alternatives for the offenders such as deferment of prosecution, deferment of sentencing, and treatment as a condition of probation. Such alternatives might make instituting and prosecuting sexual abuse cases more probable from the police report onward. Thus, although there was evidence that STTP was enlisting the support of the legal justice system, the data emphasized, too, the very complex and difficult interplay between treatment, child protection, and criminal justice involvement. (It should be noted that just prior to STTP's closing but after these data were collected, two of the cases with litigation pending were heard in court. For the first time, the court ordered treatment for the perpetrator in lieu of probation in one case and child placement in the other. In both cases, STTP's testimony and the child's statement were accepted as convicting evidence.)

Evaluation Finding: Staff Training

Staff training was the final focus of the Evaluation Plan. It was expected that in starting a new program the workers, no matter how clinically experienced, were likely to have little or no background dealing with sexual abuse of children. The cases are highly emotionally charged and generate anxiety in even the most seasoned therapist. The families are often dysfunctional and extremely resistant to treatment. Even with the support of the team treatment approach and with the guidance of a multidisciplinary team, training and supervision were assumed to be critical for effective service delivery.

Training was planned for the development of specialized diagnostic and therapeutic skills. Table 13–10 lists some of the topics for staff in-service training. Clinical consultation was also provided to the program through workshops run for STTP by a number of nationally recognized experts in child sexual abuse.

Training was to be supplemented by case supervision. All five STTP workers, despite their varied levels of clinical acumen and experience, stressed the

Table 13–10
Topics for Staff In-Service Training

Topics
Inteviewing child sexual assault victims
Dynamics and evaluations of child sexual assault
Working with unmotivated clients
Behavioral dysfunction
Family dysfunction
Psychological tests & measurements
Proper police investigation of child sexual assault
The Harborview approach to child sexual assault
Play therapy
Family therapy

importance of regular weekly supervision dealing with dynamics, assessment, case management, and treatment planning. The evaluation revealed, however, that often regular supervision was preempted by other supervisor responsibilities, case crises, and conflicting worker schedules. The optimal frequency of supervision therefore often was sacrificed to other program needs.

Even after months of experience, all the workers acknowledged a continued desire for supervision and training, particularly concerning family dynamics and treatment, child development, and legal issues of incest. Additionally, certain areas of diagnostic interviewing required periodic emphasis. At one evaluation point, for instance, questions about the incestuous parents, their backgrounds, their education, their health, and their sex lives were more frequently left uninvestigated than any other information on the POR or other record-keeping instruments. Since it was felt that this reflected worker discomfort in investigating these areas, further desensitization and training were planned. Throughout the two years the program needed to be sensitive to new areas of staff training requirements. Except for one worker who expressed immediate ease in working in the area, the staff suggested that it took at least six months before they felt comfortable in dealing with child sexual abuse. They felt this was facilitated most by increased experience with the families, reading about incest, desensitization to the sexual words and questions, and talking with other workers. Training of service providers required therefore both an initial and an ongoing effort.

Findings: Effects of the STTP Intervention

During the last six months of the program a supplementary evaluation was designed in response to staff requests. With the expiration of the federal grant and the impending termination of the program, the staff desired some indication of STTP's effects. Since further efforts at model building and program development (the goals of our formative evaluation plan) seemed superfluous as the program was preparing to terminate, an attempt was made to meet the staff's desire for information about outcomes.

As outlined earlier in this chapter, the constraints and difficulties of conducting a valid therapy effectiveness study were quite real. First, an untreated control group could not ethically be included. Second, comparisons based on other programs were unlikely given the paucity of published data on child-sexual-abuse treatment. Third, the finite granting period precluded any long-term follow-up on the victim and family. Fourth, disagreement in the field existed as to whether successful outcome should be measured by termination of the sexual contact, family separation or reintegration, better family communication, victim's academic and personal functioning, or changing family relationships. Fifth, it was unclear if any or all of the above should be assessed through family self-report, therapist assessments, or independent observations by outside evaluators of attitudinal or behavioral change. Acknowledging these limitations, an evaluation was constructed to examine some overt indicators of STTP's effectiveness. While the results may not be interpreted as findings of therapy outcome research, they did provide the staff and administration some overall idea of their impact and can also serve as a basis for comparison with other developing programs.

Problem Resolution. As a measure of treatment impact, the POR required therapists' judgments as to the status of each identified problem at termination. Each problem was deemed to be resolved, improved, unchanged, or worse than when first identified. This method of assessing outcome was specific to individual cases and did not assume that all cases should be measured by the same criteria; however, it was also general enough to view the program's effect within overall problem areas. It might also be noted that the use of therapists' assessments of problem change would lead to conservative results, compared with similar client assessments, since therapists have been shown to be less positive in their ratings of therapy outcomes (Beck and Jones, 1973).

Table 13–11 displays the degree of problem resolution of the nine problem categories. The problem areas are listed in order of decreasing treatment impact—that is, from the greatest to the least proportion of problems either settled or improved at closing. (Due to the termination date of the program, 19 cases which would have otherwise remained open had to be closed prematurely. Since it is possible that additional problems would have been remediated if these cases had been followed to their natural termination, these data should be used only to identify trends rather than provide clear indices of program impact.) Therapy was seen to have its greatest effect on the referring problem. The child was judged as being safe from further sexual abuse by the perpetrator ("settled")

Table 13–11
Closing Status of Problems Addressed in Treatment

Problem Category	Total # Cited	Settled (#)	%	Improved (#)	%	No Change (#)	%	Worse (#)	%
Child sexual relationship	81	(26)	32	(24)	30	(30)	37	(1)	1
Social/interpersonal relationships	22	(6)	27	(7)	31	(9)	41	—	—
Feelings about oneself	57	(2)	3	(29)	51	(26)	46	—	—
Criminal justice system	39	(14)	36	(5)	13	(19)	49	(1)	3
Intrafamilial interpersonal relationships	161	(29)	18	(50)	31	(79)	50	(3)	2
Health	25	(7)	28	(5)	20	(13)	52	—	—
Environmental problems	44	(8)	18	(10)	23	(23)	52	(3)	7
Adult sexual relationship	20	(4)	20	(3)	15	(13)	65	—	—
Alcohol/drug abuse	15	(3)	20	(2)	13	(10)	67	—	—

or at least protected and in little jeopardy ("improved") in 62 percent of the cases. Positive movement was also noted for the majority of cases in social relationships (58 percent) and intrapersonal difficulties (53 percent). Change was effected in fewer than half the families in the realms of criminal justice system involvement (49 percent), family interactions (49 percent), health (48 percent), education-employment-financial trouble (41 percent), adult sexual dysfunction (35 percent), and alcohol or drug abuse (33 percent). Overall, the limits to positive change as reported by therapists are sobering. Since there are, however, no available data to which STTP's rate of success can be adequately compared, the question remains as to whether this is more than, less than, or all that can be expected in treating incestuous families.

Perhaps these statistics demonstrate simply the difficulty of effecting change, that these are families not easily amenable to reorganization at least in the length of time studied here. This may be particularly true since some of the cases were evaluated for improvement prior to the natural termination of therapy which may have been many months later. On the other hand, it is possible to interpret the data as evidence that the STTP model of intervention has limited impact, particularly when assessed according to specific problem resolution. Until other studies clarify some of these issues and offer comparative information, it may be assumed that in sexually abusive families the possibility of producing change in relatively short periods of time is limited, even when utilizing a maximal impact model of therapy.

Other Outcome Indicators. A number of other outcome indicators were analyzed from data supplied by the therapists on the 41 validated cases. The variables examined were ones which STTP and other sexual abuse programs have advanced as treatment goals. Table 13–12 summarizes STTP's statistics on a number of these criteria.

Some child sexual abuse experts believe that the cornerstone of treatment is the perpetrator's admission of guilt and his acceptance of responsibility for the abuse. This was accomplished in 19 or 46 percent of the STTP cases. Denial continued in the remaining 22. Admission of guilt was not, however, the sine qua non of treatment. In at least five cases, families dropped out of treatment following an admission of guilt to the family or the therapists; conversely, problem resolution and successful therapeutic engagement of mother and victim were achieved in other cases where the perpetrator's denial was never overcome.

Maintenance of family integrity or reintegration of the family has recently been advocated as a treatment goal since family breakup is assumed to cause further trauma to the child. Traditionally the sexually abused child had been removed from the home. While perhaps protecting the child from continued abuse, such removal supposedly reinforced the child's sense of guilt and contributed to isolation and further victimization. Although 51 percent of the victims were placed outside the home at some critical time during intervention, only 14

Table 13–12
Possible Indicators of Treatment Outcome for the 41 Validated Cases of Sexual Abuse

Outcome Criteria	Cases (#)	%
Child Protection		
Child has supportive adult ally	(37)	90
Child will tell someone if abused again	(30)	73
STTP has continued access to monitor child	(33)	80
Perpetrator Admits Guilt	(19)	46
Family Integrity		
Victim		
Victim permanently removed	(7)	14
Victim temporarily removed	(19)	37
Victim never removed	(27)	49
Parents		
Marital status change[a]	(11)	42
Family		
Victim & perpetrator live together	(15)	37

[a]Number indicates a change from married or living together to separation or divorce in cases with perpetrator father, stepfathers, or boyfriends.

percent (seven children) of the victims were permanently separated from their families.

Father-daughter incest typically suggests the existence of a troubled marriage. Treatment can attempt either to salvage the marriage or to assist the family through the painful separation process. Espousing the former alternative as a treatment objective, the Santa Clara County program claims to save 78 percent of the marriages (Kroth, 1978) while Berliner, advocating the latter alternative, states that in the majority of cases treated by the Harborview Sexual Assault Center marriages end in divorce (personal communication, 1978). In the STTP program, 42 percent of the married or living together couples with husband or boyfriend perpetrators were separated or divorced during involvement with STTP. Without an indication of marital adjustment or of the perpetrator's level of impulse control, this finding is open to varied interpretations.

As a final measure of family integrity, in only 15 of the 41 cases (37 percent) was the victim living with the perpetrator at closing. In 4 cases the perpetrators had never lived with the victim. Prison, marital change, child placement, or some combination of these accounted for the other cases. Thus, viewed from a standpoint of family integrity, the majority of the STTP cases experienced some form of family disruption. Viewed from a child protection perspective, the majority of the children were in less danger by being separated from the perpetrator.

Another indication of outcome is the availability of a supportive adult to the child victim. STTP attempted to develop at least one ally for the child to whom he or she could go for support. Ninety percent of the children were assessed to have at least one supportive adult relationship, either mothers (21), foster parents (4), other relatives (8), school officials (3), or therapists (3). Further, it was expected that approximately 73 percent of the victims had built up enough trust through therapy that they would reveal the incest should it reoccur. Both figures provide some evidence of positive impact. Finally, if STTP had continued, access for ongoing monitoring of the families was available in 80 percent of the cases.

STTP was most successful, then, in accomplishing its child protection goal. A supportive, trusting relationship had been built between the victim and an adult in a large majority of the families, and most children were thought to be safe from further sexual exploitation. It was true, however, that maximizing child protection often was attained at the cost of the family's integrity. The perpetrator fathers were often separated from the child and the rest of the family at the conclusion of treatment.

Recommendations for Evaluation of Child-Sexual-Abuse Programs

The STTP example illustrates one approach to the evaluation of clinical intervention programs. A formative evaluation focusing primarily on effort and efficiency questions was consciously selected as the most effective method of assessing the project. This type of evaluation is particularly significant for treatment programs that are developing; that is, the process of collecting, tabulating, and regularly reporting information back to the staff concerning actual program operations provides the input as well as the impetus for program modification and growth. Summative evaluations with adequacy and effectiveness concerns are important, but are more appropriate to testing the efficacy of established programs and stabilized treatment techniques. It may be suggested, then, that in formulating an evaluation contract the project staff and evaluators clearly and mutually choose the type and focus of evaluation most relevant to the developmental stage and needs of the program. Unrealistic expectations of what the evaluation will do leads to failure of the evaluative venture and frustration of those involved.

In the STTP example, data were provided regarding many aspects of program functioning that revealed areas in need of further clarification or attention. For instance, issues around the timing and nature of interventions with perpetrator fathers, the sequencing of the multiple therapeutic modalities, the infrequent use of the mothers' group, and the conflict between direct service needs and time for developing community resources were some areas pinpointed as weaknesses at various times during the evaluation. Specific recommendations made on the basis of the findings were incorporated into the program to varying degrees, depending upon the difficulty of implementing the recommendation, the ability of the administration to effect the change, and the political and systems constraints impinging on the program. Because of the evaluation, however, the essential information for decision making was available when requested by program staff.

The merit of the evaluation was not limited to supplying data, nor can its value be attributed only to the implementation of specific recommendations. Additional roles that the evaluators played increased the relevance of the evaluation to STTP. In planning an evaluation, therefore, issues beyond the structure of the evaluation itself should be considered. First, administrative support is the cornerstone of a useful evaluation. Being accepted as part of the team and functioning as part of the planning process enables the evaluators both to provide critical information and have the greatest chance of effect. Second, evaluators often serve a monitoring role by informing the program about what it is doing, how many clients it is serving, how well records are being kept, and so forth. This is important since administrators rarely have enough time to monitor the program themselves. If, however, this monitoring role is accorded the evaluator without the status of first being a member of the team, the evaluator runs the risk of being a kind of watchdog without strength. A successful evaluator can also function as an administrator's support, a third evaluator role. The quasi-outside relationship of a contracted evaluator provides distance from day-to-day crises yet enough familiarity with the program to allow the evaluators to act as a sounding board for the administration. In STTP the evaluators were often an important source of support to the two administrators.

The relationship of the evaluators to the line staff must be carefully nurtured as well. This develops when the staff are included in planning and modifying the evaluation and especially in creating a record-keeping system. Evaluators must, on their part, attempt to reduce repetitive records and utilize already existing forms. For the STTP evaluation, written records were supplemented by staff interviews which not only furnished the data needed, but also gave the staff a chance openly to voice their opinions and perceptions to the evaluating team. Thus the evaluator can serve a fourth role of colleague and cooperator with the staff.

If evaluators assume these roles, taking their responsibilities seriously, they achieve credibility and promote an atmosphere of trust and cooperation. The evaluation becomes what Alkin et al. (1979) call an "information dialogue," a process of two-way communication where information is explored rather than presented. The impact of evaluation findings becomes subtle and cumulative. Change occurs as a result of comments communicated between staff and evaluators throughout the course of the program. The formative evaluation then can operate through an interplay of questions posed, information provided, and interpretations probed together.

Up to this point emphasis has been placed on the importance of evaluation to the program under study; and a number of issues have been suggested to augment the value of such an evaluation. In addition to building knowledge for the program itself, however, there is another motivation for subjecting a treatment program to the scrutiny of evaluation. In the field of mental health in general, but in the area of child sexual abuse in particular, there is a need for a data base of information. Incest and sexual abuse are relatively new areas of investigation, and data concerning treatment approaches are sparse. Evaluations which detail the characteristics of the population and describe the treatment program as implemented, not just as proposed, generate knowledge in the field. Further, since the establishment of control groups is generally impossible or unethical in "real world" evaluations, comparative program information is a vital step toward assessing therapy impact, measuring cost-effectiveness, and optimally matching the patient to the therapy model. Though data are not yet available, it is highly probable that different populations of sexually abusive or incestuous families exist and that they are differentially amenable to change. Ultimately a differentiation of sexually abusive families according to family dynamics and nature of sexual involvement (Summit and Kryso, 1978) might enhance the chances for treatment impact using alternate treatment strategies. At this time, evaluations of individual, developing, treatment programs can provide the comparative statistics necessary for such comprehensive and far-reaching studies.

Guidelines for Evaluation of Child-Sexual-Abuse Programs

1. Program administrators and evaluators should approach the evaluation as a joint venture, working closely together to formulate the most meaningful and potentially useful evaluation design.
2. The choice of the evaluation design should be geared to the stage of the project and its needs. The evaluator should clarify what evaluation can do and what information it can or cannot provide.
3. A formative evaluation is suggested for a new or developing program. This type of evaluation is aimed at program improvement and provides ongoing data feedback to encourage self-reflective program growth.
4. Following the design selection, questions relevent and important to the project staff should be identified and operationalized.
5. Methods of data collection should be carefully chosen with staff to provide information necessary for the evaluation, but at minimum cost in clinical time and program expense. Attempts should be made to use already existing forms, adding new evaluation instruments only when essential. Repetitive records should be reduced or eliminated.
6. The evaluator can provide monitoring of record-keeping since the administration and clinical staff rarely have the time.

7. As part of this monitoring role, the evaluator should function as a member of the planning team. This accords the evaluator a clearer understanding of the program and a greater opportunity to make the evaluation useful.
8. Data presentation to the staff should be timely and allow for discussion and joint interpretation of the information.
9. The evaluator-staff relationship is one which should be flexible and carefully nurtured through the life of the evaluation. An "active-reactive-adaptive" (Patton, 1978) relationship will allow for the best use of the evaluation and its findings.

References

Alkin, Marvin C., Daillak, Richard, White, Peter. *Using Evaluations: Does Evaluation Make a Difference?* Beverly Hills, California: Sage Library of Social Research, 1979.

Attkisson, C. Clifford, Broskowski, Anthony. "Evaluation and the Human Service Concept." In *Evaluation of Human Service Programs,* edited by Attkisson, C. Clifford; Hargreaves, William A.; Horowitz, Mardi J.; Sorensen, James E. New York: Academic Press, 1978.

Beck, Dorothy F., and Jones, Mary Ann. *Progress on Family Problems—A Nationwide Study of Clients and Counselors Views on Family Agency Services.* New York: Family Service Association of America, 1973.

Gelles, Richard J. "Etiology of Overcoming Fallacious Reasoning in Understanding Family Violence and Child Abuse. *Child Abuse Where Do We Go From Here?* Conference Proceeding: February 18–20, 1979. Washington D.C.: Children's Hospital National Medical Center, 1977.

Kerlinger, Fred N. *Foundations of Behavioral Research.* New York: Holt, Rinehart and Winston, Inc., 1973, p. 11.

Kroth, Jerome. "Child Sexual Abuse Treatment Program Interim Evaluation." Unpublished manuscript, 1978.

Patton, Michael Q. *Utilization—Focused Evaluation.* California: Sage Publications, 1978.

Quie, A.H. Reply to Lynn and Salasin's "Human Services: Should We, Can We Make Them Available to Everyone?" *Evaluation,* Special issue (Spring 1974):21–24.

Rape Crisis Newsletter. Cleveland: Rape Crisis Center, September–October, 1978.

Sgroi, Suzanne M. "The Sexual Assault of Children: Dynamics of the Problem and Issues in Program Development. *Sexual Abuse of Children: Implications from the Sexual Trauma Treatment Program of Connecticut.* New York: Community Council of Greater New York, 1979.

Suchman, Edward A. *Evaluative Research*. New York: Russell Sage Foundation, 1967, p. 71.

Zelen, Marvin. "A New Design for Randomized Clinical Trials." *The New England Journal of Medicine* 300, 22: 1242–45.

14 How to Start a Child-Sexual-Abuse Intervention Program

Suzanne M. Sgroi

Few communities have child-sexual-abuse intervention programs. In some places, there is no program because it has not occurred to anyone to try to start one. Perhaps the local professionals do not believe that a specialized program to handle child-sexual-abuse cases is needed in their communities. Or perhaps they realize that a need exists, but still lack the necessary initiative and motivation to begin. In many places, the local professionals have delayed getting started because they are waiting for two additional ingredients to be supplied: money and magic.

The expectation by administrators and planners that additional money must be supplied if an additional service is to be provided is both predictable and understandable. They argue that sexual abuse of children is a new and exotic problem, and that no one should expect a family service agency, community mental health center, child-protective services unit, or a child guidance clinic to be able to address unless additional funds are forthcoming. This argument is specious because the cases exist in large numbers and all of the community's tax-supported or local charitable fund-supported agencies are working with some of the families already. It is true that many of the clients who are receiving services from these agencies have not been correctly identified as cases of child sexual abuse and therefore are not being approached knowledgeably or even adequately. Nevertheless, all agencies which receive public or charitable funds already have a service mandate which includes child sexual abuse. Although supplemental program money is always welcome, a significant start can be made in most communities by redirecting or improving the services that are already being funded and provided.

What about the requirement for magic? I refer to the belief held by many that there are magical solutions for child-sexual-abuse intervention—that sometime, from somewhere, someone will sweep into the community with a simple, painless, rapid remedy for this problem. The magic approach will doubtless also be inexpensive, easily learned, and effortlessly applied. The reality is that there are no magical solutions and never will be. There is no one there just over the horizon to come riding out of the sunset and rescue either the clients or the professionals who are committed and paid to serve them.

Meanwhile, cases of child sexual abuse are managed badly in these same communities. Child-protective-services workers, police investigators, health, social services and mental health professionals are largely ignorant of the usual dynamics and mechanics of child sexual abuse, unaware that they are dealing primarily with a power problem rather than a sexual problem, insensitive to the underlying motivation of the victim's family to suppress the allegation in both intrafamily and extrafamily cases and reluctant to join forces with professionals from other disciplines for a coordinated approach to the problem.

The following scenario for child-sexual-abuse investigation is probably enacted on a daily basis in every state in the United States:

A child confides to some trusted person outside the family (perhaps a teacher or a school guidance counselor) that he or she is being sexually abused by a parent. The teacher or guidance counselor reports the case to child protective services. An intake worker from the local child protection agency visits the home and confronts the parents and the child with the child's complaint of sexual abuse. The child-protective-services worker has usually not talked directly to either the complainant or the child prior to this confrontation. He or she is thus using the tactic of confronting people who occupy a power position (the child's parents) with an allegation made by a weaker person (the child) to a third party (the teacher or guidance counselor) regarding abuse by a power figure (the offending parent). Since the child-protective-services worker has not bothered to interview the child directly, this tactic invites the child's parents to respond with denial and suppression. The child-protective-services worker thus creates a crisis by confronting all of the protagonists with the disclosure of the secret of sexual abuse.

This method of validation by confrontation and crisis encourages the persons who occupy power positions to suppress the child's allegation while conveying to all that the child-protective-services worker is prepared to believe whoever shouts loudest and proclaims innocence most vigorously. Thus encouraged by a statutory authority figure, the parents can be expected to undermine the child's credibility by calling him or her a liar and relating previous incidents in which the child has caused trouble "lying" or behaving abnormally. The child is then identified as the real problem by virtue of having made a "false" allegation of sexual abuse. The parents promise to "get help" for the child as an indication of their good faith and concern for the youngster. Reassured by the parents' response and never having bothered to develop a relationship with the child or to validate the allegation, the child-protective-services worker withdraws and closes out the case as "unfounded."

With minor variations, this scenario is enacted during police investigation of child sexual abuse. If the complaint by the child is referred to the local police, it may be a police officer who knocks on the door instead of a child-protective-services worker. In all probability, the police officer will report the child's allegation to the "nonoffending" parent (usually the child's mother). If she supports the child and is willing to swear out a complaint against the perpetrator, the police will probably obtain an arrest warrant. If not, the mother will probably support the perpetrator's protestations of innocence and join in suppressing the allegation and undermining the credibility of the victim. Case closed!

Needless to say, variations of this scenario are also enacted by health, social services, and mental health professionals every day. Members of all these disciplines lack basic understanding about the phenomenon of child sexual abuse and refuse to accept responsibility to increase their knowledge or skills. Accordingly, knowledgeable police or child-protective-services investigators find it difficult or virtually impossible to obtain comprehensive medical and psychological evaluations for victims, perpetrators, and their families. Attorneys and judges also lack basic knowledge to assess cases of child sexual abuse and make appropriate dispositions for offenders and families. Those rare cases which receive adequate investigation and medical or psychological evaluation thus are likely to fail to obtain an authoritative incentive for treatment from the legal justice system. Finally, when victims, offenders, and families *are* amenable to treatment, few, if any, treatment resources are available which are equipped to deal with involuntary clients whose problems relate to child sexual abuse.

What can be done? Chapters 2 to 12 address investigation, case management, multidisciplinary team review, and various treatment perspectives. However, successful application of these approaches requires a cadre of professionals from child protective services, law enforcement, health, social services and mental health who, working together within the community, can fulfill the basic requirements to help sexually abused children, offenders, and their families. Surprisingly, it *is* possible to start a community child-sexual-abuse intervention program without startup money and without magic. Nearly every community has the expertise within to be applied to the problem. The essential ingredients are willingness to risk time, energy, and effort, to make mistakes and painfully to learn from those mistakes.

How to begin? A few professionals who have direct case experience have to be convinced that it makes sense for them to pool their experience as an initial step. Sometimes this can occur spontaneously. It may be helpful for a local agency or professional group to sponsor an entry-level conference on child sexual abuse to stimulate interest in the problem. Sometimes an outside expert can come into a community for a day and act as a catalyst—not so much telling people what to do as by conveying confidence that the job can be done and that they can do it. Some of the steps were listed in chapter 3 as part of the basic requirements for case management. When I am invited into a professional community as a speaker or a teacher, here is what I recommend that they do to start a child-sexual-abuse intervention program.

Concentrate Case Experience

Every police department, child-protection agency, community mental health center, family service agency, and child guidance clinic has an identifiable volume of child-sexual-abuse cases to deal with every year. The usual practice is to assign cases by the "luck of the draw" or at random to those professionals who rotate intake of new clients. This practice admittedly "spreads the pain around," but it also insures that no one professional is likely to acquire enough case experience to begin to develop expertise.

Further, it is painfully apparent that working with child-sexual-abuse cases is not for everyone. Some people, for a variety of reasons, recoil at the very thought of becoming involved with this problem. Education and desensitization may help a few of these individuals to work with child sexual abuse more effectively. However, the majority of those who cannot "stomach" child-sexual-abuse cases are unlikely to be able to become effective intervenors. Inevitably, random assignment of cases will result in case management by some professionals who are so uncomfortable with this problem that it compromises their ability to deal with it.

Instead, agency administrators should identify a few staff members who are willing (and hopefully who demonstrate some ability) to work with child sexual abuse and begin to funnel cases to them. A selected group of professionals in a community can then begin to concentrate their experience with child sexual abuse. Assigning cases to those who are interested in (rather than repelled by) the problem has obvious advantages. Such individuals are more likely to approach cases with the enthusiasm and desire to improve their skills which is required. It is probably necessary for each of these professionals to be assigned a minimum of three of four cases per year in order to acquire the necessary experience. (A larger number of child-sexual-abuse cases each year would be desirable.)

The purpose of concentrating the case experience of staff members within agencies should also be obvious. Working with child sexual abuse requires the practical exercise of specialized investigative and clinical skills and judgment. No one can develop this specialized expertise without adequate case experience. This is not to equate case experience with expertise. However, it is fair to say that accumulating experience with child-sexual-abuse cases is the sine qua non for developing the necessary expertise.

Assigning cases to a few professionals within law enforcement, child protective services and mental health agencies who wish to receive such assignments and who demonstrate willingness to learn is far from being a foolproof formula for success. It is, however, a necessary first step toward building a community program. Without some focus of assignments and case experience, the effort is doomed from the start. In the absence of adequate preparation, it is totally unrealistic to expect the average police officer, child-protective-services worker, counselor, or therapist to be able to work effectively with child-sexual-abuse cases. One might as well suppose that the average family physician will be prepared to perform brain surgery in his or her office!

Use Multiple Intervenors for Intrafamily Child-Sexual-Abuse Cases

Working with child sexual abuse can be a lonely business. As described in chapter 3, there are many advantages to assigning more than one intervenor to an intrafamily child-sexual-abuse case. Since the family members tend to be highly competitive and mistrustful, it is difficult for a single intervenor to develop a meaningful relationship with more than one of them. Multiple intervenors can circumvent this difficulty. For the same reasons, multiple intervenors can collect a greater data base than a single intervenor. Having more than one intervenor working with a family enables a better response to crisis because more than one professional knows the family and can respond knowledgeably when trouble erupts. Lastly, because these cases are painful and demanding, it is a normal human response to use tunnel vision when observing the dynamics of family pathology and to assume improvement when none exists; the combined perspective of more than one intervenor tends to decrease this tendency as well as to share the burden.

Using multiple intervenors can be economical as well since some of the tasks which must be performed in investigation and case management can be performed simultaneously. The multiple intervenors do not have to be staff members from the same agency. Indeed, most intrafamily child-sexual-abuse cases are multiproblem families involved with more than one agency anyway. All that is required is for the intervenors to identify the tasks to be accomplished, to decide who will address what task, to keep in close communication at all times, and to agree to coordinate their approach.

Review Cases Regularly

A core group of professionals with "hands-on" experience with child sexual abuse is needed to review all of the cases. Chapter 12 discusses multidisciplinary team review of cases in detail. What is important is to make a beginning. For start-up, a few professionals who are working on cases simply need to agree to meet regularly and to discuss them. As they pool impressions and experience, it will quickly be apparent that input from other disciplines is necessary and helpful. If local "experts" on child sexual abuse are not available (they probably do not exist), invite professionals who are known for their competence and interest in the problem.

Why is regular case review so important? People tend to learn a great deal when they are called upon to summarize their activities to date with a given case and to present their plans and expectations for the future. It can be a positive experience to account for your own actions in an atmosphere of interest, concern, willingness to learn, and willingness to contribute to a common cause.

Great care must be exercised to avoid a punitive "kangaroo court" atmosphere. Fortunately, so few professionals can be considered "expert" in managing child-sexual-abuse cases that an atmosphere of "we're all here to learn together" is usually easy to foster and individual defensiveness is less likely.

Team review reduces the terrible isolation of those who manage cases of child sexual abuse. If cases are handled only by individuals who detest what they are doing and strive to bring them to closure as quickly and quietly as possible, a collegial relationship with others and pride in one's work have little chance to develop. The team review enables each member to acquire colleagues to share the burden and to diminish the sense of isolation as well as to receive specific suggestions for management of his or her case. Gaps in service will be identified and a stimulus to fill them will also be provided by this process.

Agencies which agree to concentrate their staff's experience by assigning child-sexual-abuse cases to a selected group who have demonstrated interest must also agree to permit case review to take place on a regular basis. Thus the impetus to prepare cases for scheduled meetings will be present. Also staff members who assume special responsibilities are entitled to the recognition and support derived from team participation.

Develop Criteria and Collect Data

The exercise of preparing for regular case review as well as the review process itself illustrates the need to develop assessment criteria. It would not be productive to allow a review of a case to degenerate into gratuitous commentary and gossip. Standards for investigation, validation, and child-protection assessment must be articulated by individuals and consensus reached as the participants become welded into a group by their common belief (hopefully allowing room for divergence of opinion). Further, as cases are reviewed, participants will begin to ask what criteria are being used to determine amenability to treatment, choice of a treatment modality, formulation of a treatment plan, and so forth.

Collecting data on the cases reviewed is a logical extension of the review process. It is not difficult to devise orderly methods of identifying problems and monitoring the success (or failure) of adhering to a treatment plan (see chapter 13). This process is essential for the growth of a community intervention program. The data collected provides the legitimate basis for assessing the impact of intervention. It is not possible to justify an effort to learn "on the job" to handle a complex problem more effectively if the participants are not also willing to collect the information that will enable them to learn from their mistakes.

Begin In-Service Education

Sporadic conferences and workshops, by themselves, contribute little to a professional's knowledge of child sexual abuse or, for that matter, to his or her capacity to intervene effectively. It is, however, possible to identify specific gaps in knowledge within a professional community and to implement a planned in-service education program designed to address these deficiencies.

It is also possible to predict in advance what topics should be addressed in the early phases of a community intervention program. The usual dynamics and mechanics of child sexual abuse, local child maltreatment and sexual assault legislation, interviewing for facts, recognition of defensive and suppressive behavior patterns exhibited by people under stress, the rudiments of working with involuntary clients—all these were identified as essential knowledge requirements for effective case management in chapter 3. These topics are logical starting points for a series of in-service education programs for professionals who are beginning to grapple with child-sexual-abuse cases in an organized fashion. Intervention modalities which can be utilized for child-sexual-abuse cases are also appropriate topics—assertiveness training, the arts therapies, sex therapy, and the like. The program's participants should be encouraged to identify their own knowledge gaps and weaknesses and to determine the direction and content of their training as much as possible.

Who should do the teaching and training? Most communities have professional people who can serve as resources for much of the training. Their credibility as trainers will depend in large measure on their degree of direct case experience with child sexual abuse as well as demonstrated professional competence in their chosen fields. The program's participants should contribute to the training as much as possible. "Outside experts" should be utilized whenever feasible to enhance the in-service education effort. It is a mistake, however, to try to substitute the occasional infusion of outside expertise for the essential component of leadership and responsibility for self-education by local professionals.

Develop Treatment Modalities

Treatment for the child, the offender and the family can be approached in a variety of ways (see chapters 4 to 10). There is no single magical "cure-all" treatment modality or approach. Instead, those who wish to provide treatment for offenders, victims, and families must be prepared to adopt existing and accepted therapeutic modalities. It is advantageous to have multiple treatment modalities for child sexual abuse in a community; nevertheless, these must usually be developed one by one.

Where to begin? It is best to utilize existing strengths and resources in the start-up phase. Is one of the team members a skilled family therapist? Good—rally around that person and encourage, cajole, stimulate, or otherwise persuade him or her to take on some cases in family therapy. Also important: figure out how best to support him or her in the process. Find another clinician who is prepared to be a cotherapist and to assist in developing this treatment modality. This approach can be used to extend the contribution of group therapists, arts therapists, sex therapists, and the like. It is unrealistic to expect any professional to develop and adapt single-handedly a treatment modality to be plugged into a community child-sexual-abuse intervention program.

Although treatment modalities must be developed one by one, it is a mistake to stop with the first one! Different clients will require different treatment modalities. It is unrealistic (as well as frustrating) to try to force the same approach to serve all the clients—it also will not work. Multiple treatment modalities should be developed; again, begin with local resource strengths, build upon them first, and then address the remaining gaps.

Summary

How to start a child-sexual-abuse intervention program? A few professional people in a community who have direct contact with cases have to be willing to stick their necks out. These enterprising individuals need to begin to review their cases together on a regular basis and to invite colleagues from other disciplines (who also have direct contact with cases) to join them. Key agencies (law enforcement, child-protective services, mental health or family services) need to permit a small number of interested staff to concentrate their case experience. As cases are reviewed by these ''hands on'' people, there is a good chance for improving interagency cooperation for case management. At the same time, these professionals must be dedicated to two concepts. First, that critical (yet supportive) review is essential to improving case mangement. Second, that they as professionals have the responsibility to design and participate in an ongoing in-service education program aimed at increasing their knowledge about the problem and improving intervention skills. Lastly, these professionals must be willing to assist their community to look within itself for the essential components of treatment for child sexual abuse. This entails identifying an existing strong local therapeutic resource and adapting it as a specialized treatment modality. The process must be repeated until multiple treatment modalities are developed.

Does this sound oversimplified? It *is* simple. Does it sound challenging? It should, because it is challenging. Does it sound expensive? It can hardly be more expensive than the current nonsystem of intervention. Does it sound frustrating? Nothing can match the frustration of the consequences of ignoring or attempting to suppress these cases. Does it sound impossible? It is not only possible but it can work. Try it and see. What do you and your professional community have to lose?

Index

Abuse of power, 2, 32–34, 182, 250–256. *See also* Child sexual abuse, treatment
Anticipatory guidance, 105, 262. *See also* Essential life support services; Initial management planning
Arts therapy, vii–x, 128, 143, 164, 166, 269–308, 353. *See also* Child sexual abuse, treatment
Authoritative intervention, 3–4

Beavers, W. Robert, 32–34, 250–251
Behavioral indicators, 40–48
Berliner, Lucy, 54, 310, 371
Blurred role boundaries, 123–124, 135–136, 194, 199–200, 207–208, 243–244, 253–254. *See also* Child sexual abuse, impact and treatment issues
Burgess, Ann, 1, 22, 54, 71, 162, 294

Case management, 81–108; and child protection assessment, 69, 92–94, 101; and court orders, 328; and diagnostic assessment, 106, 127, 303–306; and functioning adult ally, 93–94, 371–372; initial management planning of, 101–106; intervention planning in, 69; investigation and, 97–100, 316–325, 331; investigative interviewing and, 48–73, 320–324; medical examination and, 75–78, 102–103, 318; monitoring and reassessment in, 108; multidisciplinary team review in, 335–343, 364–365, 381–382; physical evidence and, 15, 318–319; preparation for court and, 105–106, 133–134, 163, 173–174, 211–212, 331; reporting, 97, 101–102; sibling incest and, 184–187; separation and, 107; treatment plan and, 107; victims and, 125–128
CENDEX, 282
Child-protection assessment, 69, 92–94, 101, 371–372
Child sexual abuse: authoritative intervention in, 3–4; behavioral indicators of, 40–48; conceptual framework of, 9–37; crisis intervention in, 18–19, 138–141; dynamics of, 13–27, 32–34, 140, 193, 250–256, 357–358; evaluation of, 6–7, 345–376; impact and treatment issues in, 112–125, 172–173; family contribution in cases of, 241–244; mechanics of, 10–12, 14–15; medical examination after, 75–78; physical indicators of, 73–75; planned intervention in, 21; treatment of, 2–3, 107, 128–138,

141–144, 147–175, 191–214, 236, 241–267, 269–308, 331, 339, 353
Child-sexual-abuse intervention programs, 1, 345–376, 377–385
Child-sexual-abuse statutes, 90–91, 309, 311–316
Communication, 200–201, 208–209, 253. *See also* Child sexual abuse, impact and treatment issues
Conceptual framework, 9–37
Connecticut Department of Children and Youth Services, 147. *See also* Sexual Trauma Treatment Program
Corroboration, 315. *See also* Investigation and validation
Court orders, 328. *See also* Case management and separation
Credibility assessment, 69–73. *See also* Investigative interviewing; Validation
Crisis intervention, 18–19, 138–141
Cunnilingus, 11. *See also* Child sexual abuse, mechanics of

Damaged goods syndrome, 112–115, 168. *See also* Child sexual abuse, impact and treatment issues in
DeFrancis, Vincent, 1
Dependent husband, 192, 218–222. *See also* Offenders, classification of
Depression, 118–119, 197. *See also* Child sexual abuse, impact and treatment issues; Mothers, treatment of; Treatment of mothers
Diagnostic assessment, 106, 127, 303–306. *See also* Case management; Investigation; Validation
Disclosure phase, 17–24; accidental disclosure, 17–18; family reaction, 21–24; purposeful disclosure, 19–21. *See also* Child sexual abuse, dynamics of
Dominant husband, 192, 222–226. *See also* Offenders, classification of
Dry intercourse, 12, 15. *See also* Child sexual abuse, mechanics of
Dyad therapy, 143–144, 276, 288. *See also* Child sexual abuse, treatment of

Engagement phase, 13–14. *See also* Child sexual abuse, dynamics of
Essential life support services, 95–96, 105, 261–262. *See also* Child sexual abuse, treatment; Initial management and planning
Evaluation, 6–7, 345–376. *See also* Problem list; Problem oriented record

385

About the Author

Suzanne M. Sgroi, M.D., is Executive Director of New England Clinical Associates, a private treatment center for child sexual abuse. She is Co-Director of the Saint Joseph College Institute for the Treatment and Control of Child Sexual Abuse in West Hartford, Connecticut. Dr. Sgroi served as program developer of The Connecticut Department of Children and Youth Services' Sexual Trauma Treatment Program from 1977 to 1979 and is a teacher and consultant on child sexual abuse for child protective services and the Municipal Police Training Council.

A physician in private practice in Suffield, Connecticut, Dr. Sgroi is also actively involved in teaching and consulting on child sexual abuse. She is the author of *VD: A Doctor's Answers* (1974) and coauthor of *Sexual Assault of Children and Adolescents* (Lexington Books, 1978).

A native of Fulton, New York, Dr. Sgroi received her A.B. in Liberal Arts from Syracuse University, and her M.D. from the State University of New York at Buffalo. Her internship was served at the Millard Fillmore Hospital, Buffalo, and residency in internal medicine at the Rochester General Hospital, Rochester, New York. Before moving to Connecticut in 1972, she served as a Rotating Physician, Internal Medicine, on the Hospital Ship Hope mission to Natal, Brazil.